ARLINGTON
NATIONAL CEMETERY

ARLINGTON
NATIONAL CEMETERY
Shrine to America's Heroes

3rd Edition
James Edward Peters

Woodbine House   2008

Copyright © 2008 by James Edward Peters
Third edition
All rights reserved under International
and Pan-American Copyright Conventions.
Published in the United States of America
by Woodbine House, Inc., 6510 Bells Mill Road,
Bethesda, MD 20817-1636. 800-843-7323.
http://www.woodbinehouse.com

Cover Photograph: Warren G. Miller
Photos: Library of Congress, United States Archives,
Warren G. Miller, and James Edward Peters
Book Design and Typesetting: Shala Stevenson

The author wishes to thank the staff of Arlington National Cemetery,
for providing critical information for this book.
http://www.arlingtoncemetery.org.

Library of Congress Cataloging-in-Publication Data

Peters, James Edward, 1951-
    Arlington National Cemetery : shrine to America's heroes / James Edward Peters. – 3rd ed.

    p. cm.
    Includes index.
    ISBN 978-1-890627-92-8 (pbk.) : $19.95

    1. Arlington National Cemetery (Arlington, Va.) 2. Heroes–United States–Biography. 3.
Soldiers–United States–Biography. I. Title.

    II.
    Title: Arlington National Cemetery, shrine to America's heroes.
    F234.A7P47 2008 973.09'9--dc22

2008033261

Manufactured in the United States of America

10   9   8   7   6   5   4   3   2

Dedication

To my parents,
Kathleen and Richard Peters,
who gave me the most important things in life:
love, support, encouragement, and seven siblings.

Table of Contents

Author's Notes i

Introduction...v

Arlington's History: Washington to Lee to Today.......................................1

American Heroes at Arlington:
Profiles in Patriotism..37

Other Notable Persons Buried at Arlington 219

Arlington's Major Monuments and Memorials 241

Arlington's Living Memorials:
Tree Dedications 303

Arlington: A Visitor's Guide 309

Appendices..323

Index..341

Author's Notes

As I was growing up in Quincy, Illinois, there were two cemeteries near my family's home. The larger of the two, Woodland Cemetery, provided my brothers and sisters and me with hours of adventure exploring the cemetery's rolling hills along the bluffs overlooking the Mississippi River. Here family burial plots became army fortresses and tombstones provided hiding places for grand-scale games of hide-and-seek, as long as we were able to avoid detection by the caretaker. However, we paid little attention to the unfamiliar names on the endless rows of headstones.

Then one day, as I was using the cemetery as an unauthorized shortcut between the municipal swimming pool and our home, I spotted a name on a headstone that was familiar to me—John Wood. I had learned recently in school that John Wood had been the first settler of Quincy, later becoming governor of Illinois. Of course. **Wood**land Cemetery! I stopped and stared at the headstone, struck by the thought that right in front of me was the grave of someone important, someone I knew something about. Suddenly it occurred to me that all of those names on all of those headstones were real people with real pasts. And I found myself reading each one, searching for clues among the names and dates, trying to solve the mysteries of who these people were. If a book is born at the instant one discovers a genuine interest in the subject matter, then this book on Arlington Cemetery was born that day in Quincy's Woodland Cemetery because I have never stopped looking at headstones nor searching for clues.

I was an elementary school student in November 1963 when I became aware of Arlington National Cemetery. Like millions of other Americans that dark weekend in November, I watched the televised burial services for President **John Kennedy.** A few years later, as a delegate to the American Legion's Boys' Nation in Washington, D.C., I paid my first visit to Arlington. There I saw the Eternal Flame and read the simple inscription on the stone tablet above John Kennedy's grave, remembering the story of his life and the tragedy of his death. Looking over my shoulder as we climbed back on the bus that day, I realized that the endless rows of headstones that dot the hillsides of Arlington Cemetery represent thousands of men and women whose stories were left untold.

My interest in cemeteries is simply an extension of my interest in history. To me, reading headstones is not some morbid obsession with the dead. Rather, it is a celebration of the memories of people who lived at another time. And at Arlington, there are hundreds of thousands of people whose lives deserve celebration. Even now, when I visit the graves of famous Americans at Arlington, I feel somehow that I am in the presence of these legendary figures, and I am daunted by the memory of their achievements.

When I moved to Washington, I made several expeditions to Arlington, each time discovering new and more interesting facts about the people buried there. The ornate headstones of Civil War-era veterans revealed plenty of clues about the persons whose names they bear. Even the thousands of simple, white regulation headstones divulge some small part of the lives of the men and women they name. But there was so much more to know.

I looked for publications that would answer my many questions about the cemetery. How had it become the home of Robert E. Lee? Why is there a cemetery on Lee's estate? Who's eligible to be buried here? And how do I learn more about the numerous monuments and memorials? I rummaged through bookstores and scoured library shelves, but was unable to find a current definitive guide to this national shrine. Finally, a search at the Library of Congress revealed that there simply was no current book on Arlington National Cemetery that would answer the questions of a visitor like me. That was in 1985.

The first edition of this book was published the following year, and throughout its preparation, I relied heavily upon the contributions of others. And if I have been successful in my goal to better inform visitors about our greatest national cemetery, then literally dozens of people must share in that success.

During my initial research, Raymond Costanzo was superintendent of the cemetery. He and his staff provided more help than I can ever recount. Today Mr. Costanzo is buried among the other heroes at Arlington (Sec. 7, Lot 191, Grid U-24). As I prepared to write the second and third editions of this book, Superintendent John Metzler, Jr. also provided help and offered a truly historic perspective—he lived in the cemetery as a child. His father, John Sr., was cemetery superintendent, and as such, his family lived on the cemetery grounds. Mr. Metzler, Sr. is well remembered for the vital role he played in the preparation and administration of the funeral for President **John Kennedy** in 1963. He can be seen in the photographs of the funeral on pages 108–109.

Cemetery historians Kerri Childress and Tom Sherlock also were important resources for the first edition, and Tom has continued to offer help and assistance to the thousands of American families who bury their loved ones at Arlington every year.

On a personal note, there is a long list of people to whom I am very grateful. The longest part of the list is my family, always there to offer support and advice (wanted or not); Gary Mohrman, providing a lifetime of encouragement and support; and Ron and Maria Lefrancois, extraordinary people and very dear friends. Finally, my special thanks goes to the staff at Woodbine House whose advocacy of this project has not wavered in more than 20 years; Shala Stevenson, whose keen eye and creative talents designed this book; and Warren Miller, whose photographs grace its cover and interior.

Cemeteries are like libraries; they perpetuate knowledge. And if this book advances the public's knowledge of Arlington National Cemetery and spurs greater interest in this shrine to America's heroes, then all of us have achieved our goal.

Introduction

"Let us here highly resolve that these honored dead shall not have died in vain."
— Abraham Lincoln, The Gettysburg Address

President Lincoln spoke these words on November 19, 1863, at the dedication of the national cemetery on the Civil War battleground at Gettysburg, Pennsylvania. In 1920, that sentiment was reaffirmed when his words were engraved in the Memorial Amphitheatre at Arlington National Cemetery. Lincoln's words remind all who visit here that for more than 200 years, thousands of men and women have given their lives in defense of this great nation, and that their contributions to our liberty must never be forgotten.

Arlington National Cemetery is dedicated to the memories of those gallant men and women. This cemetery is more than just a military burial ground; it is one of the most important national shrines in America, and as such, it is visited by millions of people every year. Yet, whether or not the reader visits Arlington, this book hopes to present a vivid picture of the cemetery and serve both as an historical text, as well as an on-site guide to present-day Arlington.

Unlike the White House, the Capitol, or the other great monuments that grace the Washington area, the creation of Arlington National Cemetery did not result from years of careful planning. It was not the product of a commission specially appointed to review prospective plans and select the most appropriate site before unveiling the shrine in a blaze of patriotic glory. Rather, it was born of tragic necessity.

During the Civil War, thousands of soldiers and civilians lost their lives in the unrelenting battles in and around Washington. As a grim testament to the human costs of that war, there was a shortage of space in which to bury the dead. Therefore, on an afternoon in June 1864, without public fanfare or formal ceremonies, and only with the simple affixing of his signature, the secretary of war designated the estate of Robert E. Lee's wife as a military burial ground—Arlington National Cemetery. Unlike the great buildings of government across the Potomac, the marble stones at Arlington were not used to create large public structures; instead, they were placed side by side in seemingly endless rows, adorned simply with names and dates.

At that time in America's history, it was no honor to be buried at Arlington. Only those who died unknown or whose families could not afford the costs of private burial were interred here. Yet, during that period of battles and mass burials, no one foresaw that Arlington Cemetery would become this nation's greatest shrine to our fallen heroes.

Today, as visitors approach Arlington National Cemetery, they are struck by its grandeur even as they cross the Potomac River. Rising before them is Arlington House, standing majestically on a hillside like a proud sentinel diligently guarding those left in its charge. They travel along Memorial Drive, the broad avenue over which so many caissons have borne America's sons and daughters. And even before they enter the cemetery's gilded gates, they see monuments dedicated to those heroes.

This book helps you share the greatness of Arlington National Cemetery from its checkered history to its present glory. It guides you through the days when the land was purchased by the stepson of George Washington; when **George Washington Parke Custis,** Washington's adopted son, built Arlington House as a memorial to our first president; and when, as the home of Robert E. Lee, it was confiscated by the Union government and used as a burial ground during the darkest days of the Civil War. This book traces Arlington's history following the war, from the establishment of the Freedman's Village; through the successful Supreme Court battle waged by Lee's son to regain title of the property; to its development as this country's most important national cemetery.

Although the history of the Lee estate parallels the rich history of our nation, it is the stories of the tens of thousands of men and women buried at Arlington that truly illustrate the colorful past of the American people. Within its walls Arlington perpetuates the memories of those who are famous and not-so-famous; known and unknown; honored or forgotten. Together on these hillsides overlooking the Potomac lie presidents and privates, officers and enlisted men, Supreme Court justices and unknown slaves, each with a past. It is impossible to tell the story of all those buried here, yet it is both possible and important to tell the story of the spirit that has guided America for nearly 250 years.

Walking among the gravestones at Arlington, a visitor discovers such names as Lingan, L'Enfant, Sheridan, Doubleday, Holmes, Lincoln, Westinghouse, MacArthur, Bryan, Delano, Taft, Pershing, Donovan, Hammett, Marshall, Bradley, Halsey, Forrestal, Dulles, Kennedy, Evers, Grissom, Scobee, Muskie, and Rehnquist.

It becomes increasingly clear while reading the names on these headstones, that a visit to Arlington is like scanning the history shelves at the public library or browsing the biography section of a good bookstore.

To assist the reader in a better appreciation of Arlington's place in our nation's history, a collection of approximately 100 short biographies or descriptive sketches is included in this volume. The stories of these people, many of them well known and some less well known, illustrate the diversity of the 300,000 people buried at Arlington. With each biography, the grave's section and lot number is provided to facilitate finding the grave's location.

Also, within Arlington's 657 acres are numerous memorials dedicated not to an individual, but to the memory of a group, an event, or cause. One section in this volume describes the history and purpose of approximately 40 of those memorials.

In addition, an extensive index is provided to allow the reader quick reference to the people, places, and events represented in the book. Any name appearing in **bold** type indicates that person is buried at Arlington.

To accommodate cemetery visitors, a map is located inside the back cover. With this map, the reader can utilize the clearly marked grid coordinates to assist him or her in locating a specific grave or memorial.

Today, Arlington National Cemetery performs two very important functions. It maintains one of America's most revered shrines, and at the same time, administers a large, modern cemetery where as many as 30 burials take place each weekday. The final chapter of this book explains the types of services regularly performed at Arlington, from military burials to the laying of wreaths by visiting dignitaries. Interment requirements, the columbarium, and tombstone regulations also are discussed in this section.

While many of the people buried at Arlington are not best known for their military careers, it is important to remember that Arlington is a military cemetery, and as such, military symbols and abbreviations are used on the headstones. A glossary is included to explain those symbols and abbreviations, as well as religious designations. Other appendices provide information regarding the designation of military rank, the requirements for burial at Arlington, and the use of private headstones.

A person cannot casually visit Arlington National Cemetery and hope to visit its many impressive sights. It is a vast, beautifully landscaped memorial to those Americans who have served our country, and, in many cases, have sacrificed their lives in its defense. The story of Arlington is a wondrous one and no one volume could tell it all. Yet, the reader will learn much about Arlington's past and present from this book, and in this it will have fulfilled its objective.

Arlington's History:
From Washington to Lee to Today

"When we assumed the soldier, we did not lay aside the citizen."
— George Washington

"Arlington...where my affection and attachments are more strongly placed than at any other place in the world."
— Robert E. Lee

"I could stay here forever."
— John F. Kennedy,
speaking at Arlington House on November 11, 1963

On a hillside rising above the Potomac River overlooking Washington, D.C., stands Arlington House—the focal point of Arlington National Cemetery. For many of the millions of people who annually visit our nation's most important national cemetery, it seems incongruous that this magnificent mansion should be located in the middle of a military burial ground. But in 1802, when construction of Arlington House began, it was not intended to be the centerpiece of a cemetery. Rather, it was designed to be a living memorial to George Washington, the father of our country.

Here on a 1,100-acre estate, Washington's adopted son—**George Washington Parke Custis**—proudly housed the largest collection of Washington memorabilia in the world. Tragically, that collection and Arlington House itself became victims of America's bloody Civil War.

Prior to the Civil War, Washington Custis occupied the home with his wife, their daughter, and their daughter's husband, Robert E. Lee—then a little-known, but highly respected lieutenant colonel. Arlington was Lee's home for nearly 30 years before it was confiscated by the Union Army at the outbreak of the Civil War. Today the restored mansion has been designated the Robert E. Lee Memorial, and continues to reflect its stature during the period before the war.

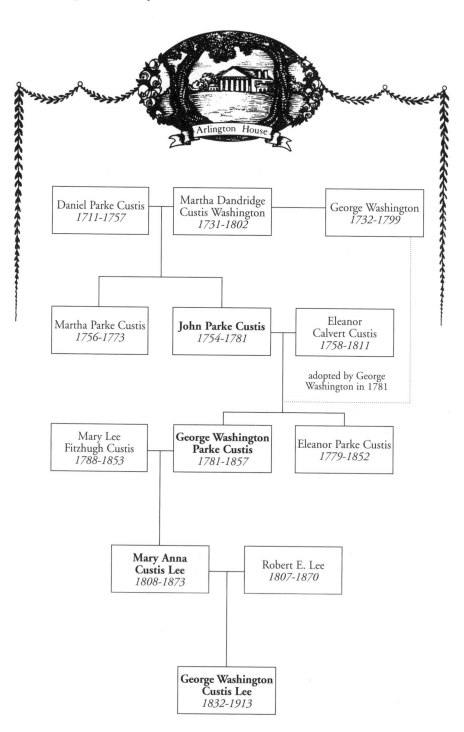

Arlington House

Daniel Parke Custis *1711-1757*	Martha Dandridge Custis Washington *1731-1802*	George Washington *1732-1799*

Martha Parke Custis *1756-1773*	**John Parke Custis** *1754-1781*	Eleanor Calvert Custis *1758-1811*

adopted by George Washington in 1781

Mary Lee Fitzhugh Custis *1788-1853*	**George Washington Parke Custis** *1781-1857*	Eleanor Parke Custis *1779-1852*

Mary Anna Custis Lee *1808-1873*	Robert E. Lee *1807-1870*

George Washington Custis Lee *1832-1913*

Names appearing in **bold** print signify holders of title to Arlington House.

George Washington was an up-and-coming, 27-year-old Virginia planter when he married Martha Dandridge Custis, a widow one year his senior, on January 6, 1759. Martha Custis was rumored to be the richest woman in the colonies, having inherited 15,000 acres and a considerable fortune upon the death of her first husband, Daniel Parke Custis. Her marriage to Custis had produced four children, only two of whom survived infancy, John Parke Custis and Martha Parke "Patsy" Custis. They were ages 6 and 4 respectively when their mother married Washington.

George and Martha's union produced no children of their own, but Washington worked hard to raise young John, or Jackie, as he was sometimes called. As young John grew, he watched and learned as his stepfather skillfully managed the large Mount Vernon plantation, retaining what he learned for the day when he, too, would own such an estate. In 1778, 25-year-old John invested money he had inherited from his natural father in a 1,100-acre tract of land about 15 miles north of Mount Vernon. The property was purchased from one John Alexander. It was on this land, later known as Arlington, that Custis intended to build his home after the Revolutionary War.

During the siege of Yorktown in 1781—while serving as an aide to General Washington—John Parke Custis died. He had contracted camp fever, the name given to a wide range of maladies from malaria to tuberculosis. Like so many other wartime families, Washington and his family were devastated by the loss of John Parke Custis, who was survived by a wife and four children. To assist in the rearing of those children, George and Martha Washington adopted the two youngest, George Washington Parke Custis and Eleanor Parke Custis.

George Washington Parke Custis, who as a child was known as Tub, and was later called Washington, was just six months old when he was adopted by the future president. Just as Washington had raised John Custis 20 years earlier, he again found himself in the position of role model, this time for his young adopted son. But the role Washington played was unlike any other in history, and while constantly at Washington's heels, young Washington Custis witnessed the historic events surrounding the birth of our nation. When prominent citizens and heads of state journeyed to Mount Vernon to call on the first president, young Washington Custis was ever present.

From an early age, Washington Custis was awestruck by his famous father, and throughout his life he tried to emulate George Washington, not only in the way he managed his estate, but in his political views as well.

George Washington Parke Custis was only 18 years old when President Washington died in 1799, but he promptly directed his energies to

George and Martha Washington are shown with young George Washington Parke Custis and Eleanor Parke Custis, who were adopted by Washington in 1781.

perpetuating the memory of the man whose name he bore. After Martha died in 1802, Custis attempted to buy Mount Vernon to establish the first national historic site as a memorial to his adopted father. Unfortunately for Custis, Washington's nephew, Bushrod Washington, inherited the property and was unwilling to sell. So Custis looked elsewhere for a memorial site and discovered that among the 15,000 acres of land he owned was the 1,100-acre tract north of Mount Vernon that his natural father John Parke Custis had purchased in 1778. Just across the Potomac River from the new federal capital, Washington City, Custis found the perfect site to build his home. He resolved that it would serve as a national memorial to George Washington, and that he would be its self-appointed curator. Initially Custis wanted to name the property "Mount Washington," a title he deemed equal to its purpose. However, he was persuaded by members of his family to settle on "Arlington House." Arlington had been the name of the original Custis family estate on Virginia's Eastern Shore which had been acquired by a grant from the Earl of Arlington.

Like many other Virginia planters at that time, Parke Custis was land rich but cash poor. Although he owned several plantations throughout Virginia, and had inherited more than 200 slaves, he did not have sufficient liquid assets that would allow him to build his home immediately. Undaunted, he forged ahead, planning his home and collecting more Washington memorabilia to exhibit there. In 1802, when he moved onto the site to begin construction of the house, Custis called upon George Hadfield to build it. Hadfield was an English architect who had come to America in 1785 to help construct the U.S. Capitol. He provided Custis with plans for a Greek revival structure, which due to Custis' financial situation would take 16 years to complete.

Also contributing to Washington Custis' financial woes was his obsession with obtaining more Washington relics. Although he had inherited many portraits, papers, and even clothes that had belonged to Washington, he doggedly pursued more. At one Mount Vernon auction, Custis bid more than $4,500 for a variety of items that ranged from axes, corn drills, and a brick-making mold to Washington's coach, British and Hessian battle flags, and the red-trimmed tent that Washington used at Yorktown. It took him many years to retire the debt from that single auction. Nevertheless, he succeeded in acquiring the most extensive collection of Washington's personal effects in the country. Among Custis' possessions were Washington's punch bowl, pocket telescope, umbrellas, and the bed in which the first president had died.

All Custis lacked was the proper environment to display his collection. Unfortunately, the magnificent mansion he envisioned to house both himself and his treasures could only be built in stages. This was not only customary at that time, but, considering Custis' poor cash situation, necessary.

The north wing was the first structure completed and Custis, who was a bachelor, made that section his home in late 1802. It consisted of only six rooms, a significant portion of which was used to store his Washington collection. By 1804, the south wing was finished, providing Custis with two additional rooms. The area that would ultimately contain the large center section and the now-famous portico was nothing more than an open yard and a home for Custis' chickens. Nonetheless, these two completed, but detached, wings of Arlington House were home to George Washington Parke Custis when he married **Mary Lee Fitzhugh** in July 1804.

Like her new husband, Mary descended from old, established Virginia families—the Lees, Randolphs, and Fitzhughs. And though she was only 16 when she married her "dear Washington," she assumed her position as lady of the house with grace and finesse. During the 14 years it took to complete the house, the couple lived in the north wing. The south wing served as an office for Custis and a repository for the Washington relics, which Custis continued to accumulate. Four Custis children were born to Washington and Mary Custis, but only one, Mary Anna Randolph Custis, would live to maturity.

As the mansion was being built, Custis also was developing the lands surrounding Arlington House, using what he had learned from George Washington at Mount Vernon. He rotated his crops and kept records to document his successes and failures. Custis also established a good reputation in animal husbandry. He bred fine mules and developed a highly acclaimed breed of woolly sheep known as Arlington Supremes or Arlington Improved. He encouraged other farmers to develop domestic breeds in light of the high cost of importing sheep. It was his early agricultural successes that earned Custis the cash he needed to improve the land and finish his mansion.

In 1818, the large central section of the house was completed. Now the mansion stretched 140 feet from north to south. The newly completed section provided a large central hall on the first floor that served as a parlor during hot summer months. Between the hall and the north wing now stood a formal dining room and a sitting room. Much of the area south of the hall was used for storage and Custis' studio. The vast portico with its eight majestic columns, each five feet in diameter at the base, stood like an honor guard greeting the many visitors to Arlington House. At last, Custis had completed his own "Washington monument," more than 60 years before the now-familiar towering obelisk was completed across the Potomac River. Arlington House could be seen for miles up and down the river, prompting Robert E. Lee to note later that it was "a house that any one might see with half an eye."

With the completion of the house, visitors began coming in droves to view the Washington collection and to hear George Washington Parke Custis discourse on his famous father. The gregarious Custis welcomed any opportunity to tell stories about President Washington, and established a park for picnickers by the large spring on his estate. Sometimes he would spot a group gathered by the spring and would canter down from the mansion with his violin tucked under his arm, ready to entertain his guests with his music and a repertoire of stories. Often to his delight, and that of his guests, he would drag out and set up the huge tents Washington used at Yorktown.

Not only did the local farmers and folks from the capital come to Arlington House, but admirers of George Washington traveled from all over the globe to show their respect for the late president. The Marquis de Lafayette, who served with Washington during the Revolutionary War, twice made the pilgrimage to Arlington, and during an 1825 visit, Custis presented him with an umbrella and Masonic sash that belonged to Washington. In honor of President Andrew Jackson's visit, Custis gave Jackson Washington's pocket telescope. Custis always enjoyed distributing souvenirs of Washington, often cutting

Arlington House shown from the "Great Oak" shortly after the estate was designated a national cemetery.

Washington's signature from documents and giving them as remembrances.

Arlington House was the scene of many colorful events during the life of George Washington Parke Custis. Not only was he a famous farmer and teller of Washingtonian tales, but also an amateur artist and playwright. Several of his most accomplished battle scene paintings, including "The Battle of Monmouth," which is seven feet tall by 11 feet wide, can be seen at Arlington House. In 1827, Custis wrote his first play entitled 'Indian Prophecy," but his best known play is "Pocahontas," which he finished in 1830.

So it was in this antebellum environment filled with its receptions and cotillions, servants and socials, teas and tales that Washington Custis reared his daughter, Mary Anna Randolph Custis. As his only surviving child, Mary Custis was the beneficiary of her father's undivided attention. She received an excellent education, and life at Arlington House provided her with all of the luxuries a young woman her age could have desired. Yet her father insisted that she always remember one important fact, she was the foster granddaughter of George Washington. As Custis' only heir, Mary alone would be entrusted with the preservation of this living memorial to Washington. Of course, the collection of Washington memorabilia and the many visitors who came to Arlington to see it were constant reminders to Mary Custis of the responsibility that she accepted with pride. It also was one

George Washington Parke Custis, the man who built Arlington House as a memorial to his foster father, George Washington.

that later caused her overwhelming sorrow when she was unable to fulfill it.

In 1830, many young men sought to win the heart and hand of Mary Anna Custis, but it was a childhood friend and distant cousin, Robert E. Lee, who finally captured her affections. Lee was the son of former three-term Virginia Governor Henry "Light Horse Harry" Lee, and had graduated from West Point in 1829. Mary's father, however, did not favor his only daughter marrying a career military man, and voiced concern over Lee's ability to support Mary on a second lieutenant's salary. Nonetheless, the young couple found a strong ally in Mary's mother. Mrs. Custis had known Robert E. Lee and his family since Robert was just a child, and held him in highest regard. But Mr. Custis remained reluctant. For him, the custody of his two greatest joys was at stake—his daughter and his memorial to Washington. However, finally succumbing to the overwhelming desires of his wife and daughter, Washington Custis blessed the marriage.

The wedding of Mary Anna Randolph Custis and Robert E. Lee was the grandest event ever at Arlington House. June 30, 1831, was chosen as the date, and the house was decorated to reflect the magnificence of the occasion. Flowers from Mrs. Custis' famed gardens bedecked the halls. Friends and neighbors from all over Virginia and the Potomac Valley made their way up the hill to Arlington House. It was a grand day for the Custises and the Lees. Even the steady rain that fell during the afternoon could not dampen the spirits of those who had gathered to witness the ceremony. It was in this idyllic setting that Robert E. Lee realized that he had married not only Mary Anna Custis, but Arlington House as well. And although his military career would lead him away from Arlington, it was on this estate that his life would be rooted for the next 30 years.

Lee readily shared his wife's custodial responsibility for the Washington memorabilia. He welcomed the opportunity to preserve George Washington's memory. Having been raised in Washington's hometown of Alexandria, Virginia, Lee had long been an admirer of the first president, and except for his own father, he respected Washington more than any other man in the world. Of course Arlington and its Washington collection remained

Mary Anna Custis Lee, the only child of George Washington Parke Custis, married Robert E. Lee in 1831, and inherited Arlington House just prior to the Civil War. Colonel Lee is pictured during his days as superintendent of West Point.

under the watchful eye of Washington and Mary Custis. Washington Custis continued to manage the estate for more than 25 years after his daughter's marriage. The new Mrs. Lee usually accompanied her husband on his military assignments, but returned to Arlington House to give birth to six of their seven children.

Robert E. Lee served in the Army Corps of Engineers, and to his family's delight, most of his military assignments were near Arlington. His first major assignment away from the area came in 1837, when he was ordered to supervise engineering work for the harbor at St. Louis, Missouri. Knowing he would be gone for an extended period, he requested and received permission to take his family with him to the Far West, which is what St. Louis was considered. So in 1837, Robert E. Lee and his family left the Custises and Arlington House for St. Louis. Washington Custis was then 57 years old, and no longer the aggressive estate manager that he had been 30 years earlier. Unfortunately, the condition of the estate declined markedly until Lee returned to assume its management.

Between 1841 and 1857 Lee was away from Arlington for several extended periods. In 1846, he served in the Mexican War under General Winfield Scott with whom he developed a lifelong friendship. It was during the Mexican War that Lee distinguished himself as a brave and courageous engineer and soldier. The Mexican War has often been called the "training field" for the Civil War because so many of the Civil War's future officers got their training in the Mexican campaign. That was true for Lee.

In 1852, Lee was appointed superintendent of the U.S. Military Academy at West Point, his alma mater. He had preferred a field command, but welcomed the opportunity to serve where his family could join him. No sooner had Mrs. Lee and their children arrived at West Point than Mrs. Lee was called back to Arlington to care for her ailing mother. Mary Custis Lee was at Arlington House when her mother, Mary Fitzhugh Custis, died in 1852. Mrs. Custis was buried in the family plot which is located in Section 13 (Grid N-30) of Arlington Cemetery. Following her mother's burial, Mrs. Lee remained at Arlington with her father, then in his seventies, before rejoining her husband at West Point.

In 1855, Lee was transferred from New York to Texas to command the Second U.S. Calvary. While the transfer earned him a promotion to lieutenant colonel and gave him the field command he sought, it also separated him from his family. Although Mrs. Lee and the younger children returned from West Point to the familiar surroundings of Arlington, Lee was very concerned for his wife's health. He knew that she suffered from chronic arthritis and was fast becoming an invalid. So during the next two years, he returned to Arlington as often as he could.

While in Texas in the fall of 1857, Lee received word from Arlington that Washington Custis had died. He had admired and respected his father-in-law, and the loss affected him deeply.

Custis had named Lee as executor of his estate, and upon learning of the terms of his will, Lee quickly realized that his new responsibility would demand his full attention. Immediately he applied for leave to return to Arlington House to join his family. Upon his return, Lee was dismayed to find the estate badly neglected. He was even more shocked by his wife's rapidly deteriorating health. Lee requested a year's leave, but the monumental task that confronted him took more than two years to complete.

Arlington House figured centrally in the terms of Washington Custis' will. His daughter, Mary Anna Custis Lee, was given the right to inhabit and control Arlington House for the rest of her life. Upon her death, full title to the property would pass to her eldest son, George Washington Custis Lee. Contrary to what many people still believe, Robert E. Lee never owned Arlington House.

Further complicating Lee's burden as executor of the estate, Custis had bequeathed $10,000 to each of his four granddaughters, and left other plantations to his remaining two grandsons. However, Custis left no cash and was in debt at the time of his death. He also had provided that if there was not enough cash to fulfill the bequests to his granddaughters, the plantations

The Custis Family plot as it exists today in Section 13. Only two graves are located within the plot—those of George Washington Parke Custis (on the left) and his wife Mary Fitzhugh Custis.

should be sold to raise the requisite money. Custis did leave 196 slaves as personal property, but he provided that they be emancipated within five years of his death. This left Robert E. Lee in a serious financial and familial quandary. To raise the cash intended for his own daughters, he might have to sell the land left to his sons.

He could have sold the nearly 200 slaves, which would have raised more than enough funds to satisfy the terms of Custis' will, but it was his strong belief that the slaves should be educated, trained, and freed. Therefore, under the terms of Custis' will, which called for the manumission of the slaves within five years, Lee planned to use the slaves during that five-year period to earn the money necessary to satisfy specific bequests.

Washington Custis had become completely indulgent in the last decade of his life. He had lived the comfortable lifestyle he sought without enforcing fiscal discipline on himself or his operators. Though Custis claimed to have despised slavery, calling it "the mightiest serpent that ever infested the world," he had always operated his lands with their extensive use, often renting them out to other farmers. As for the domestic slaves at Arlington House, he always referred to them as "servants," treated them with great affection, and demanded little of them.

After Custis' death, Lee attacked the complex problem before him with the same efficient methods he had used as an army engineer. He carefully plotted his strategy, attempting to cover every area in detail. He dealt with his field workers as if they were troops under his command, not indulging or coddling them as Custis had done. Lee himself also undertook the physical labors of restoring the estate. During daylight hours, he could be seen repairing the roofs, replacing fences, or rebuilding roads, and after the sun had set, he literally burned the midnight oil doing the necessary bookkeeping.

In an attempt to ease the tremendous administrative and probate burden, Lee's oldest son, Custis Lee, offered to convey his rights in Arlington to his father, but the elder Lee declined. It was Custis land and Custis land it would remain. However, in one letter to his son, Lee facetiously suggested that the best thing he could do for Arlington was to marry a rich woman. Custis Lee never married.

The one benefit which Lee allowed himself and his wife was to finish furnishing the house. The Lees redecorated most of the house in their own tastes, especially the rooms south of the center section that had been used primarily for storage. Many of the furnishings that Lee had purchased while living away from Arlington now found their way here. Among other pieces, the red velvet Victorian settee, which had adorned his home at West Point, was now placed in the large room just south of the central hall. Today Arlington House has been restored to reflect this period.

By 1859, Lee had returned a semblance of order to the estate. The other plantations were now showing profits, and even Arlington was breaking even. Also important to Lee, however, was the once magnificent grounds of Arlington had been restored, and its position as a showplace redeemed. He was pondering the possibility of resuming his military career when in October 1859, J.E.B. Stuart, a young officer who had been a cadet at West Point during Lee's superintendency, appeared at Arlington. He carried an urgent message from the war department for Lee to appear there as soon as possible.

Without changing his clothes, Lee and Stuart headed across the Potomac to Washington. There Lee was offered command of a detachment ordered to capture John Brown, who had just seized the federal arsenal at Harper's Ferry, Virginia. Without hesitation, Lee accepted the command and ultimately captured Brown. The incident brought Lee considerable recognition and accelerated his return to duty. Lee also felt that he could safely leave Arlington because he had secured a Washington assignment for

The study in Arlington House where George Washington Parke Custis wrote and painted.

his oldest son, Custis, which would enable him to oversee the estate. So, in February 1860, Arlington House once again witnessed the departure of Robert E. Lee on a military assignment to Texas.

What greeted Lee upon his return to command in Texas disturbed him greatly. Throughout Texas and the entire South, there was serious talk of secession. To Lee, secession was "nothing but revolution." For more than a year he bitterly argued against the destruction of the Union, even as he watched the possibility grow more likely each day. In December 1860, South Carolina voted to secede. There was talk in Congress and among members of President Buchanan's administration of an invasion of the South. To this apparent escalation of hostilities, Lee reacted by saying,

> "A Union that can only be maintained by swords and bayonets, and in which strife and civil war are to take the place of brotherly love and kindness, has no charm for me. I shall mourn for my country and for the welfare and progress of mankind. If the Union is dissolved, and the Government disrupted, I shall return to my native state, and share the miseries of my people, and save in defense draw my sword on none."

The threat of secession became a reality on February 1, 1861, when Texas seceded. On February 13, unsure of his fate or that of his country, Lee received orders to return to Washington. The next 90 days changed the course of life for the Lees, and Lee's decisions changed the course of our nation.

Lee arrived at Arlington on March 1, 1861, to find his ailing wife walking with a cane, and his home state of Virginia threatening to secede. On March 28, word came that Lee had been promoted to full colonel by General-in-Chief of the Army Winfield Scott, with the approval of Abraham Lincoln, the newly inaugurated president. With this promotion came command of the First U.S. Cavalry. Scott, who was then 75 years old and nearly immobilized by obesity, looked to Lee as his field commander should any action be required against the South. Lee accepted his promotion and waited. As war became more probable, Lee agonized over what position he would take. Virginia still had not taken any action toward secession, and it was Lee's home state that claimed his first allegiance. He knew, however, that regardless of Virginia's decision, Arlington House would never be allowed to remain the serene and stately homestead it had been for him and his family. Its location on that strategic ridge overlooking Washington would make its occupation vital for either side of the conflict.

Events unfolded rapidly in April 1861, and as Lee waited at Arlington, news arrived daily both from the Virginia state convention in Richmond regarding secession, and from Washington as the Lincoln administration responded to the actions of the Southern states.

Friday, April 12. Southern soldiers fired the first shots at Union troops at Fort Sumter in Charleston Harbor.

Monday, April 15. President Lincoln called for 75,000 volunteers, and Virginia was called upon to furnish her share to suppress the rebel states.

Tuesday, April 16. An ordinance of secession was introduced into the Virginia convention in response to President Lincoln's call for volunteers from Virginia. The sponsors argued they would rather secede than take up arms against fellow Southerners.

Wednesday, April 17. At the same time the Virginia convention went into secret session to further debate secession, Lee received a letter to report to General Scott's office the following day. He was told to call first upon Francis P. Blair at his home on Pennsylvania Avenue before he appeared at the war department to see Scott. Blair was considered an insider in the Lincoln administration although he held no official post.

Thursday, April 18. Lee left Arlington for Washington on what would be his last such journey. He went directly to Blair's house near the White House. Blair explained that President Lincoln had authorized him to offer Lee command of the new army that was being raised. This was the very command for which Lee had waited a lifetime, but without hesitating he replied, "Though opposed to secession and deprecating war, I could take no part in an invasion of the Southern states."

With that, Lee left Blair House and proceeded across Pennsylvania Avenue to the war department. There he met with his old friend, General Scott. He quickly related to the general the substance of his encounter with Blair, to which Scott uttered his famous reply, "Lee, you have made the greatest mistake of your life. But, I feared it would be so."

A gray mood accompanied Robert E. Lee on his ride back to Arlington. The United States Army was his life. He had spent 32 years as an Army officer, protecting and defending the Union that his father had fought to establish. With all his heart, he wanted to preserve that Union, but he did not want to fight against his fellow Southerners. How could he stay in the Army, but not be forced to fight? he wondered. And he feared for Arlington House and its future.

Friday, April 19. Lee learned that Virginia had voted to secede, though it had not yet decided to join the Confederacy. It was springtime as Lee walked the grounds of Arlington pondering his next move. He could smell

the flowers in the gardens, and see the apple blossoms in the orchard
the river. From the front portico, Lee also could see across the river to
still unfinished dome of the Capitol and the new Washington Monumen
construction of which had been halted for lack of funds, both symbols of the
Union he so strongly wanted to preserve.

That afternoon he went to his room on the second floor of Arlington
House and remained there until well after midnight. In the parlor below,
Mrs. Lee and some of their family and friends waited quietly for his decision.
They could hear his footsteps as he paced across the room's wooden floor.
They could hear when he stopped, probably to ponder or pray, only to pace
again. Well after the clock had struck midnight, in the early morning hours
of April 20, Lee reappeared downstairs and silently handed his wife a letter
which he had written. It was addressed to General Scott:

General:

Since my interview with you on the 18th instant I have felt that
I ought not longer to retain my commission in the Army. I therefore
render my resignation, which I request that you recommend for
acceptance.

It would have been presented at once, but for the struggle it has
cost me to separate myself from a service to which I devoted all the
best years of my life and the ability I possessed.

During the whole of that time, more than 30 years, I have
experienced nothing but kindness from my superiors, and a most
cordial friendship from my companions. To no one Genl have I
been as much indebted as to yourself for uniform kindness and
consideration, and it has always been my ardent desire to meet your
approbation.

I shall carry with me to the grave the most grateful recollections
of your kind consideration, and your name and fame will always be
dear to me. Save in defense of my native State, I never desire again
to draw my sword.

Be pleased to accept my most earnest wishes for the continuance
of your happiness and prosperity and believe me most truly yours,

/s/ R. E. Lee

Later that same day, still tormented by his decision, Lee wrote another
letter, this one to his sister:

devotion to the Union and the feeling of loyalty
rican citizen, I have not been able to make up
hand against my relatives, my children, my

....day, April 22. Upon the request of Virginia Governor John Letcher, Lee left Arlington House to catch a train for Richmond. He was unaware of the reason he was being summoned to the state capital, but contrary to a widely held belief, it was not to take command of the Confederate Army. Virginia still had not joined the Confederacy, and all Lee desired at this time was to offer his services to his state. Of course, as he left Arlington that day, he could not have known that this would be the last time that he would ever set foot on the grounds of the place he considered more dear to him than any other. It still was his hope that this threat to the Union could be resolved, and that he shortly would be able to return home.

Likewise Lee did not know that he would not see his beloved wife for more than 14 months, during which time he would undertake a crusade that would reshape a nation. When next they met, Mary Custis Lee, hardly recognized her husband because during this period of separation, Lee at age 54, had grown the stately gray beard that has come to characterize him. In fact, at no time during his nearly 30 years at Arlington House did Robert E. Lee ever wear a beard.

Late in the afternoon of April 22, 1861, Lee met with Governor Letcher in the Virginia state capitol. The governor informed him that an ordinance had been passed calling for the appointment of a commander of Virginia's military forces to serve under the governor's authority and bear the rank of major general. Letcher further stated that Lee had been recommended to him for the position. Lee accepted it immediately. He had not resigned his U.S. Army commission in anticipation of this appointment, nor was this an appointment to the Confederate ranks because Virginia was still not part of the Confederacy.

Wednesday, April 24. Virginia entered into a military alliance with the Confederacy. This alliance ultimately led to the state's formal incorporation into the newly formed confederation of states that occurred on May 24 when Virginia voters ratified the ordinance of secession.

Saturday, April 27. Although he had been gone for only five days, Lee was deeply concerned about those members of his family still at Arlington. He was well aware of the estate's strategic importance to the Union Army, but feared that his wife did not fully appreciate the danger. Lee knew what soldiers might do to the personal property found on occupied premises. With this weighing on his mind, Lee wrote to his wife:

"War is inevitable, and there is no telling when it will burst around you... You have to move and make arrangements to go to some point of safety which you must select. The Mount Vernon plate and pictures ought to be secured. Keep quiet while you remain, and in your preparations.... May God keep and preserve you and have mercy on all our people."

Mrs. Lee heeded her husband's warning and began making arrangements for her and her daughters to leave Arlington. She sent the portraits of President Washington and other family members to relatives who lived in safer quarters farther South. But other than those paintings and the family silver, she shipped little more than her basic personal effects. No extensive transfer of valuables was undertaken because she, like her husband, believed that they would ultimately return to her home and that no one, whether Northerner or Southerner, would even consider disturbing her treasured possessions.

Mary Custis Lee left Arlington House on May 15, 1861, for temporary shelter at the plantation home of Anne Maria Fitzhugh, who was Mrs. Lee's aunt by marriage and a close friend of Robert's since childhood. The plantation, known as Ravensworth, was located in Fairfax County, Virginia.

Following the ratification of the ordinance of secession by the voters of Virginia on May 24, federal troops finally crossed the Potomac River into Virginia. Under the command of Brigadier General Irvin McDowell, they took up positions around Arlington House as well as other points along the Potomac. From Ravensworth, Mrs. Lee, ever mindful of her obligation to protect her home and secure the Washington memorabilia, wrote to both General McDowell and to General-in-Chief Winfield Scott in Washington. In her letters, she reminded both men that Arlington was the home of George Washington's adopted son, that it should be well protected, and that the slaves who were left there should be looked after.

McDowell politely and courteously replied to Mrs. Lee saying that she could rest assured that the mansion would come to no harm and that the personal possessions would be protected. Unfortunately, though that communication must have given Mrs. Lee some comfort, McDowell was unable to keep his promise. Arlington became a headquarters for the Union Army charged with the defense of Washington, and a great number of troops trafficked in and around the estate. At first, a few personal items belonging to the Lees began vanishing. Later, when it became clear that great quantities of the Lee's property had disappeared, McDowell ordered that the remaining

Brigadier General Irvin McDowell (fifth from right with hand on sword) standing with his troops on the steps of Arlington House during its occupation by the Union Army in 1861.

items be packed and stored at the patent office in Washington under the label, "Captured at Arlington." Sadly, many irreplaceable heirlooms of the Washington, Custis, and Lee families were gone.

Following the occupation of Arlington by Union soldiers, military installations were erected at several locations around the 1,100-acre estate, including Fort Whipple (on the site of present-day Fort Myer), Fort McPherson (now Section 11), and around the mansion. With the establishment of Arlington House as headquarters for the defense of Washington, and with the large number of troops stationed upon the land, the character of the once-stately plantation changed. Instead of a productive, self-sustaining estate which had always replenished resources as they were used, Arlington was now occupied by military forces which were rapidly depleting its trees, crops, and other natural and man-made resources, and making no effort to replace them.

General Lee foresaw the probable transformation of his home during the early stages of the war. In the fall of 1861, he wrote to Mrs. Lee about Arlington,

> "...It is better to make up our minds to a general loss. They cannot take away the remembrance of the spot, and the memories of those that to us rendered it sacred. That will remain to us as long as life will last, and that we can preserve...."

Lee felt that he still was legally responsible for the estate under the terms of his father-in-law's will, though the war made it impossible to exercise his authority. Nonetheless, he remained particularly concerned about the status of the slaves who had been left behind, and he continued to hope that they would be trained and freed within the five years prescribed in Washington Custis' will.

The appearance of the Arlington estate remained primarily that of a military camp until 1864. Prior to that time, actions taken by the government in Washington proved to have a direct impact on Arlington's future. On June 7, 1862, Congress passed "An Act for the Collection of Direct Taxes in the Insurrectionary Districts of the United States." Outwardly the bill appeared to be a means to raise revenue from those areas of the Confederate states that were under Union control. In reality the measure proved to be a method of confiscating private property for governmental use. That was exactly its effect on Arlington.

Under the Act, the government established a commission charged with assessing "insurrectionary properties," and taxing them. The regulations further required that the legal titleholder of the property appear personally to pay the taxes. Since most property owners were Confederate sympathizers and could come forth only under threat of arrest, they were forced either to place themselves in personal jeopardy or fail to pay the taxes. In most cases the taxes went unpaid, and the properties of the Confederate sympathizers were sold at public auctions.

The Arlington property had been assessed at a value of $26,810 against which a tax of $92.07 was levied. Because the law required the legal owner to appear personally, Mary Custis Lee would have had to travel behind Union lines to Alexandria to pay the taxes. Mrs. Lee, already wheelchair-bound and frail, could not physically make the journey, even if she chose to disregard the danger to her personal safety as the wife of the South's commanding general. So in her stead, she authorized her cousin Philip R. Fendall to travel to Alexandria with the necessary funds to pay the taxes, interest, and costs. This payment was refused, and the taxes subsequently were declared delinquent. On January 11, 1864, the Arlington property was offered for public sale at an auction with the tax commissioners themselves as the only bidders. They "purchased" the property, consisting of 1,100 acres, the mansion and all the outbuildings for the exact assessed value of $26,810 "for Government use, for war, military, charitable, and educational purposes."

Now that Arlington was owned by the government and used as a military installation, it came under the jurisdiction of Secretary of War

Edwin M. Stanton. More specifically, it fell under the direct control of the quartermaster general of the Army. Since the nation was at war, the secretary of war and the quartermaster general were given extraordinary powers. The quartermaster general was charged with overseeing any government land used for military purposes. He controlled the construction of barracks, depots, hospitals, cemeteries, and roads. He also supplied military units with food, clothing, and all equipment except ordnance, and was responsible for providing transportation by pack animal, roads, rail, river, or sea. At this crucial time, the person in whom these extraordinary powers were vested was Brigadier General **Montgomery Meigs.**

By all accounts, Meigs was a hard-working, efficient but vindictive man who tended to exaggerate his own importance. He espoused a particularly anti-Southern attitude although he had been born in Georgia. Meigs had even served with some of the South's most eminent leaders, benefiting from his close association with Jefferson Davis while Davis was secretary of war during President Pierce's administration. Meigs had served under Robert E. Lee in the Corps of Engineers while working on the river improvements at St. Louis. Still, Meigs expressed a deep hatred for Southerners who left the Union, including his own brother, who had become a Confederate soldier. He considered them traitors and was particularly hostile toward Lee.

At about the same time the insurrectionary tax bill was passed by Congress, another piece of legislation found its way to President Lincoln's desk. Buried in an omnibus bill was a clause that provided "the President of the United States shall have power, whenever in his opinion it shall be expedient, to purchase cemetery grounds and cause them to be securely enclosed to be used as a national cemetery for the soldiers who shall die in the service of the country." It was signed into law on July 17, 1862, as the result of the inadequate preparations made for the burial of the massive number of Union casualties.

Early in the war, much of the fighting centered around Washington, which, by necessity, became a city of hospitals where many wounded soldiers were treated, and where many of them died. Soon burial space became scarce, and the public reacted to the scandalous manner in which the burial of soldiers was conducted. This public outcry resulted in the passage of the cemetery authorization bill, and President Lincoln directing his secretary of war to establish the necessary burial grounds. During 1862, military cemeteries were established in Alexandria, Virginia, and in the District of Columbia. But by 1864, with the continuation of the war and its heavy Union casualties, burial space again became scarce. Therefore, to avoid another scandal, Secretary of War Stanton ordered his quartermaster general to survey additional sites and to submit suggestions for his approval.

General Meigs made no surveys. To him it was obvious where the next military cemetery should be established: on the grounds of Arlington House. Therefore, on June 15, 1864, he proposed Arlington as his site. In his letter to Stanton, Meigs stated that "the grounds about the Mansion are admirably adapted to such a use." Stanton shared Meigs' enthusiasm for the choice, and replied with uncharacteristic speed, informing Meigs the very same day:

> "The Arlington Mansion and the grounds immediately surrounding it are appropriated for a Military Cemetery....The Quartermaster General is charged with the execution of this order. He will cause the grounds, not exceeding two hundred acres, to be immediately surveyed, laid out, and enclosed for this purpose...."

Even if Arlington was the only available location capable of satisfying the need for additional burial space, there were many plots within its 1,100 acres that clearly were better suited for a cemetery than the 200 acres surrounding the mansion. It was clear that Meigs' intention was to bury soldiers within the immediate proximity to Arlington House, rendering the mansion uninhabitable should the Lee family attempt to return.

There also may have been a secondary reason for Meigs' selection of the Arlington estate for a military burial ground. Records indicate that more than a month prior to his proposal to Stanton, Meigs had ordered the first burial of military dead on Arlington's ground. On June 15, when Meigs had written to Stanton, more than a dozen soldiers were already buried there. To be exact, it was on May 13, 1864, that Private **William Christman,** a farmer from Pennsylvania and a member of Company G of the 67th Pennsylvania Infantry, became the first soldier to be buried at Arlington National Cemetery. Private Christman's grave is among other Civil War dead in Section 27 near the north boundary of the cemetery.

Whatever the reason for Montgomery Meigs' decision to convert the grounds around the Arlington mansion to a cemetery, it was his purpose to bury as many people as quickly as possible. At first, the soldiers quartered at the mansion objected to the placement of graves near the house, and ordered the burial details to inter bodies far from the house. But this did not meet with General Meigs' approval. When he visited the cemetery in August 1864, he expected to find the house nearly unapproachable due to the number of new graves. Instead he found the mansion much as it had been when it was

The grave of the first soldier buried at Arlington National Cemetery–Private William Christman of Pennsylvania (Sec. 27, Lot 19, Grid CC-47/48). The "19" indicates a later-designated lot number. The earliest burials took place in Section 27, far from Arlington House.

During the Civil War, there were at least three fortifications on the original Arlington estate, including Arlington House where Union soldiers gathered shortly after the estate was designated a national cemetery in 1864.

first occupied by federal troops in May 1861. Furious, Meigs demanded that 26 bodies be brought immediately from Washington, and in the heat of that mid-August day, he personally supervised the burial of these fallen soldiers around Mrs. Lee's once-famous rose garden. Those graves remain in their original locations and can be seen encircling the restored garden.

Montgomery Meigs did not stop there. In April 1866, to assure the destruction of Arlington as a habitable dwelling, he requested sealed proposals for the construction of a stone and masonry burial vault, 20 feet in diameter and 10 feet deep, also to be constructed in the rose garden of Arlington House. In this vault, Meigs placed the remains of 2,111 unknown soldiers who were found in trenches or scattered over battlefields within a 25-mile radius of

Washington. Nearly 1,800 remains were collected from the battlefield at Bull Run, and it can be assumed that it included Confederate soldiers as well, since in some instances only a few bones or a skull were recovered. However, despite its checkered origin, this monument proudly stands today as Arlington's memorial to the Unknown Dead of the Civil War.

The vault that contains the remains of the Civil War unknowns was not the only structure that Montgomery Meigs placed on the site of Mary Custis Lee's garden. He also constructed a colonnaded gazebo called the Temple of Fame, which was dedicated to the memory of George Washington and 11 Union generals. After approximately 100 years, however, the gazebo had become structurally unsound and was removed to facilitate the restoration of the Arlington House grounds.

It also is interesting to note that Montgomery Meigs is buried within 100 yards of the Lee's rose garden at Arlington National Cemetery. Interred with him are his wife, father, and son, Lt. **John Rodgers Meigs,** who, like his father, was an Army engineer and who was killed late in the war. It has been reported that Meigs' son was killed in cold blood by Southern guerillas.

The Tomb of the Unknown Dead from the Civil War is a vault containing the remains of 2,111 soldiers. It was purposely placed in the Lees' rose garden by Quartermaster General Montgomery Meigs. Meigs also erected the Temple of Fame (at right) as a monument to George Washington and 11 Union generals. The Temple of Fame was dismantled as a part of the restoration of the grounds of Arlington House, at left.

The manner of young Meigs' death further contributed to his father's bitter hatred toward the South.

From its establishment as an official military cemetery in June 1864, until nearly the end of the century, the large Arlington estate accommodated many purposes. Not only was it fast becoming one of the largest military cemeteries in the area, but it was the site of several permanent military installations (which today are part of Fort Myer), and the site of an encampment for freed slaves known as Freedman's Village.

The Freedman's Village

Freedman's Village resulted from President Lincoln's emancipation of all slaves living in the District of Columbia on April 16, 1862. With this action, and given Washington's proximity to the Southern states, many fugitive slaves, as well as those liberated by advancing Union troops, found their way to Washington in search of freedom and a new way of life. Liberated slaves came to be known as "contraband," following a precedent set by Major General Benjamin Butler. Butler refused to return fugitive slaves to their civilian owners in the belief that, like wagons or horses, they were property that might be used to support the Confederate war effort. As "contraband of war," he was justified in releasing them.

These "contrabands" joined large numbers of free African Americans already in Washington. They were housed in several camps, including at the U.S. Capitol. Eventually disease and overcrowding forced the government to relocate many of them. The federal government decided to establish a camp on the Arlington estate in the area which now contains Sections 8, 47, and 25 along Eisenhower Drive. Its initial purpose was to provide a temporary refuge for freed slaves, but the camp grew to be known as Freedman's Village, providing permanent housing and other community services to liberated African-American men, women, and children for nearly 30 years.

By May 1863, the idea of a village to harbor freed slaves had gained widespread support within the Lincoln administration and construction of shelters began. When the village was dedicated on December 4, 1863, members of Congress, the Cabinet, and Army officials were present at the ceremonies. Throughout its early years, Freedman's Village entertained numerous government officials who took an interest in the welfare of the people living there. Vice President Hannibal Hamlin, Secretary of the Treasury Salmon P. Chase, Secretary of the Navy Gideon Welles, and Secretary of State William H. Seward all spent time at the camp, lending both their moral and physical support. Seward, in particular, demonstrated his interest in the intellectual well-being of the residents by his personal support of its school.

From its inception, the village came under the jurisdiction of the U.S. Army and was governed by a military commander. Many residents complained that life under military rule was not much better than slavery. In March 1865, the situation improved somewhat when the Bureau of Refugees, Freemen and Abandoned Lands, commonly known as the Freedmen's Bureau, assumed jurisdiction of the village. From its beginning as little more than a tent camp, the village grew into a large community, not only for refugees from other states, but for many of the former Arlington slaves who found a home here. The community counted among its institutions a school, a training center, a home for the aged and disabled, a hospital, churches, and farms.

The first school opened soon after the camp was dedicated. Starting with 150 students, it grew to as many as 900 students, and classes were conducted, not only for primary-age children, but for adults as well.

The training center, known as the Industrial School, provided training for blacksmiths, wheelwrights, carpenters, shoemakers, and tailors. The carpenters made the desks for the school, while tailors made clothing for the residents of the home for the aged and disabled. That "home" was a large structure that provided shelter for those people unable to care for themselves, including the very old, permanently disabled, and those needing custodial care. Also assisting in the care of the residents was Abbott Hospital, which was established in November 1866. It provided 50 beds and a staff of 14 medical officers who cared for hospitalized patients, but also provided health care for the general village population.

In addition to providing for the cultural, intellectual, and physical needs of its residents, the village also established several churches to fulfill their spiritual needs. The first structures were small wooden facilities, but in 1878, the residents built a brick church. People who did not work in the schools, home, or hospital worked as field laborers on the adjacent farms. These farms produced corn fodder, wheat, potatoes, and vegetables that were sold by the villagers for a profit.

While the village provided many necessary services to its residents, it was not without its problems. Situated at first in a low-lying area, it was necessary to move the village to the higher ground of Section 4 when it was discovered that the water supply was contaminated by nearby marshes, causing frequent outbreaks of fever and disease. Also during its early days, the refugees were unhappy with the Army rations they were fed. Known as "contraband's" rations, they were smaller portions than those served to soldiers.

After the war, the desire to assist freed slaves lost a great deal of its appeal among the general public and fewer and fewer resources were made available to the villagers. Neighboring residents complained of the crime associated with the village, and of the financial burden they were being forced to assume as federal assistance to the residents was reduced. All of these circumstances seriously threatened the existence of Freedman's Village, but it was a decision of the United States Supreme Court in 1882 that finally forced its closing. That Supreme Court decision resulted in the government obtaining legal title to the entire former Custis estate. The land, including the village and cemetery, became a military reservation and federal law prohibited civilians from living there. On December 7, 1887, the residents were notified that they had 90 days to vacate the premises.

Nearly a generation had passed since the end of the Civil War and public sentiment in the United States had changed. No longer were the villagers considered refugees from slavery, and without the financial and moral support of the public, the village could not sustain itself. By 1890, after nearly 30 years, Freedman's Village was dismantled and the residents forced to leave.

On April 9, 1865, General Lee surrendered to General Ulysses S. Grant at Appomattox Courthouse, Virginia, effectively ending the Civil War, but as head of a defeated Confederate Army, Lee's future was uncertain. He and Mrs. Lee wanted desperately to return to their home at Arlington House, but were unaware of its current condition. They knew that the property had been confiscated by the federal government, and that there was a military cemetery somewhere on the grounds. They knew that the house had been used as a military headquarters, but neither was yet aware of the nearly wholesale loss of their personal property, including the treasured Washington collection.

Neither Robert E. Lee, as executor of the estate of George Washington Parke Custis, nor Mary Anna Custis Lee, as titleholder to the property, ever attempted to publicly recover control of Arlington House. However, Lee did contact Attorney Francis L. Smith of Alexandria to investigate the status of the property, and to make overtures regarding its recovery. These inquiries, which were performed with utmost discretion, were entirely unsuccessful and generally unknown during Lee's lifetime.

There were two factors that governed Lee's decision not to bring a legal action against the government to reclaim Arlington. First, for more than three years following the cessation of hostilities between the North and the South, Lee considered his status as that of a "paroled prisoner of war." Under the law, as a former Confederate soldier, Lee had no civil rights, including the right of suffrage. For this reason he felt he was without standing to bring

Students from the Freedman's Village school assemble on the grounds of the village, which was established on the Arlington estate to provide refuge for former slaves. Founded in 1863, it was dismantled in 1890.

any legal action in a Virginia state court or Federal district court, and he was not willing to test the point. However, there was an even greater concern deterring him from any action.

More than anything, Lee wanted desperately to heal the wounds between North and South, and to restore the Union envisioned by earlier Virginians like Washington, Jefferson, and Lee's father. He repeatedly advised his fellow Confederates to accept the outcome of the war, and to "help build up the shattered fortunes of our old state." Lee recognized the symbolic importance that he played in rallying Southern support for reconciliation, and he did not wish to present even the appearance of contention between himself and the federal government. So his family's right to recover the Arlington estate was considered secondary to the reunification of the country. He and his wife resigned themselves never again to live at Arlington.

Abandoning recovery of Arlington was not the only gesture Lee made to advance his desire for national unity. He also rejected scores of personal and business opportunities after the war that would have guaranteed his financial future. He wished to avoid any political or social position that might be used to jeopardize national reconciliation. Instead he accepted the presidency of Washington College, a small institution in Lexington, Virginia, where he could "be of some service to the country and the rising generation."

Lee and his wife did work to recover the personal effects that had been confiscated by the government in 1861, and were being stored in Washington. An opportunity presented itself late in 1868. On Christmas Day of that year, President Andrew Johnson proclaimed a general amnesty for all former Confederates. This action restored Lee's civil rights and lifted the indictment of treason that still shadowed the former Confederate general. Following Johnson's conciliatory gesture, and prompted by Illinois Congressman James May, Lee suggested to his wife that she write personally to the president, appealing for the return of her personal property. Because the president was in the last few weeks of his term in office, Lee believed Johnson might be free of political considerations and be more disposed to release the property. His belief was affirmed.

The president acceded to Mrs. Lee's request, and with the approval of his Cabinet, he informed the secretary of the interior to turn the items over to whomever Mrs. Lee designated to receive them. Included among the items held by the government were a set of china that Lafayette had given to Mrs. Lee's great-grandmother, Martha Washington, a punch bowl from Mount Vernon, a mirror, a dresser, and some miscellaneous items, including the Yorktown tents and a strong box. Unfortunately, the transfer was discovered by a group of Radical Republicans before it could be concluded.

Prompted by a story in the February 28 edition of *The Washington Evening Express,* the Republicans acted swiftly. The story had implied that "the Rebel General Lee" himself was going to invade Arlington National Cemetery amid the buried Union soldiers, and abscond with the priceless possessions of George Washington. This was all the fuel the Radicals needed for their *cause celebre,* designed again to embarrass President Johnson. Led by Illinois Senator John A. Logan, a former Union general, the Radicals claimed that Johnson, who had survived their earlier impeachment attempt, was in collusion with his fellow Southerner Lee to deprive the nation of its rightful historic property. A resolution was passed by the Congress during the evening of March 3, the day before Johnson was to leave office, declaring that the property belonged to the federal government and that "to deliver the same to the Rebel General Robert E. Lee is an insult to the loyal people of the United States." That fateful resolution effectively ended any effort to regain any portion of the Arlington estate, either real or personal, during the lifetime of Robert or Mary Custis Lee. Lee later wrote with regard to the Washington relics:

"I hope their presence in the capitol will keep in the remembrance of all Americans the principles and virtues of Washington."

Today, many of these items, including Washington's Yorktown tent, are in the permanent collection of the Smithsonian Institution.

Unable to return to Arlington, Robert E. Lee and his wife, Mary Custis Lee, spent their remaining years on the campus of Washington College (now Washington and Lee University), where he served as that institution's president until his death. General Lee never again visited Arlington House. He did see the mansion from a distance during two trips to Washington after the war. In 1866, Lee was called to testify before a Congressional committee. In May 1869, he was invited to the White House by his old foe and the new president, Ulysses S. Grant. As he left Washington, Lee traveled across the Potomac River toward Alexandria where he planned to visit with old hometown friends. From the window of his passing railroad car, he caught a glimpse of the abandoned mansion which was once his beloved home.

Robert E. Lee died in Lexington, Virginia, on October 12, 1870, and is interred in the chapel on the campus of the university that now bears his name.

For Mary Custis Lee, the fate of Arlington House caused even greater sorrow. She was the granddaughter of George Washington, and never fully recovered from the loss of her ancestral home. Following her husband's death, Mrs. Lee was determined to see her home once more and visit the burial plot of her parents. In 1873, nearly three years after General Lee's death, Mary Custis Lee rode in a carriage up the winding road to Arlington House. She could not help but notice the sad changes. Tombstones dotted the grounds; the rose garden she had cherished was now encircled with the graves of Union soldiers; and saddest of all, the mansion that her loving father had worked so long and hard to build, not only to house his family, but also to enshrine the personal effects of his father, George Washington, now stood abandoned and in dire disrepair.

As she drew near to the front of the house, she was recognized by Selina Gray, a woman who had been a servant in her home. Selina offered her a drink of water, which she gratefully accepted, but Mrs. Lee was physically unable to leave her carriage to look inside her former home. She died three months later. But before her death, she wrote that she would never have recognized her former home except for a few oak trees that the Union troops "had spared and trees planted on the lawn by the General and myself... My dear home was so changed it seemed but as a dream of the past." Mary Anna Randolph Custis Lee died November 5,1873, and is buried next to her husband in the chapel at Washington and Lee University.

General Robert E. Lee and his oldest son, George Washington Custis Lee, shortly after Lee's surrender at Appomattox Courthouse. George Washington Custis Lee inherited Arlington House from his mother. This photograph marks the last time that Lee wore his Confederate uniform.

Upon Mrs. Lee's death, the title to the property passed to her eldest son, George Washington Custis Lee, under the terms of the will of Mary Lee's father, George Washington Parke Custis.

George Washington Custis Lee, known simply as Custis Lee, graduated from the United States Military Academy in 1854. Like his father, he served in the U.S. Army Corps of Engineers until resigning his commission to join the Confederate forces. During the war he served as an aide-de-camp to Jefferson Davis and attained the rank of major general.

After the war, he was appointed a professor of civil and military engineering at the Virginia Military Institute. When Robert E. Lee died in 1870, Custis Lee was named to succeed his father as president of the new Washington and Lee University, serving in that capacity until 1897. It was during his tenure as president of the university that he challenged the government's title to Arlington.

Lee had been advised by his legal counsel that because of the questionable procedure used in obtaining the title, the government's claim to the property was tenuous at best. He, therefore, made overtures to the government to recover the property, or, if actual recovery of the land was impossible, to receive just compensation for it. In April 1874, his formal claim was presented to the United States Senate, where it received an unsympathetic reception. Unfortunately, Lee's name still triggered a hostile response from the Radical Republicans, the same faction that had denied his mother the recovery of her personal property five years earlier. The Radical Republicans contended that the government rightfully owned the property, and that as long as soldiers continued to be buried there, the government would not relinquish its title to the estate. After a failed three-year attempt to achieve a peaceful settlement, Custis Lee filed suit against the United States of America.

He brought an action for ejectment in the Circuit Court of Alexandria (now Arlington) County, Virginia, in April 1877. A host of defendants were listed in the suit because the law required that every alleged trespasser be made a party to the action. This included all the cemetery personnel, the Army personnel at Fort Whipple, and the residents of the Freedman's Village. This initial legal step began a process that would slowly wind its way through the Virginia State Court system into the Federal Courts, and would finally reach its climax before the United States Supreme Court five years later.

To say that the case was complicated by procedural quagmires is a gross understatement. The United States attorney general opposed Lee at every turn, attempting to derail the action before its scheduled jury trial. Eventually the matter was presented to a jury in January 1879. After a six-day trial, the jury found in favor of the plaintiff, Custis Lee. The government, dissatisfied with that judgment, appealed the verdict, and the matter was not resolved until the case reached the United States Supreme Court in October 1882. After only two months of deliberation, Mr. Justice Miller delivered the decision of the court in a 46-page opinion. By a 5-4 decision, the Court ruled that the United States had denied Mary Custis Lee her property without due process when its tax commissioners had refused to accept the payment of taxes from anyone but the owner.

Accordingly the Supreme Court granted Lee his request for ejectment and thereby reaffirmed his right to require all trespassers to leave the premises.

Of course, the legal solution only raised the practical question of what was to be done with the nearly 17,000 graves and the military post located on the estate. Under the Court's ruling, Custis Lee could have ordered the government to dismantle the military post and disinter the remains of every soldier buried there. Fortunately, reasonable minds prevailed. Custis Lee reissued his original offer to accept compensation for the property and on March 3, 1883, the Forty-Seventh Congress appropriated the agreed sum of $150,000 to be paid to Major General Custis Lee.

Upon receipt of this payment, Custis Lee executed the deed, and following the approval of the Secretary of War **Robert Todd Lincoln,** it was recorded at the Alexandria County Courthouse on May 14, 1883. At last, nearly 22 years after Union troops had first occupied the estate, Arlington became an official national cemetery of the United States of America.

From the end of the Civil War, Arlington House served as the administrative center of the cemetery, as well as the residence of the superintendent of the cemetery. At the end of the War, the cemetery only

George Washington Custis Lee during his tenure as president of Washington and Lee College in Lexington, Virginia. It was during this period that Custis Lee successfully challenged the United States government's title to the Arlington estate.

consisted of 200 acres and contained 17,260 burials, of which 11,911 were known and 5,349 were unknown.

By 1897, the size of the cemetery more than doubled, growing to 408 acres. In 1981, it had acquired the land formerly known as the South Post of Fort Myer and had grown to 612 acres. The number of persons buried at Arlington has increased significantly after every war. By 1957, nearly 93,000 American military personnel and their dependents had been buried at Arlington. In just over 40 years, by 2000, that number had nearly tripled again to 250,000. In 1999, the neighboring, 37-acre Navy Annex property and eight acres from Fort Myer were transferred to the cemetery.

The desire of Armed Services personnel and their families to be laid to rest at Arlington has been heightened by the significant number of national figures who have chosen to be buried here. This wish for an Arlington burial reflects the dramatic change in the cemetery's status from its early days when it was considered little more than a potter's field. The original burials took place in Arlington by necessity, not by design. Few families chose to bury their dead here, but as more and more of the nation's heroes chose Arlington as their resting place, more of the men and women with whom they served followed their example. Today burial at Arlington is restricted by official government regulation. A copy of the rules for eligibility for burial at Arlington can be found in Appendix III.

Also contributing to the honored status of Arlington Cemetery are the ceremonies that have become a tradition here in the shadow of the United States capital. As early as 1868, the first Memorial Day services were held on an open grassy area following a declaration by the former Commander of the Grand Army of the Republic, General John A. Logan. He declared that May 30 be set aside as a day to remember "comrades who died in the defense of their country." This early commemoration of a memorial day evolved into grand, day-long ceremonies that found thousands of people journeying to the cemetery

In December 1899, 164 victims of the explosion that destroyed the *USS Maine* in February 1898 were reinterred at Arlington National Cemetery from Colon Cemetery in Havana, Cuba.

to decorate graves and to listen to the nation's greatest speakers deliver their stirring orations in the Old Amphitheatre. The custom continues today as thousands of Americans visit Arlington each year on Memorial Day.

Arlington also gained prominence as it became home to many celebrated memorials and monuments. In 1912, the mast of the battleship *USS Maine* became a permanent memorial to the 260 men who lost their lives in Havana Harbor when their ship exploded and sank in 1898. In 1914, the Confederate Monument was unveiled, honoring those soldiers who died fighting for the South during the Civil War. At its dedication, it was hailed as the memorial that made Arlington, at last, a truly national cemetery.

The need for a larger, permanent gathering site prompted the construction of the Memorial Amphitheatre, dedicated in 1920. However, the most memorable ceremonies at Arlington have been the interments of the Unknowns. On November 11, 1921, an unknown soldier of World War I was buried with full military honors on the east plaza of the Memorial Amphitheatre. In 1958, that honored soldier was joined by unknown servicemen from World War II and from the Korean Conflict. And in 1981, an unknown soldier of the Vietnam War was interred on the plaza.

On May 14, 1998, the unknown American of the Vietnam Era was exhumed from the Tomb for possible identification. Using the most sophisticated science available, the unknown was identified as First Lieutenant Michael J. Blassie, U.S. Air Force. In accordance with the wishes of his family, he was reinterred in Jefferson Barracks National Cemetery near St. Louis, Missouri. The crypt at the Tomb of the Unknowns is empty, but a marble tablet marking the crypt states, "HONORING AND KEEPING FAITH WITH AMERICA'S MISSING SERVICEMEN, 1958–1975."

In 1922 former Confederate soldiers appeared at the Confederate monument to remember their fallen comrades-in-arms. Completion of the monument in 1914 symbolically brought North and South together, making Arlington a truly national cemetery.

In 1926, the daylight civilian Tomb guard was replaced with a military guard, and in 1937, the guard became a 24-hour vigil. The Third United States Infantry, known as the Old Guard, undertook the full-time guardianship of the Tomb in 1948. It has continued uninterrupted since that time.

In 1925, Congress designated Arlington House as a permanent memorial to Robert E. Lee. The War Department, which still had jurisdiction over the mansion, was instructed to restore it to reflect the condition in the pre-Civil War period when the Lees made the mansion their home. Arlington House, as the Robert E. Lee Memorial, was reopened to the public in 1929. In 1933, the mansion and its immediate environs were transferred from the jurisdiction of the United States Army to the National Park Service in the Department of the Interior.

But it was in 1963 that Arlington gained widespread recognition as millions of Americans watched the televised burial services for President John F. Kennedy. Kennedy's assassination stunned the world, and an international audience stayed glued to television sets as he was laid to rest with full military honors while Jacqueline Kennedy lit the Eternal Flame. During the next

The east entrance to the Memorial Amphitheatre as it appeared at the time of its dedication in 1920. This photograph shows the East Plaza before it became the site of the Tomb of the Unknown Soldier the following year.

year, eight million visitors came to John Kennedy's gravesite. The cemetery also received hundreds of requests for burials each week. That great influx of vehicular and foot traffic and demand for burials forced the cemetery to alter its visitation and burial policies to accommodate the public.

Arlington was again propelled into the spotlight on September 11, 2001. American Airlines Flight 77 had just taken off from Dulles International Airport headed for Los Angeles when a group of terrorists hijacked the plane, and crashed it into the west side of the Pentagon, just a few hundred yards from Arlington Cemetery. Today, 64 of the 184 victims of that tragedy are buried here. A monument in Section 64 honors all who lost their lives that day.

When George Washington Parke Custis began building Arlington House in 1802, he intended the estate to serve as a national shrine. Unfortunately his dream of a memorial to George Washington was eclipsed by the tragedy of the Civil War, and his monument to Washington was destroyed. However, that war forced the creation of a strikingly different national shrine—Arlington National Cemetery. Today Arlington is visited annually by more than four million people who are drawn to the cemetery out of respect for the hundreds of thousands of men and women who are buried here—men and women who dedicated their lives to the preservation of this great nation. Although it is not the monument that Custis envisioned, Arlington proudly fulfills Custis' dream of honoring America and our nation's heroes.

American Heroes at Arlington: Profiles in Patriotism

On the Virginia hillsides overlooking Washington, D.C., lie the graves of hundreds of thousands of men and women who have dedicated at least a portion of their lives to the defense and preservation of liberty. Here at Arlington lie Americans and friends of America; paupers and presidents; soldiers and civilians; warriors and peacemakers. Many we can never forget; most we will never know. The lives of these people reflect the history of our nation. Though it is impossible to tell the life stories of every man, woman, and child who now rest at Arlington, discovering more about even a few of them will illustrate the high caliber of people who have earned their place here. Therefore, outlined below are short profiles of more than one hundred of these patriots.

THE APOLLO ONE ASTRONAUTS

Virgil "Gus" Grissom
(April 3, 1926–January 27, 1967)
Sec. 3, Lot 2503–E, Grid Q–15/16

Roger Bruce Chaffee
(February 15, 1935–January 27, 1967)
Sec. 3, Lot 2502–F, Grid Q–15/16

Edward H. White II
Buried at the United States Military Academy
West Point, New York

It was 6:31 p.m., January 27, 1967. The last traces of sunlight had disappeared over Cape Kennedy. Strapped into their command capsule atop the giant Saturn rocket, three Apollo One astronauts prepared for a full-scale simulated liftoff. This was the dress rehearsal for the scheduled

February 21 launching of the first Apollo mission, a mission that would carry the three Americans on a 14-day journey into space. With this mission, America would launch its program to put the first person on the moon.

Veteran astronaut Gus Grissom was in the command seat on the left, Ed White sat in the middle, and Roger Chaffee, the rookie of the team, occupied the right-hand seat. They had been strapped into these positions for more than five hours, testing various launch procedures and receiving commands from ground control until just ten minutes remained before their simulated launch. All hatches were sealed as the men readied for liftoff. Suddenly, a bright flash erupted across the darkness atop the booster rocket. Communication with the astronauts went silent. Instantly, emergency crews scrambled to the capsule to investigate, but dense black smoke billowing from the cockpit blocked their approach. Even using a high-speed elevator, ten full minutes passed before the first rescuers reached the top of the rocket. Once inside the capsule they discovered that the three men had died, apparently instantaneously.

An intensive investigation by the National Aeronautic and Space Administration revealed that the fire, which had been ignited by a spark from faulty wiring and had fed on nylon netting and other flammable materials, had swept through the cockpit's pure-oxygen environment with lethal speed. The emergency escape system had been rendered useless because it could only be triggered by an on-board astronaut. In this case, there had been no time to activate the escape system. As a result of this tragedy, NASA engineers undertook to redesign the entire spacecraft, installing more safety features, and utilizing nonflammable or flame-retardant materials inside the cockpit.

On that fateful day in January 1967, Colonel Virgil I. ("Gus") Grissom, a native of Mitchell, Indiana, was preparing for his third space voyage. As one of the original seven Mercury astronauts, Grissom had eluded a disaster on his first flight in 1961. Returning to earth after becoming only the second American in space, he and his capsule splashed down in the Atlantic Ocean. The hatch opened, the capsule filled with water and began to sink. Grissom succeeded in scrambling out of the sinking capsule, and was later rescued by a helicopter search team. His second space mission was the first two-man Gemini flight in 1965, during which he became the first person to make a second voyage into space.

Following his graduation from Purdue University in 1950 with a degree in mechanical engineering, Grissom entered the United States Air Force. During the Korean War, he served as a fighter pilot with the 334th Interceptor Squadron in 1951 and 1952, flying 100 combat missions, and earning the Distinguished Flying Cross. By 1956, he had graduated from the

Test Pilot School at Edwards Air Force Base, California, and was assigned to Wright-Patterson Air Force Base, Ohio, in the fighter branch. He remained with the fighter branch until his selection as one of the original Mercury astronauts in 1959.

Roger Bruce Chaffee was preparing for his first flight in space when the aborted test launch claimed his life. Born in Grand Rapids, Michigan, Chaffee, like Grissom, was a graduate of Purdue University who had earned his degree in aeronautical engineering in 1957. During that same year Chaffee undertook postgraduate work at the Air Force Institute of Technology at Wright-Patterson Air Force Base, and joined the Navy. He became a Navy pilot, rising to the rank of lieutenant commander before being chosen for the third group of astronauts in 1963.

The third member of the Apollo One crew, Lt. Colonel Edward H. White II, a native of San Antonio, Texas, was the first man ever to walk in space. He accomplished this historic feat during his first flight in 1965. The Apollo flight was to have been his second mission in space. He is buried on the grounds of his alma mater, the United States Military Academy at West Point.

All America mourned the tragic loss of these three space pioneers as President Lyndon Johnson expressed the nation's sorrow at the burials of Colonel Grissom and Lt. Commander Chaffee in Arlington National Cemetery. Although they are buried in adjoining graves, their burial ceremonies took place four hours apart allowing each man to receive full

military honors. Colonel Grissom's honorary pallbearers included many of the major figures in America's space program. John Glenn, Donald Slayton, Scott Carpenter, Alan Shepherd, Gordon Cooper, and Walter Schirra all escorted Grissom to his final resting place.

Roger Chaffee and Virgil Grissom rest side by side in graves marked with simple government-issue headstones. Nothing on those stones tells the tragic story of how these men lost their lives. However, the decision to place them in Section 3 is significant: the two astronauts were assigned graves in this section to put them in close proximity to the grave of Lt. **Thomas Selfridge** who died on December 17, 1908, while testing a Wright brothers' plane at nearby Fort Myer. Selfridge was the first air fatality among American Armed Services personnel, just as Grissom, Chaffee, and White were the first fatalities of the American space program.

Henry Harley "Hap" Arnold
American Military Aviation Pioneer, Five-Star General
(June 25, 1886–January 15, 1950)
Sec. 34, Lot 44–A, Grid UV–11/12

The story of General Henry "Hap" Arnold is the story of American military aviation. Learning to fly from the Wright brothers, he became the only man in American history to attain the rank of general in both the Army and the Air Force. It was largely through his efforts that the United States Air Force became a separate branch of military service. In fact, his role in transforming the old Army Air Corps into a modern air force won him the unofficial title of "Father of the United States Air Force."

Born and raised in Gladwyne, Pennsylvania, Arnold received an appointment to the United States Military Academy, where he was given the nickname "Hap" because of his cheerful disposition. His graduation from West Point in 1907 fatefully coincided with the birth of modern aviation. Four years later, Arnold found himself assigned to the Aeronautical Division of the Signal Corps. Thereafter, for nearly 40 years, his name would be synonymous with flying.

In 1911, after completing flight training with Orville and Wilbur Wright, Arnold became only the 29th pilot to be licensed in the United States. His career was highlighted by one first after another. In September 1911, he carried the first U.S. air mail shipments; on June 1, 1912, he attained the record altitude of 6,540 feet; and in October 1912, he won aviation's

first MacKay Trophy for a 30-mile round-trip flight from College Park, Maryland, to Fort Myer, Virginia. On that flight, Arnold piloted an early Wright biplane powered by a 40-horsepower engine. It had two propellers driven by a chain-and-sprocket device. He also pioneered air refueling techniques, as well as airborne patrolling of forest fires. On July 6, 1924, Arnold established a new speed record of 113 miles per hour between Rockwell, California and San Francisco, and in 1934, he received a second coveted MacKay Trophy for outstanding achievement in flying—this time for commanding ten bombers on a round-trip flight from Washington, D.C., to Fairbanks, Alaska.

During World War I, Arnold was appointed head of the Army's Aviation Training School, and following several flight-related commands, gained promotion to lieutenant colonel. By 1938, he rose to major general, chief of the Army Air Corps. By the time the United States entered World War II, the aircraft industry had increased its production capabilities sixfold, due primarily to Hap Arnold's influence and leadership. He was promoted to lieutenant general in 1941, and was commissioned as aviation's first full general in 1943. Serving on both the Joint Chiefs of Staff and the Allied Combined Chiefs of Staff during World War II, he was recognized by President Harry Truman in 1945 with a promotion to the rank of five-star general of the Army, joining Douglas MacArthur, **George C. Marshall,** Dwight Eisenhower, and **Omar Bradley.**

Hap Arnold retired to his farm in Sonoma, California, in March 1946. Nevertheless, in 1949 in recognition of his unequaled contribution to the United States' flying forces, he was commissioned general of the Air Force, the first such commission ever given, and one which made him the only person in American military history to attain that rank in both the Army and Air Force. Arnold published his autobiography, *Global Mission,* in 1949, and died on his Sonoma ranch in 1950. His tomb is marked by a simple regulation tombstone, near the grave of another great American general, **John Pershing.**

Hap Arnold's sons are buried near their father—**U.S.A.F. Colonel William Bruce Arnold** (West Point 1943), Sec. 34, Lot 3.A (UV-11/12), and **U.S.A.F. Colonel David Lee Arnold** (West Point 1949), Sec. 34, Lot 101.A (U-12).

Constance Bennett (Coulter)
Stage and Screen Actress
(October 22, 1905–July 25, 1965)
Sec. 3, Lot 2231–A, Grid P–13

A military cemetery is an unusual place to find the grave of the glamorous movie queen of the 1930s, Constance Bennett. The whirlwind career of this film legend mirrored the Golden Age of Hollywood. Married five times during her life, Bennett's longest lasting marriage was to her fifth husband, an Air Force colonel.

Daughter of silent film idol Richard Bennett and sister of Joan Bennett, another movie great, Constance Bennett was born in New York City. Samuel Goldwyn launched her movie career in 1924 with the silent film, *Cytherea,* the first of more than 50 films in which she appeared. She survived the transition to "talkies" and played opposite many of Hollywood's greatest leading men, including Clark Gable, Frederick March, Joel McCrea, Herbert Marshall, and Cary Grant.

In *Topper,* the 1937 comedy hit, she and Grant were cast as a pair of well-intentioned ghosts who come to the aid of a downtrodden bank president, brilliantly portrayed by Roland Young. The same trio also starred in the film's sequel, *Topper Takes a Trip.* Her final picture was *Madame X,* which also starred Lana Turner, John Forsythe, Ricardo Montalban, and Burgess Meredith.

Bennett's private life was almost as entertaining as her movie roles. At age 15, she eloped with a University of Virginia student whom she met over Easter weekend. That marriage ended in divorce. At 19, she married millionaire Philip Plant, and at 26, divorced from Plant, she married the Marquis Henri de la Falaise, former husband of screen star Gloria Swanson. Ten years later she wed her fourth husband, movie actor Gilbert Roland. In 1946, she married Air Force Colonel John Coulter. An advisor for Air Force training films, Coulter met Bennett in Hollywood, and persuaded her to try the life of a career military wife. That life seemed to have agreed with her because she remained married to Coulter until her death in 1965 in New York City. John Coulter attained the rank of general before he retired. He died in 1995.

Film making was not Constance Bennett's only forte. She also was known as a shrewd businesswoman, creating her own cosmetics firm and designing Constance Bennett originals for a Cincinnati dressmaker. When she died, Bennett was buried in Arlington National Cemetery, exercising her right to be interred with her husband, who had attained the rank of brigadier general before his death. The plain black marble stone which marks her grave makes no mention of her sparkling film career or of her business successes; rather, it simply reads: Constance Bennett Coulter.

Hiram Bingham
Teacher, Explorer, Statesman
(November 19, 1875–June 6, 1956) Sec. 1, Lot 357, Grid M–35/36

Hiram Bingham enjoyed a long and eclectic life. He taught history at three ivy league colleges, led highly successful expeditions to the wilds of South America, commanded an aviation instruction center in France during WWI, and was governor of Connecticut for two days before joining the United States Senate.

Bingham was born in Honolulu in 1875. His father—also Hiram Bingham—was a well-known missionary who instilled a profound sense of adventure in his son. Young Hiram was educated at Harvard and Yale universities and the University of California, earning a PhD in South American history. In 1900, Hiram Bingham married **Alfreda Mitchell,** heir to the Tiffany fortune. He was able to draw on his wife's wealth to help subsidize his later explorations.

In 1906, he traveled to South America, attempting to retrace the route taken in 1819 by Simon Bolivar from Venezuela to Colombia. Two years later he followed an old Spanish trade route from Buenos Aires across the Andes Mountains to Lima, Peru. But his greatest discovery came in 1911 while leading the Yale Peruvian Expedition. Bingham was determined to find Vilcabamba, the storied "lost city of the Incas." There were few clues regarding the location of this 16th-century Incan stronghold, and traversing the Andes was a formidable challenge. Yet on July 24, 1911, Bingham and his guide Melchor Arteaga discovered the ruins of Machu Picchu, an Incan Empire site built around 1450.

He returned the following year on behalf of Yale and the National Geographic Society, and spent three years excavating the site, uncovering well-preserved stonework and an Incan temple.

In 1917, Bingham earned his pilot's wings and became chief of the Air Personnel Division of the Air Service in Washington, D.C. Later he commanded the Aviation Instruction Center at Issoudun, France, during WWI.

Hiram Bingham taught history at Harvard and Princeton universities, but spent the greatest part of his teaching career at Yale, 1910–1923. In 1922, Bingham was elected lieutenant governor of Connecticut. He won the governorship in 1924, but served just two days before being chosen to fill a vacant seat in the United States Senate. He was reelected to a full term in the Senate in 1926.

He left the Senate in 1933 and devoted himself to his business interests. In 1951, President Harry Truman appointed him to the Civil Service Loyalty Review Board, which investigated cases of suspected subversion in the state department. He died in Washington, D.C., on June 6, 1956.

Hugo L. Black
U.S. Senator, Supreme Court Justice
(February 27, 1886–September 25, 1971)
Sec. 30, Lot 649 LH, Grid WX–39

During his 34 years on the Supreme Court, Justice Hugo Lafayette Black earned a solid reputation as a staunch defender of the Bill of Rights, but his position on the nation's highest court was jeopardized when it was disclosed that he had once been a member of the Ku Klux Klan.

Black, a native of Harlan, Alabama, was one of eight children whose father was a storekeeper and farmer. Young Hugo attended the University of Alabama, where he received his law degree in 1906. He practiced law in Birmingham until he was selected as a police court judge in 1910. In 1915, he served as county prosecutor, but joined the U.S. Army when the United States entered the first World War. A member of the Eighty-first Field Artillery, Black served his tour of duty without leaving the country.

After the war, Black resumed his law practice in Birmingham. In 1926, he was elected to the United States Senate from Alabama, and won praise for his investigation of utility lobbyists and for leading the drive for the Fair Labor Standards Act. He also was a staunch supporter of President Franklin Roosevelt's New Deal legislation, and favored FDR's initiative to increase the number of Supreme Court justices. In 1937, when Justice Willis Van Devanter retired from the Supreme Court, President Roosevelt appointed Senator Black to fill the vacancy.

Black's nomination was quickly confirmed by the Senate, but shortly came under fire when it was learned that during the 1920s, he had been a member of the Ku Klux Klan. In a nationally broadcast radio statement—an act almost unheard of by a Supreme Court Justice—Black dramatically acknowledged that he had indeed been a member of the Ku Klux Klan, but that he had resigned many years earlier, prior to his election to the Senate. Following his broadcast, Black made no further comment on the subject, and immediately undertook his duties on the Court. Within a short period of time, the furor over the disclosure calmed and Black's position on the Court never again was challenged.

On the bench, Black became a strong advocate for the absolute authority of the Bill of Rights, especially the freedom of speech. Justice Black voted to strike down mandatory school prayer statutes, and to guarantee the right to legal counsel for suspected criminals. In 1971, his last major opinion upheld the right of *The New York Times* to publish the so-called "Pentagon Papers."

Black suffered from ill health during the later years of his life, and was forced to resign from the Supreme Court on September 17, 1971. He died eight days later at Bethesda Naval Hospital in Maryland. President Richard Nixon nominated Lewis Powell, Jr. to succeed Black.

Government regulation tombstones mark the graves of Justice Black and his wife, **Josephine Foster Black.** Adorning the site is a small marble bench inscribed with the simple epitaph: "Here lies a good man."

Harry A. Blackmun
Supreme Court Justice
(November 12, 1908–March 4, 1999)
Sec. 5, Lot 40-4, Grid W–35

Richard Nixon was looking for a strict constructionist when he nominated Harry Blackmun to the United States Supreme Court in 1970. Chief Justice **Warren Burger** had suggested Blackmun, a friend since childhood, and Nixon felt sure that he had found a candidate who would take the court in a more conservative direction. Not so. By the time Blackmun retired from the Court in 1994, he was considered its most liberal member and had enraged conservatives with his 1973 majority opinion in *Roe v. Wade.* That decision found an implicit right of privacy broad enough to encompass a woman's choice to end a pregnancy—the right to have an abortion.

Harry Blackmun was born in Nashville, Illinois, on November 12, 1908, but his family moved to Saint Paul, Minnesota, while he was still a boy. He received his undergraduate degree in mathematics from Harvard University in 1929, and earned his law degree from Harvard in 1932. He returned to

Minnesota to practice law, and eventually counted the Mayo Clinic among his clients. He married **Dorothy Clark** in 1941 and they had three children.

In 1959, President Dwight Eisenhower appointed Blackmun to the United States Court of Appeals for the Eighth Circuit on the recommendation of then-Senator Hubert Humphrey.

In 1969, Justice Abe Fortas was forced to resign from the Supreme Court following a disclosure by Life magazine that he had accepted and then returned a questionable fee of $20,000. Fortas' resignation gave President Nixon his second chance to appoint a justice, but the United States Senate rejected Nixon's first two candidates—Clement Haynsworth of South Carolina and G. Harold Carswell of Florida. Then at Chief Justice Burger's suggestion, Nixon nominated Harry Blackmun.

Justice Blackmun had been on the Court just three years when he wrote the majority opinion in the landmark case of *Roe v. Wade.* The 7-to-2 ruling is considered among the most influential decisions of the Court in the twentieth century. It galvanized supporters and opponents alike, but Blackmun stated after his retirement, "It's a step that had to be taken...toward the full emancipation of women." Not everyone agreed.

Blackmun's opinion brought repeated threats on his life. He received more than 60,000 pieces of "hate mail," calling him everything from "low-down scum" to a "murderer" and comparing him to the Nazi overseers of genocide.

Blackmun championed other causes as well, including the strict separation of church and state and expanding the freedom of speech. Two months before he announced his retirement in 1994, Blackmun, who had consistently voted to uphold the death penalty, said he had come to believe that the capital punishment system was fraught with discrimination and mistakes. "From this day forward," he said, "I no longer shall tinker with the machinery of death."

Justice Blackmun resigned from the Court on August 3, 1994, and was succeeded by Justice Stephen G. Breyer. In 1997, Blackmun appeared as Justice Joseph Story in the movie "Amistad." On February 22, 1999, he fell at his home and underwent hip replacement surgery. He died on March 4 at the age of 90 from complications of the surgery.

Gregory "Pappy" Boyington

Black Sheep Squadron Commander
(December 4, 1912–January 11, 1988)
Sec. 7A, Lot 150, Grid U–24

Pappy Boyington was one of WWII's most colorful and daring pilots. He organized a group of replacement and inactive pilots into one of the most successful units in the war, and personally shot down a record 28 enemy planes before he was shot down and taken prisoner.

Gregory Boyington was born in Coeur d'Alene, Idaho, in 1912, the son of apple ranchers. He earned a degree in aeronautical engineering from the University of Washington in 1934, enlisted in the Marine Corps in 1936, and became a pilot. In 1941, he was a first lieutenant stationed in Pensacola, Florida, when he resigned from the Marine Corps to join General **Claire Chennault's** American Volunteer Group, the Flying Tigers, in China.

Following the Japanese attack on Pearl Harbor on December 7, 1941, Boyington rejoined the Marines and was allowed to organize the 212 Squadron. He called them Black Sheep Squadron because they were a collection of unattached or replacement pilots, who, for one reason or another, were not a part of any other unit. Just 10 years older than most of his recruits, Boyington became "Pappy" to the men in his unit.

The Black Sheep Squadron flew its first combat mission on September 16, 1943. In just 84 days, they compiled a record 203 planes destroyed or damaged, troop transports and supply ships sunk, and ground installations destroyed.

On January 3, 1944, Boyington encountered 10 Japanese fighter planes over Rabaul Harbor, New Britain. After shooting down three of them, Boyington's plane was hit. With his F4U fighter plane on fire, Boyington bailed into the Pacific. While in the water, the Japanese strafed him for 20 minutes before he was captured by a Japanese submarine.

As a Medal of Honor recipient, Pappy Boyington's headstone is engraved in gold.

He was transported to a prison camp in Japan where he remained for nearly two years. With his fate unknown, President Franklin Roosevelt awarded Major Boyington the Congressional Medal of Honor. Shortly after the fighting ceased in 1945, his fellow POWs painted "PAPPY BOYINGTON HERE!" on the top of their barracks. This led to his speedy release and return to the United States where President Harry Truman presented him with his Medal of Honor.

Boyington was promoted to colonel and retired from the military in 1947.

Pappy Boyington was married four times and had three children, one of whom was a pilot and fought in Vietnam. In 1958, he wrote his autobiography, "Baa Baa Black Sheep," which became the basis for a popular television series during the 1970s. He died in Fresno, California, on January 11, 1988, and was buried with full military honors at Arlington National Cemetery.

Omar Nelson Bradley
Five-Star General, World War II's "GI General"
(February 12, 1893–April 8, 1981)
Sec. 30, Lot 428–1, Grid AA–39

Omar Bradley did not have a field command in World War II until April 1943. At that time, he assumed command of the II Corps from General George Patton, and following a successful D-Day landing at Normandy, he led the largest force ever commanded by an American field officer—1.3 million men—across Europe into Germany. Throughout his campaigns, he had a policy of keeping his command posts near the front lines; he visited his troops regularly; and he cared greatly about the morale of his men. His conduct earned him the unofficial title of "The GI General." In an official statement, Army Chief of Staff General **George C. Marshall** called Bradley "the finest Army group commander" in the United States Army.

Born in the small Missouri town of Clark,

Bradley moved to Moberly, Missouri, as a child, living there until he left for West Point in 1911. Upon graduation from the military academy in 1915, in a class that included Dwight Eisenhower and **James Van Fleet,** he earned a commission in the infantry.

After various stateside assignments during World War I, Bradley was made a professor of military science at South Dakota State University in 1919, but was transferred to instruct at West Point the following year. By 1941, he had risen to the rank of brigadier general and commandant of the Infantry School of the Eighty-second Infantry (later of the Eighty-second Airborne Division) at Camp Claiborne, Louisiana. After a year commanding the Twenty-eighth Infantry Division at Camp Livingston, Louisiana, Bradley was ordered to North Africa as an aide to General Dwight Eisenhower in 1943.

It was then, in April 1943, that he was ordered to relieve General Patton of his command of the II Corps. Under his command, the II Corps captured Bizerte and Tunis, and Bradley became a lieutenant general. From North Africa, he led his troops in a landing near Scoglitti, Sicily; then in September 1943, he was called to England to assist in the cross-channel invasion. While in England, he was appointed commander of the Provisional First U.S. Army Group (FUSAG) for the historic D-Day invasion.

On June 6, 1944, he landed his First Army at Utah and Omaha Beaches. In July, he directed the crucial breakthrough at St. Lo, which allowed the advance of the Allied Forces and ultimately liberated Paris from Nazi control. During this advance, Bradley commanded the Twelfth Army Group, the largest force ever led by an American commander. Following the surrender of Germany, Bradley was promoted to full general in August 1945. At that same time, because of his widely publicized and widely praised concern for enlisted men, he also was named Administrator of Veterans Affairs in what later became known as the Veterans Administration.

He stayed at the V.A. until February 1948, when he was named to succeed General Eisenhower as Army Chief of Staff. The following year, he became chairman of the first permanent Joint Chiefs of Staff in the new U.S. Department of Defense. In 1950, he was promoted to five-star general of the Army, joining **George C. Marshall,** Dwight Eisenhower, **Hap Arnold,** and Douglas MacArthur as the only persons to hold that rank.

In 1951, Omar Bradley published his memoirs, *A Soldier's Story,* and two years later retired from the Army. Following his retirement, he served as chairman of the board of the Bulova Watch Company. Omar Nelson Bradley died in 1981 while on a visit to New York City. His wives—**Mary Quayle Bradley** (1892–1965) and **Esther "Kitty" Bradley** (1922–2004)—are buried with him.

William J. Brennan, Jr.
Army Colonel, Supreme Court Justice
(April 25, 1906July 24, 1997)
Sec. 5, Lot 40, Grid W–36

William J. Brennan, Jr. served with distinction during WWII and holds the highest military rank of the Supreme Court justices buried in Arlington National Cemetery. It was following his military career that Brennan served nearly 34 years on the United States Supreme Court, writing 1,360 opinions—more than any other justice except **William O. Douglas.**

Brennan was born in 1906, in Newark, New Jersey, the second of eight children of Irish immigrants. He graduated with honors from the Wharton School of Finance and Commerce at the University of Pennsylvania, and received his law degree from Harvard University in 1931, graduating at the top of his class. He returned to New Jersey to practice law, but joined the Army in 1942 following the attack on Pearl Harbor.

Brennan was a major in the Ordnance Department in Washington, D.C., serving as a legal aide specializing in labor and industrial problems. He was discharged with the rank of colonel in 1946, and returned to his law practice in New Jersey. He served as a trial and appellate judge before being appointed to the New Jersey Supreme Court in 1952.

In 1956, when Justice Sherman Minton retired, President Dwight Eisenhower appointed William Brennan to the United States Supreme Court, although Brennan had strong ties to the Democratic Party.

During his tenure on the Court, Brennan supported a broad interpretation of the First Amendment's right to free speech. He wrote the majority opinion in *Baker v. Carr,* establishing the principle of "one person, one vote," and wrote rulings favoring affirmative action, abortion rights, and separation of church and state. He strongly opposed sex discrimination and the death penalty.

Justice Brennan retired from the Court on July 20, 1990, citing ill health. He was succeeded on the Court by Justice David H. Souter. In 1993, President Bill Clinton awarded Brennan the Presidential Medal of Freedom. He died at the age of 91 on July 25, 1997, and was buried in Arlington National Cemetery next to his first wife **Marjorie Leonard Brennan** who died in 1982.

William Jennings Bryan

Presidential Candidate, Secretary of State
(March 19, 1860–June 26, 1925)
Sec. 4, Lot 3121, Grids Y/Z–11

At age 36, William Jennings Bryan became the youngest person ever to be nominated for president by a major political party. Though he would be nominated twice more, the nation's highest office would elude him.

A statue of William Jennings Bryan represents Nebraska in the United States Capitol's Statuary Hall because of his long association with that state, though he was born in Marion County, Illinois. He attended public schools in Jacksonville, Illinois, and graduated from Illinois College in 1881. He returned to Jacksonville to practice law after completing his legal studies at Union College in Chicago in 1883. In 1887, Bryan moved to Nebraska, where he maintained his residence for nearly 35 years. After serving two terms in Congress from 1891 to 1895, he declined to be a candidate for reelection in order to run for the United States Senate in 1894, an election he lost.

Following his Senate defeat, Bryan returned to Nebraska, becoming editor of the *Omaha World-Herald*. In 1896, he went to the Democratic National Convention in Chicago as a virtual unknown, but he left the convention as that party's nominee for president. This startling turn of events occurred as a result of the trait that made William Jennings Bryan one of the most famous men of his time: his dramatic talent as an orator.

During the convention's platform debate, Bryan addressed the question regarding the free silver plank. The resulting "Cross of Gold" speech is considered one of the most famous orations ever made before an American political convention. It left the convention hall in pandemonium and led to Bryan's nomination. He had to face Republican William McKinley in the general election, and knew that he could not rely upon traditional campaign tactics to win.

Prior to that election, presidential candidates had not personally campaigned for votes, relying instead on surrogates to campaign for them. Bryan, however, knew that his most powerful weapon was his talent for communicating directly with people, so he stumped the countryside traveling 18,000 miles, facing five million voters along the way. The Republicans feared Bryan's ability to sway voters almost as much as they feared the populist positions he had taken. Therefore, the giants of industry rallied to McKinley's cause and outspent the Democrats and Bryan by more than 20 to one. The result was a victory for McKinley, though he garnered only four percent more of the popular vote than Bryan.

When war broke out with Spain in 1898, Bryan raised the Third Regiment of the Nebraska Volunteer Infantry, and although he saw no overseas duty, he was commissioned a colonel. Two years later, Bryan again was ready to take on McKinley. He again was nominated by the Democrats, and again lost to McKinley, this time by a larger margin than in 1896.

In 1901, Bryan established *The Commoner,* a newspaper in Lincoln, Nebraska, which he used as a forum for his political viewpoints. Theodore Roosevelt became president following the assassination of President McKinley, and enjoyed great popular support. Bryan chose not to challenge the popular president in 1904, believing that such a race could not be won. During 1905–06, Bryan toured the world in recognition of the United States' new position as an international power, and in preparation for his third try for the presidency. In 1908, again winning his party's nomination and hailed as "The Great Commoner," Bryan faced **William Howard Taft.** Taft won the election by a sizable margin.

Despite his three failed attempts at the presidency, Bryan continued to exercise great influence within the Democratic Party, playing a pivotal role in the nomination of Woodrow Wilson in 1912. Following Wilson's victory, Wilson named Bryan as his secretary of state on March 4, 1913. Bryan remained in that position, negotiating more than 30 treaties during his tenure, until June 9, 1915, when he resigned in disagreement with President Wilson's strong protest against the German sinking of the *Lusitania.* Bryan felt that such a vehement response would serve only to pull the United States into the war already raging in Europe. However, once the United States entered the war in 1917, Bryan was a loyal supporter.

Out of office, Bryan resumed his writing and his popular lecture series in which he advocated the literal interpretation of the Bible and the prohibition of liquor. It was his fundamentalist religious beliefs that involved him in the famous Scopes monkey trial. John Scopes, a high school biology teacher in Dayton, Tennessee, was charged with teaching evolution, contrary to state law. Bryan, recruited to assist in the prosecution of the case, was put head-to-head against the country's foremost defense attorney, Clarence Darrow. Bryan was called to testify; Darrow, of course, relished the opportunity to cross-examine him. By the time the legal sparring ended, Darrow had humiliated Bryan, forcing him into ideological corners, often leading Bryan to contradict his own testimony. Immediately following the trial, Bryan set to work writing his rebuttal to Darrow, a rebuttal he did not have a chance to deliver at the trial. Bryan intended to publish his remarks hoping to vindicate his position. Sadly, he died within a week of the trial's conclusion, the manuscript still incomplete.

William Jennings Bryan is buried on a hillside overlooking the southern sections of Arlington near Bryan Circle, named in his honor. Buried with him is **Mary Baird Bryan,** his "Wife and Helpmate." His tombstone bears the inscription: "Statesman, yet friend to truth! Of Soul sincere, In action faithful, and honor clear."

Warren E. Burger
Chief Justice of the United States
(September 17, 1907–June 25, 1995)
Sec. 5, Lot 7015, Grid VW-35

President Richard Nixon nominated Warren Burger to be chief justice of the United States, but it was Burger who later spoke for a unanimous court upholding a subpoena for the Watergate tapes that resulted in Nixon's resignation in 1974.

Warren Earl Burger was born in Saint Paul, Minnesota, in 1907. As one of seven children, Burger knew the only way for him to attend college and law school was to earn his way. He went to the University of Minnesota, and in 1931 graduated from the St. Paul College of Law (now the William Mitchell College of Law). He practiced law for more than 20 years, and taught at his law school. He married Elvera Stromberg in 1933. They had two children.

He was a strong supporter of Dwight Eisenhower during his bid for the presidency in 1952. Following the election, Burger joined the Eisenhower administration as assistant attorney general in charge of the justice department's civil division. In 1956, Eisenhower appointed him to the United States Court of Appeals for the District of Columbia. His conservative rulings gained Burger the reputation of advocating a strict construction of the Constitution, which was exactly what President Richard Nixon wanted when he nominated Burger to succeed **Earl Warren** as chief justice in 1969.

During his tenure on the Court, Burger and the three other Nixon appointees were expected to steer the Court away from the liberal activism of the Warren court, but they upheld the 1966 Miranda decision requiring a criminal suspect be informed of his or her rights, and the decision that validated busing as a means of desegregating schools. Generally conservative in his rulings, Burger joined the majority in the landmark *Roe v. Wade* decision that established a woman's constitutional right to have an abortion. And in 1974, Burger's ruling sealed Nixon's fate when the Court decided that the president must turn over secret White House tape recordings to the Congressional committee investigating the Watergate break-in. Burger also unsealed court records that named Nixon as an "unindicted co-conspirator." Nixon resigned within days of the rulings.

Burger modernized the Court with computers and overhauled the entire judicial system. He was the longest-serving chief justice of the 20th century when he unexpectedly resigned on September 26, 1986, to chair the commission planning the bicentennial celebration of the U.S. Constitution in 1987. **William Rehnquist** succeeded him as chief justice.

In 1988, President Ronald Reagan presented Burger with the Presidential Medal of Freedom. He died on June 25, 1995, in Washington and was buried at Arlington. His wife **Elvera Stromberg Burger** preceded him in death in 1994.

Richard Evelyn Byrd, Jr.
Polar Explorer
(October 25, 1888–March 11, 1957)
Sec. 2, Lot 4969, Grid WX–32/33

Richard Evelyn Byrd, Jr. began his adventures at an early age. When he was only 12 years old, he took an unescorted trip around the world, which convinced him to spend his life as an adventurer. By the time he died at age 69, Byrd had achieved what no other person had achieved. He had flown over both poles, led several extended expeditions into the Antarctic interior (one of which nearly cost him his life), received more than 20 commendations for bravery or conspicuous conduct, and won the adulation of his country.

Born in Winchester, Virginia, Byrd attended the University of Virginia before entering the United States Naval Academy, from which he graduated in 1912. In 1915, after only three years of active service, Byrd was forced to retire, abandoning his dream of a naval career. The Navy had determined that he was physically unable to serve because of a leg injury he had

This state of Richard E. Byrd, Jr., erected by the National Geographic Society, is located on Memorial Drive just outside the main gate to Arlington.

suffered while captain of the academy gymnastics team. However, upon the United States' entry into World War I, Byrd returned to duty in the Navy's aviation branch. He earned his wings in 1918, flying solo with only six hours instruction. During the war, he served as commander of a Navy patrol squadron based in Canada.

After flying over sea, ice, and glaciers in western Greenland during an expedition with Commander D.B. MacMillan in 1924, Byrd set his sights on an airborne expedition to the North Pole. On May 9, 1926, he and his copilot **Floyd Bennett** left their base in Spitsbergen, Norway, aboard their Fokker trimotor plane, *Josephine Ford.* They completed the 1,500-mile flight to the Pole, suffering no greater malfunction than a minor oil leak. The explorers returned to a heroes' welcome, and were each presented a Congressional Medal of Honor by President Calvin Coolidge, a rare peacetime achievement.

Next Byrd attempted an Atlantic crossing. In June 1927, with three companions, including **Bernt Balchen,** Byrd reached the coast of France, but was forced to crash-land his plane at Ver-sur-Mer after 42 hours of flight. For this extraordinary flight he was named a commandant in the Legion d'Honneur.

Searching for other uncharted skies, Byrd announced his intention to explore the unknown regions of the Antarctic from the air. In 1928, he sailed to the area known as Bay of Whales, Antarctica, and established Little America, a base that remains today. On November 29, 1929, during the Antarctic spring, Byrd, Balchen, and two other men took off from their base at Little America, and flew to the South Pole. The plane, named *Floyd Bennett,* after Byrd's friend and polar companion, took 19 hours to complete the world-record flight. For this achievement Byrd was promoted to rear admiral, retired.

In 1933, Byrd headed yet another expedition to the Antarctic to map and explore new regions around the Pole. During the winter of 1934, Byrd stayed alone in a weather observation shed 125 miles from any other human being. We know from Byrd's notes that with temperatures between -58 and -76 degrees

Fahrenheit, he could hear his breath freeze as it drifted from his lips, making crackling noises like little firecrackers. After five months in this self-imposed solitary confinement, during which he made no mention of any problems in his radio transmissions to Little America, Byrd became seriously ill. When crew members of the base camp became alarmed by incoherent reports from Byrd, a rescue team set out to investigate. They arrived to find Byrd suffering from frostbite and carbon monoxide poisoning, a result of an improperly vented oil-burning stove. Too weak to travel, Byrd was cared for in the hut for two months before he could return to Little America.

This episode permanently impaired his health and restricted his future activities. Admiral Byrd recounted this grueling adventure in his book, "Alone," published in 1938.

Byrd went on to lead three more expeditions to the Antarctic as director of the newly established Antarctic Service. During World War II, he served on the staff of the chief of naval operations. In 1955, he was named head of "Operation Deep Freeze," which was the United States' contribution to the International Geophysical Year of 1957–58. It was during this project that Byrd took his last flight over the South Pole on January 8, 1956. He died in Boston the following year and was buried with full military honors at Arlington.

Two monuments honor Admiral Byrd at Arlington. The first marks his grave in Section 2. It is a regulation headstone, engraved in gold to signify his receipt of the Congressional Medal of Honor. The other monument is located on the north side of Memorial Drive along the approach to the cemetery's main gates. Erected by the National Geographic Society, it is a life-size statue of Admiral Byrd and the base is inscribed: "Upon this bright globe he carved his signature of courage." The sculpture was created by Felix de Weldon (who also sculpted the Seabees Monument and the Marine Corps Memorial) in 1961.

Claire Lee Chennault
Commander of the Flying Tigers of World War II
(September 6, 1893–July 27, 1958)
Sec. 2, Lot 873-4, Grid PQ–31

Claire Chennault was both a fighter and a flyer. And when World War II forced the forging of those two qualities, he became commander of one of the most famous flying groups in aviation history, the Flying Tigers.

Chennault's career started neither as a soldier nor a pilot, but rather as a teacher and principal of a small rural school in Louisiana. Born in Commerce, Texas, Chennault attended Louisiana State Normal College (now Northwestern State College of Louisiana). When the United States entered World War I in 1917, Chennault enlisted in the Army, attending officers training camp at Fort Benjamin Harrison, Indiana. In November of that year, he was commissioned a first lieutenant in the Infantry Reserve and soon became both a pilot and flight instructor.

By 1929, Chennault had been promoted to captain, and in 1931, he graduated from the Air Corps Technical School at Langley Field, Virginia. It was during this period that he and two friends formed a barnstorming-style air stunt show billed as "Three Men on a Flying Trapeze." He remained a flight instructor until 1937, by which time his hearing had become so severely impaired that the Army forced him to retire. Disappointed, Chennault sought other skies, eventually being hired by Madame Chaing Kai-shek, wife of the Nationalist Chinese leader, to assume command of the Chinese air defenses against Japan.

In 1940, prior to the United States' declaration of war against Japan, Chennault recruited American pilots and mechanics to fight for the Chinese. In 1941, he began training what was known as the American Volunteer Group at Kun Ming. On December 20, 1941, just 13 days after the attack on Pearl Harbor, the AVG flew their first mission. Their successes against the Japanese won them worldwide acclaim, and they became known as the Flying Tigers.

In 1942, disregarding his hearing impairment, the U.S. Army recalled Chennault to active duty as a colonel in the Army Air Corps. Shortly thereafter, he was promoted to brigadier general, and in July of that year, the Flying Tigers officially became part of the Twenty-third Fighters Squadron, with Claire Chennault named chief of Army Air Forces in China. By March 1943, he had risen to major general and had been placed in command of the Fourteenth Air Force. Following Japan's unconditional surrender on September 2, 1945, Chennault retired from the Army.

Claire Chennault's tombstone bears his name in two languages–English on one side and Chinese on the other. Chennault's son, Colonel John S. Chennault, is buried next to his father.

Chennault publicly criticized the United States for failing to support the government of Chiang Kai-shek. He rejoined the Nationalists in 1946 to organize the Chinese National Relief and Rehabilitation Air Transport. Later he formed a contract cargo carrier known as the Civil Air Transport Service based on Taiwan. The Central Intelligence Agency eventually purchased this air transport company, and Chennault continued in a management role with the service until ill health forced his retirement in 1955.

Returning to the United States in June 1958 to seek medical treatment for lung cancer, Chennault received an extraordinary recognition. By special legislation, Congress promoted him to lieutenant general just nine days before his death in New Orleans on July 27. He was buried with full military honors at Arlington, and as a special tribute to his achievements, Chennault's tombstone bears his name inscribed in two languages: English on one side and Chinese on the other. His son, Colonel **John S. Chennault,** a veteran of World War II and Korea, was laid to rest next to his father in 1977.

One final postscript: Claire Lee Chennault is buried in what was once part of the rose garden of his mother's distant cousin, Robert E. Lee.

John Lincoln Clem
Drummer Boy of Chickamauga, Major General
(August 31, 1851–May 13, 1937)
Sec. 2, Lot 993, Grid S–32/33

O n May 24, 1861, a 9-year-old boy ran away from his Newark, Ohio, home to join the fighting that had recently erupted in what would become the Civil War. His mother had been killed in a train accident, and he was now free to do his part to protect the Union. The Twenty-second Michigan Infantry allowed him to serve as their drummer boy, but within two years, he achieved the rank of sergeant at the tender age of 12. He was Johnny Clem, the youngest soldier ever to fight in the United States Army.

His proper name was John Joseph Klem, but he was so enamored with Republican candidate Abraham Lincoln during the presidential campaign of 1860 that he changed his middle name to "Lincoln." It is unclear when he chose to start spelling his last name with a C rather than using the K, which was used by his German immigrant family.

The first major action in which young Clem was involved was the Battle of Pittsburg Landing, near Shiloh, Tennessee. During a rout by Confederate

troops, Union soldiers were rapidly retreating from their positions. With his drum rendered useless by Rebel gunfire, Clem picked up a musket with a sawed-off barrel and returned the Confederate fire.

The Union troops, inspired by the young drummer boy's bravery, regrouped. Following the battle, Clem was cited for his valiant conduct, and officially inducted into the Army. During the battle of Chickamauga, Johnny wounded a Confederate colonel, then eluded capture by playing dead. Once reunited with his regiment, he was promoted to the rank of sergeant, becoming the youngest American soldier ever to hold that rank. The remainder of the war found young Johnny at Murfreesboro, Lookout Mountain, Missionary Ridge, and Atlanta. He was captured by Confederate forces shortly after Chickamauga, but was exchanged two months later. Twice ponies were shot from under the young soldier, and once he was wounded in the hip by a shell fragment. But his military career did not end with the Civil War.

In 1869, an old wartime friend—Ulysses S. Grant—became president of the United States. Two years later, President Grant personally handed Clem his second lieutenant's commission. Clem also saw action during the Spanish-American War. In 1915, he was promoted to brigadier general; in 1916, he retired as a major general after 53 years of active duty. But when the United States entered World War I, 65-year-old Clem sought permission to be reactivated to join the fighting in France. President Woodrow Wilson flatly refused his request, sending the disappointed "drummer boy" into permanent retirement at his home in San Antonio, Texas. John Lincoln Clem, the youngest soldier ever to serve in the United States Army, died in 1937 at the age of 86.

He is buried among many other great soldiers of that war, including **Sheridan, Wheeler, Schofield, Crook, Ord,** and 2,111 unknown Civil War soldiers. His stone proudly displays his military career in just three lines:

THE DRUMMER BOY OF CHICKAMAUGA

MAJOR GENERAL U.S. ARMY

1851–1937

George Crook
Veteran of the Civil War and Indian Campaigns
(September 9, 1830–March 21, 1890)
Sec. 2, Lot 974, Grid S–32

When he died at the age of 59, General George Crook was still on active duty after 38 years. His career was highlighted by his courageous service to the North in the Civil War, as well as by his equitable treatment of Native Americans while stationed in the West after the war.

Born in Dayton, Ohio, Crook was a member of the West Point graduating class of 1852. He first was assigned to explore and defend the Northwest frontier, where he began his lifelong study of Indians, their environment, cultures, languages, and ways of warfare. In 1857, he was wounded in a skirmish with the Pit River Indians.

In September 1861, Crook was recalled from the western frontier to command a company of Ohio Volunteers in the Civil War. He took part in the battles of South Mountain and Antietam, earning himself a promotion to brigadier general of volunteers in 1862. In September of that year, he commanded a division of cavalry under General **William Starke Rosecrans** at Chickamauga; in October, he pursued the Confederate cavalry under General **Joseph Wheeler** to Farmington, Tennessee, where Crook defeated them. During the Shenandoah campaign in 1864, he saw action at Winchester under General **Philip Sheridan;** and in March 1865, while leading a cavalry division in the battle of Petersburg, Crook was captured and held at Richmond's Libby Prison. Following his release in an exchange of prisoners, he served with the Army of the Potomac.

Crook returned to the western frontier after the war, and initially took a hard line against Native Americans. In 1871, he was ordered to Arizona to deal with the Apache Indians. Under Chief Cochise, the Apaches were terrorizing white settlers believed to be encroaching on Indian territory. In 1875, Crook was commander of the Department of the Platte when gold was discovered in the Black Hills.

Gold fever sparked an invasion of Indian territories by white settlers. Crook was heavily engaged throughout 1876, trying to pacify the Sioux and Cheyenne Indians. On June 17, at Rosebud Creek, Crook fought nearly 1,500 Sioux and Cheyenne Indians under Chief Crazy Horse, but was forced to retreat.

This failed campaign changed Crook's attitude toward dealing with Indians. He felt that they needed protection from corrupt Indian agents and hostile frontiersmen, and over time he gained a reputation among the Indians as an equitable frontier army commander. In 1882, Crook returned to Arizona to quell an uprising by the Apaches under Geronimo. He chased the Indian warrior into the Sierra Madre Mountains of Mexico before capturing and returning him to his reservation. Geronimo escaped in 1885, but Crook was relieved of his command by General **Nelson A. Miles** before he could recapture the Apache chief.

Crook spent his last years as commander of the Department of Missouri stationed in Chicago. He spent much of his time on public crusades criticizing government Indian policy because Indians were often unjustly treated. George Crook died in Chicago and was brought back to Washington, D.C., for burial at Arlington.

General Crook's tombstone, erected by the Society of the Army of West Virginia, displays a bas-relief of the surrender of Geronimo, as well as a list of Crook's Civil War campaigns. Like many of the tombstones of Union soldiers in Arlington, the Civil War is referred to as the War of the Rebellion. Also of note: The Crook Walk in Arlington Cemetery, which leads from Arlington House to the Tomb of the Unknowns, is named for George Crook.

Mounted on the tombstone of George Crook is a bas-relief depicting the 1883 surrender of Apache Chief Geronimo to General Crook, shown at right.

Jane Delano
Army Nursing Pioneer
(March 12, 1862–April 15, 1919)
Sec. 21, Lot 6, Grid LM–20

During the first quarter of this century, Jane Delano was instrumental in providing qualified nurses for service in the United States Armed Forces. She personally supervised the training and preparation of more than 20,000 nurses who came to the aid of American troops during World War I.

Delano, a native of Montour Falls, New York, graduated from Bellevue Hospital of Nursing in 1886. The following year she became superintendent of nurses at a hospital in Jacksonville, Florida, where she pioneered the use of mosquito netting to prevent the spread of yellow fever before the mosquito was proven to be the carrier of the disease. She later established a hospital in Arizona for coal miners suffering from scarlet fever. In 1902, Jane Delano returned to Bellevue Hospital to assume the position of director of the School of Nursing. In 1909, she became chairman of the National Committee of the American Red Cross, serving simultaneously as president of the American Nurses Association and as superintendent of the Army Nurse Corps. She authored the American Red Cross textbook, "Elementary Hygiene and Home Care of the Sick."

Full military honors accompanied the burial of Army nurse and former Red Cross official Jane Delano following her death in 1919.

During her tenure as superintendent of the Army Nurse Corps, Jane Delano implemented a program that made the Red Cross Nursing Service a reserve for the military nursing corps. This plan resulted in the availability of 8,000 nurses ready for duty when the United States entered World War I. Delano was chosen to direct the wartime Department of Nursing, an organization established to select and assign all nursing units. Believing that she could better fulfill her obligations by being close to the nurses treating combat victims, she left her safe quarters in this country and went to France. She died at Savenay in 1919, but her body was returned to this country for burial with full military honors at Arlington National Cemetery.

Sir John Dill
British Field Marshal
World War II Allied Combined Chiefs of Staff
(December 25, 1881–November 4, 1944)
Sec. 32, Lot S–29, Grid X–33

British Prime Minister Winston Churchill visited Washington, D.C., in December 1941 to confer with President Franklin Roosevelt soon after the United States entered World War II. Accompanying Churchill as a military advisor was Field Marshal John Dill. When Churchill returned to England, Dill remained in the United States as chief of the British Joint Mission to the United States and as senior British representative on the Combined Chiefs of Staff.

Sir John was born John Greer Dill in Lurgan, Northern Ireland, on Christmas Day 1881. He was educated at Cheltenham College in Sandhurst, England, and joined the First Battalion Leinster Regiment in South Africa in 1901. He was promoted to captain in 1911 and to brigade-major by 1914, while serving in France during World War I. Following the war, he was assigned to India, and later commanded forces in Palestine in 1936 and 1937.

When Britain declared war on Germany in 1939, Dill was promoted to general and given command of the I Corps in France. He received his promotion to field marshal in 1941, and was named chief of the Imperial General Staff. However, Prime Minister Churchill considered him to be obstructive and overly cautious in that position. At that time, it was widely speculated that was the reason Dill was assigned to Washington. Nevertheless, he proved to be a valuable asset while in the United States capital. His services were of great importance in securing the necessary cooperation between the American and British armed

Sir John Dill is the highest-ranking foreign military officer buried at Arlington. His is one of only two equestrian statues in the cemetery.

forces, not only in Washington, but at conferences in Casablanca, Quebec, Cairo, and Tehran. He earned the trust and confidence of everyone with whom he worked, especially President Roosevelt and Chief of Staff General **George C. Marshall.** Both the United States and Great Britain recognized the great contribution of John Dill. On behalf of the British people, King George VI knighted Dill in 1942. The United States Congress, on behalf of all American citizens, granted Dill the Distinguished Service Cross posthumously.

Sir John died while stationed in Washington in 1944, and received the extraordinary honor—as a foreign soldier—of being buried at Arlington National Cemetery. His is one of only two equestrian statues in the cemetery.

William Joseph "Wild Bill" Donovan
World War I Hero, World War II Spymaster
(January 1, 1883–February 8, 1959)
Sec. 2, Lot 4874, Grid V–33

For bravery in the battle trenches of World War I, William Joseph Donovan received the Congressional Medal of Honor. When World War II started in Europe, however, he traded his helmet and rifle for a cloak and dagger.

Donovan, the son of Irish immigrants, was born in Buffalo, New York. He entered Niagara College, then transferred to Columbia University where he played quarterback for the football team and became acquainted with classmate Franklin Roosevelt. He received his BA from Columbia in 1905, earned his law degree in 1907, and practiced law in Buffalo.

The cavalry troop which Donovan organized for the New York National Guard served under General **John Pershing** on the Mexican Border in 1916, and then followed General Pershing to France during World War I. As part of the Twenty-seventh Division, Donovan became a colonel of the 165th Infantry (formerly known as the Fightin' 69th). During the Meuse-Argonne Offensive, Donovan was wounded three times as he led his regiment against the seemingly impenetrable Hindenburg Line at Landres-et-St. Georges on October 14, 1918. He inspired his young recruits as he moved among his men in exposed front-line positions. For his uncommon valor in that war, Donovan was awarded the Congressional Medal of Honor.

Exactly when Donovan picked up his nickname, "Wild Bill," is unclear. Some reports place its inception during his college football days while others credit his conduct during the war as its source. In any event, the press correspondents covering the First World War picked up the name, tagged him with it, and it remained his sobriquet throughout his life.

Throughout the war, Donovan was greatly respected by his men. Among his sergeants was the well-known poet, Joyce Kilmer. Speaking of Donovan, Kilmer, who later was killed in action, stated that he would rather be a sergeant under Donovan than "a lieutenant in any other regiment."

Donovan resumed his law practice in 1920, and actively involved himself in Republican Party politics. Serving as U.S. Attorney for Western New York from 1922 to 1924, he was defeated in his bid for lieutenant governor of New York. He moved to Washington to serve as an assistant U.S. attorney general, a post he held for four years. Donovan worked hard in the election campaign of Herbert Hoover in 1928, hoping to be named attorney general after Hoover's victory. However, because Donovan was a Catholic and an antiprohibitionist, Hoover did not name him to the post. A disappointed Donovan declined the president's offer to be governor of the Philippines.

"Wild Bill" again sought public office in 1932 when he ran for governor of New York against Herbert Lehman, but Lehman was swept into office by Franklin Roosevelt's landslide. Donovan returned to his law practice, devoting much of his time to assisting the American Legion in its efforts to find employment for military veterans.

As war ravaged Europe in 1940, Donovan undertook his first clandestine journey to Britain on behalf of President Roosevelt. There he met with Sir William Stephenson, the British intelligence agent known as "Intrepid," who was a confidant of Prime Minister Winston Churchill. Following their meeting, Donovan reported to Roosevelt that the British, with the aid of American ships and munitions, could survive the Nazi sweep across Europe. The United States ultimately provided that crucial military support.

It also was at this time that Donovan strongly urged the creation of an intelligence network for the United States. In July 1941, President Roosevelt appointed Donovan to head the Office of Coordinator of Information, charging him with the task of developing a comprehensive plan for a military intelligence agency to operate throughout the world. In June 1942, the Office of Strategic Services (OSS) was created, and Donovan named as its director. He oversaw operations which gathered intelligence behind enemy lines in every theater in World War II. He also participated in counterintelligence, sabotage, underground activities, propaganda, and psychological warfare. The legends credited to Donovan as "America's Spymaster" rival any novel.

As head of the OSS, Donovan was privy to highly classified information, and therefore not only required personal protection, but also carried the infamous OSS cyanide capsule, prepared to kill himself rather than face enemy interrogators. One feat credited to Donovan occurred after his office had perfected a quiet pistol. As the story goes, an excited Donovan—eager to demonstrate his new discovery for the president—stormed into the Oval Office, and in front of a startled FDR, tossed a sandbag on the floor, and proceeded to empty six rounds of ammunition into the sandbag.

After the war the OSS was dissolved, and when the CIA was created in 1947, Donovan held no position in the agency. He served as an aide to Robert H. Jackson, who was the chief prosecutor during the Nuremberg trials. In 1946, he ran unsuccessfully for the U.S. Senate, and in 1953, at the age of 70, he was appointed by President Dwight Eisenhower as ambassador to Thailand, where he served for two years. Then in 1957, with his receipt of the National Security Medal, he became the first American to be awarded this country's top four decorations: The Congressional Medal of Honor, the Distinguished Service Cross, the Distinguished Service Medal, and the National Security Medal.

Donovan died on February 8, 1959, at Walter Reed Hospital in Washington, D.C. His grave is marked with a regulation government headstone, inscribed in gold to reflect his Medal-of-Honor status. Buried next to him is his son, **William James Donovan,** a U.S. Army veteran who served in Vietnam.

James "Jimmy" Doolittle, PH.D.
Aviation Pioneer, WWII Flying Ace
(December 14, 1896–September 27, 1993)
Sec. 7A, Lot 110, Grid U-24

After the Japanese attacked Pearl Harbor in December 1941, Americans were dismayed at the tremendous loss of life and property, and were eager to retaliate. Their spirits were lifted on April 18, 1942, when Lieutenant Colonel James Doolittle led a daring daylight air raid on Tokyo and Yokohama. Although his raid inflicted little damage, it bolstered American morale and showed Japan that the U.S. was within striking range. Doolittle received the Congressional Medal of Honor for his mission and was promoted to brigadier general.

Although James Doolittle was born in Alameda, California, in 1896, his family moved to Nome, Alaska, when he was just 4 years old. He demonstrated a keen interest in flying from an early age. At 15, he built a glider from plans he found in Popular Mechanics magazine. Doolittle studied mining engineering at the University of California, but left college with one year remaining to join the U.S. Army Signal Corps as part of the American Expeditionary Forces headed to Europe in WWI.

After the war, Doolittle set a series of aviation records, including being the first pilot to fly coast to coast in less than a day. In September 1922, Doolittle took off from Jacksonville, Florida and landed 20 hours and 30 minutes later in San Diego, California. In 1925, he set a seaplane speed record of 232 miles per hour. He also made the first instrument flight—taking off, flying, and landing without seeing beyond his instrument panel. In 1927, Doolittle earned his PhD in aeronautical engineering from the Massachusetts Institute of Technology.

Throughout the 1930s, Doolittle worked for Shell Oil Co., but was recalled to active duty in 1940 with the rank of major. He was placed in command of a flying unit that came to be known as "Doolittle's Raiders." On April 18, 1942, 80 aviators flew 16 B-25s from the deck of the aircraft carrier *Hornet* under the command of **William F. Halsey, Jr.** It was a daring one-way mission that required the pilots to bail out over mainland China after their attacks on Japan. Sixty-nine of them landed in friendly territory. The attack was the subject of a 1944 movie, "Thirty Seconds over Tokyo," starring Spencer Tracy.

Doolittle was placed in command of the 12th Air Force in Britain, the 15th Air Force, which took part in the invasion of North Africa and Italy, and the 8th Air Force, which later attacked Germany. He was promoted to lieutenant general in 1944, and held the rank of general when he left the Army in 1946.

Doolittle returned to work for Shell Oil after the service. In 1989, President George Bush awarded Doolittle the Presidential Medal of Freedom. He died in Pebble Beach, California, on September 27, 1993, and was buried with full military honors at Arlington National Cemetery.

Abner Doubleday
Civil War General, Inventor of Baseball?
(June 26, 1819–January 26, 1893)
Sec. 1, Lot 61, Grid NO–32/33

Although Abner Doubleday did establish the first cable car company in America, he did not—contrary to popular belief—invent baseball. In fact, Doubleday never claimed to have invented the game that has become our national pastime. He considered his greatest achievement to be his distinguished military career.

Doubleday was born in Ballston Spa, New York, and grew up in Cooperstown. The grandson of a Revolutionary War veteran and the son of a newspaper editor, young Abner entered the United States Military Academy at West Point, graduating in 1842.

Like many other Civil War veterans, Doubleday got his first significant military experience in the Mexican War, where he served under General (and later President) Zachary Taylor. In 1856, he saw action again against the Seminole Indians in Florida. It was in 1861, after he was assigned to Charleston Harbor in South Carolina, that he was an eyewitness to the start of our nation's greatest domestic conflict. For it was at Charleston Harbor that soldiers of the young Confederacy first fired upon Union troops. The date was April 12, 1861, and Abner Doubleday is credited with manning the first of Fort Sumter's guns to respond to this attack by the South.

Within two months he was promoted to major, and served with an infantry regiment in the Shenandoah Valley until the following year when he was assigned to assist in the defense of Washington, D.C. Promoted to brigadier general of volunteers in February 1862, he took part in major battles in Maryland and northern Virginia, including the Second Battle of Bull Run, Antietam, and Fredericksburg. In November of that same year, he became a major general of volunteers and was recognized for his command of the I Corps during the first day of battle at Gettysburg. Today, a statue in his honor

stands on the Gettysburg battlefield. Following his heroic performance at Gettysburg, Doubleday hoped for a more important command, but his hopes were frustrated when he was reassigned to Washington, where he was stationed for the remainder of the war.

Following the Civil War, Doubleday reverted to the rank of lieutenant colonel, receiving a final promotion to full colonel in September 1867. He retired from the Army in 1873, and moved to San Francisco, where he started the first cable car company in America. Some years later, he relocated to Mendham, New Jersey, where he died in 1893.

Abner Doubleday's association with the invention of baseball is nearly a legend in itself. As our nation entered a new century, baseball had become widespread and a group of enthusiasts, led by former major leaguer and sporting goods kingpin Albert G. Spalding, established a commission under Spalding's direction to verify the origin of the sport. Relying upon very thin evidence, the commission decided that baseball had been founded in the United States, and was "devised by Abner Doubleday at Cooperstown, New York, in 1839." It is widely believed today, however, that a form of baseball had been played in the United States—and in England—long before Doubleday appeared on the scene. In Britain, the sport was known as "rounders," in colonial America it was called "townball." No doubt this information was discovered by Spalding's group, but they could hardly claim that the roots of our national pastime were found in Great Britain. What they did correctly verify was that Doubleday had codified some of the rules of the game, which they considered sufficient cause to declare Abner Doubleday, an American, the father of baseball.

Doubleday Field and the Baseball Hall of Fame and Museum were established in honor of Abner Doubleday during the celebration of baseball's centennial in 1939 by the citizens of Cooperstown, New York. It is presently under the jurisdiction of Major League Baseball.

William O. Douglas
Supreme Court Justice, Environmentalist
(October 16, 1898–January 19, 1980)
Sec. 5, Lot 7004–B–1, Grid W–36

William O. Douglas served on the United States Supreme Court longer than any other justice in history, and although his lengthy tenure evoked fierce devotion from many supporters, he twice faced impeachment by those who opposed his lifestyle and liberal viewpoints.

Born into an impoverished farm family just before the turn of the 20th century, Douglas moved with his family from Maine, Minnesota, to Yakima, Washington, where he spent his youth. It was in Yakima that Douglas suffered an attack of polio. His therapy included hiking in the mountains near his home to strengthen his crippled legs, an activity that kindled his lifelong love of the outdoors.

Refusing to allow polio to keep him from serving his country during World War I, Douglas enlisted in the United States Army to fight in Europe. He also refused to let poverty forestall his formal education, so he worked full time to support himself and to pay his tuition at Whitman College in nearby Walla Walla. Following graduation in 1920, he was encouraged by his academic success to pursue a career in law, and set his sights on Columbia University in New York City. Again, working hard to support himself and to underwrite the costs of his own education, Douglas soon became one of Columbia's top law students, graduating Phi Beta Kappa in 1925.

Remaining in New York, Douglas joined a prestigious Wall Street firm. However, after two years, he realized that practicing corporate law was not what he desired. So, he returned to Yakima to enter private practice, but a year later Douglas again found himself in New York as a faculty member of Columbia University's School of Law. By 1933, as the Great Depression gripped the nation, he was teaching at Yale University Law School in New Haven, Connecticut, and had developed a solid reputation as an expert in financial law. He also had gained the attention of President Franklin Roosevelt. Roosevelt, who was looking to staff the newly created Securities and Exchange Commission, turned to Douglas for his assistance. Joining the Commission in 1936, Douglas became its chairman in 1937, and remained in that position until 1939.

On March 20, 1939, Roosevelt nominated Douglas to fill a vacancy on the United States Supreme Court created by the retirement of Justice Louis D. Brandeis. Within two weeks, his nomination won confirmation in the Senate. Despite this initial display of overwhelming Senate confidence, members of that body twice attempted to impeach Justice Douglas.

Douglas became renowned as a champion of liberal causes and this reputation, coupled with his flamboyant personal lifestyle, fueled the fires of impeachment. Douglas married four times during his life; each of his first three marriages ending in divorce. In 1966, shortly after his third divorce, at the age of 68 he married Cathleen Heffernan, a 23-year-old waitress whom he met in Portland, Oregon. This marriage was viewed by some as utterly inappropriate for a Supreme Court justice; others felt that marriage was a personal and private matter and that conservative critics of Douglas were exploiting his marriage for political reasons. The fourth Mrs. Douglas finished law school and was a prominent Washington attorney at the time of her husband's death.

Impeachment articles were first drafted against Douglas in 1953, but gained little support. Again in 1970, there was talk of impeachment. That threat was spurred by resentment on the part of several conservative senators over the rejection of two of President Richard Nixon's nominees for the Court. Like the earlier attempt, however, there proved to be little support to unseat Justice Douglas.

During the last years of his life, William O. Douglas suffered from ill health, relying on the use of a heart pacemaker. Yet, he refused to retire from the Court. It was widely reported that he was unwilling to allow President Nixon to name his successor. In January 1975, however, Douglas suffered a paralytic stroke. And although he valiantly tried to continue his work on the bench, the burden was too great. In November of that same year, he resigned. Seventy-seven years old, Douglas had served 36 years and seven months on the Supreme Court, eclipsing the career record of Justice **Oliver Wendell Holmes, Jr.** And if it was Douglas' intent to deny President Nixon the nomination of his successor, he succeeded. A year before Douglas retired, Nixon resigned from office, and Justice John Paul Stevens was named by President Gerald Ford to fill the vacancy on the Court.

Douglas' love of nature was memorialized in 1980 when the historic Chesapeake & Ohio Canal, which runs along the Potomac River near Washington, was renamed in his honor. He is buried near the graves of seven other Supreme Court justices—**Oliver Wendell Holmes, Jr., Potter Stewart, William Brennan, Thurgood Marshall, Harry Blackmun, Warren Burger and William Rehnquist.**

John Foster Dulles
Senator, Secretary of State
(February 25, 1888–May 24, 1959)
Sec. 21, Lot 31, Grid MN–20/21

John Foster Dulles was the grandson of John Watson Foster, secretary of state during the administration of President Benjamin Harrison, and the nephew of Robert Lansing, President Woodrow Wilson's secretary of state. So, when President Dwight Eisenhower named him secretary of state in 1953, it was a post for which, by his own account, he had trained, and one he had sought throughout his lifetime.

Dulles, the son of a Presbyterian minister, was a brilliant student, both in the public schools of Watertown, New York, and at Princeton University where he received his undergraduate degree. In 1908, he studied at the Sorbonne in Paris, then received his law degree in 1911 from George Washington University in Washington, D.C. That same year he joined the New York law firm of Sullivan and Cromwell.

Dulles' desire for a diplomatic career began in 1907, when, at the age of 19, he accompanied his grandfather, the former secretary of state, to the Peace Conference at The Hague where the young Dulles served as a secretary to the Chinese delegation. Following his service as a major in the United States Army in World War I, Dulles was appointed legal counsel to the U.S. delegation to the Versailles Peace Conference.

Soon he returned to his international law

practice with Sullivan and Cromwell, and, by 1927, was head of the firm. His diplomatic portfolio further expanded in 1945 when he participated in the Dumbarton Oaks Conference at which the United Nations Charter was drafted. After chairing the U.S. delegation to the United Nations General Assembly in Paris in 1948, Dulles was chosen the next year by Governor Thomas Dewey of New York as United States senator to fill the term of Robert F. Wagner. Wagner had retired due to ill health. In the subsequent election, Dulles sought to retain that Senate seat but was unsuccessful.

America's postwar diplomatic efforts were stalled in 1946. The United States could not successfully seal a peace treaty with Japan that would also include the Soviet Union. So President Harry Truman and his secretary of state, Dean Acheson, charged Dulles with the extraordinary task of negotiating the Japanese peace treaty. Circumnavigating the globe, Dulles gained international acclaim for successfully managing the complex negotiations which resulted in a treaty signed by 49 nations. Following Dwight Eisenhower's victory in the presidential election of 1952, the new president announced his first Cabinet appointment: John Foster Dulles, secretary of state. During his tenure as America's chief diplomat, Dulles guided American foreign policy through the early days of the Cold War. A man of deep religious beliefs, he detested Communism, assailing its shortcomings at every opportunity. Dulles used his mastery of negotiating techniques to seek and conclude vital pacts which remain today as cornerstones of American foreign policy, including the Southeast Asia Treaty Organization (SEATO).

Critically ill with cancer, John Foster Dulles resigned his office on April 15, 1959. He was awarded the Medal of Freedom shortly before he died on May 24, 1959. His funeral at Arlington was attended by President Eisenhower, Vice President Richard Nixon, and the many members of the foreign diplomatic corps.

Medgar Wiley Evers
Civil Rights Activist
(July 2, 1925–June 12, 1963)
Sec. 36, Lot 1431, Grid BB–40

On June 12, 1963, President **John F. Kennedy** made a televised address to the nation on the subject of civil rights. Kennedy's message was clear: There must be equal rights and equal opportunities for all Americans, regardless of race. The president's statement was prompted by a variety of circumstances, but the most recent and dramatic event occurred the day before when Alabama Governor George Wallace had denounced integration and symbolically blocked the entrance to the University of Alabama. Across America that evening, people gathered in front of their television sets to hear President Kennedy's message. Many welcomed the president's steadfast commitment to civil rights, while others resented the president's interference in a local system they felt should be maintained. Joining the millions of Americans who watched the president's message that evening was Medgar Evers, field secretary of the National Association for the Advancement of Colored People (NAACP) in Mississippi. When the president finished speaking, Evers himself addressed a rally of civil rights proponents in Jackson, Mississippi. Just after midnight, on his way home from that rally, he was murdered.

At the time of his tragic death, Medgar Evers was not a nationally known civil rights leader. Though he worked tirelessly traveling across the state to recruit members, register voters, and organize economic boycotts, outside of Mississippi he was a relatively obscure figure. Born in Decatur, Mississippi, in 1925, Evers was the son of a lumberjack. He attended segregated schools in Newton County and enlisted in the Army following his high school graduation. During the war, Evers took part in the landing at Normandy on D-Day (June 6, 1944), and for his gallant service, was awarded two Bronze Stars.

After being honorably discharged in 1946, Evers entered Alcorn A&M College in Lorman, Mississippi, under the GI Bill. He played halfback on the football team, and in 1952 earned a degree in business administration. Following graduation, he embarked on a career as an insurance salesman. It was during this period that Evers began organizing local chapters of the NAACP on a part-time basis. In 1954, he left his insurance job to become the first full-time field secretary for the NAACP in Mississippi, dedicating his life to the advancement of the rights of African Americans. So, it was with great interest that Medgar Evers listened to the words of John Kennedy on that June night in 1963.

Later that night, the civil rights leader arrived home, parking his car in his driveway. As he turned toward the side entrance to his house, he was silhouetted by the overhead light that hung under the carport. A shot rang out as a bullet pierced Evers just below the right shoulder blade, passing through his body. He staggered toward the doorway, but collapsed near the steps to the house. His wife and three children rushed to the door, their screams waking a neighbor. Together they lifted the wounded Evers into the neighbor's station wagon, rushing him to University Hospital in Jackson.

There was little the doctors could do; Medgar Evers died of his wounds just after 1:00 a.m.

Byron de la Beckwith, a self-avowed segregationist, was indicted for the murder of Medgar Evers and was twice tried for the crime. In both cases, all-white juries were unable to reach a verdict, and de la Beckwith was set free.

In 1994, 31 years after the death of Medgar Evers, Byron de la Beckwith again stood trial for murder. This time, a jury found him guilty. De la Beckwith appealed the conviction, but the Mississippi Supreme Court upheld the decision. Writing for the majority, Justice Mike Mills wrote, "Miscreants brought before the bar of justice in this state must, sooner or later, face the cold realization that justice, slow and plodding though she may be, is certain in the state of Mississippi."

Upon hearing the Supreme Court's decision, Medgar Evers' widow, Myrlie Evers-Williams, then national chairwomen of the NAACP, said, "It's like taking a deep breath and letting the air out of your lungs very slowly and saying, 'it's over' and really meaning it."

From relative obscurity, Evers became a nationally known figure, the symbol of black pride and a martyr of the civil rights struggle in America. He was posthumously awarded the 1963 Springarn Medal of the NAACP. Medgar Evers was buried in June 1963, with full military honors, at Arlington National Cemetery.

Sir Moses J. Ezekiel
Sculptor of the Confederate Monument
(October 28, 1844–March 27, 1917)
Sec. 16, buried at the base of the Monument

Following his service in the Confederate Army, Moses Ezekiel studied art and music in Berlin, then took up residence in Rome for 40 years. Yet, with roots steeped in Virginia soil, he was drawn back to America to design and sculpt what was—by his own account—his favorite work: The Confederate Monument at Arlington National Cemetery.

Born in Richmond, Virginia, Moses Ezekiel's propensity for art became evident at an early age. At 10, he was cutting out shadow pictures; by age 14, he was drawing and painting as well as writing poetry. Initially Ezekiel's love of art was of great concern to his parents because—as Orthodox Jews—their religion forbade the creation of graven images. But young Moses' artistic talents could not be suppressed, and his parents came to recognize their son's extraordinary gifts.

Ezekiel was a cadet at the Virginia Military Institute when the Civil War erupted in 1861, and left school to fight for the Confederacy. Joining other VMI cadets, he took part in the battle of New Market, Virginia, under General John C. Breckinridge. Ezekiel returned to graduate from VMI in 1868, then studied anatomy at the Medical College of Virginia. Living briefly in Cincinnati, Ohio, he went to Berlin in 1869 to study at the Royal Academy of Art.

While living in Berlin in the 1870s, Ezekiel supplemented his income by acting as a news correspondent during the Franco-Prussian War. He was arrested by the Prussians, and imprisoned for a short time under suspicion of spying for the French. In 1874, the Jewish order, Sons of the Covenant, commissioned Ezekiel to execute a sculpture for display at the Centennial Exhibition in Philadelphia. The result was *Religious Liberty*, a marble grouping, considered one of his greatest and best-known works. While living in Europe, Ezekiel also studied music under Franz Liszt, and eventually executed a bust of the music master.

After moving to Rome in 1874, Ezekiel was eventually knighted by Italian King Victor Emmanuel for his outstanding contribution to art. Ezekiel received numerous international awards during his lifetime, including a decoration by the German emperor.

On March 6, 1906, Secretary of War **William Howard Taft** approved plans of the United Daughters of the Confederacy to erect a memorial to the Confederate dead in Arlington National Cemetery. Ezekiel was chosen to design and sculpt the monument because, as a Civil War veteran, he brought to the work an unparalleled knowledge of the subject. The magnificent monument was dedicated on June 4, 1914. (See page 248.)

Moses Ezekiel died in Rome on March 27, 1917, but with hostilities raging in Europe, his remains could not be transported back to the United States. Four years later, on March 30, 1921, funeral services for Ezekiel were held in the recently completed Memorial Amphitheatre at Arlington National Cemetery—the first funeral ever to be held there. President Warren G. Harding called Ezekiel, "A great Virginian, a great artist, a great

American and a great citizen of world fame." The Italian ambassador to the United States, who participated in the funeral services, claimed Ezekiel as an "adopted son of Italy." Following the solemn services, Sir Moses Ezekiel was laid to rest at the base of the monument that he created.

James Vincent Forrestal
First Secretary of Defense
(February 15, 1892–May 22, 1949)
Sec. 30, Lot 674, Grid X–39

James Vincent Forrestal, a tireless worker and dedicated public servant, not only served valiantly as secretary of the navy during World War II, but also undertook the massive reorganization of the armed forces into the Department of Defense, which he headed after the war. Tragically, the nonstop pace and hard-driving demands of his life finally took their toll. Suffering from severe fatigue and depression, Forrestal took his own life in 1949, becoming the highest ranking government official in American history ever to do so.

James Forrestal, the third son of Irish immigrants, was born in Beacon, New York. He entered Dartmouth College in 1911, but transferred to Princeton University the following year. Without explanation, he left school six weeks before graduation, never receiving his degree. However, the lack of academic credentials did not hinder his career. In 1916, he joined the well-known Wall Street investment firm of William E. Read & Company (later Dillon, Read & Company, then a part of USB AG). A year later, when the United States entered the war in Europe, Forrestal enlisted in the Navy and won his aviator's wing, seeing action from several U.S. bases. He resigned in 1919 as a first lieutenant and returned to Dillon, Read, where his career skyrocketed. Within weeks of his rejoining the firm, he made investment headlines resulting in his being promoted to partner in 1923, vice president in 1926, and ultimately president in 1938. His success did not escape the attention of President Franklin Roosevelt, another New Yorker, who appointed him the first under secretary of the Navy in 1940. In 1941, Forrestal represented Roosevelt in London, establishing a close liaison with the British Admiralty. Then, when **William Franklin Knox** died in April 1944, Forrestal succeeded him as secretary of the Navy, a Cabinet-level position at the time.

Applying proven business management techniques to his responsibilities as Navy secretary, Forrestal established himself as a tireless administrator with an indefatigable drive to succeed. He continued as secretary of the

Navy under President Harry Truman, gaining special notoriety for his vocal opposition to Truman's decision to use atomic weapons against the Japanese toward the end of World War II. He was integrally influential in allowing the Japanese emperor to retain his throne after the war to provide stability for the Japanese people.

On September 17, 1947, Forrestal accepted the position of secretary of defense, becoming the first person to serve in that capacity. He was charged with the immense responsibility of bringing all the branches of the armed forces under a single department head, and at the same time, coping with massive postwar demilitarization. Many believed the challenge to oversee these responsibilities was more than any one person could have managed. Forrestal was confronted with the opposition from every direction. The military branches, steeped in the separate traditions, opposed the unification that Forrestal was mandated to achieve. He fought regularly with the president and Congress over the size of the budget he was given. The 1946 defense appropriation of $45 billion shrank to $14.5 billion in 1947, and to $11.25 billion in 1948. Forrestal argued that this was inadequate to guarantee a strong national defense. He also waged a public campaign against the Truman administration's decision to recognize Israel, a stance which cost him widespread support.

By 1949, Forrestal's behavior was becoming noticeably erratic; his physical health was deteriorating. Increasingly irate in public, and unwilling to make necessary decisions, he resigned on March 1, 1949. For his long and valued public career, he was awarded the Distinguished Service Medal by President Truman. Shortly thereafter, he was admitted to Bethesda Naval Hospital for psychiatric care. Sadly, on May 22, 1949, after several prior attempts at suicide, James Forrestal threw himself from a 16th floor window to his death.

Forrestal was buried at Arlington with full military honors before a large crowd that included President Truman. His grave lies on a small hilltop beneath towering oak trees and is marked by a simple granite stone bearing the epitaph: "In the Great Cause of Good Government."

Arthur J. Goldberg

Cabinet Member, Supreme Court Justice, U.N. Ambassador
(August 8, 1908–January 19, 1990)
Sec. 21, Lot S-35, Grid M–20/21

The son of Russian immigrants, Arthur Goldberg dedicated his life to public service—as a labor representative, secretary of labor, Supreme Court justice, and United States ambassador to the United Nations.

Born in Chicago in 1908, Arthur Goldberg was admitted to the Illinois bar at age 20. He attended DePaul and Northwestern universities, where he graduated from the law school in 1929. In 1931, Goldberg married Dorothy Kurgans. They had two children.

Arthur Goldberg first attracted national attention as legal counsel for the Chicago Newspaper Guild during its strike in 1938. By 1948, he had become general counsel for the Congress of Industrial Organizations and the United Steelworkers.

In 1955, he played a pivotal role in the merger of two giant labor groups—the American Federation of Labor and the Congress of Industrial Organizations—to form the AFL-CIO.

President **John Kennedy** named him secretary of labor in 1961, and then nominated him to the United States Supreme Court on August 29, 1962. In July 1965, President Lyndon Johnson persuaded Goldberg to leave the Court to succeed Adlai Stevenson as United States ambassador to the United Nations. But by 1968, Goldberg had become frustrated with the escalation of the conflict in Vietnam and resigned his U.N. post.

In 1970, Arthur Goldberg made his first run for elective office. He challenged incumbent Nelson Rockefeller for governor of New York, but was defeated. He returned to Washington, D.C., to practice law, and served as ambassador-at-large during the administration of President Jimmy Carter.

Former Justice Goldberg died in Washington, D.C., on January 19, 1990, at the age of 81.

Adolphus Washington Greely
Arctic Adventurer
(March 27, 1844–October 20, 1935)
Sec. 1, Lot 129, Grid NO–32/33

A dolphus Greely received a Congressional Medal of Honor on his 91st birthday, but he nearly lost his life during a treacherous adventure that killed 18 other men and left him and his crew stranded in the Arctic for nearly two years.

In their 1879 meeting at Hamburg, Germany, the International Geographical Congress recommended the establishment of a chain of 13 circumpolar stations in the Arctic. Following that recommendation, the United States Congress in 1881 authorized the appropriation of $25,000 to undertake the "Lady Franklin Bay Expedition." Given command of the expedition was Lieutenant Adolphus Greely, who volunteered for the service, and was authorized to take two officers and 21 volunteer enlisted men with him on this dangerous journey. He was further authorized to charter a steam vessel for transport, and to hire Eskimo hunters as guides.

The vessel he selected was the *Proteus*, an ironclad whaler he felt could negotiate the treacherous icy waters of the Arctic. The *Proteus* was to deliver the expedition to its proposed encampment on Ellesmere Island and to return with supplies the following year. In the 1880s, it was necessary to arrange relief expeditions prior to getting underway so that if an expedition should run into difficulty, a rescue vessel would arrive eventually. For Greely's expedition, arrangements had been made for the *Proteus* to retrieve them in 1882. If that mission should fail, a second relief effort would be launched in 1883. Fully supplied, the *Proteus* set sail for the Arctic on July 4, 1881.

Greely's scientific expedition landed on the previously uncharted northeastern side of Ellesmere Island, north of Greenland in August 1881. Here they established Fort Conger where they conducted daily observations of weather and tides and collected samples of minerals, flora, and fauna for study. Sledge trips were made to the western side of the island during which Greely and his men set a new farthest north record by reaching 83 degrees and 24 minutes north of the equator. But sadly, the adventure ended in tragedy.

One year later, in August 1882, the party desperately awaited the arrival of the *Proteus*, but the ship never came. It was later learned that the ship had sunk in the Arctic waters on its way to meet Greely. Trapped then in the Arctic for another winter and with no new supplies, Greely and his crew rationed their food as they counted the days until the second relief vessel's scheduled arrival. When that vessel also failed to reach them in August 1883, the brave band of explorers abandoned their settlement and traveled southward in five small boats. In 51 days, the party covered 500 miles, landing at Bedford Pym Island in Smith Sound, still well within the Arctic Circle. Unable to travel farther, the weary crew, left with less than 40 days rations, faced the long and brutal Arctic winter of 250 days.

During the journey, one Eskimo drowned; another was shot on Greely's orders for pilfering what was left of the meager rations. Throughout the ordeal, Lt. Greely kept a diary in the sad belief that if no one survived, someday someone might know their fate. The diary provides the gruesome details of their plight. Surviving the most arduous conditions, the remaining crew attempted to find what food they could to save their own diminishing food supplies. They ate frozen lichens and searched for any form of animal life. Occasionally, they killed a polar bear or a seal only to see it disappear beneath the floes. By April 3, 1884, their rations were reduced to five pounds of meat and three pounds of dried bread for a dozen men.

By June—without food of any kind and forced to eat their boots and the remnants of their seal skin clothing—only seven men were left alive. Finally, near death, Greely and his six crewmen spotted the relief ship *Thetis* on June 23. Under the command of **Winfield Scott Schley,** the crew of the *Thetis* revived Greely and his men, and returned them to a somber but happy welcome in the United States. For his extraordinary survival efforts, Greely was awarded medals from the Royal and the French Geographical Societies.

Greely was born in Newburyport, Massachusetts, where he graduated from high school in 1860. Only 17, he bluffed his way into the Massachusetts Infantry as a volunteer private during the Civil War, seeing action in several major battles, including Antietam and Fredericksburg. During that war he was wounded three times.

After Greely's return from the Arctic, most of his military service was spent building telegraph lines throughout the western United States, Cuba, Puerto Rico, and the Philippines. By 1906 he was promoted to brigadier general—the first volunteer private ever to reach that rank—and was placed in charge of all relief operations after the San Francisco earthquake. He retired in 1908.

In 1911, President **William Howard Taft** selected Greely to head the delegation to the coronation of King George V of England. He also was a founder of the National Geographic Society, serving on its board for 47 years. Fifty-one years after he was rescued from the Arctic, on his 91st birthday—March 27, 1935—Greely accepted the Congressional Medal of Honor, awarded to him for a "life of splendid service." Six months later, he died in his home in Washington, D.C.

William Frederick "Bull" Halsey, Jr.
Fleet Admiral of the United States Navy
(October 30, 1882–August 16, 1959)
Sec. 2, Lot 1184, Grid T–31

William Frederick Halsey, Jr. was the son of a career naval officer, and, like his father, attended the United States Naval Academy at Annapolis. Graduating in 1904, Halsey was first assigned to the battleship *Kansas* as part of President Theodore Roosevelt's Great White Fleet, which steamed around the world in a show of American naval strength. During World War I, he served aboard patrol and escort vessels based in Ireland, earning a Navy Cross for his brilliant maneuvers in seas occupied by enemy submarines and laden with mines.

After the war, Halsey's career turned to diplomacy. He served as naval attaché to the U.S. embassies in Germany, Sweden, Denmark, and Norway. Then in 1935, Halsey returned to active sea duty, commanding the carrier *Saratoga,* and later completing flight training. He earned his wings as a naval aviator at the age of 52, becoming the oldest American service personnel ever to do so. Subsequently he was named commandant of the Pensacola Naval Air Station, attaining the rank of rear admiral. By 1940, he was a vice admiral, commanding all aircraft carriers in the Pacific Fleet.

When the Japanese attacked Pearl Harbor, Halsey was with his force aboard the carrier *Enterprise,* 150 miles west of Oahu. He anchored the vessel at Pearl Harbor only long enough to refuel. On December 9, he set out to sea with orders to hunt Japanese submarines. He directed surprise forays against Japanese positions in the Marshall and Gilbert islands, as well as on Wake Island. In April 1942, it was from one of his ships, under the command of Captain **Marc Mitscher,** that Colonel **Jimmy Doolittle's** famed B-25 bombers were able to maneuver close enough to the Japanese mainland for air raids on the city of Tokyo.

In October 1942, Halsey was chosen to command the South Pacific Area Force and played an important role in the pivotal battles of Santa Cruz and Guadalcanal. Promoted to commander of the Third Fleet in June 1944, Halsey teamed with the Seventh Fleet and provided support for Douglas MacArthur's invasion of the Philippines, defeating the Japanese fleet in Leyte

Gulf. With the Philippines liberated, Halsey's bombers conducted more raids on Tokyo and other naval installations, and when the Japanese surrendered, the official ceremonies took place aboard Halsey's flagship *USS Missouri* on September 2, 1945, in Tokyo Bay.

In December 1945, President Harry Truman elevated Halsey to five-star status, naming him fleet admiral of the Navy, and making him one of only five men in our nation's history to hold that rank. Retiring from the Navy in 1947, Halsey turned his attentions to the private sector where he served as president of International Telecommunications Laboratories for six years. He died in 1959 and was buried next to his father, **William Frederick Halsey, Sr.,** a Navy captain.

Samuel Dashiell Hammett
Detective Novelist
(May 27, 1894–January 10, 1961)
Sec. 12, Lot 508, Grid YZ-23

Samuel Spade's jaw was long and bony, his chin a jutting V under the more flexible V of his mouth. . . . He said to Effie Perine: 'Yes, sweetheart?. . .'" Thus Dashiell Hammett introduced his most famous detective in his most popular novel, *The Maltese Falcon,* published in 1930. Dash Hammett was no stranger to Sam Spade's lifestyle; he had been a detective during the 1920s, leading the same hard-boiled life he wrote about.

Hammett was born in St. Mary's County, Maryland, and grew up in Baltimore. By age 13, he had dropped out of school, choosing to work at low-paying jobs from messenger boy to stevedore. At 21, he joined the Pinkerton Detective Agency, interrupting his 8-year detective career to serve in World War I. Although Hammett reached the rank of sergeant during WWI, he also contracted tuberculosis and spent much of his time in Army hospitals immediately after the war.

It was in 1928 that Hammett emerged as a pioneer of the "hard-boiled" detective novel. His first books, *Red Harvest* and *The Dane Curse,* set the stage for his finest work, *The Maltese Falcon.* That book, which was the basis for the classic 1941 film starring Humphrey Bogart, propelled Dashiell Hammett into literary stardom as a fiction writer. Another of his works that spawned a motion picture and later a television series, was *The Thin Man* (1934), in which Hammett introduced witty amateur detectives, Nick and Nora Charles. Hammett also tried his hand at creating comic strips for a time, but his "Secret Agent X-9" could never match the success of Dick Tracy.

During the 1930s, Hammett began to take interest in left-wing political activities and the defense of civil liberties. His appearance at Marxist rallies prompted the FBI to place him under surveillance. Nevertheless, Hammett—who bitterly opposed Hitler and Mussolini—enlisted for military service in World War II. It is reported that under suspicion by the Army, he was assigned to the remote Aleutian island of Adak, 800 miles off the Alaskan coast. There, on that barren island, he edited a military newspaper for nearly two years.

After the war, he resumed his political activities and became a trustee of the Civil Rights Congress. As such, he knew the names of persons who had contributed to its bail bond fund. Amidst the widespread anti-Communist furor of the postwar period, he was subpoenaed and questioned about these contributors. When he refused to divulge their names, he was sentenced to six months in jail, which he dutifully served. Commenting on his sentence, Hammett displayed some of Sam Spade's defiance: "If it were more than jail, if it were my life, I would give it for what I think democracy is, and I don't let cops or judges tell me what I think democracy is."

The government headstone marking the grave of Samuel D. Hammett yields few clues that this is the grave of detective novelist Dashiell Hammett.

Throughout his adult life, Dash Hammett maintained a close, romantic relationship with playwright Lillian Hellman, who he acknowledged was the model for his fictional character, Nora Charles. At age 39, he virtually stopped writing, and his later years were marked by chronic ill health. By the time he died in 1961, he had become a veritable recluse in his cottage in Katonah, New York. Hammett's burial at Arlington National Cemetery prompted objections from the FBI, but burial here was what Dashiell Hammett wanted; and it was an honor he had earned. His grave is marked by a standard government tombstone, just one in a long line of similar stones. It reads simply, "Samuel D. Hammett."

Matthew A. Henson

First Person to Reach the North Pole
(August 8, 1866–March 9, 1955)
Section 8, Lot 15, Grid X–8/9

A s an African American, Matthew Henson was banned from joining the United States Navy, received little recognition for accompanying **Robert Peary** to the North Pole, and when he died, was buried without fanfare in an obscure shared grave. It was not until he was reinterred at Arlington National Cemetery in 1988 did Matthew Henson finally receive the public recognition he deserved for his part in the discovery of the North Pole.

Matthew Henson was born in Charles County, Maryland, in 1866. His mother died when he was just a child. His father, who was a tenant farmer, remarried but also died before Matthew turned 11 years old. He ran away from his stepmother, and eventually became a cabin boy on the sailing ship *Katie Hines*. For six years he sailed, teaching himself to read, write, and navigate. When the captain of the ship died, Matthew landed in Washington, D.C. He was working as a clerk in a hat store when he met Robert Peary in 1887.

Peary hired Henson as an aide to accompany him on a surveying mission to Nicaragua. Impressed with Henson's ability and resourcefulness, Peary knew that Henson would be an asset on his venture to locate the North Pole. The first expedition began in 1891, lasted nearly a year, but ended without reaching the Pole. Six more times Henson accompanied Peary, each time they pioneered new methods of travel in the Arctic. They carried minimal equipment, foregoing heavy tents and sleeping bags. Instead, they built igloos and wore heavy fur suits day and night.

Peary came to rely heavily on Henson's ability to navigate and to communicate with the Eskimos.

In July 1908, Peary, Henson, and their six sledge teams again set out for the North Pole. By February 1909, the group left Cape Columbia on the northern edge of Ellesmere Island behind them. The plan was simple. Each team would take turns breaking the trail, leave supplies, and then turn back. Peary, Henson, and four Eskimos comprised the last team.

The travel was treacherous. Temperatures rarely rose above -50°F and extreme winds whipped across the barren ice cap. But the intrepid explorers inched their way northward until April 6, 1909, when Peary, Henson, and their Eskimo companions stood at the North Pole—on top of the world.

As a result of the achievement, Robert Peary was praised as a great explorer and compared to Marco Polo, Magellan, and Columbus. Matthew Henson received little acclaim.

Although Peary repeatedly acknowledged Henson's contributions to the success of the expeditions, Henson did not benefit from his participation. He was denied membership in the famed Explorers Club, although Peary was its president. Three times Congress refused to grant Henson a pension, and because he was not a member of the military, Henson was denied burial at Arlington at the time of his death.

In 1912, Henson published his memoir, "A Negro at the North Pole." In 1913, President **William Howard Taft** appointed Henson a clerk at the New York Customs House where he worked in near obscurity until he retired in 1936.

Eventually, Henson received some recognition. In 1944, Congress voted to give Henson the same Congressional medal that Peary received for his achievement. Henson also was awarded honorary degrees from Howard University in Washington, D.C., and Morgan College in Baltimore.

When he died on March 9, 1955, at the age of 88, Matthew Henson was buried in a shared grave in Woodlawn Cemetery in New York City. In 1968, his wife **Lucy Ross Henson** was buried nearby.

On April 6, 1988—79 years to the day that Admiral Robert Peary, Matthew Henson, and their Eskimo companions stood at the North Pole—Matthew Henson was reinterred with full military honors at Arlington National Cemetery, just a few yards from Admiral Peary's grave.

In 1987, Dr. S. Allen Counter, a professor of neurophysiology at Harvard University, petitioned President Ronald Reagan to allow Henson and his wife to be reinterred in Arlington Cemetery. On April 6, 1988—79 years to the day that Peary, Henson, and their Eskimo companions stood at the North Pole—Matthew Henson was reinterred with full military honors at Arlington National Cemetery, just a few yards from Admiral Peary's grave. At the ceremonies, Professor Counter stated that Henson's burial was "long-overdue recognition for our hero." Also attending were four descendants of Anaukaq Henson, a son Matthew Henson fathered by an Eskimo woman while in the Arctic.

The five-foot black granite memorial marking the graves of Matthew Henson and his wife Lucy Ross Henson includes an excerpt from Henson's own account of his adventure. It also has large bas-reliefs of Henson in his Arctic gear and an image showing Henson flanked by the four Eskimo adventurers at the North Pole. The image is based on a photograph taken by Peary, which supports the belief that Henson was the first person to plant an American flag at the Pole.

Marguerite Higgins (Hall)
Pulitzer Prize-winning Journalist
(September 5, 1920–January 3, 1966)
Sec. 2, Lot 4705, Grid UV–32/33

Marguerite Higgins knew that women were not welcome into the fraternity of war correspondents, but that made her even more determined to join them. And when she did, she covered every major war during her lifetime, earning a coveted Pulitzer Prize.

Born in Hong Kong in 1920, Higgins graduated from the Columbia University School of Journalism in 1942 and went to work for the *New York Herald Tribune.* In 1945, the newspaper sent her to Paris to cover the end of the war. She was with Allied troops as they neared the Nazi concentration camp at Dachau, Germany. Higgins entered the camp while it was still under German control, and was nearly crushed by the rush of prisoners trying to escape. When she attempted to interview the German guards, they tried to surrender to her. For her participation in that event, she was awarded the U.S. Army campaign ribbon.

Higgins covered the war trials at Nuremberg and then was named Berlin bureau chief for the *Herald Tribune* in 1947. In 1948, she was in Berlin during the Soviet blockade.

When the Korean War erupted in 1950, Higgins was sent to cover it. Army officials tried to prevent her from having the same access as her male colleagues, but General Douglas MacArthur intervened on her behalf and ordered that she be treated the same as male correspondents. For her coverage of the war, Marguerite Higgins was awarded the Pulitzer Prize in 1951. She also was named Associated Press Woman of the Year.

She became a columnist for *Newsday* in 1963. On a visit to Vietnam in 1965 to investigate the fall of the Diem regime, Higgins contracted a tropical disease. She died from complications of the disease on January 3, 1966, in Washington, D.C.

Marguerite Higgins was married to U.S. Air Force Lieutenant General William Hall. They had three children.

Oliver Wendell Holmes, Jr.
Civil War Veteran, Supreme Court Justice
(March 8, 1841–March 6, 1935)
Sec. 5, Lot 7004, Grid VW–36

To say that Oliver Wendell Holmes, Jr. had a long and distinguished career is to understate the achievements of a man who served every president from Abraham Lincoln to Franklin Roosevelt. Wounded three times during the Civil War, Holmes later taught law at Harvard University, sat on the Massachusetts supreme court for 20 years and another 30 years on the United States Supreme Court.

Growing up in Boston, Holmes was the product of an aristocratic family that stressed character and accomplishment. The descendant of two established Boston families, he was the maternal grandson of Charles Jackson, a justice of the Massachusetts supreme court, and the son of Oliver Wendell Holmes, Sr., the physician and celebrated poet who penned such noted works as "Old Ironsides" and "The Autocrat of the Breakfast Table." The senior Holmes exercised great influence over his eldest son, especially by acquainting him with a circle of friends that included such literary giants as Ralph Waldo Emerson, Nathaniel Hawthorne, Henry Wadsworth Longfellow, and Herman Melville.

Oliver, Jr. attended private schools, and entered Harvard University at age 16. During his last year at Harvard, the Civil War erupted. Expecting to be drafted before he could graduate, Holmes enlisted in the Army. He did, however, receive his degree and was chosen class poet, just as his father had been 32 years earlier. Upon graduation, Holmes was commissioned a lieutenant in the Twentieth Massachusetts Regiment of Volunteers, and began a wartime experience that affected his entire life.

During the Civil War, Holmes was wounded three times. The first was near Leesburg, Virginia, at the Battle of Ball's Bluff, where he was shot in the chest. Survival meant a treacherous trip down the bluff above the Potomac and across the river in the midst of enemy gunfire. Miraculously Holmes survived, only to be wounded again at Antietam, this time in the throat. Slower to recover from this wound, Holmes nonetheless returned to the front and was wounded a third time at Chancellorsville when his foot was hit with shrapnel.

The best-known tale of Holmes' Civil War experience occurred later in the war. In July 1864, Confederate General Jubal Early's forces were threatening Washington, D.C. Holmes, now under the command of General

Horatio Wright, was chosen to escort President Abraham Lincoln to Fort Stephens on the outskirts of the city. Lincoln, anxious to witness his first battle confrontation, was so intrigued by the fighting that he climbed up on the rampart to get a better view. The sight of the tall, lanky president in his stovepipe hat immediately drew fire from the Confederate troops, but Lincoln was unfazed. In a gentlemanly and subordinate manner, General Wright attempted to convince the president to take cover, but he met with little success. It was obvious to Holmes that the president was not going to guard himself against the clear and present danger of the Confederate gunfire. Exasperated, Holmes shouted at Lincoln, "Get down, you fool!" The president immediately obeyed the command and later expressed his gratitude to Holmes. "Captain," he said, "I'm glad that you know how to talk to a civilian."

The war finally over, Holmes returned to Harvard to study law, his wartime experiences having irrevocably deepened his passion for life. He was admitted to practice law in 1867, but found a certain rigidity in the precedent-oriented law of the mid-19th century. To Holmes, too many concepts were kept alive long after they had lost their relevance. Addressing this problem, he published his classic treatise, "The Common Law," in 1881. In this legal masterwork, he advocated a legal system which is fluid and flexible enough to change with the needs of society instead of being bogged down by antiquated precedents.

In December 1882, Holmes was appointed to the Supreme Judicial Court of Massachusetts, becoming its Chief Justice in 1899. In 1902, Justice Horace Gray resigned from the United States Supreme Court, and President Theodore Roosevelt asked then-governor of the Philippines, **William Howard Taft,** to accept the appointment, but Taft declined. Roosevelt then turned to Holmes. The president was impressed with Holmes' opinions in corporate antitrust cases, as well as his progressive labor views at a time when the labor movement was rapidly expanding. At age 61, Holmes accepted the appointment.

For 29 years Holmes remained on the Court, and although he disappointed Roosevelt with many of his opinions, he became one of the most respected jurists in American history. Justice Holmes was known as "the

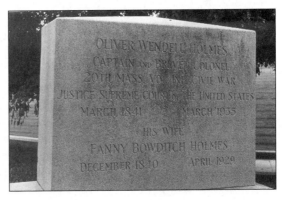

Great Dissenter," not because he frequently dissented (fewer than one in ten of his opinions were in the minority), but because of the brilliant legal reasoning found in his written opinions. He strongly advocated the doctrine of "judicial restraint," which discourages judges from allowing their personal opinions to influence their legal decisions.

Oliver Wendell Holmes, Jr. remained on the Supreme Court until January 12, 1932, just two months short of his 91st birthday, the oldest person ever to sit on the bench. Amazingly, most legal scholars agree that many of Holmes' best decisions were written when he was well past 80 years of age.

For 25 years Holmes did not miss a single session of the Court, walking every day the two and one-half miles from his home to the Capitol building, where the Supreme Court met until its present building was completed in 1935. Also, though justices were exempted, he voluntarily paid federal income tax every year. Regarding taxes, he said, "Taxes are what we pay for a civilized society." That statement now is inscribed on the frieze of the Internal Revenue Service building in Washington, D.C.

After Holmes retired in 1932, President Franklin Roosevelt called upon the former justice to discuss a possible successor. The president found Holmes in his living room reading Plato, and wondered aloud why a 92-year-old man would read Greek philosophy. Without missing a step, Holmes quipped, "Why, to improve my mind, Mr. President." Roosevelt appointed Benjamin Cardozo to succeed Holmes.

Holmes and his wife, **Fanny Bowditch Holmes,** had been married for 57 years when she died in 1929. Upon her death Chief Justice William Howard Taft made arrangements for her burial at Arlington, knowing that Justice Holmes desired to be buried there himself, but was too modest to request it. Holmes died six years later on March 6, 1935, just two days before his 94th birthday. He was buried next to his wife with full military honors, a privilege he had earned 70 years earlier during the Civil War.

Juliet Opie Hopkins
Florence Nightingale of the South
(May 7, 1818–March 9, 1890)
Sec. 1, Lot 12, Grid N–33

Juliet Opie Hopkins was a genuine Confederate heroine. So great was America's respect for her, that 25 years after the Civil War she was awarded full military burial honors by the United States Army at Arlington National Cemetery.

Born in Jefferson County, Virginia, she was married at the age of 19 to A.G. Gordon, a Navy lieutenant who died in 1849. She later met Arthur F. Hopkins, a justice of the Alabama Supreme Court, and although he was 24 years her senior, they were married in 1854. Living in Mobile, Alabama, at the outbreak of the Civil War, Juliet Hopkins offered her services to the state and was sent to Richmond, Virginia, where she took charge of the Alabama section of the Chimborazo Hospital.

In November 1861, the Alabama legislature named Judge Hopkins to be state hospital agent, though the state's true intent was for Mrs. Hopkins to fulfill the duties of the office while her husband held the title. Immediately she set about the task of staffing, supplying, and managing base and field hospitals, proving herself to be an effective and resourceful administrator. Juliet Hopkins was so dedicated to her cause that she expended much of her personal fortune and that of Judge Hopkins' to staff and equip the hospitals she established.

Her care and concern were not confined to the hospitals. She frequently left the security of her hospital office to go onto the battlefields to treat the wounded. On May 31, 1862, at Seven Pines (Fair Oaks), while assisting a wounded Confederate soldier, she was hit by a wayward bullet that left her with a permanent limp.

The high quality of health care in the hospitals under Hopkins' supervision won widespread acclaim. She received the profound gratitude of many commanding generals, including Robert E. Lee who once wrote to her: "You have done more for the South than all the women." Hopkins is now buried on the grounds of Lee's former home. She was further honored when her likeness was put on the $100 bill issued by the Confederate state of Alabama.

In 1890, Juliet Hopkins died while visiting her adopted daughter in Washington, D.C. She is buried with her son-in-law, General **Romeyn E. Ayers,** who preceded her in death. For nearly 100 years the grave of Juliet Opie Hopkins was marked only by the headstone of her son-in-law. Finally, in 1987, the oversight was corrected when a new government regulation headstone was erected to mark the grave of the woman known as the Florence Nightingale of the South.

Grace Murray Hopper
Computer Pioneer
(December 9, 1906–January 1, 1992)
Sec. 59, Lot 973, Grid EE-24

G race Hopper was a computer pioneer who helped develop early programming languages; is credited with coining the phrase "computer bug" more than 50 years ago; and predicted in the 1950s that computers would go from room-size to desk tops. At the time of her death, Rear Admiral Hopper was the highest ranking woman buried at Arlington National Cemetery.

Grace Brewster Murray was born in New York City on December 9, 1906. Her maternal grandfather was a U.S. Navy admiral. Her paternal grandfather was an engineer. So, perhaps it was no surprise that she combined a Naval career with her great interest in science and mathematics. She graduated from Vassar College in 1928 with degrees in mathematics and physics. She taught math at Yale University from 1931 to 1941 where she also earned her master's degree and her PhD. In 1930, Grace Murray married Vincent Hopper. They were divorced in 1945.

After the United States entered WWII, Grace Hopper joined the Naval Reserves and was soon commissioned a lieutenant, junior grade. She was assigned to the Bureau of Ordnance's Computation Program at Harvard University where she work on Mark I, the first large-scale automatic calculator and forerunner to modern-day computers.

Following the war, Hopper was refused a regular Naval commission because of her age (40), so she reverted to inactive reserve status. She remained at Harvard as a civilian research fellow in engineering science and applied physics. One morning in 1947, her computer failed to start. Upon investigation, she found a moth had caused an electrical relay to fail. She described the malfunction as a computer bug, and the phrase soon came to describe any unexplained failure.

Hopper left Harvard in 1949 to join the Eckert-Mauchly Computer Corporation, which later was a part of Sperry Rand. There she worked on the Universal Automatic Computer, or UNIVAC. At that time, programming was a time-consuming, tedious operation, so Hopper undertook a project to develop the first compilers, or programs that convert simple human statements into complex computer instructions. One of her creations was the basis for COBOL (Common Business Oriented Language), the most widely used programming language for 20 years.

In 1966, Grace Hopper retired from the Navy with the rank of commander, but she was recalled a year later for service in the Naval Automation Command to standardize their various computer programming languages.

By a special act of Congress, she was promoted to captain in 1973 at the age of 66, and at a special White House ceremony, President Ronald Reagan promoted her to the rank of rear admiral in 1983. At the age of 79, she was the oldest officer on active duty in the U.S. Navy when she again retired in 1986.

Her many honors include being named 1969 Man of the Year by the Data Processing Management Association, the Navy Meritorious Service Medal in 1980, the Navy Distinguished Service Medal in 1986, and in 1991, President George Bush presented Rear Admiral Hopper with the National Medal of Technology. She died on New Year's Day 1992 in Arlington, Virginia.

IWO JIMA MARINES

On February 23, 1945, Associated Press photographer Joe Rosenthal happened to be nearby as a group of six Marines planted the United States flag atop Mount Suribachi on the tiny island of Iwo Jima. The resulting photograph has become the single most famous photograph taken during World War II. The six men captured in that photo became instant celebrities. Those Marines are Corporal Harlan H. Block, PM2/C John H. Bradley, PFC **Rene Gagnon,** PFC **Ira Hayes,** PFC Franklin R. Sousley, and Sgt. **Michael Strank.** Three of these men died on Iwo Jima, and three are buried in Arlington National Cemetery. They are:

Rene Arthur Gagnon
(March 7, 1926–October 12, 1979)
Sec. 51, Lot 543, Grid DD–47/48

Rene Gagnon was born in Manchester, New Hampshire, where he attended local schools before leaving high school to work in a textile mill. On May 6, 1943, Gagnon was inducted into the Marine Corps Reserve and sent to Parris Island, South Carolina. Promoted to first class on July 16, 1943, he was assigned to the Twenty-eighth Marines when they assaulted the beaches of Iwo Jima on February 19, 1945, and he was atop Mount Suribachi on the 23rd when the United States' colors were planted. Following the Marines' victory on Iwo Jima, Gagnon was ordered to Washington, D.C. because of the

51 543

FOR GOD AND HIS COUNTRY
HE RAISED OUR FLAG IN BATTLE
AND SHOWED A MEASURE OF HIS
PRIDE AT A PLACE CALLED 'TWO JIMA'
WHERE COURAGE NEVER DIED.

A bronze plaque that recreates the famous flag-raising on Iwo Jima Island during World War II is mounted on the grave of Rene Gagnon, one of the six men shown and one of three who are buried at Arlington.

public interest generated by Rosenthal's photo. He joined the other two survivors to make public appearances in connection with the Seventh War Loan Drive, which featured the photo on its publicity poster. When the tour was completed, Gagnon was married in Baltimore and reassigned to San Diego.

Gagnon again was sent overseas on November 7, serving in China until he was discharged on April 27, 1946, after three years in the Marines. Following his discharge he returned to Manchester, where he resided until his sudden death on October 12, 1979. Gagnon was buried in Mount Calvary Mausoleum in Manchester until permission could be obtained to allow his reinterment at Arlington. Since Corporal Gagnon did not meet burial requirements for Arlington at the time of his death, a waiver of policy was necessary. It was granted on April 16, 1981, and on July 7 of that year he was buried at Arlington.

Ira Hamilton Hayes
(January 12, 1923–January 24, 1955)
Sec. 34, Lot 479A, Grid U–11

Ira Hayes is probably the best known of the six men in Joe Rosenthal's famous 1945 photo of the flag-raising on Iwo Jima. His Native American heritage added a dimension to his background that intrigued a public already very interested in the six men. Unfortunately, Hayes could not cope with the celebrity status that was thrust upon him. On January 24, 1955, suffering from alcoholism, he was found dead from exposure near his home in Arizona.

Hayes, a Pima Indian, was born on the Gila River Indian Reservation in Arizona. He left high school after two years to serve in the Civilian Conservation Corps in 1942 and then worked as a carpenter. On August 26, 1942, he enlisted in the United States Marine Corps Reserve, and following boot camp in San Diego, was assigned to the Parachute Training School. He was promoted to first class and sailed for New Caledonia on March 14, 1943. Hayes took part in the Bougainville campaign, but was ordered back to San Diego on February 14, 1944, when he was reassigned to the 28th Marines.

With the 28th when they landed on Iwo Jima on February 19, 1945, Hayes joined five of his comrades to plant the colors on Mount Suribachi on February 23. When it became clear that those six men were becoming the focus of international attention, Hayes tried very hard to conceal his identity, even swearing the other five men to secrecy. He was inordinately shy and came to dread the notoriety. He remained on Iwo Jima until it was secured on March 25, 1945, but after his identity became known he was ordered to Washington, D.C. to take part in the promotional tour for the Seventh War Loan Drive. Hayes remained with that public tour for less than three weeks, at which time he was returned to the 28th in Hawaii. On December 1, 1945, Ira Hayes was honorably discharged.

Following his military career, Hayes had difficulty keeping a steady job because of the widespread discrimination against Native Americans and because of his alcoholism. When the U.S. Marine Corps Memorial was dedicated in the fall of 1954, he was working as a cotton picker and again was pulled unwillingly into the national limelight. His indigent status was widely publicized; two months later, Hayes was found dead of exposure.

After his tragic death, Ira Hayes' body lay in state in the Arizona State Capitol before he was buried with honors at Arlington National Cemetery. Hayes' life story later became the subject of a motion picture. He now rests in Section 34 very near the grave of General of the Armies **John J. Pershing** and **General Hap Harold.**

Michael Strank

(November 10, 1919–March 1, 1945)
Sec. 12, Lot 7179, Grid ZAA–25/26

Sergeant Michael Strank was the oldest of the six men in Joe Rosenthal's famous Iwo Jima photograph. He was 25 when they planted that flag on February 23, 1945, but Strank soon became one of the nearly 6,000 men who lost their lives on the island. On March 1, during fighting on the northern side of Iwo Jima, he was killed; the same day that another of the six men, Harlan Block, died.

Michael Strank was born on November 10, 1919, in Conemaugh, Pennsylvania, the son of Czechoslovakian immigrants. Following high school, he spent nearly 18 months with the Civilian Conservation Corps and then worked as a laborer for the state highway department. Strank enlisted in the United States Marines on October 6, 1939, for a four-year term. During 1942 and 1943, he participated in campaigns in the Wallis Islands, the Russell Islands, and on Bougainville Island. On January 12, 1944, he was reassigned to the Twenty-eighth Marines and stormed ashore with them at Iwo Jima on February 19, 1945. After helping to capture Mount Suribachi, Strank moved northward on the island with his unit. While attacking Japanese positions on March 1, Strank was fatally wounded by enemy artillery fire. He was initially buried in the Marine Cemetery on Iwo Jima, but he was reinterred in Arlington National Cemetery on January 13, 1949, nearly six years before the Marine Corps Memorial was dedicated.

Daniel "Chappie" James, Jr.
First African-American Four-Star General
(February 11, 1920–February 25, 1978)
Sec. 2, Lot 4968-B, Grid V–33

At the end of his military career in 1977, Daniel James, Jr. reflected on his life in the Air Force, stating that early in his career he had realized the importance of setting an example for younger recruits to follow, especially young African Americans who wished to pursue military careers. James had experienced firsthand some of the obstacles encountered by blacks in the military. When he entered the Army in January 1943, he was a member of a segregated unit in Alabama. Once he was barred from leaving the base in his uniform so that white enlisted men would not have to salute a young black flight officer. Nevertheless, he held firm to his dream of a military flying career, choosing to fight the racial inequality in the U.S. Armed Forces and to change the system from within. When James retired from the Air Force, he had become the first black American in our nation's history to achieve the four-star rank of general.

Raised in a family of 17 children, "Chappie," as he was known, left his home in Pensacola, Florida, to attend Tuskegee Institute in Alabama. Following his graduation in 1942, he continued his education in the field of civilian flight training until he received his appointment as a cadet in the Army Air Corps in January 1943. Assigned to a segregated unit in Alabama, and remaining with that unit throughout World War II, he trained pilots for the all-black Ninety-ninth Pursuit Squadron. During the Korean

War, he flew 101 missions in fighter planes, and from 1953 until 1956, he commanded the 437th and then the Sixtieth Fighter Interception Squadrons. In 1957, James graduated from the Air Command and Staff College and was assigned to duty in Washington, D.C. After tours of duty in England and Arizona, James was ordered to Vietnam in 1966. There he flew 78 combat missions, earning promotion to colonel. When he left Vietnam the following year, he was named vice commander of the Thirty-third Tactical Fighter Wing at Elgin Air Force Base, Florida. His rise in rank continued. In 1969, he was promoted to brigadier general and given command of Wheelus Air Force Base in Libya. Returning to the United States in 1970, he served as deputy assistant secretary of defense for public affairs and achieved the rank of major general. In 1974, climbing to the rank of lieutenant general, he became vice commander of the Military Airlift Command at Scott Air Force Base, Illinois.

The pinnacle of James' distinguished career was reached in December 1975, when he became the first black American in any branch of the service to gain promotion to full general. At that time, General Daniel James, Jr. was named commander of the North American Air Defense Command (NORAD), a distinction which gave him responsibility for all aspects of the air defense of the United States and Canada.

Unfortunately, James suffered from heart problems which forced his retirement from the Air Force in 1977. He died in Colorado Springs, Colorado, on February 25, 1978, and following a funeral mass attended by military and civilian leaders at the National Shrine of the Immaculate Conception in Washington, D.C., General James was buried with full military honors at Arlington National Cemetery.

Philip Kearny

Mexican War Hero, Civil War Hero
(June 1, 1814–September 1, 1862)
Special Lot S-8, Grid OP–32

The lifelike equestrian statue of Philip Kearny in Arlington Cemetery dramatically tells the story of a man who was determined to be a professional soldier. Sculptor E. C. Potter has captured the scrappy little general poised in his saddle, nearly standing in his stirrups. His horse appears caught in midstride, its tail and mane blowing in the wind. With the reins in his only hand, Kearny seems ready to bark orders to his men as he leads the charge. His proud military career is graphically summarized by the inscription on its base:

Gave his left arm

at

Churubusco, Mexico

August 18, 1847

and his life at Chantilly, Va.

September 1, 1862.

Kearny was born in New York City to a very wealthy family, but was orphaned as a young child. Although reared by a grandfather who wanted a career in the ministry for his grandson, Kearny's heart was set on being a soldier. As soon as he was old enough, he left for France to become a student at the French Cavalry School at Saumur. He later served with the Chasseurs d'Afrique, returning to the United States to enlist in the Army and serve on the western frontier.

Kearny always believed that in order to be a good soldier you must look like a good soldier. So, while commanding a troop of dragoons during the Mexican War, he purchased matching dapple gray horses for his men with his own funds. It was also during that war that Kearny lost his left arm. While leading an assault in the battle of Churubusco, Kearny's arm was shattered by gunfire and later required amputation. Yet he could do with one arm what many men could not do with two.

Following the Mexican campaign, undaunted by the loss of his arm and searching for more battles, Kearny returned to France to take part in the

Franco-Italian War under Napoleon III. When the Civil War broke out in the United States, he came back to fight for the Union. Initially unwilling to offer him a commission, the Army relented and Kearny took command of the First New Jersey Brigade as part of the Third Division of the Army of the Potomac.

Kearny demanded strict discipline of his men, but he demanded even more of himself. He was often seen holding his reins in his teeth and directing his men with his free right arm. Kearny's men, who were fiercely loyal to him, could always count on the general leading the charge, not following as so many other commanders did. But his unbridled gallantry cost Kearny his life. Just prior to the Second Battle of Bull Run, Kearny inadvertently crossed the Confederate lines and was killed.

Even among the Confederate soldiers Kearny commanded such deep respect that, under a flag of truce, General Robert E. Lee immediately ordered the return of Kearny's body and later returned his horse and sword. Kearny is now buried in what was once part of Lee's garden at Arlington.

Following his death, Kearny's men decided to establish a tribute to their fallen leader. For that reason, Kearny's successor, Major General David Birney, created the Cross of Honor, also known as Kearny's Cross, to be awarded to noncommissioned officers and privates for exceptional valor in battle. That commendation has evolved into the Medal of Honor, the highest decoration that can be given to American military personnel.

Major General Philip Kearny was buried in Trinity Church Yard in New York City following his death at Chantilly, Virginia, at the age of 48. His remains were reinterred in Arlington Cemetery on April 12, 1912. He was later placed in his current grave when his statue was completed in 1914 during the centennial of his birth. Kearny is one of only two persons honored with an equestrian statue in Arlington. The other is Sir **John Dill.**

Edward M. (Ted) Kennedy
"Lion of the Senate"
February 22, 1932 – August 25, 2009
Sec. 45, Grid TU-23/33

During his inauguration celebration in January 1961, **John F. Kennedy** gave his youngest brother, Teddy, a silver cigarette case engraved with the words, "And the last shall be first" from the gospel of St. Matthew. Although it is unclear what the new president was trying to convey then, today when assessing which Kennedy brother—John, Robert, or Edward—has had the greatest impact on the lives of Americans. Most historians would conclude that President Kennedy was prophetic, Edward Kennedy would be first.

Edward Moore Kennedy was born on February 22, 1932—the 200th anniversary of George Washington's birth. He was the youngest of nine children born to Joseph P. Kennedy and Rose Fitzgerald Kennedy, both products of prominent Irish-Catholic families in Boston. Joseph was a wealthy financier, investing in movies, liquor, real estate and the stock market.

The Kennedy children lived in affluence. And while their millionaire father held a variety of important positions in business and government, he always put his family first. He and Rose stressed high academic performance from their children, although Teddy preferred sports to school work. Because of his father's frequent moves, Teddy attended 10 prep schools in the United States and England in 11 years, landing finally at Milton Academy near Boston. There he played football and participated in debate, drama and the glee club.

In 1950, Ted entered Harvard. A football standout as a freshman, he often allowed the sport to supersede his studies. Fearful of failing a Spanish final, he enlisted another student to take the exam. Harvard expelled him, allowing him to return if he exhibited good behavior for two years. So he joined the Army.

With a little influence from his father, Private Kennedy was assigned to a unit guarding NATO Headquarters in Paris. He served honorably and was discharged in 1953. He returned to Harvard, where he took his studies more seriously, although he was the first-string end on the Crimson football team. His notable football performance drew the interest of the Green Bay Packers, who tried unsuccessfully to recruit him in 1955.

Ted Kennedy graduated from Harvard in 1956 and eventually enrolled at the University of Virginia Law School, where his brother **Robert Kennedy** had studied. He earned his degree in 1959 and returned to Massachusetts. While still in law school, Ted managed his brother John's successful reelection campaign for the U.S. Senate in 1958. That same year, he married Joan Bennett, a debutante whom he had met years earlier while living in New York.

In 1960, John Kennedy resigned his Senate seat to become president. Many thought that Bobby would seek the seat, but he chose instead to serve as his brother's attorney general. At 28, Edward was two years too young to qualify, but one month after his 30th birthday in February 1962, Edward Kennedy declared his candidacy for his brother's former seat.

Kennedy easily won the general election on Nov. 6, 1962. He was sworn in the next day when Benjamin Smith resigned the seat he had been appointed to fill. Kennedy would serve more than 46 years, becoming the third-longest serving Senator in U.S. history behind Robert Byrd of West Virginia and Strom Thurmond of South Carolina.

Edward Kennedy was in the Senate for just a year when John Kennedy was assassinated in Dallas, and like his brother Bobby, Ted Kennedy was committed to fulfilling the programs President Kennedy had pursued. Early in his career, he played an important role in the passage of Medicare, immigration reform, and civil rights legislation.

After voting for the historic Civil Rights Act of 1964, Kennedy boarded a private plane on June 19 heading to a convention in Springfield, Mass. But while landing in fog, the plane struck treetops, killing the pilot and an aide. Indiana Senator Birch Bayh and his wife, Marvella, received minor injuries. Senator Kennedy, however, suffered a broken back and collapsed lung. He was bedridden for five months.

Tragedy struck again when his brother Bobby was assassinated in Los Angeles in 1968. Now the family's political mantle fell on Teddy. By this time, Kennedy had openly questioned America's policies in Viet Nam, and when Hubert Humphrey lost to President Richard Nixon that fall, many Democrats saw Teddy as their next standard bearer. That expectation was thrown into question on July 18, 1969.

Kennedy had invited some former workers from Bobby's presidential campaign to a reunion on Chappaquiddick Island off Martha's Vineyard. Just before midnight Kennedy left the gathering with one of the workers,

Mary Jo Kopechne. The car he was driving went off the side of a small unrailed bridge and landed upside down in the water. Kennedy escaped, but Kopechne drowned.

Many people questioned Kennedy's explanation of the event, and although he received a short suspended sentence for his negligent driving, his chances to win the presidency in 1972, and, later, 1976 were severely damaged.

So Kennedy threw himself into his work in the Senate. In the 1970s, he introduced bills to establish universal healthcare, deregulate airlines, begin arms-control talks with the Soviets, extend voting to 18-year-olds, reform campaign financing, and extend the voting rights and fair housing acts. By 1980 he had regained his stature among Democrats, and with President Jimmy Carter falling in the polls, Kennedy announced his candidacy for president. But his inability to clearly articulate why he wanted to be president stalled his campaign and Carter was easily renominated.

By 1982 his marriage to Joan, which produced three children, had collapsed and they divorced. Suspecting that he would never gain the White House, Kennedy again focused on his work in the Senate. Considered the voice of liberal causes in the Senate, Kennedy was able to work across the aisle to pass AIDS legislation, the Americans with Disabilities Act, the State Children's Health Insurance Program, and No Child Left Behind.

It was during this period that Kennedy renewed his acquaintance with Victoria Reggie, a 37-year-old attorney who had been an intern in Kennedy's office years earlier. Their relationship flourished, and in 1992 they married. Many people credit Victoria for bringing stability to Kennedy's personal life.

In May 2008 Kennedy was diagnosed with brain cancer. Although he was absent from the Senate for long periods, he worked tirelessly in support of President Barack Obama's healthcare reform bill—a bill Kennedy called, "the cause of my life." Sadly, he did not live to see the bill pass. On August 26, 2009, Kennedy died at his beloved home in Hyannis Port. He was laid to rest near his brothers John and Robert on the hillside below Arlington House.

Jacqueline Kennedy (Onassis)
(July 28, 1929–May 19, 1994)
Sec. 45, Grid U–35

Jackie Kennedy was just 31 years old when **John F. Kennedy** became president of the United States. Yet she forever transformed the role of first lady when she moved into the White House, and touched the hearts of a nation when she left it.

Jacqueline Lee Bouvier was born in Southhampton, New York, in 1929. Her parents, Janet Lee and John Vernou Bouvier III, were divorced when Jacqueline was just a child. Her mother then married Hugh Auchincloss, a wealthy stockbroker, and the family moved to Washington, D.C.

Jackie, as she became universally known, graduated from Miss Porter's School before attending Vassar College in Poughkeepsie, New York, the Sorbonne in Paris, and earning her bachelor's degree from George Washington University in Washington, D.C., in 1951. She then spent a year touring Europe where she perfected her French and Spanish.

Jackie Bouvier returned to the United States to work as a photographer for the Washington Times-Herald newspaper. In 1953, she was invited to a dinner party at the home of Charles Bartlett, a columnist for the Saturday Evening Post. At that dinner she was introduced to the newly elected senator from Massachusetts, 35-year-old John F. Kennedy. Kennedy later recalled the encounter, "I leaned across the asparagus and asked her for a date."

On September 12, 1953, John Fitzgerald Kennedy and Jacqueline Lee Bouvier were married in a spectacular wedding in St. Mary's Church in Newport, Rhode Island. The reception was held on the Newport estate of Jackie's stepfather, Hugh Auchincloss.

During their first year of marriage, the Kennedys encountered tragedy. Jackie suffered her first miscarriage, and Senator Kennedy was plagued by debilitating back pain. He was forced to undergo an experimental lumbar fusion operation. It was not successful, and twice in the month following the operation, he was so close to death that a Catholic priest was called to administer the last rites.

In 1956, tragedy struck again when Mrs. Kennedy delivered a stillborn daughter. However, in 1957, she gave birth to her second daughter, Caroline Bouvier Kennedy.

Meanwhile, Senator Kennedy's political career flourished. On January 2, 1960, he announced his candidacy for president of the United States. Shortly after the announcement, Jackie had an announcement of her own. She was pregnant again, due shortly after the general election in November. Despite her pregnancy, she actively campaigned for her husband, and in the early morning hours of November 9, 1960, the Kennedys learned that John had won a narrow victory over Vice President Richard Nixon. Sixteen days later, Jacqueline Kennedy gave birth to a son, John Fitzgerald Kennedy, Jr.

On January 20, 1961, John Kennedy took the presidential oath of office and Jacqueline Kennedy assumed the role of first lady. As first lady, she dedicated herself to her public duties, but never forgot her most important responsibility.

As unofficial White House curator, Jacqueline Kennedy refurbished America's best-known residence with historic furnishings and artwork. And when she finished, Mrs. Kennedy conducted the first-ever television tour that gave millions of Americans their first glimpse inside the president's home. For that milestone, she received an Emmy award for public service.

Mrs. Kennedy also took advantage of her role as hostess for state dinners and official receptions to showcase American artists and performers. She often accompanied her husband overseas where she impressed foreign dignitaries with her command of languages and great interest in the arts, history, and literature. And she inspired men and women all over the world with her sense of style and fashion.

In May 1994, Jacqueline Kennedy Onassis was buried next to her former husband and their two children. Above them burns the Eternal Flame that Jacqueline Kennedy lit at John Kennedy's funeral in 1963.

But the greatest role Jacqueline Kennedy saw for herself was as a mother. Although she was proud of her achievements as first lady, she once said "if you bungle raising your children, I don't think whatever else you do well matters very much." Throughout her life, Mrs. Kennedy was devoted to her children. In August 1963, she gave birth to a son, **Patrick Bouvier Kennedy.** Born five weeks prematurely, he developed breathing complications and died less than two days later.

Following Patrick's death, Mrs. Kennedy restricted her public appearances while she convalesced. After several weeks, she agreed to accompany the president on a politically important trip to Dallas, Texas. It would be her last trip as first lady.

The image that most Americans have of Jacqueline Kennedy—her grace, dignity, composure, and courage—was etched into our minds as a result of the assassination of her husband on November 22, 1963, in Dallas. During the days following President Kennedy's death, Mrs. Kennedy touched the hearts of every American as she led the nation in mourning. She personally oversaw the details of her husband's funeral and burial, knowing that she had to share her grief with the rest of the world.

Mrs. Kennedy and her two children moved to New York City shortly after the president's death. As the most famous and admired woman in America, she diligently tried to shield her children from the glare of intense public interest. In 1968, she married one of the world's wealthiest men, Greek shipping magnate Aristotle Onassis, and moved to Greece. When Onassis died in 1975, Mrs. Onassis returned to New York and became an editor with Viking Press and then Doubleday and Co.

She dedicated herself to rearing her children, working, promoting the arts, and assisting historic preservation. She never wrote a memoir of her White House years, although she did record tapes on the subject of President Kennedy's assassination. They will remain sealed until 50 years after the death of her last surviving child.

On May 19, 1994, Jacqueline Kennedy Onassis died of cancer in her New York City apartment at the age of 64. At her request, she was buried next to President Kennedy in the grave site that she helped design 30 years earlier. Buried near her are their son, Patrick, and their unnamed baby girl.

Their son, John F. Kennedy, Jr., died when the plane he was piloting crashed into the Atlantic Ocean off Martha's Vineyard, Massachusetts, on July 16, 1999. John, Jr.'s wife Carolyn Bessette also was killed. They were cremated and their ashes were scattered over the Atlantic Ocean near where they died.

John Fitzgerald Kennedy
35th President of the United States
(May 29, 1917–November 22, 1963)
Sec. 45, Grid U–35

It was 12:30 p.m. CST on November 22, 1963, when President John F. Kennedy was assassinated in Dallas. Word of that tragedy spread rapidly around the world, and for anyone who heard that shocking news, that moment was frozen in time. Anyone old enough to remember that day recalls exactly where he or she was when the first report of the president's death was broadcast.

President Kennedy had traveled to Dallas to forge a united political front in Texas in anticipation of the 1964 presidential election. Kennedy knew that a win in the Lone Star State would help him secure a victory in 1964, and give him the mandate he sought for his social programs. While riding in an open limousine, two bullets struck John Kennedy and he slumped helplessly into his wife's lap. He was raced to Parkland Memorial Hospital for emergency treatment, but was pronounced dead on arrival. Vice President Lyndon Baines Johnson took the oath of office as president at 2:38 p.m., November 22, 1963.

The life that ended so tragically in Dallas began with such hope and promise in Brookline, Massachusetts, a suburb of Boston, in 1917. "Jack" Kennedy, as he was known to his family and friends, was the second son of Boston banker and financier Joseph P. Kennedy and his wife Rose, who was the daughter of Boston Mayor John F. "Honey Fitz" Fitzgerald, after whom John was named. Young Jack was raised in a very affluent environment, and like each of his eight brothers and sisters, was given a million-dollar trust fund by his father. His life, however, was not always easy.

Joseph Kennedy served as chairman of the Securities and Exchange Commission in the mid-1930s and later as U.S. ambassador to Great Britain. He was a strict disciplinarian who taught his children to be fiercely competitive in all aspects of their lives, whether they were playing touch football or running for public office. John did not foresee a political career for himself; that career had been reserved for his older brother, Joseph, Jr. When Jack graduated from Harvard in 1940, his eye was on a career in Academe or journalism. In fact, during the year he graduated from Harvard, he expanded his senior thesis on the subject of British military unpreparedness prior to World War II into a best-selling book, "Why England Slept."

In the spring of 1941, more than six months before the Japanese attack on Pearl Harbor, Jack Kennedy attempted to enlist in the United States Navy, but was denied because of a back injury that he suffered while playing football at Harvard. He underwent physical therapy and treatment, and was finally accepted into the Navy in September 1941. In August 1943, Lieutenant John Kennedy was in command of a torpedo boat, *PT-109*, patrolling the waters off the Solomon Islands. Running with lights out through heavy fog, Kennedy's boat was rammed and ripped in half by a Japanese destroyer. The impact threw the young lieutenant and his crew into the dark Pacific Ocean. Kennedy risked his life to save the lives of his men, even towing one injured sailor for three miles, holding that man's life jacket between his teeth. For this heroic deed, Jack Kennedy was awarded the Navy and Marine Corps Medal, but he also was hospitalized with further injury to his back.

While recuperating, Kennedy learned of the death of his older brother, Joe, a Naval aviator shot down over the English Channel. It was Joe who was to carry the family's political standard; John now knew that that responsibility had passed to him. This special family belief regarding public service was later expressed by Kennedy after he was elected to the Senate: "Just as I went into politics because Joe died, if anything happened to me tomorrow, my brother Bobby would run for my seat in the Senate. And if Bobby died, Teddy would take over for him."

Kennedy's first campaign for elective office came in 1946 when he ran for Congress from Massachusetts. He easily won the primary and registered a landslide victory in the November general election. He had won his first election at age 29, and would never lose one. After serving three terms in the House of Representatives, he chose to give up his safe House seat to challenge the popular incumbent senator from Massachusetts, Republican Henry Cabot Lodge. With his brother, **Robert Kennedy,** managing his campaign, and his family working in full force, Jack Kennedy succeeded in unseating Lodge, though Dwight Eisenhower recorded a statewide presidential victory. Kennedy entered the Senate in January 1953, and eight months later married **Jacqueline Bouvier.**

In 1956, Kennedy underwent one of three major surgeries on his back. While convalescing he conceived *Profiles in Courage,* an anthology of eight great American political leaders that was awarded the 1957 Pulitzer Prize. Also in 1956, Kennedy was considered as a running mate for Democratic presidential candidate Adlai Stevenson. When Kennedy was not selected for the vice president's slot in favor of Estes Kefauver, some politicos felt this was a blow to Kennedy's desire for national office. However, given the national exposure he received, Kennedy found himself the front runner for his party's presidential nomination in 1960.

John F. Kennedy formally announced his presidential candidacy in January 1960, and undertook the drive to win the nomination from his chief rivals, fellow Senators Hubert Humphrey and Lyndon Johnson. In overcoming their challenge, he dealt effectively with the question about his religion (Roman Catholic) and won the nomination on the first ballot. Then, with Senator Johnson as his running mate, he faced Vice President Richard Nixon and Henry Cabot Lodge in the general election.

The 1960 campaign introduced several new campaign techniques to American political life, including extensive use of air travel, heavy reliance on television advertising, and televised debates between the candidates. Analysts uniformly agree that the four televised debates greatly aided Jack Kennedy who appeared poised and demonstrated a firm grasp of the issues. By contrast, Vice President Nixon suffered from poor makeup and a fatigued appearance. It was early in the morning after election day before all the votes were counted, and Kennedy declared the winner by a razor-thin margin of victory, winning by just over 100,000 votes out of a total of nearly 69 million votes cast nationwide.

John F. Kennedy was inaugurated president of the United States on January 20, 1961, becoming the youngest man ever elected to that office and the first Roman Catholic. His administration was a relatively short one, lasting only 1,037 days. Yet during that time, President Kennedy faced several major foreign policy tests and proposed wide-ranging domestic legislation. Kennedy also began televised press conferences—which have since become commonplace—where he often disarmed his critics by displaying an unusually candid sense of humor.

Soon after his inauguration the CIA sponsored an invasion of Cuba by a brigade of Cuban exiles intent on inciting rebellion against Fidel Castro. John F. Kennedy had allowed the covert operation on the recommendation of the Joint Chiefs of Staff, and accepted full responsibility when the rebel forces failed in their objective and every member was either killed or captured by Castro's troops.

The most serious challenge of Kennedy's administration, however, came in October 1962, when it was learned that the Soviet Union had installed missiles in Cuba. President Kennedy demanded that the missiles be removed. When his warnings went unheeded, he ordered the U.S. Navy to blockade the island. For 13 days the two superpowers appeared on the brink of war, but then the Soviets yielded, agreeing to withdraw their missiles and handing President Kennedy a major foreign policy victory. In his own estimation, his greatest foreign policy achievement was the Nuclear Test-Ban Treaty, signed by Great Britain, the Soviet Union, and the United States in December 1962.

Domestically, Kennedy envisioned greatly expanded civil rights and social programs. The president knew he could not marshal the support he needed unless he could win a strong mandate in his bid for reelection. This was his purpose for visiting Dallas in November 1963. After John Kennedy's assassination, President Lyndon Johnson won the electoral mandate that Kennedy sought, and many Kennedy-inspired programs became part of Johnson's "Great Society."

Following reports of President Kennedy's assassination in Dallas, the world watched for three days as our nation prepared to bury its fallen leader. On Monday, November 25, 1963, as a worldwide television audience viewed the proceedings, John Fitzgerald Kennedy was laid to rest on the hillside below Arlington House in a 20 feet by 30 feet plot surrounded by a white picket fence.

Two other sites in Arlington had been considered for his burial: one near the *USS Maine* Memorial and the other in Dewey Circle, near where the U.S. Coast Guard Memorial sits today. But Mrs. Kennedy chose the current site because it provided easier access to the public.

More than 3,000 people an hour were visiting President Kennedy's grave, so the family decided to construct a more suitable memorial than the small fenced plot. Construction began in 1965 and was completed on July 20, 1967. The grave site consists of a circular walkway which approaches a small elliptical terrace. From this terrace visitors can look over a low wall toward the Lincoln Memorial across the Potomac. The wall is inscribed with passages from President Kennedy's speeches. President Kennedy's grave lies on a slightly elevated terrace, marked by a marble tablet which simply proclaims:

John Fitzgerald Kennedy

1917–1963

Today that grave is the single most visited site in Arlington National Cemetery.

Above his grave stands the Eternal Flame that was lit by **Jacqueline Kennedy** at her husband's burial service. Two infant children—a boy, **Patrick Bouvier Kennedy,** and an unnamed baby girl who predeceased the president—were reinterred on either side of him on December 4, 1963. When this permanent grave site was completed, the bodies of President Kennedy and his two children were removed to their final resting places on the evening of March 14, 1967, and were blessed by Richard Cardinal Cushing in a private ceremony attended by Mrs. Kennedy, Senators Robert and Edward Kennedy, and President Lyndon Johnson.

In 1968, Jacqueline Kennedy married Greek shipping magnate Aristotle Onassis, who died in 1975. Jacqueline Kennedy Onassis died of cancer on May 19, 1994, and was buried alongside President Kennedy. Their son, John F. Kennedy, Jr., died when the plane he was piloting crashed into the Atlantic Ocean off Martha's Vineyard, Massachusetts, on July 16, 1999. John Jr.'s wife Carolyn Bessette also was killed. They were cremated and their ashes were scattered over the Atlantic Ocean near where they died. John Kennedy's brother, **Robert Francis Kennedy,** also is buried at Arlington a short distance from the president's tomb in a grave marked by a simple white cross.

A horse-drawn caisson bears the body of President John F. Kennedy during his funeral services in November 1963.

Representatives of every branch of the United States Armed Forces served as pall bearers, carrying the slain president to his grave in Section 5.

Mrs. Jacqueline Kennedy is escorted by Arlington Cemetery Superintendent John Metzler and the president's brothers, Robert and Edward. The president's mother Mrs. Rose Kennedy, and other members of his family follow.

The flag that draped the casket throughout the services for President Kennedy is folded and presented to Mrs. Kennedy as part of the Combined Armed Forces Honors.

Jacqueline Kennedy prepares to light the Eternal Flame, which continues to light the permanent memorial to John F. Kennedy.

A never-before-published photograph of John F. Kennedy's original gravesite, taken on November 29, 1963, just four days after his burial. More than eight million people visited Arlington National Cemetery during the year following President Kennedy's burial. The large number of visitors required a redesign of the area around the gravesite. A steeper slope was created for the hill above the grave to discourage access from above and vehicular traffic was prohibited in the cemetery.

Robert F. Kennedy
Attorney General, Senator, Presidential Candidate
(November 20, 1925–June 6, 1968)
Sec. 45, Grid U–33/34

After Robert Kennedy graduated from Harvard University in 1948, he foresaw a career dedicated to advancing the political ambitions of his older brother, John. Having already managed John's successful campaign for Congress, Robert Kennedy looked forward to working to get his brother elected president of the United States. Only during those dark days following **John Kennedy's** assassination did Robert Kennedy decide to consider elective office for himself.

Robert F. Kennedy was the seventh of nine children born to Joseph and Rose Kennedy, a wealthy and prominent Boston couple. Joseph Kennedy was a banker and financier who had accumulated great wealth in the stock market before its crash in 1929. The elder Kennedy chaired the Securities and Exchange Commission in the mid-1930s during the Franklin Roosevelt administration, and then served as U.S. ambassador to Great Britain. Rose Kennedy was the daughter of John F. "Honey Fitz" Fitzgerald, the long-time mayor of Boston.

Robert Kennedy's early years were spent developing the fierce competitive drive for distinction which typified his father, and the love, compassion, and serenity that were the result of his mother's influence. Spared the economic hardships that befell many American families in the 1930s, Robert grew up in an affluent environment. With his three brothers and five sisters, Robert enjoyed touch football, sailing, and tennis. After entering Harvard University, he interrupted his studies to serve in the U.S. Navy during World War II. Following the war, he returned to graduate from Harvard in 1948 and continued his education at the University of Virginia Law School, graduating in 1951.

It was no surprise that Robert joined the successful congressional campaign of his older brother, John, in 1946. Following John to Washington, D.C., Robert was named assistant counsel to the Senate Permanent Committee on Investigations, a powerful committee chaired by Senator Joseph McCarthy. Robert stayed in that position for only a short time, resigning because of the nature of the investigations undertaken by the committee. He returned the following year as majority counsel when McCarthy was no longer chairman. Then in 1957, Robert was chief counsel for the special Senate committee investigating labor racketeering. It was in this position that he first encountered Teamsters Union leader, Jimmy Hoffa. This encounter led

Robert Kennedy's grave is the only gravesite in Arlington marked with a simple wooden cross.

to a longstanding feud between Kennedy and Hoffa, a battle which continued into Kennedy's days as U.S. attorney general. It was during Kennedy's tenure as attorney general that Hoffa was imprisoned for jury tampering, fraud, and conspiracy.

In 1960, Robert Kennedy directed his brother's successful campaign for president of the United States. Subsequently, Robert was named as JFK's attorney general amid loud public cries of nepotism. Although Bobby—as he was universally known— was only 35 years old at the time, President Kennedy brushed aside criticism of his appointment with such quips as "I can't see that it's so wrong to give him a little legal experience before he goes out to practice law." The president's confidence was confirmed by his younger brother's performance. Bobby established a record that advanced civil rights across our country, fought relentlessly against organized crime, and improved life for Americans. When he resigned from that post in 1964, *The New York Times* (which had criticized his appointment three years earlier) editorialized about Robert Kennedy:

> He named excellent men to most key posts, put new vigor into protecting civil rights through administrative action, played a pivotal role in shaping the most comprehensive civil rights law in this country. ...Mr. Kennedy has done much to elevate the standard.

When John Kennedy was assassinated in Dallas in 1963, Robert was overcome with grief. He and his brother had spent much time together, working closely on many issues as national leaders and sharing personal thoughts and feelings as friends. After considerable soul searching, Robert resigned from the Justice department in September 1964 to enter the race for the United States Senate from New York.

In that election Kennedy easily defeated incumbent Senator **Kenneth Keating** (Sec. 5, Lot 141) and became a major political figure in the Democratic Party, championing liberal causes and opposing President Lyndon Johnson's wartime policies in Vietnam. As a younger man, Robert had never viewed himself as potential presidential material. He had left that to his older brother, Joseph, who had been killed during World War II, and then to John. But Robert Kennedy believed America was heading away from the ideals set by his brother, so on March 16, 1968, he announced his candidacy for the Democratic nomination for President.

Embarking on an uphill fight against incumbent President Lyndon Johnson, the race opened up for Kennedy when President Johnson announced that he would neither seek nor accept his party's nomination. Kennedy's campaign gained great momentum, as he won five of six primary contests, including the final and most important preconvention election, the delegate-rich California primary on June 4, 1968.

It was a Robert Kennedy filled with hope and confidence who addressed his supporters following his victory in California. As he stood before them at the Ambassador Hotel in Los Angeles just after midnight on June 5, he exhorted his followers, promising to take the fight for the nomination to the floor of the National Democratic Convention in Chicago. He left them cheering in the ballroom as he slipped out through a kitchen hallway. There, with the cheers still echoing in the air, Robert Kennedy was met by Sirhan Sirhan, a Palestinian immigrant, who shot and critically wounded him. Senator Kennedy died the following morning. Surviving Kennedy were his ten children and his wife, Ethel, who was expecting another child. Sirhan Sirhan was convicted of murder and was sentenced to death by a California court, but his sentence was commuted to life imprisonment when the United States Supreme Court declared the death penalty unconstitutional.

At Robert's funeral Senator Edward Kennedy said of his older brother, "Some men see things as they are and ask, 'Why?' He saw things that never were and asked, 'Why not?'" Robert now is buried near his brother, John, in the only grave at Arlington marked by a simple white cross. Passages from Robert Kennedy's speeches are inscribed on a wall above a fountain which forms a part of the burial site.

photo by Warren Miller

Ethel Kennedy (left), widow of Robert F. Kennedy, is joined at his gravesite with Sargent Shriver, Ethel Kennedy Shriver, and Edward M. Kennedy and his wife, Victoria Reggie Kennedy.

William Franklin Knox

Rough Rider, Newspaper Publisher,
Secretary of the Navy
(January 1, 1874–April 28, 1944)
Sec. 2, Lot 4961, Grid WX–32/33

The inscription on his tombstone reads "Secretary of the Navy," leaving unlisted the other remarkable achievements of William Franklin Knox. Nowhere is it engraved, for example, that Knox was with Teddy Roosevelt on San Juan Hill, or that he saw combat in World War I, or that he published the *Chicago Daily News,* or that he ran for vice president of the United States.

Born in Boston, Knox moved to Michigan at an early age. He attended Alma College in Alma, Michigan, and when war broke out with Spain in 1898, enlisted in the First U.S. Volunteer Cavalry—better known as the Rough Riders. Knox was sworn into the Army by Theodore Roosevelt himself, and not only did he fight at Las Guasimas, but also saw action in the battle up San Juan Hill near Santiago de Cuba. Sunstroke and malaria forced Knox to return home before the conclusion of that war. He received his honorable discharge in September 1898.

Following the war, he began a successful career in journalism, publishing the *Sault Ste. Marie (Michigan) News* in 1902. He launched his political career in 1910 when he successfully managed the Michigan gubernatorial campaign for Republican Chase Osborn. Unfortunately, he would never again be associated with a successful campaign, although he tried on several occasions, including the 1912 election in which he supported Teddy Roosevelt in his unsuccessful bid for a third term as President.

When World War I erupted across Europe, Knox—then 43 years old—volunteered for active service again. Following completion of Officer's Training School, he was commissioned a captain and took part in the battles of the St. Mihiel Salient and the Meuse-Argonne. The war's end marked his return to journalism and politics.

In 1920, Knox went to work for publisher William Randolph Hearst, taking charge of Hearst's paper *The Boston American and Advertiser* seven years later. While handling Hearst's newspapers in New England in 1924, Knox ran for governor of New Hampshire, but lost in the Republican primary. In 1931, Knox purchased the *Chicago Daily News* and remained its publisher until 1940. In 1936, Governor Alf Landon of Kansas, the Republican nominee for president, picked Knox as his running mate, but their ticket lost overwhelmingly to Democrat Franklin Roosevelt in the November general election.

In spite of his defeat by Roosevelt and his staunch Republican ties, Knox supported FDR's military and foreign policies regarding the war in Europe in 1939. At that time, Roosevelt asked Knox to join his Cabinet as secretary of the Navy. Knox refused, however, claiming that it would take more than one Republican to make a good Cabinet. Following the German successes in Denmark, Norway, and the Low Countries during the spring of 1940, FDR again asked Knox to take the Navy post. This time Knox accepted and was sworn in on July 11, 1940.

His term as secretary of the Navy, then a Cabinet-level position, was highlighted by his frequent and candid press conferences that reflected his journalistic background. He tied American survival with the survival of Great Britain, and played a key role in arranging the "Destroyers for Bases" exchange with Britain in 1940. FDR credited him with winning the necessary support for the war effort among Republicans just prior to America's entry into World War II.

Knox died while secretary of the Navy in Washington, D.C. in 1944. He was succeeded by **James V. Forrestal.** Knox was buried with full military honors on the slope below the mansion at Arlington Cemetery.

William D. Leahy
Five-Star Fleet Admiral of the Navy
(May 6, 1875–July 20, 1959)
Sec. 2, Lot 932, Grid R–31/32

Though William D. Leahy's long naval career spanned four decades, it was not until he retired from the Navy that he undertook the task which earned him the highest rank ever conferred upon a U.S. Navy officer.

Leahy's father, a Civil War veteran, moved his family from their home in Hampton, Iowa, to Ashland, Wisconsin, where young Leahy attended high school. Entering the Naval Academy and graduating in 1897, William Leahy was on board the *Oregon* when it made its famous dash around Cape Horn to join the American fleet under the command of **William T. Sampson** and **Winfield Scott Schley** at Santiago, Cuba, during the Spanish-American War.

After various assignments in the Philippines, China, Santo Domingo, Mexico, and Nicaragua, Leahy received his first command on the transport *Dolphin*. It was during this period that Leahy became acquainted with the assistant secretary of the Navy, Franklin Roosevelt, who often traveled on the *Dolphin*. Then, when the United States entered World War I, Leahy took command of an expropriated German liner, the *Princess Matoika,* and undertook the dangerous task of transporting troops and supplies to France. For his courageous and successful efforts, he was awarded the Navy Cross.

Leahy's career eventually turned to administrative duties but not before he spent two years on the faculty of the Naval Academy in the Department of Physics and Chemistry. In 1927, Leahy earned promotion to rear admiral and was named chief of the Bureau of Ordnance. In 1933, he was appointed chief of the Bureau of Navigation, becoming one of the few people ever to hold both positions. Elevated to vice admiral in 1935, he was promoted to admiral the following year. On January 2, 1937, Leahy was awarded the highest command in the Navy, chief of naval operations, becoming only the second person in American history ever to attain that position after heading both Navy Bureaus. He retired from the Navy in August 1939, and was awarded the Distinguished Service Medal.

His retirement was short-lived. Almost immediately, Leahy was called upon by his old friend and now president, Franklin Roosevelt, to serve as governor of Puerto Rico. He accepted the appointment, serving only until the next year when he resigned to assume the delicate diplomatic post of U.S. ambassador to the Vichy government. That was the government in the part of France not occupied by the Germans after the French defeat early in World War II. Here Leahy walked a diplomatic tightrope, dealing with the Petain government while under close scrutiny by the Germans. When the United States went to war against Germany in December 1941, Leahy returned to the U.S. to assume the newly created position of chief of staff to the president.

In this position, Leahy advised President Roosevelt on military affairs. He also served as a member of the U.S. Joint Chiefs of Staff and as U.S. representative on the Allied Command Combined Chiefs of Staff. In December 1944, in recognition of Leahy's invaluable service to our country, the president elevated him to the venerable rank of five-star fleet admiral of the Navy, placing him in the elite company of only four other men ever to hold that rank—George Dewey, Chester Nimitz, Ernest J. King, and **William F. Halsey, Jr.**

Upon FDR's death in 1945, Leahy retained his position under President Harry Truman until March 1949, at which time he retired for the second time. Completing his memoirs in 1950, he continued to advise the secretary of the Navy on international strategic matters. Fleet Admiral William D. Leahy died in Bethesda, Maryland, on July 20, 1959, at the age of 84.

Pierre Charles L'Enfant
Designer of the United States Capital
(August 2, 1754–June 14, 1825)
Sec. 2, Lot S-3, Grid S–34

The tombstone of Pierre Charles L'Enfant invites comparison between his original plan for the new federal city and present-day Washington, D.C. L'Enfant's design of the nation's capital is permanently engraved in stone atop a table-like monument which marks his grave. From its position near Arlington House on the hilltop overlooking Washington, the comparison between his original concept and today's Washington is simple. But it was not always so. When L'Enfant was called upon by our nation's first president to plan this city, the area was little more than wilderness.

Pierre L'Enfant was born in Paris and studied art under his father at the *Academie Royale de Peinture et de Sculpture*. In 1776, he left France to join the American fight for independence against Great Britain. At age 22, he enlisted in the corps of engineers; by the end of the war he had risen to the rank of captain. (The tombstone indicates he was a Major, but this error in engraving was not changed for fear of disfiguring the stone.)

Following the Revolutionary War, L'Enfant joined other veterans headed by General Henry Knox to form the Society of the Cincinnati, a military and fraternal society. L'Enfant designed the Certificate and Insignia of the Society and is one of three founding members buried at Arlington.

L'Enfant eventually returned to France, but remained only a short time, finally settling in New York in 1784. In 1787, he renovated New York's old city hall under authority from the United States Congress. It was on the steps of the new Federal Hall that George Washington took his first oath of office. In 1791, Congress authorized the new president to hire a designer to plan the new federal city, which was to be built on the banks of the Potomac River on land ceded from Virginia and Maryland. Trying to build a nation's capital out of this 100 square miles of wilderness promised to be a difficult task. President Washington entrusted Pierre Charles L'Enfant with this historic undertaking.

While L'Enfant drew ideas from the great cities of Europe, his concepts and designs were uniquely his own. In a prophetic pronouncement, he promised President Washington that he was going to design a city magnificent enough not for just "thirteen states, but fifty." The focal points of his city were the "Congress House" and the "President's House" with a grand mall connecting them. There would be wide avenues crisscrossing and encircling the city

The gravesite of Pierre L'Enfant overlooks the magnificent city he designed.

to form squares, circles, and triangles where parks, fountains, and monuments could be placed.

In 1792, while much of L'Enfant's plans were still only on paper, President Washington dismissed him. L'Enfant had become defiant of the city commissioners and highhanded in his methods, especially in removing a prominent citizen's house to make way for one of his avenues. L'Enfant further enraged the populace when he pressed a claim for payment of his fees totaling $95,000. Congress authorized $3,800 to be paid to him, but he continued throughout his life to demand more money, alienating many former friends in the process.

Pierre L'Enfant spent his last days residing at Chilharn Castle Manor, the estate of his friend and benefactor, William Dudley Digges, located in Green Hills, Maryland. L'Enfant died there penniless on June 14, 1825 and was buried on the estate.

Like many great artists, however, the value of L'Enfant's creations was appreciated only many years after his death. In 1908, the Board of Commissioners for the City of Washington made overtures to remove his body from its resting place in Prince Georges County, Maryland, to a suitable site in Arlington National Cemetery, and requested the secretary of war to make such a site available. On April 28, 1909, his remains were conveyed by military escort to the United States Capitol where they lay in state for three hours. During that time, thousands of Americans paid their respects to the man who had planned this nation's capital city. At noon on that date, the military escort carried the body of the Revolutionary War veteran to the hilltop in front of Arlington House in Arlington Cemetery. There, overlooking the magnificent city, Pierre Charles L'Enfant was buried with the full military honors due an officer of the United States Army.

On May 22, 1911, with President **William Howard Taft** presiding, the tombstone that now marks his grave was dedicated. By Act of Congress, the stone was designed and sculpted as a belated tribute to L'Enfant. The focal point of the monument is the reproduction of L'Enfant's original plan for the city sculpted into the white marble top. Accompanying the map on top of the stone is a tribute to L'Enfant: "Engineer–Artist–Soldier."

The monument remains a visual testament to the achievement of L'Enfant's dream. The city he planned stands proudly across the Potomac and the comparison between the dream and the reality is simple. The Capitol rises majestically above Jenkin's Hill where L'Enfant envisioned the "Congress House," and across the wide expansive mall can be found the "President's House" just as L'Enfant had dreamed.

John Archer Lejeune
World War I Field Commander, Marine Corps Commandant
(January 10, 1867–November 20, 1942)
Sec. 6, Lot 5682, Grid VW–22/23

John Archer Lejeune was known as "The Greatest of All Leathernecks," and he earned that sobriquet the hard way. After surviving a deadly hurricane that wrecked his ship and killed several of his crew members, he became the first marine to command an Army division, ultimately serving as Commandant of the Marine Corps under three presidents.

Lejeune was born in Pointe Coupee, Louisiana, the son of a former Confederate officer who had lost his home during Reconstruction. The younger Lejeune attended Louisiana State University, which at that time was both a military preparatory school and college. After three years at L.S.U., he attempted to gain entry to West Point, but finding no openings in his class, he chose instead to attend the United States Naval Academy at Annapolis, Maryland, graduating in 1888.

Sent to sea aboard the *Vandalia,* Lejeune and his shipmates suffered through a devastating hurricane near Samoa that destroyed their vessel in March 1889. Convinced that sea life was not for him, he applied for a transfer into the Marines. His initial request was denied, but his continued pleas resulted in his eventual transfer to the Corps in July 1890.

Promoted to first lieutenant in 1892, Lejeune was given command of the Marine attachment aboard the *Cincinnati* during the Spanish-American War. While in that post, he took part in the occupation of Puerto Rico. By 1903, he had advanced through the ranks to major and had been given command of the Marine Battalion attached to the Atlantic Fleet.

In 1905, Lejeune was named commander of the Marine Barracks in Washington, D.C., and then was sent to the Philippines in 1907. In 1909, having risen in rank to lieutenant colonel, Lejeune became the first Marine officer admitted to the Army War College, graduating in 1910. He then was granted the prestigious command of the New York Navy Yard, a command he retained until 1913, when he was promoted to full colonel, taking command of the Advanced Base Brigade at New Orleans in his home state. Among his military credits, he led the Marine brigade that occupied Veracruz, Mexico, in 1914. Then in August 1916, promoted to brigadier general, he served as assistant to Marine Corps Commandant General George Barnett.

In 1917, Lejeune assumed the critically important post of commander at Quantico, Virginia. This base served as a training center and staging area for Marines on their way to the European front in World War I. Lejeune himself went to France in June 1918 to take command of the Fourth Marine Brigade, the only Marine brigade in the American Expeditionary Force. In July, he was promoted to major general, succeeding General **Omar Bundy** as commander of the Second Infantry Division, and becoming the first Marine ever to command an Army division. He led that Division in the St. Mihiel Offensive in the battle of Blanc Mont Ridge on October 3, 1918, and throughout the Meuse-Argonne operation.

Following the war, Lejeune served with the Army of Occupation in Germany, returning in 1919 to resume command of the Quantico Marine base. Named 13th Commandant of the Marine Corps in June 1920, he is credited with modernizing the Corps, as well as with establishing the Marine Corps School at Quantico. Lejeune retained his command throughout the terms of three U.S. presidents: Woodrow Wilson, Warren Harding, and Calvin Coolidge. Upon his retirement from the Marine Corps in 1929, he accepted the position of Superintendent of the Virginia Military Institute, serving in that capacity until 1937.

General John Lejeune died of cancer in Baltimore, Maryland, on November 20, 1942. The sprawling Marine base in North Carolina has been named in his honor.

Robert Todd Lincoln
Son of the President, Lawyer, Secretary of War, Diplomat
(August 1, 1843–June 26, 1926)
Sec. 31, Lot 13, Grid Y–38

During his lifetime, Robert Todd Lincoln often wondered if history might have been different had he accepted his father's invitation to accompany the president and Mrs. Lincoln to Ford's Theatre the night his father was assassinated. Instead, the young soldier, fresh from the battlefields of the Civil War, chose to visit friends that fateful night in April.

Robert Lincoln returned to Washington to visit his parents on April 13, 1865, just four days after Robert E. Lee surrendered to Ulysses S. Grant at Appomattox Courthouse, Virginia. Lincoln, who was a member of Grant's staff, was present at the courthouse as Lee offered his sword in surrender. The grueling Civil War that had crippled the country finally was over, and the nation's capital was filled with the sights and sounds of celebration. Young Lincoln commented that even his father, normally drawn and weary, seemed noticeably relieved. Having recently graduated from Harvard College, the 21-year-old Robert had been commissioned a captain and had joined the staff of General Grant in February 1865.

President Lincoln mentioned to his son that General and Mrs. Grant would be joining the Lincolns on the evening of April 14 at a performance of "Our American Cousin" at nearby Ford's Theatre. When the afternoon papers reported that both the Lincolns and the Grants were going to be at the theatre that same evening, tickets to the performance sold out. However, later in the day Grant informed the president that he and Mrs. Grant would be unable to attend, and instead were planning to take an afternoon train to Burlington, New Jersey, to visit their children. The president then asked Robert to accompany him and his mother, but Robert declined, having previously planned to visit with friends in Washington.

The gravesite of Robert Todd Lincoln, Mary Harlan Lincoln, and their son, Abraham Lincoln II, assumes a park-like atmosphere in this photograph taken in 1932, six years after Robert's death.

It was nearly midnight before Robert learned that his father had suffered a single gunshot wound to the head and lay dying in a house at 453 Tenth Street in northwest Washington. He rushed to the site to find his father near death, stretched diagonally across a single bed in a rear bedroom, and his grieving mother secluded in a front parlor. Robert kept vigil with his mother throughout the night, but the man known as The Great Emancipator died the following morning at 7:22 a.m., the first American president to be killed in office.

Robert Todd Lincoln was the eldest of President Abraham Lincoln's three sons and the only child to live to maturity. He shared his father's Midwestern roots, having been born and raised in Springfield, Illinois. In 1859, seeking the education denied his father, Robert attempted to enter Harvard but was unsuccessful, failing 15 of the 16 subjects in the entrance examination. Following a year at Exeter Academy in New Hampshire, Robert again attempted and gained admission to Harvard where he was studying when his father was elected president in 1860.

Following the Civil War, Robert studied law in Chicago, and was admitted to practice in 1867. The following year he married Mary Harlan, daughter of Iowa's senator. Lincoln became a well-known and skillful lawyer, representing many major corporations and railroads. He was named secretary of war by President James Garfield in 1881, and retained that position under President Chester Alan Arthur after Garfield's assassination. From 1889 to 1893, he served as minister to Great Britain, the last American to serve with that title. All later envoys to the Court of St. James were elevated to the rank of ambassador. Upon returning to this country, Lincoln resumed his legal practice, and ultimately was named president of the Pullman Company of Chicago, one of his major clients. Lincoln served as Pullman's president from 1897 until 1911.

Robert Todd Lincoln's life was filled with many ironies. Prior to his father's assassination, young Lincoln was saved from falling from a speeding train by Edwin Booth, the brother of his father's assassin. Lincoln also was present when two other presidents were assassinated. While serving as secretary of war, he was waiting on the platform at a Washington railroad station to greet President Garfield when Garfield was shot in 1881. In 1901, Lincoln was at the Buffalo Pan-American Exposition when President William McKinley was fatally wounded. This series of events later led Lincoln to refuse a presidential invitation with the comment, "No, I'm not going, and they'd better not ask me, because there is a certain fatality about presidential functions when I am present."

After 1912, Robert Todd Lincoln lived in Washington and was present during the dedication of the memorial to his father in 1925. He died at his retreat Hildene in Manchester, New Hampshire, on June 26, 1926.

Mary Harlan Lincoln (1846–1937) is buried with her husband on this hillside in Arlington. Their grave is marked by a pink marble stone that bears another familiar name. Buried here with his parents is the namesake of our sixteenth president, **Abraham Lincoln II,** who was the only son of Robert Todd Lincoln, and who died at the age of 17 in 1890. Robert Lincoln was survived by two daughters. The last direct descendant of Abraham Lincoln, a great-grandson, died in 1985 at the age of 83.

James McCubbin Lingan
American Revolutionary, Defender of Free Speech
(May 13, 1751–July 28, 1812)
Sec. 1, Lot 89-A Grid JK–32

J ames McCubbin Lingan fought alongside thousands of other colonists during the American Revolution to gain independence for this nation and to ensure certain basic freedoms, including the right of free speech. Although he was held by the British as a prisoner of war for more than three years, Lingan survived the Revolution. Later in 1812, he again fought for the right of free speech, this time defending a newspaper editor's right to publish antiwar sentiments. But this battle for freedom of the press was not against the British; it was against a violent mob of Americans and it cost Lingan his life.

On July 13, 1776, just nine days after the United States of America declared its independence from Great Britain, 25-year-old James McCubbin Lingan was commissioned a second lieutenant in the Rawlings Additional Regiment. On November 16, during a battle at Fort Washington, he was stabbed with a bayonet and taken prisoner. For nearly three and one-half years he was held captive aboard the British prison ship *Jersey.*

During his imprisonment, Lingan was approached by British Admiral Sir Samuel Hood, a distant cousin, who offered Lingan 10,000 pounds and a high commission in the British Army if he would renounce the revolution and support King George III. Sitting in his cell, a space in which he could neither stand up nor lie down, Lingan unequivocally replied, "I'll rot first."

On another occasion, while Lingan was aboard the prison ship, a fellow prisoner died during the night. When the guards arrived to retrieve the body, they brought along a coffin which was too short to hold the remains. One

James McCubbin Lingan's tombstone proudly displays his record of service in the Revolutionary War. He is one of 11 veterans of that war reinterred at Arlington.

of the guards suggested that they simply cut off the dead prisoner's head and be done with it. At that, Lingan stood astride the body, stating in no uncertain terms that he would kill with his bare hands any person who would dare to touch the dead man's body with a knife. The guards found a larger coffin.

By the end of the American Revolution, Lingan had risen to the rank of general. Following the war, he was appointed by President George Washington to be collector of the Port of Georgetown, which is now a part of the District of Columbia. He also was a founding member of the famed Revolutionary War veterans group, the Society of the Cincinnati.

During the War of 1812, Lingan found himself defending the First Amendment to the U.S. Constitution which he had fought so hard to establish more than 30 years earlier. But this time he was not fighting against British soldiers; instead it was American citizens who opposed the freedom of the press. On June 19, 1812, the United States declared war on Great Britain, a decision that did not have the unanimous backing of the American people, including Alexander Contee Hanson. Hanson, a close friend of Lingan, was the editor of the *Federal Republic,* a newspaper in Baltimore, Maryland, which ran an editorial denouncing the call to arms against Britain. That editorial ignited the fierce opposition of several readers who felt that Hanson's opinion was treasonous. A large group of angry citizens congregated in front of the newspaper's office. Excited by loud denunciations of Hanson, the mob raided the offices and destroyed its presses. Hanson was forced to run for his life.

On July 27, 1812, Hanson resumed publication of his paper from a house in Georgetown. Within a few hours a mob again gathered and shots were fired. Among the supporters who had come to the defense of Hanson were James Lingan and "Light Horse Harry" Lee, another famous general of the

American Revolution and former governor of Virginia. Only the arrival of the militia prevented further bloodshed. For their own protection, Hanson and his supporters were escorted to the jail in Baltimore where they intended to stay until the mob dispersed.

However, the mob did not disperse. Instead they broke into the jail during the night where a fierce battle ensued. Although Alexander Hanson survived the attack, James McCubbin Lingan was beaten to death. Harry Lee, father of Robert E. Lee, was severely beaten, but miraculously managed to escape almost certain death by remaining motionless as several of the rioters rummaged among the victims. One of the scavengers even poured hot wax into Lee's eye, searching for any sign of life. Lee was left blinded and permanently disabled by the episode.

Lingan's death produced great public indignation. St. John's Church in Georgetown was to have been the site of his funeral but the size of the crowd forced the ceremony to be held outside. Called upon to deliver Lingan's eulogy was the son of George Washington, **George Washington Parke Custis.** Custis acknowledged that he only knew Lingan by reputation, but quickly pointed out that President Washington had held Lingan in the highest regard. Praising Lingan for his defense of freedom of the press, Custis—his voice trembling—chastised every citizen for having allowed this massacre to have taken place, "Oh, Maryland! Would that the waters of the Chesapeake could wash this foul stain from thy character!" No one knew at that time that James McCubbin Lingan's final resting place would be on Custis' former estate. Lingan originally was buried in a private burial ground in Georgetown. His body was reinterred in Arlington National Cemetery on November 5, 1908.

Joe Louis (Barrow)
"The Brown Bomber," Heavyweight Champion of the World
(May 13, 1914–April 12, 1981)
Sec. 7A, Lot 177, Grid U–24

During the 1930s and 1940s, the name of Joe Louis probably was as well known as that of the president, Franklin Roosevelt, because between 1937 and 1949, Joe Louis was boxing's "Heavyweight Champion of the World." He held that title longer and defended it more often than any boxer in history, becoming the first great African-American idol for a whole generation of Americans.

Joe Louis' proper name was Joe Louis Barrow, but when he fought his first amateur fight, he signed up as "Joe Louis." His career skyrocketed and soon the whole world knew him simply as Joe Louis. Born in Lexington, Alabama, Joe moved with his six older brothers and sisters and their widowed mother, Lilly Barrow, to Detroit when he was a young boy. He was working in Detroit as an automobile assemblyman when he won the U.S. Amateur Athletic Union crown in 1934 and turned professional that year.

Joe Louis suffered only one defeat in his first 69 fights, and that was on June 19,1936, at the hands of Germany's great Max Schmeling, the reigning world heavyweight champion. Schmeling knocked out Louis in the 12th round of that title fight. Louis became world champion, however, one year later when he knocked out James J. Braddock in the eighth round of their bout. He defended his title 25 times, more than any champion in boxing history, scoring knockouts 20 times.

On June 22, 1938, in what was touted as "the fight of the century," a rematch between Joe Louis and Max Schmeling drew a crowd of 70,000 to Yankee Stadium in New York. This time it was Louis who entered as champion and Schmeling as challenger. President Roosevelt met with "The Champ" before the fight to wish him well; everyone knew that more was at stake on that night than just the title. In that ring Joe Louis represented America's best, and he was squaring off with Schmeling, the pride of Nazi Germany, at a time when the Nazis were professing to be a superior race. While none of the American spectators was disappointed in the outcome, they may have been disappointed that the fight did not last longer. Louis pummeled Schmeling, knocking him to the canvas in just over two minutes into the first round. Schmeling was hit so hard and so often in that short time that he spent a week in a New York hospital.

Joe Louis was heavyweight champion for 12 years with a record of 68-1.

When the United States finally went to war against Germany in 1941, Louis enlisted in the Army, serving in the same segregated unit as Jackie Robinson, the first African American later to play major league baseball. During the war, Louis fought 96 exhibition matches before more than two million troops. He also donated more than $100,000 to Navy and Army relief efforts. He left the Army with the rank of sergeant.

Joe Louis retired from boxing on March 1, 1949, with a record of 68 wins and one loss. During his fabled career, he had earned about $5 million, most of which he either gave away or spent. In the late 1940s, the Internal Revenue Service assessed Louis more than $1,000,000 in back taxes and penalties. This arose as a result of a divorce settlement in which Louis agreed to pay his ex-wife a portion of the purse from his biggest fight, $650,000. It was based on a percentage of his winnings, as a manager's fee would be computed, but the IRS considered it to be alimony, ruling that Louis owed taxes and considerable penalties on that money. Louis knew only one way to earn that kind of money, so he returned to the ring.

Coming out of retirement on September 27, 1950, he challenged the new champion, Ezzard Charles, but was beaten decisively in 15 rounds. He attempted another major bout on October 26, 1951, against future champion Rocky Marciano; this time Louis was knocked out in the eighth round. He never fought again, ending his extraordinary 17-year career with a record of 68 wins and three losses, winning 54 of his fights by knockouts.

Louis is remembered for the famous "Bum-of-the-Month" tour, during which Joe defended his title with a fight each month for a full year. He spent his final years confined to a wheelchair as a result of open heart surgery. He also worked as a greeter at a Las Vegas hotel.

When Joe Louis died on April 12, 1981, he had not been champion for more than 32 years. But still people throughout the world paid him homage. To them he would always be "The Champ." President Ronald Reagan waived the technical requirements for burial at Arlington to allow Joe Louis to be interred there. During a service with full military honors, the hundreds of people who came to the funeral heard three volleys fired into the quiet, spring air as a salute to the former boxing great, signaling his last round. Since his death, thousands of visitors have come to view the tombstone that bears a bas-relief of the famous fighter and the inscription "The Brown Bomber."

Arthur MacArthur
Medal of Honor Recipient, Highest Ranking Army Officer
(June 2, 1845–September 5, 1912)
Sec. 2, Lot 879, Grid P–31

Arthur MacArthur foresaw a military career for himself, but was unable to secure the appointment to West Point he so strongly desired. Not to be deterred, he volunteered his services to his country, earning a Congressional Medal of Honor for gallantry during the Civil War, and by

1906, becoming the highest ranking officer in the Army. His proud military record set an example for his son, Douglas MacArthur, who was able to enter West Point and rose to the rank of Five-Star General.

Arthur MacArthur was the son of a prominent Scottish immigrant who had settled in Springfield, Massachusetts. The elder MacArthur developed a successful law practice by the time Arthur was born in 1845. In 1849, the family moved to Wisconsin where the senior MacArthur continued his legal and political interests becoming lieutenant governor and then governor of the state. Arthur attended Milwaukee public schools, and when he was unable to obtain an appointment to West Point, he volunteered for service during the Civil War with the Twenty-fourth Wisconsin Volunteer Infantry.

MacArthur saw combat at Perryville, Kentucky, where his conduct earned him a citation for bravery and a promotion to captain, although he was just 17 years old. During the siege of Murfreesboro in December 1862, MacArthur quickly assumed command of the troops when his regimental commander fell. Issuing timely orders, MacArthur held the Twenty-fourth together. He led the assault on Missionary Ridge, planting the regimental colors and giving confidence and direction to his men. For his action, he was awarded the highest military combat decoration, the Congressional Medal of Honor, although it was not presented until June 30, 1890.

On January 24, 1864, MacArthur was given command of his regiment and later was wounded during the battle of Kennesaw Mountain on June 27 of that year. On November 30, 1864, MacArthur was wounded again in the battle of Franklin, Tennessee, the result of hand-to-hand fighting. His injuries were so severe that he was unable to return to active duty for the remainder of the war. Nonetheless, he was promoted to lieutenant colonel of volunteers, and when he mustered out of the Army in June 1865, he was an experienced field commander commonly called "the boy colonel of the West." He had just celebrated his 20th birthday.

MacArthur began the study of law, but soon realized that his real love was the military. He reenlisted in February 1866, and received a commission as a second lieutenant in the regular Army. By the end of 1866, he was a captain and began a three-year tour of the Western frontier. During the next 30 years, MacArthur's tours of duty found him in New York, the Utah Territory, Louisiana, Pennsylvania, and New Mexico, where he took part in the campaign against the Apache chief, Geronimo, in 1885. MacArthur became an instructor at the Infantry and Cavalry School at Fort Leavenworth, Kansas, in 1889, and was promoted to lieutenant colonel in 1896. He finally had reached the same regular Army rank at the age of 51 that he had achieved as a volunteer more than 30 years before.

Arthur MacArthur was stationed in the Dakotas when the Spanish-American War started in 1898. On May 27 of that year, he was commissioned a brigadier general and assigned as adjutant general of III Corps. He ultimately commanded a brigade of volunteers headed for the Philippine Islands where he took part in the capture of Manila in August. President William McKinley named him military governor of the Philippines on May 6, 1900, which ultimately put him at odds with the civilian governor appointed the following year, **William Howard Taft.** MacArthur combined an aggressive military presence with humane civic actions such as establishing public education and revising the harsh Spanish civil code. Nevertheless, MacArthur favored military rule for at least another decade, an idea which ran contrary to Taft's desire for a quick return to civilian government. By this time, however, Taft's good friend and mentor, Theodore Roosevelt, was president and Taft remained as civilian governor while MacArthur was transferred back to the United States.

During the next eight years, MacArthur held several commands and toured American posts overseas. He went to Manchuria in 1905 to observe the final stages of the Russo-Japanese War, and served as military attaché to the American embassy in Tokyo. He returned to the U.S. in 1906 to resume his previous post as commander of the Pacific.

In 1906, the position of Army chief of staff, the highest position in the Army, became vacant. At that time, MacArthur was the highest ranking officer in the Army and would normally have been elevated to the post. Instead, he was overlooked by his former nemesis and now secretary of war, William Howard Taft.

Although he was promoted to lieutenant general, the highest rank available at the time, MacArthur never achieved his dream of being Army chief of staff. He retired from the Army on his 64th birthday, June 2, 1909. On September 5, 1912 MacArthur returned to Milwaukee to address a reunion of veterans of the old Wisconsin Twenty-fourth Volunteer Regiment from the Civil War. He suffered a seizure while on the dais and died. He was buried with full military honors at Arlington National Cemetery.

George C. Marshall
Five-Star General, Secretary of State, Nobel Laureate
(December 31, 1880–October 16, 1959)
Sec. 7, Lot 8198, Grid VW–24

As a soldier, he was more than a victor, he was a healer; in government, he was greater than a politician, he was a statesman; and in international affairs, he rose above routine diplomacy to become a peacemaker. President Harry S Truman called him "the Greatest of the Great." He is General of the Army George C. Marshall.

George Catlett Marshall, Jr. shared his birthplace—Uniontown, Pennsylvania—with another American general, Revolutionary War hero **Thomas Meason.** A distant cousin of early Supreme Court Chief Justice John Marshall, George Marshall entered Virginia Military Institute in 1897. When he graduated in 1901, Marshall held the position of first captain of the Corps of Cadets. He applied for a commission in the United States Army and was named first lieutenant of infantry in February 1902.

Marshall's first assignment was in the Philippines, his station until 1903. In 1906, he entered the Infantry School, graduating first in his class, then went on to serve as an instructor at Fort Leavenworth, Kansas. In June 1917, Captain Marshall accompanied the First Division to France at the outbreak of World War I. His mastery of military logistics allowed him to move hundreds of thousands of troops in the Meuse-Argonne Salient, and earned him recognition from the commander of the American Expeditionary Force, General **John J. Pershing.** Pershing was so impressed with this young lieutenant colonel that he made Marshall his aide, and kept him in that position until he retired as Army chief of staff in 1924. When Marshall married in 1930, he chose Pershing to serve as his best man.

Following his assignment with Pershing, Marshall spent three years in Tientsin, China, as executive officer of the Fifteenth Infantry Regiment. Returning to America in 1927, he was placed in charge of instruction at the Infantry School at Fort Benning, Georgia, where in the following five years, 165 future generals passed under his command, among them **Omar Bradley** and **Walter Bedell Smith.**

From 1933 through 1936, Marshall served as senior instructor of the Illinois National Guard and was promoted to brigadier general. Two years later he was head of the War Plans Division (WPD) in Washington, D.C., rising to deputy chief of staff. Ironically, Marshall was promoted to full general and sworn in as Army chief of staff on September 1, 1939, the same

George C. Marshall is one of three five-star generals buried at Arlington, but the only Nobel peace laureate.

day that Nazi troops invaded Poland to begin the second world war.

When Marshall assumed the position of chief of staff, it was clearly with an eye on the events in Europe. Although the U.S. did not enter that war until two years later, Marshall directed his efforts toward preparing for our nation's entry. In 1939, the United States forces numbered fewer than 200,000 men. Under Marshall's direction, that number increased to more than 8 million men and women in less than four years. Not only did he oversee the expansion of our Armed Forces, but the improvement of their training and equipment as well.

It was George C. Marshall who coordinated the U.S. military efforts throughout the world during World War II. Every theatre of operation—whether in Europe, the Pacific, or the Far East—benefited from Marshall's influence and presence. He traveled throughout the world, meeting with Winston Churchill and Allied commanders in London, and with Douglas MacArthur in the Pacific. From Washington he planned and directed the successful invasion of Normandy on D-Day, though sharing very little in the glory given to the generals who were present on the beaches of France.

On December 16, 1944, President Franklin Roosevelt elevated Marshall to the five-star rank of general of the army. Only five men were so honored in that war, three of whom now rest at Arlington: Marshall, **Omar Bradley,** and **Henry "Hap" Arnold.** The others were Dwight Eisenhower (buried on the grounds of his library in Abilene, Kansas) and Douglas MacArthur (buried in Norfolk, Virginia).

Marshall resigned as chief of staff on November 21, 1945; just one week later, President Truman persuaded him to tackle the challenge of resolving the difficult political situation in China. As President Truman's special envoy, Marshall returned to the country where he had lived during the 1920s, and dedicated himself to bringing the Nationalists and Communists together. After a year of unsuccessful diplomatic maneuvering, he returned to the United

States in 1947 to accept another top-level assignment from the president.

President Truman appointed him to succeed James R. Burns as secretary of state. Marshall assumed the Cabinet post during a period of international realignment in the aftermath of the war. During his two-year tenure, the U.S. provided support for the anticommunist forces in Greece and Turkey, and the state of Israel was recognized as an independent nation. He began the discussions that led to the formation of the North Atlantic Treaty Organization (NATO) and the Organization of American States (OAS); in 1949, he oversaw the Berlin Airlift, the action that defused the threat of a Soviet Union blockade of West Berlin.

Marshall's greatest triumph, however, was his European Recovery Program, universally known as the "Marshall Plan." Proposed in a commencement address at Harvard University in June 1947, this plan contributed billions of dollars toward the economic recovery of 16 war-torn European nations. It was Marshall's belief that the Soviet Union was simply awaiting the economic collapse of Western Europe before attempting to expand its sphere of influence in Europe. As a testament to his efforts, Marshall was awarded the Nobel Prize for Peace in 1953, becoming the only professional soldier ever to receive that most coveted award.

George Marshall resigned as secretary of state in 1949, following surgery to remove a kidney and became president of the American Red Cross. As war in Korea neared, President Truman again summoned Marshall to his Cabinet, this time as secretary of defense. Nearly 70 years old, Marshall agreed to serve for one year. Special legislation was passed by Congress waiving—in Marshall's case alone—the prohibition against a military man serving as head of the defense department. During his tenure, Marshall rebuilt American military manpower, and increased production of war materials before permanently resigning from public service in September 1951.

Marshall adamantly refused offers to publish his memoirs, including one offer for a million dollars. It was his belief that such memoirs would require the truthful recitation of events and he did not wish to tarnish the image of people he would have felt compelled to include. In addition to the numerous decorations presented by this country, Marshall received recognition from at least a dozen other nations, including the Soviet Union. These awards and his many honorary degrees are housed at the George C. Marshall Research Library in Lexington, Virginia.

Early in his career, it was clear that George C. Marshall possessed the attributes of command. Those who served with him recognized his quiet self-confidence and his desire to shun flamboyance. He could communicate effectively with soldier and civilian alike, and inspire any subordinate to do his or her best. Few Americans have done more to further the cause of democracy and world peace than he did. George Marshall died at Walter Reed Hospital in Washington, D.C., on October 16, 1959, and was buried with honors at Arlington National Cemetery.

Buried with Marshall are his first wife, **Elizabeth Carter Coles Marshall**, her mother, **Elizabeth Pennington Coles**, and his second wife, **Katherine Tupper Brown Marshall** (1882–1979). Katherine Marshall's autobiography, *Together: Annals of an Army Wife*, was published in 1946.

Thurgood Marshall
Civil Rights Advocate, Supreme Court Justice
(July 2, 1908–January 24, 1993)
Sec. 5, Lot 40, Grid W–36

Thurgood Marshall spent his entire life in public service, fighting for equal rights for African Americans. In 1954, he successfully argued for the plaintiff in *Brown v. Board of Education*.

Born in Baltimore, Maryland, in 1908, Marshall was the son of William and Norma Williams Marshall. He attended Lincoln University, a historically black college in Chester County, Pennsylvania, where he graduated in 1930. In 1933, he was first in his class at Howard University Law School in Washington, D.C.

In 1929, he married Vivian Burey, who died in 1955. They had two children. After his first wife's death, Marshall married Cecelia Suyat.

From 1936 until 1961, Thurgood Marshall was legal counsel for the National Association for the Advancement of Colored People. In that position, he won 29 of the 32 cases he argued before the United States Supreme Court,

including *Brown v. Board of Education,* the 1954 landmark decision that declared unconstitutional the "separate but equal" policy used to justify public school segregation. As counsel for the NAACP, he also won cases against poll taxes, racial restrictions in housing and whites-only primary elections. He was awarded the Springarn Medal in 1946.

In September 1961, President **John Kennedy** nominated Marshall to the U.S. Court of Appeals for the Second Circuit, and although his nomination was delayed by opposition from Southern senators, he took his seat several months later.

In 1965, President Lyndon Johnson appointed Marshall to be solicitor general, the lawyer who represents the United States government before the Supreme Court. Two years later, Johnson nominated him to be associate justice of the Supreme Court to succeed Justice Tom C. Clark. Thurgood Marshall was the first African American to serve on the United States Supreme Court.

Marshall served on the Court for 24 years during which time he opposed discrimination and the death penalty and championed free speech and civil liberties.

Ill health forced Marshall to retire from the Court in 1991 at the age of 83. At the time of his retirement, Justice Marshall asked that he be remembered by these ten words: "That he did what he could with what he had." President George H. W. Bush nominated Clarence Thomas to fill his seat.

Thurgood Marshall died on January 24, 1993 in Bethesda, Maryland. He is buried in Section 5 near seven other justices—**Harry Blackmun, William J. Brennan, William O. Douglas, Oliver Wendell Holmes, Jr., Warren Burger, William Rehnquist,** and **Potter Stewart.** His headstone reads, "Civil Rights Advocate."

Lee Marvin
Actor, Purple Heart Recipient
(February 19, 1924–August 29, 1987)
Sec. 7A, Lot 176, Grid U–24

Most people are surprised to learn that Lee Marvin is buried at Arlington National Cemetery. But as a Marine during World War II, he served with distinction in the Pacific and earned a Purple Heart when a bullet severed his sciatic nerve.

Born in New York City in 1924, Lee Marvin's father was an advertising executive and his mother a fashion writer. He was an incorrigible child and a difficult student. Expelled from several New York schools, his parents enrolled him in St. Leo's Preparatory School near Dade City, Florida. By the time that school also dismissed him, the country was at war. So Marvin enlisted in the United States Marine Corps.

In June 1944, during the battle of Saipan, Lee Marvin was hit by enemy fire which severed the sciatic nerve in his hip, sending him back to the United States. When he recovered, he took a job as a plumber's apprentice in Woodstock, New York, and found himself in the right place at the right time. While repairing a toilet in a local community theatre, he was asked to take the part of an actor who had become ill. He fell in love with the theatre.

He moved to New York, studied acting, and got roles in small, off-Broadway productions. He made his Broadway debut in "Billy Budd."

Lee Marvin landed several television roles and finally moved to Hollywood. There he began to develop the tough-guy image that earned him movie roles as cops and bad guys. He played a detective on the successful TV series "M Squad."

In 1965, Marvin surprised Hollywood pundits when he won the Academy Award for best actor for his role in "Cat Balou." During his career, he made more than 60 movies, including "The Caine Mutiny," "The Dirty Dozen," "Sergeant Ryker," "Paint Your Wagon," "Gorky Park," and "Delta Force."

Marvin also gained notoriety when his long-time companion, Michelle Triola, sued him. Though they were never married, Triola asked for a substantial portion of his assets. Triola failed to get the assets she sought, but the case established the precedent for the rights of unmarried co-habitors, the so-called "palimony" law.

Lee Marvin was still making movies and was still a star when he died of a heart attack at his home in Arizona in 1987. He was 63 years old.

Actor Lee Marvin is buried next to Heavyweight Champ Joe Louis in Section 7A.

Anthony C. McAuliffe
WWII General, Hero of Bastogne
(July 3, 1898–August 11, 1975)
Sec. 3, Lot 2536, Grid P-16

Anthony Clement McAuliffe was a man of few words, but he needed only one when he replied to a German ultimatum to surrender during the Battle of the Bulge in World War II. That terse one-word rebuttal became the most famous response of the war.

Anthony McAuliffe was born in Washington, D.C. in 1898. While a student at West Virginia University in 1917, he received an appointment to the United States Military Academy at West Point, New York. Graduating in 1919, he was commissioned a second lieutenant. Following West Point, McAuliffe served in various field and school positions until he found himself commander of division artillery for the 101st Airborne Division during World War II.

Under the command of General **Maxwell Taylor**, McAuliffe and the 101st Airborne Division parachuted into Normandy as part of the D-Day invasion of France on June 6, 1944. Throughout that summer, the Allied troops moved quickly across northern France into Belgium, but stalled near the German border in September. By late fall, the 101st Airborne Division was in Bastogne, Belgium, part of the Allied forces that stretched along a 600-mile front from the North Sea to Switzerland.

Suddenly on December 16, 1944, taking advantage of bad weather that kept Allied planes on the ground, Germany launched a surprise counteroffensive. General Gerd von Rundstedt's 5th and 6th Panzer Armies struck parallel attacks in the wooded Ardennes region of southern Belgium. Hoping to pierce the Allied lines and recapture the Belgian port of Antwerp, the German Army advanced through Belgium, surrounding Bastogne and the 101st Airborne Division.

With General Maxwell Taylor away, Anthony McAuliffe was acting commander of the division. Surrounded, outnumbered, and with no relief in sight, the German command demanded McAuliffe surrender. Undaunted by the odds and steadfastly refusing to relinquish his position, McAuliffe replied with perhaps the most famous and defiant one-word response in military history, "NUTS!"

For more than a week, the 101st Airborne Division stubbornly withstood the German siege. Finally on December 26, the United States 3rd Army under the command of General George S. Patton relieved Bastogne and McAuliffe.

On January 3, 1945, the U.S. 1st Army launched a counteroffensive that ultimately ended Germany's desperate battle of the bulge.

In 1945, McAuliffe was given command of the 103rd Infantry Division, which he held until the end of the war in Europe. After the war, he headed the Army Chemical Corps, and in 1953 he returned to Europe to command the U.S. 7th Army. Two years later, he was named commander in chief of the U.S. Army in Europe. He retired from military service in 1956 to work for American Cyanamid Corp.

General Anthony Clement McAuliffe died on August 11, 1975. He was buried with military honors in Section 3 of Arlington National Cemetery. His grave is marked with a regulation headstone.

Montgomery Cunningham Meigs
Soldier, Engineer, Architect
(May 3, 1816–January 2, 1892)
Sec. 1, Lot 1, Grid N–32/33

Although Montgomery Meigs played a pivotal role in the creation of a national military cemetery on the grounds of the Arlington estate in 1864, he is better known for his architectural and engineering feats in and around Washington, D. C.

A native of Augusta, Georgia, Meigs attended the University of Pennsylvania, and then transferred to the U.S. Military Academy where he graduated fifth in his class in 1836. Commissioned into the Artillery, Meigs held a degree in engineering and soon was transferred to the Corps of Engineers. In 1837 he accompanied Robert E. Lee to St. Louis, Missouri, to undertake navigational improvements of the Mississippi River.

During the 1850's, Meigs initiated and completed several engineering projects in Washington, D.C., which greatly changed the city. He supervised the construction of the Washington Aqueduct that extended 12 miles from Great Falls on the Potomac River to a reservoir near Georgetown. The Cabin John Bridge, which he designed to carry Washington's main water supply and vehicular traffic, was for 50 years the longest single masonry arch in the world. Meigs also oversaw the construction of the wings and dome of the U.S. Capitol building.

The best known architectural accomplishment of Meigs, however, is the Old Pension Building in Washington's Judiciary Square. That building was intended originally as a pension distribution center for Union soldiers. It is a large brick shell covering an interior space of 30,000 square feet; its exterior displays a terra cotta frieze depicting Union forces in battle. The Old Pension Building has been used for inaugural balls and is officially classified a National Historic Monument. Indeed, in October 1985, it was rededicated as the National Building Museum.

Other buildings designed, at least in part, by Montgomery Meigs are the War Department Building, now called the Executive Office Building near the White House, and the National Museum Building, now known as the Centennial Building of the Smithsonian Institution.

It was in May 1861 that Montgomery Meigs was promoted to brigadier general and named quartermaster general. He was placed in charge of equipping all Union forces for every need, except ordnance; history has credited him with performing efficiently and with competence. Meigs also has been credited with holding a rather high opinion of himself, and with possessing a violent, sometimes irrational, temper.

Although a Southerner by birth, Meigs considered the secessionists as revolutionaries and the soldiers who fought for the South as traitors. Among those he hated most were his former mentor Jefferson Davis when Davis was serving as secretary of war under President Franklin Pierce, his former commanding officer, Robert E. Lee, and his own brother, who fought for his family's native Georgia. It was his hatred of Lee that prompted him to recommend that Lee's home be made a military cemetery.

Meigs retired from the Army in 1882, but remained involved in Washington civic affairs. It was after his retirement that he designed the Old Pension Building. He also served as a regent at the Smithsonian Institution, and was an early member of the National Academy of Sciences. Meigs died in Washington on January 2, 1892, and was buried at Arlington, the cemetery he had personally established. Interred with him are his wife and his son, Lieutenant **John Rodgers Meigs.** Lieutenant Meigs' grave is marked by a bronze

Montgomery Meigs–the person responsible for recommending the Arlington estate be used as a military cemetery–is buried in Section 1. A statue depicting Meigs' slain son, Lt. John Meigs, marks the young Meigs' grave next to his father's.

statue depicting the dramatic scene of young Meigs' death during the Civil War on October 3, 1864. He was killed by a band of Confederate guerillas.

Also buried near Montgomery Meigs is his father, **Josiah Meigs,** who had served as a commander of the General Land Office and who died on September 4, 1822, and was buried in Congressional Cemetery in Washington. He was later reinterred at Arlington beside his son.

Nelson Appleton Miles
Civil War Veteran, General in Chief of the Army
(August 8, 1839–May 15,1925)
Sec. 3, Lot 1873, Grid U-16

Nelson Appleton Miles entered the Army as a volunteer captain during the Civil War, and despite his lack of formal military training, rose to the military's highest rank, general in chief of the Army. Yet his record was tarnished when troops under his command undertook one of the most tragic massacres of Native Americans in our country's history.

Born near Westminster, Massachusetts, in 1839, Miles was a 21-year-old captain in the Twenty-second Massachusetts Regiment when the Confederates fired on Fort Sumter to begin the Civil War. He first was wounded at Fair Oaks (Seven Pines) on May 31, 1862. Undaunted, he returned to combat at Antietam, and under fire, assumed command of his regiment, earning a promotion to lieutenant colonel. Just three months later at Fredericksburg, Miles was severely wounded when he was shot through the throat. In May 1863, he was wounded a third time while fighting at Chancellorsville. For his continued bravery throughout the Civil War, Miles was belatedly awarded the Congressional Medal of Honor in 1892.

Controversy first touched his career immediately after the war while he was commanding Fortress Monroe, Virginia. He was entrusted with the custody of Jefferson Davis, the former president of the Confederacy. Under Miles' strict orders, Davis was denied any privileges and kept manacled in a dark, musty cell. Leaders of both the North and the South roundly criticized Miles for this harsh treatment of his prisoner.

Miles' career as a reputed Indian fighter began in 1869 when he was transferred to the Fifth Infantry on the western frontier. Following the defeat of Lieutenant Colonel George Armstrong Custer in 1876, Nelson Miles was given the command of one of the columns that forced the Sioux and Northern Cheyenne Indians either into Canada or onto existing reservations. His reputation preceded him to Arizona where he succeeded General **George Crook,** and captured the elusive Apache leader Geronimo in 1886.

In 1890, Miles commanded federal troops responsible for keeping the peace with the Sioux Indians in South Dakota. The government became alarmed when a religious movement known as the Ghost Dance spread among the Sioux. Fearing an uprising, Indian police were sent to take Sioux Chief Sitting Bull into custody, hoping to disarm the movement. Sitting Bull resisted and was killed. A large group of his followers fled and joined Chief Big Foot's band of Sioux on the Cheyenne River. There they were captured by Miles' troops and taken to a cavalry camp at Wounded Knee Creek. While disarming the Indians, a shot was fired and a bloody battle followed. Two hundred men, women, and children were massacred by the soldiers. Later, as a result of the controversy with the Sioux at Wounded Knee, Miles was reassigned to Chicago where he led the federal troops that suppressed the Pullman strike in 1894.

The following year, upon the retirement of **John McCallister Schofield,** Miles inherited the title of general in chief of the Army, joining a distinguished list of other men who had held that position—Ulysses S. Grant, William Tecumseh Sherman, and **Philip Henry Sheridan.** Due to a reorganization of the Army, he was the last person to bear that title. When the war with Spain

This 1930's photograph shows the mausoleum of Nelson A. Miles (at left), which is located on a cul-de-sac at the end of Miles Drive in Section 3. Also located atop this hill overlooking the old South Post of Fort Myer and the city of Washington are the graves of Vinnie Ream and Edmund Rice.

broke out in 1898, Miles expected to be named commander of all combat forces. However the secretary of war, who had long been at odds with Miles, prevailed upon President William McKinley to deny Miles the position.

Unwilling to retire on his own, Miles was forced into retirement at the mandatory age of 64 in 1903 by President Theodore Roosevelt. Having finished his first autobiography in 1896, Miles wrote a second in 1911. As the Army's most senior officer, General Miles was honored as grand marshal of the parade that preceded the dedication of the Memorial Amphitheatre at Arlington in 1920. He died in 1925 at the age of 85 in Washington, D.C., and is buried in one of only two family mausoleums in Arlington National Cemetery. The other mausoleum belongs to the family of Brigadier General **Thomas Crook Sullivan** (Sec. 1, Lot 236, Grid MN–34).

(Alton) Glenn Miller
Big Band Leader
March 1, 1904–December 15, 1944
Memorial Section H, Lot 464-A, Grid O-28

Glenn Miller was arguably the most popular band leader in America in 1942, but he suspended his booming civilian career when the United States entered WWII. Miller never played as a civilian again. On December 15, 1944, on a flight from London to Paris, Miller's plane disappeared and neither the plane nor Glenn Miller were ever found.

Alton Glenn Miller was born in 1904 in Clarinda, Iowa. He attended the University of Colorado, and in 1924 moved to Chicago to join the Ben Pollack orchestra. By 1928, he was in New York carving out a career as an orchestra trombonist, studio musician, and arranger. He worked with such well-known band leaders as Red Nichols, the Dorsey Brothers, and Ray Noble.

In 1937, he formed his own band. It didn't last. He tried again a year later, and within two years he had achieved stardom with such hits as "Moonlight Serenade" and "In the Mood." He and his band also starred in two Hollywood films, "Sun Valley Serenade" (1941) and "Orchestra Wives" (1942). In February 1942, his recording company RCA Victor presented Miller with the first gold record ever awarded for his recording of "Chattanooga Choo-Choo."

When the United States declared war on Germany in 1941, Miller felt he could best serve our men and women in uniform by enlisting. At 38, he knew he was too old to be drafted, and the Navy couldn't use him. So, he persuaded the Army to allow him to enlist.

Ultimately, he became a captain in the Army Air Corps where he formed the 418th Army Air Force Band. This 50-member band, often working 18 hours a day, did as many as 40 radio broadcasts and 35 concerts in just one month. And although they were a musical unit, they still faced the dangers of war.

The band was attached to the allied forces supreme headquarters in London. During 1944, London and its environs were regularly attacked by German V-1 bombs causing massive casualties and heavy damage. Searching for safer quarters, Miller petitioned his superiors to move his band out of London. On Sunday, July 2, the men were moved to Bedford. That night their former quarters were destroyed and more than 100 people killed. Miller was credited with saving his men and later promoted to major.

By the fall of 1944, allied forces were moving across Europe. To celebrate their successes, Miller planned to broadcast a Christmas concert from Paris. Normally, his manager Lt. Don Haynes would go ahead to make arrangements. On this trip, however, Miller decided to go himself. With Flight Officer John Morgan and Lt. Colonel Norman Baesell, Miller took off in the Norseman UC-64 from a foggy Twinwood Farm Air Field on the evening of December 15, heading toward Paris. The plane never reached France, and was never found. Miller was listed as missing in action.

Glenn Miller's Army Air Force Band made the scheduled broadcast on Christmas, under the direction of Jerry Gray, and it continued to perform during the remainder of the war. They performed their last concert on November 13, 1945, at a National Press Club dinner for President Harry Truman. Also in attendance were generals Dwight Eisenhower and **Henry "Hap" Arnold.**

In 1953, Miller's reputation was enhanced with the release of the movie "The Glenn Miller Story" starring Jimmy Stewart, and the Glenn Miller Orchestra continued to perform more than 40 years after Miller's death.

As a soldier missing in action, Miller was eligible for a memorial headstone

As an MIA, Glenn Miller was eligible for a memorial headstone in Arlington National Cemetery.

in Arlington National Cemetery. In 1992, at his daughter's request, a stone honoring the memory of big band legend and Army Major Glenn Miller was placed in Memorial Section H, Lot 464 near Wilson Drive.

Marc Andrew Mitscher
Commander, World War II's Task Force 58
(January 26, 1887–February 3, 1947)
Sec. 2, Lot 4942, Grid W–32/33

Although he was not a model plebe at the Naval Academy, Marc Andrew Mitscher became a model commander who contributed invaluable service in the Pacific Theatre during World War II, serving as commander of the inimitable Task Force 58.

Marc Mitscher moved from his hometown of Hillsboro, Wisconsin, to Oklahoma City when he was still a child. There his father was elected mayor, and through the efforts of a friend in Congress, the elder Mitscher secured for his son an appointment to the Naval Academy. Never a serious scholar, Marc Mitscher nevertheless graduated in 1910 and was assigned to the Pacific Fleet. In October 1915, he reported for naval aviation training, becoming naval aviator No. 33 the following year when he received his wings. World War I saw Mitscher serving in three different stateside naval stations.

In 1919, Mitscher participated in the first transatlantic flight when three NC-1 Flying Boats attempted the crossing. Piloting one of the planes, Mitscher was forced down short of the Azores, but earned the Navy Cross for his efforts. In 1926, he was transferred to the U.S. Navy's first aircraft carrier, *Langley.* He was later named to head the air department of another carrier, *Saratoga,* and Mitscher himself landed the first plane on its deck in 1928.

When the new aircraft carrier *Hornet* was commissioned in October 1941, Mitscher was given that command and found himself in the Atlantic when the Japanese attacked Pearl Harbor. Ordered to the Pacific, Mitscher's carrier became the secret "Shangra La" from which Colonel **Jimmy Doolittle's** famed B-25 bombers made their morale-boosting raids on Tokyo in April 1942. Later that year he led the *Hornet* to the first important U.S. victory over Japan at Midway Island where his planes sank four Japanese carriers. In July 1941, he rose to the rank of rear admiral, directing all U.S. aircraft during the bitter Solomon Islands campaign in 1943.

Mitscher's greatest achievements occurred, however, following his appointment as commander of the legendary Fast Carrier Task Force, Pacific Fleet, or Task Force Fifty-eight as it came to be known around the world. From his flagship *Yorktown,* Mitscher led air strikes from his fast carriers against the island of Truk in the Carolinas in February 1944. That success was followed by equally impressive performances in the battle of the Philippine Sea in June (during which Mitscher provided air support for Douglas MacArthur's invasion of the Philippines); the battle of Leyte Gulf in October; and the capture of Iwo Jima and Okinawa in early 1945. Also during this period, planes under Mitscher's command struck the Japanese mainland and sank the super battleship, *Yamato.* Fighting deadly kamikazes, Mitscher twice was forced to transfer his flagship when first the *Bunker Hill,* and then the *Enterprise* suffered damage. He ended the encounter aboard the *Randolph.*

Mitscher returned to Washington, D.C. in July 1945, having earned the respect and trust of his pilots. He took extraordinary risks to save the lives of airmen as, for example, on the evening of June 20, 1944. During the battle of the Philippine Sea, many of Mitscher's pilots were returning after dark. Knowing that they were inexperienced in night landings and that they would be low on fuel, he ordered all the ship's lights turned on so that the pilots could see the flight deck. This move, unheard of during war, endangered all on board, including Mitscher himself, but his concern first was for his pilots' welfare. He was a pilot himself who had survived three crashes and he would not let his own pilots down.

In 1946, Mitscher earned promotion to the four-star rank of admiral and was given command of the Atlantic Fleet. While still in active service, Mitscher died of a chronic heart ailment at Norfolk, Virginia, in 1947. He is buried at Arlington near other great naval heroes of World War II.

Audie Murphy

World War II's Most Decorated Soldier, Actor
(June 20, 1924–May 28, 1971)
Sec. 46, Lot 366-11, Grid O/P–22/23

He wanted to join the Marines, but he was too short. He tried the paratroopers, but they wouldn't have him either. Reluctantly, he settled on the infantry, enlisting to become nothing less than the most decorated hero of World War II. He was Audie Murphy, the baby-faced Texas farm boy who became an American legend.

Murphy grew up on a sharecropper's farm in Hunt County, Texas. Left to help raise ten brothers and sisters when his father deserted their mother, Audie was only 16 when his mother died. He watched as his brothers and sisters were doled out to an orphanage or to relatives. Seeking an escape from that life in 1942, he looked to the Marines.

War had just been declared, and like so many other young men, Murphy lied about his age in his attempt to enlist. But it was not his age that kept him out of the Marines; it was his size. Not tall enough to meet the minimum requirements, he tried to enlist in the paratroopers, but again was denied entrance. Despondent, he chose the infantry.

Following basic training Murphy was assigned to the Fifth Regiment, Third Infantry Division in North Africa preparing to invade Sicily. It was here in 1943 that he first saw combat, proving himself to be a proficient marksman and highly skilled soldier. Consistently his performance demonstrated how well he understood the techniques of small unit action. He landed at Salerno to fight in the Volturno River campaign and then at Anzio to be part of the Allied force which fought its way to Rome. Throughout these campaigns, Murphy's unmatched skills earned him advancements in rank while many of his superior officers were being transferred, wounded, or killed. After the capture of Rome, Murphy won his first decoration for gallantry.

Shortly thereafter his unit was withdrawn from Italy to train for Operation Anvil-Dragoon, the invasion of southern France. During seven weeks of fighting in that successful campaign, Murphy's division suffered 4,500 casualties, and he became one of the most decorated men in his company. But his biggest test was yet to come.

On January 26, 1945, near the village of Holtzwihr in eastern France, Lieutenant Murphy's forward positions came under fierce attack by the Germans. Against the onslaught of six Panzer tanks and 250 infantrymen, Murphy ordered his men to fall back to better their defenses. Alone, he mounted an abandoned burning tank destroyer and, with a single machine gun, contested the enemy's advance. Wounded in the leg during the heavy fire, Murphy remained there for nearly an hour, repelling the attack of German soldiers on three sides and single-handedly killing 50 of them. His courageous performance stalled the German advance and allowed him to lead his men in the counterattack which ultimately drove the enemy from Holtzwihr. For this Murphy was awarded the Congressional Medal of Honor, our nation's highest award for gallantry in action.

By the war's end, Murphy had become the nation's most-decorated soldier, earning an unparalleled 28 medals, including three from France and one from Belgium. Murphy had been wounded three times during the war, yet in May 1945, when victory was declared in Europe, he had still not reached his 21st birthday.

Audie Murphy returned to a hero's welcome in the United States. His photograph appeared on the cover of LIFE magazine, and he was persuaded by actor James Cagney to embark on an acting career. Still very shy and unassuming, Murphy arrived in Hollywood with only his good looks and—by his own account—no talent. Nevertheless, he made more than 40 films. His first part was a small one in "Beyond Glory" in 1948. The following year he published his wartime memoirs, "To Hell and Back," which received good reviews. Later he portrayed himself in the 1955 movie version of the book. Most film critics, however, believe his best performance was in "Red Badge of Courage," Stephen Crane's Civil War epic.

After nearly 20 years, he retired from acting and started a career in private business. But the venture was unsuccessful, eventually forcing him into bankruptcy in 1968. Murphy—who once said that he could only sleep with a loaded pistol under his pillow—was haunted by nightmares of his wartime experiences throughout his adult life. In 1971, at the age of 46, he died in the crash of a private plane near Roanoke, Virginia.

Audie Murphy lies buried in Arlington Cemetery just across Memorial Drive from the Memorial Amphitheatre. A special flagstone walkway has been constructed to accommodate the large number of people who stop to pay their respects to America's most decorated soldier. Located at the end of a row of graves, his tomb is marked by a simple, white, government-issue tombstone that lists only a few of his many military decorations. The stone is, as he was, too small.

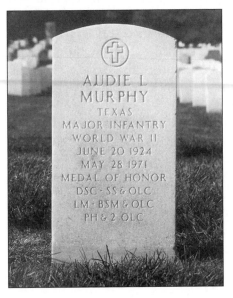

Following the death of Audie Murphy in 1971, a special walkway was built to accommodate the large number of visitors to his grave. The government regulation headstone of Murphy—the most decorated soldier in World War II—is not large enough to display all his commendations.

Simon Newcomb
Astronomer, Rear Admiral (Retired)
(March 12, 1835–July 11, 1909)
Sec. 1, Lot 527, Grid KL–34/35

Simon Newcomb was no ordinary seaman. The only courses he wanted to chart were those of the planets and the stars. He was a sailor who avoided the sea.

Simon Newcomb was born in Wallace, Nova Scotia, and was educated by his father, an itinerant schoolteacher. By the age of 5, young Simon was spending several hours a day calculating multiplication and division problems. At the age of 16 he was apprenticed to an herb doctor in Salisbury, New Brunswick, but he ran away from the "doctor" when he realized that the man was a quack who never saw patients. Simon joined his father who had settled in Maryland. He took up teaching in rural Maryland schools, spending his free time in nearby Washington, D.C., where he studied mathematics and developed an interest in astronomy.

In January 1857, Newcomb applied for and received employment with "The American Ephemeris and Nautical Almanac" in Cambridge, Massachusetts. The almanac was an annual handbook for astronomers, which included the predicted positions of the principal celestial bodies and other astronomical phenomena. While working there, Newcomb enrolled in Harvard's Lawrence Scientific School, graduating in 1858. In 1861, he was commissioned as a professor of mathematics in the United States Navy and was assigned to the Naval Observatory in Washington, D.C. His primary task was to find and correct errors in published values for the positions and motions of various celestial objects. During this period, Newcomb also negotiated the contract for the new 26-inch telescope at the Naval Observatory, which was built in 1873.

In 1877, Newcomb was promoted to captain and named senior mathematics professor in the Navy as well as superintendent of the American Nautical Almanac Office. It was in the latter position that Newcomb undertook his greatest work—the thorough revision of the motion theory and position tables for all major celestial bodies in the solar system. The result of his work, which took more than 20 years to complete, became a standard reference which was recognized throughout the world, and is still in use today. He also led several field expeditions, including one to the Cape of Good Hope to observe the Venus transit of 1882.

As contributing editor of the *American Journal of Mathematics,* Newcomb was named a professor of mathematics and astronomy at Baltimore's Johns Hopkins University in 1884. He led an international conference in Paris in 1896 that adopted a common system of ephemerides—the tables of computed places of celestial bodies over a period of time. Another such conference was held in 1950 that reaffirmed the validity of Newcomb's tables.

In 1897, Newcomb reached the age of mandatory retirement for Navy captains, but was allowed to continue his work under grants from the Carnegie Institute of Washington. In 1899, he founded the American Astronomical Society, serving as its president for six years. Then in 1906, after he had been retired for nine years, he was granted the extraordinary promotion to rear admiral. Throughout his lifetime, Simon Newcomb was the recipient of numerous honorary degrees and of foreign and domestic civilian commendations, also gaining election to the National Academy of Sciences. He died in Washington, D.C. on July 11, 1909.

Ignace Jan Paderewski
President-in-exile of Poland, Composer
(November 18, 1860–June 29, 1941)
Sec. 24 [The *USS Maine* Memorial]

On September 1, 1939, World War II erupted when Adolph Hitler's troops invaded Poland. Within a few short weeks, that country fell to German domination, forcing the legitimate Polish government into exile. The Polish leaders who sought refuge in the United States selected 79-year-old Ignace Jan Paderewski as its president. Paderewski never saw Poland again, dying in exile in 1941. President Franklin Roosevelt authorized the "temporary" interment of the Polish patriot in the vault of the *USS Maine* Memorial at Arlington, specifying that his body was to remain here until Poland again was free of foreign domination, and his body could be returned to his homeland. More than five decades later, Paderewski's remains were finally returned to Poland.

For 50 years, Ignace Paderewski's remains were entombed in the *USS Maine* Memorial.

Ignace Jan Paderewski was born in Podolia, in the Ukraine region of the Soviet Union. At a very early age he displayed extraordinary musical talent; at the age of 12, he entered the Warsaw Conservatory, achieving the remarkable distinction of being named a professor just six years later. In 1884, Paderewski became a pupil of the famed pianist Theodor Leschetizky in Vienna, and in 1887, he began his career as a concert pianist, a career that would flourish for more than 50 years. He toured throughout Europe, beginning a concert tour of the United States in 1891, during which he gave 117 recitals in 90 days. Yet his greatest love was not music; it was his homeland, Poland.

During World War I, he gave concerts to raise relief funds for Polish refugees and to help inspire men to enlist in the Polish army. It was Paderewski who represented Poland at the Versailles Peace Conference where he convinced President Woodrow Wilson to include the cause of Polish independence in his Fourteen Points. He served as both prime minister and foreign minister of the Polish Republic.

During the 1920s, Paderewski resumed his musical career, publishing his memoirs in 1938. When Germany invaded Poland, he dedicated himself to raising thousands of dollars for the relief of Poles throughout the world. He was named president of the Polish National Council, the government in exile. He died in New York City in 1941, leaving behind a grand legacy of music.

It was to this country that Ignace Jan Paderewski fled in search of freedom during World War II. Upon his death, the people of the United States honored this Polish native son with interment in our nation's most important military cemetery, where he remained until 1992. Following Poland's denunciation of Communist rule and Soviet influence, Paderewski's remains were returned to his free homeland. Although he now is buried in a crypt in St. John's Cathedral in Warsaw, Poland, by his own wishes, his heart is encased in a bronze sculpture in the Shrine of the Czestochowa in Doylestown, Pennsylvania, where it will remain.

His former tomb at Arlington is marked by several plaques dedicated to his memory, including one placed by the American Legion and another by the Polish Legion of American Veterans and Auxiliary.

James Parks
Former Arlington Estate Slave
(?, 1843–August 21, 1929)
Sec. 15, Lot 2, Grid G–26

Only one person buried in Arlington National Cemetery was also born on this property. That person is James Parks, born to slave parents living on the Arlington estate at the time it was owned by **George Washington Parke Custis.** The exact date of Parks' birth remains uncertain, though he is believed to have been born in 1843. (An interesting note: Neither

Washington Custis nor his wife, **Mary Lee Fitzhugh Custis,** was born at Arlington. Custis moved here when he built the first wing of Arlington House in 1802; his wife joined him after their marriage in 1804.)

Under the terms of George Washington Parke Custis' will, all of his slaves were to be trained and freed by 1862, five years after his death. When the Civil War erupted, Robert E. Lee, as executor of Parke Custis' will, was making provisions for the training and manumission of Parks and the other slaves on the Arlington estate. In April and May 1861, Lee and his family left the estate. Parks, then about 18 years old, remained behind attaching himself to the military unit that occupied the premises.

When Secretary of War Edwin M. Stanton designated Arlington as a national military burial ground in 1864, Parks was still living on the property. He became a grave digger and maintenance man for the cemetery, continuing in that work until his death in 1929. When Parks died, the secretary of war, in recognition of Parks' lifelong service to Arlington, and in full awareness that Parks did not meet the formal burial qualifications, granted special permission to inter Parks' body in Arlington. James Parks died in Arlington County on August 21, 1929. He was believed to be about 86 years old at the time of his death. His grave in Section 15 is marked with a special commemorative headstone.

Robert Edwin Peary
Explorer
(May 6, 1856–February 20, 1920)
Sec. 8, Lot S-15, Grid X–8/9

Engraved on the tombstone of Robert Edwin Peary is the Latin phrase: *Inveniam Viam Aut Facium,* meaning "I shall find a way or make one." These words describe the lifelong quest of Admiral Peary to become the first person to reach the North Pole. Enduring unimaginable hardship, Peary—accompanied by his longtime friend and assistant, **Matthew Henson,** and four Eskimo aides—did indeed "find a way" across the Arctic icecap, and on April 6, 1909, they stood together on top of the world.

Peary and his mother moved from Pennsylvania to South Portland, Maine, after his father died. As a child he lived the outdoors life. He graduated with Phi Beta Kappa honors from Bowdoin College in 1877, receiving a degree in civil engineering. Then, after working a short time with the United States Coastal and Geodetic Survey, Peary joined the U.S. Navy Civil Engineering Corps in 1881 as a lieutenant.

It was in 1886 that Peary discovered his true vocation on an exploratory trip into the unknown interior of Greenland. That trip whetted his appetite for other expeditions to explore the uncharted Arctic regions. During the next 11 years, Peary made four more trips to Greenland, some of them lasting for more than a year. These expeditions earned him great fame as an explorer and scientist. He proved that Greenland was an island, and he returned from his 1893 expedition with three gigantic meteorites, among them the largest the world has ever seen. It weighs 90 tons and remains on permanent display at the Hayden Planetarium in New York City.

As an explorer Peary pioneered new methods of travel in the Arctic. He traveled with minimal equipment, foregoing the traditional heavy tents and sleeping bags. Instead, he built igloos along the way and wore thick fur suits day and night. He also restricted the size of his parties so that he could move quickly over long distances. However, his feats of exploration did not come without a physical cost.

In an area where the temperature rarely climbs above -50 degrees F, and where high winds whip across frozen seas, frostbite was a constant threat. In the course of one treacherous search for a route to the North Pole, during which the temperature registered -60 degrees F, Peary noted in his journal, "a suspicious 'wooden' feeling in the right foot...and I found, to my annoyance, that both feet were frosted." Shortly thereafter, Peary's toes were amputated. His physical hardships, however, did not halt his explorations.

In 1897, granted a leave of absence from the Navy, Peary announced his intention to reach the Pole. One year later, his ship *Windward* set out on a voyage of discovery, but that voyage—which lasted four years—was unsuccessful. Not deterred, Peary again set sail in 1905 aboard the *Roosevelt,* an icebreaker built to his specifications. His exploration party left the ship on the north coast of Ellesmere Island and pushed northward on sledges over the icebound Arctic Ocean. At 87 degrees, 6 minutes, Peary set a new "farthest north" record, just 175 miles short of the Pole, but he and his crew were forced to turn back when supplies ran so dangerously low that they nearly starved to death.

Undaunted by the failures and physical hardships, Peary courageously set out in July 1908 on what he knew would be his last chance to reach his elusive goal. In February 1909, Peary and six sledge teams left Cape Columbia on the northern coast of Ellesmere Island. His plan was simple. Each team would take turns breaking the trail, then they would leave supplies and fall back. Peary, Henson, and four Eskimos comprised the last team. On February 28, severe temperatures, driving snow, and physical exhaustion once again threatened the lives of the explorers. But they would not give up. They inched their way northward until, on April 6, Peary, Henson, and their Eskimo companions stood where no persons had ever stood before—the North Pole.

Expecting a hero's welcome upon his return to the United States, Peary found instead a former assistant, Dr. Frederick Cook, claiming that he had reached the Pole nearly a year earlier. Peary's reaction: "Cook has simply handed the public a gold brick." Charges and countercharges followed until the testimony of Cook's companions (that during their expedition they never lost sight of land) showed that Cook had perpetrated a malicious hoax.

In 1911, the United States Congress officially recognized Peary's achievement and voted him their thanks. In March of that year, he was granted the rank of rear admiral, retired. The recipient of numerous medals, awards, and honorary degrees, Peary continued a heavy schedule of speaking engagements throughout his life, also serving as president of the American Geographical Society.

When Peary died on February 26, 1920, in Washington, D.C., he was buried at Arlington. On April 6, 1922, exactly 13 years following his discovery of the North Pole, a memorial erected by the National Geographic Society was dedicated on his grave site. President Warren G. Harding presided over the ceremonies, which were attended by a large crowd including **William Howard Taft,** Chief Justice and president of the United States at the time of Peary's discovery. The memorial depicts a large globe of the world with the North Pole vividly marked by a bronze star. Engraved in Latin on the monument is Peary's motto: *Inveniam Viam Aut Facium* (I shall find a way or make one).

A bronze star marks the North Pole on this globe erected by the National Geographic Society in honor of Arctic explorer Robert Peary. The monument was dedicated on this site in 1922 as shown in this old photograph. Peary's grave later was moved nearer to Jesup Drive.

Buried with Peary is his wife, **Josephine Diebitsch Peary,** who was the first woman to spend a winter in the Arctic when she accompanied her husband there in 1891.

The remains of his friend and partner, **Matthew Henson,** were reinterred near his grave in 1988.

John J. "Black Jack" Pershing
General of the Armies, Pulitzer Prize-winning Author
(September 13, 1860–July 15, 1948)
Sec. 34, Lot S-19, Grid U–12

The United States Congress conferred upon John J. Pershing the highest rank ever awarded an American, that of general of the armies. Previously only one person in our history was permitted that rank: General of the Armies George Washington. Such was the esteem in which General Pershing was held following the Allies' victory in Europe in World War I. Yet, when this great general died, his last request was that he be buried with the men he had fought beside, and that his grave be marked with the same white regulation tombstone marking their graves.

General of the Armies Pershing began his life in modest surroundings. He was born in Laclede, Missouri, the son of a railroad switchman. At age 17, Pershing taught in a rural school for African-American children to earn enough money to pay for his college education at Kirksville Normal School (now Truman State University). In 1881, answering an advertisement for the Military Academy's entrance exam, Pershing sat for the exam and won entry to West Point in 1882. Graduating in 1886 as president of his class and captain of cadets, he was commissioned in the cavalry.

After receiving his commission, Pershing was ordered to the Western frontier where he earned his first combat citation. From 1891 until 1895, he served as a professor of military science at the University of Nebraska, earning a law degree there in his spare time. From Nebraska, Pershing returned to West Point as a tactical officer.

In 1898, at the outbreak of the Spanish-American War, Pershing was sent to the Philippines where he earned a Silver Star. In 1904, he was assigned as military attaché of the American embassy in Tokyo after the Russo-Japanese War broke out. Returning to the United States the following year, Pershing married **Helen Frances Warren,** the daughter of Senator Francis E. Warren of Wyoming.

Although John Pershing's military prowess stands unquestioned, his promotion to brigadier general in 1906, in which he leapfrogged 862 other officers, prompted a great deal of professional resentment. The promotion raised rumors of favoritism and political dealing, fueled by the fact that his father-in-law was chairman of the Senate Military Affairs Committee. Nevertheless, Pershing continued to serve with great distinction—returning to the Philippines as military commander and remaining there until 1913.

In 1914, Pershing returned to the U.S. where President Woodrow Wilson assigned him to "pursue and disperse" the band of Mexican guerrillas under Pancho Villa that was terrorizing the Southwestern United States. Leaving his family in San Francisco, Pershing went to El Paso, Texas, to coordinate his campaign. But just prior to his incursion into Mexico, he received the tragic news that a fire had swept through his family's quarters, killing his wife and three daughters. Only his 6-year-old son had survived. Despite this tragic personal loss, Pershing pressed on with his assignment and effectively thwarted Villa's terrorism. He was promoted to major general. During this campaign, Pershing commanded the 10th Calvary, a distinguished regiment of African-American troops, often called the "Buffalo Soldiers." (See page 245.) It was his advocacy of these black soldiers that earned him the nickname "Black Jack."

Upon the heels of Pershing's return to Washington in 1917, President Wilson named him to command the American Expeditionary Forces being sent to France after America's declaration of war against Germany. The army he was ordered to command did not yet exist; his task was to create it. No one knew better than Pershing how long and arduous a fight this would be. He recommended an army of one million men by 1918, to expand to three million men by the following year.

General of the Armies John J. Pershing shared that rank with only one other person–George Washington.

One of Pershing's first actions upon arriving in France was to pay respects at the tomb of the Marquis de Lafayette, the French general who had provided invaluable assistance to American forces under General George Washington during the American Revolution. Lafayette became a close friend and confidant of Washington. As Pershing laid a wreath on the French soldier's grave, his aide announced, "Lafayette, we are here!" This gesture signified to the French people that the United States was ready to assist them as Lafayette had assisted the struggling young American republic in 1776.

Once engaged in Europe, Pershing fought diligently to maintain the integrity of his American forces. He did not, and would not, concur with the plan to use American forces only as replacements for depleted French and British units. Indeed, it was Pershing and his American troops who defeated the Germans in the St. Mihiel Salient in September 1918. Then in October, the Americans fought bravely and bitterly against the Germans along the seemingly impenetrable Hindenburg Line during the Meuse-Argonne Offensive until at last the German ranks were ruptured, and the Allies marched toward the armistice on November 11, 1918.

Upon his return to the United States, Pershing received a hero's welcome. Congress conferred upon him the rank of general of the armies, a rank which had been created by Congress in 1799 explicitly for George Washington. Interestingly, it was later learned that Washington had never accepted the rank, so the Congress conferred it upon General Washington posthumously in 1976, maintaining Washington's place as the senior ranking officer on the U.S. Army roster. Therefore, only two men in American history have received this highest rank.

Pershing served as Army chief of staff from 1921 until his retirement in 1924. He went on to chair the American Battle Monuments Commission and to write his two-volume memoirs. Published in 1931, "My Experiences in the World War," earned him a Pulitzer Prize. Although retired and living at Walter Reed Hospital in Washington, D.C., Pershing was called upon during World War II for advice and counsel by the Army chief of staff, General **George C. Marshall.** It was during World War I in France that Pershing met Marshall as a young logistics officer. Marshall became an aide to Pershing for the duration of the war and remained on the general's staff until Pershing's retirement.

When John Pershing died in Washington in 1948, his funeral cortege was led by the president of the United States, Harry S Truman, himself a veteran "doughboy" from World War I. After the funeral service in the Memorial Amphitheatre at Arlington, Pershing was buried on top of a grassy knoll near the other veterans of the Great War; and as he had requested, his grave was marked by a simple white stone. Buried beside him are his grandsons, **Richard W. Pershing,** killed in Vietnam in 1968, and **John Warren Pershing III,** who died in 1999.

David Dixon Porter
Rear Admiral, Civil War Hero
(June 8, 1813–February 13, 1891)
Sec. 2, Lot S-5, Grid S/T–35

D avid Dixon Porter's life as a seaman seemed preordained. Even as a child in Chester, Pennsylvania, Porter lived a life that many young boys only dream about. The son of a naval hero from the War of 1812, young Porter accompanied his famous father on a mission to fight pirates in the West Indies at the age of 11. By the time he was 13, and while his father was serving as commander-in-chief of the Mexican Navy, Porter was appointed a midshipman in the United States Navy. As a young teenager, he served on the warship *Congress,* which sailed in both Mediterranean and Brazilian waters.

David Porter, at the age of 33, played a diplomatic role in 1846 when he was dispatched to the Dominican Republic on an observation mission for the state department. In 1847, as a first lieutenant, he sailed on the war steamer, *Spitfire,* and led the landing party that captured the main fort at Tabasco, Mexico. For his heroics, Porter was given command of the *Spitfire.* He then left the Navy for a short time to captain civilian vessels, but rejoined the Navy in 1855 to command the steamship *Supply.* Among his exotic exploits was sailing to North Africa to undertake transporting camels to the American Southwest for experimentation by the U.S. Army. But it was his conduct during the Civil War that earned him a place of distinction in American history.

At the outbreak of that war, Porter served under another famous American admiral, David Glasgow Farragut, who was none other than Porter's adopted brother. Porter's father had adopted the homeless Farragut child, and had raised both future naval heroes side by side, the same way they fought during the Civil War. Porter commanded Union gunboats on the Mississippi River and succeeded in breaking through the crucial Confederate blockade of the river at Vicksburg, Mississippi, a task at which so many other commanders had failed. He eventually commanded the largest fleet of the war—60 vessels—in the blockade of the Confederate Atlantic coast, and led the assault on Fort Fisher, North Carolina.

After the war, Porter became only the second U.S. naval officer in our nation's history to attain the rank of admiral. His adopted brother, Admiral David Farragut, was the first. Porter later served as superintendent of the Naval Academy, and wrote several books on naval history, including a biography of his father.

He died in Washington, D.C., on February 13, 1891, and was buried on the hillside below Arlington House. Although his tombstone bears the inscription "temporarily erected," that same marker has sufficed for more than 100 years.

John Wesley Powell
Explorer, Geologist, Native American Linguist
(March 24, 1834–September 23, 1902)
Sec. 1, Lot 408, Grid L–35

Adventure was the hallmark of John Wesley Powell's life. From his early childhood in Mount Morris, New York, he traveled widely with his minister father, cultivating a desire to explore and discover, a desire which inspired him throughout his life. It was this adventuresome spirit that led Powell to undertake his dangerous exploration of the Colorado River.

Powell's father, a Methodist minister, traveled with his young son throughout the Midwest spreading the gospel. Young John was educated in schools in Ohio, Wisconsin, and Illinois. After attending Oberlin College in Ohio and Wheaton College in Illinois, Powell graduated from Illinois Wesleyan University, which was named—as was Powell himself—for the founder of Methodism, John Wesley.

With the outbreak of the Civil War, Powell joined the Second Illinois Artillery in 1861, climbing to the rank of major. However, Powell did not survive that war without injury. During the bloody Battle of Shiloh in 1862, he lost the lower part of his right arm.

Following the war, Powell returned to Illinois Wesleyan to teach geology. It was there in Bloomington, Illinois, that he began planning his exploration of the Colorado River and its canyons. By 1869, much of America's Western frontier had been explored and charted, but the Colorado River remained unexplored. It was still the subject of mysterious folk tales filled with uncharted dangers. For Powell, it also represented an untapped source of geological treasures. The river, which carves its way through the Grand Canyon, had never been navigated, nor had anyone studied the canyon's unique geological formations. Powell was eager to undertake the challenge.

On May 24, 1869, Powell and his companions launched their boats into the Green River in Wyoming to begin a thousand-mile journey over the uncharted, rapid white water of the Green and Colorado rivers. That journey did not end until August 30 when Powell and six members of his crew arrived at the junction of the Colorado River, and what is now known as Lake Mead in southern Nevada. The survivors were sunburned and nearly starved. However, the expedition brought recognition to Powell and kindled in him the hopes of another, more scientific journey. The one-armed adventurer did attempt another expedition down the river, but impassable high water forced him to terminate the trip prematurely.

From 1871 until 1879, Powell directed a government-sponsored geological and geographical survey of public lands in the western United States. It also was during this time that Powell undertook a study of Native American languages, publishing *An Introduction to the Study of Indian Languages*. Then, when the U.S. Bureau of Ethnology of the Smithsonian Institution was established in 1879, Powell was named its first director. He also served as director of the U.S. Geological Survey from 1881 until 1892.

Although Powell retired in 1894, he remained active in the National Geographic Society, of which he was a founding member. He died in 1902 in Haven, Maine. His wife **Emma Dean Powell** is buried with him.

Francis Gary Powers
Spy Pilot
(August 17, 1929–August 1, 1977)
Sec. 11, Lot 685-2, Grid OP–15/16

Just as the long Cold War between the United States and the Soviet Union began to thaw in 1960, the Soviet Union shot down a U-2 reconnaissance plane deep within its borders. The Soviets charged it was an American spy plane. The United States claimed it was just a NASA weather plane which had strayed off course. The incident not only severely strained relations between the two superpowers, forcing the cancellation of a scheduled summit meeting between President Eisenhower and Soviet Communist Party chief Nikita Khrushchev, but it also changed the life of Francis Gary Powers forever.

Powers was the only boy among the six children of a Kentucky coal miner. Born in Jenkins, Kentucky, he graduated from nearby Pikeville College, joined the Air Force as a private, and went into flight training. After two years, he was commissioned his wings and stayed in the Air Force until

1956, at which time he went to work as a civilian pilot for Lockheed Aircraft Corporation, the company that developed the U-2 plane. In actuality, Powers was working for the CIA.

Eventually Powers joined a group of pilots who were CIA operatives stationed at a base in Adana, Turkey. From there the pilots flew surveillance missions into the heart of the Soviet Union, photographing Soviet long-range ballistic missile installations. Both the CIA and the pilots believed that at an altitude of 60,000 feet they were beyond the range of Soviet missiles. They were wrong. On May 1, 1960, a Soviet missile found its intended target, a U-2 plane piloted by Powers near the city of Sverdlovsk.

In the heated exchange between the governments following the downing of the plane, the Eisenhower administration maintained that the plane had been on a routine weather reconnaissance flight and strongly denied that the flight had been a spy mission. To rebut the American claim, the Soviets not only produced the American pilot at a highly publicized press conference, but they also displayed the extensive photographic and surveillance equipment found on board the American plane. Ultimately, our government acknowledged the mission's true purpose, but stated that the surveillance flights had been undertaken to monitor Soviet missile advances that threatened world security.

Powers was publicly tried for espionage in Moscow. He appeared as a quiet man who didn't quite understand the full ramifications of his actions. Convicted and sentenced to ten years in a Soviet prison, he served less than two years, gaining his freedom as part of a dramatic exchange for a convicted Soviet spy being held by the United States. Colonel Rudolf Abel, an alleged member of the Soviet KGB, was convicted in New York City in 1957 for espionage activities against the U.S. He was given a 30-year sentence, which was commuted in 1962 by President **John F. Kennedy** in order to arrange the swap for Powers. On February 10, 1962, in a theatrical ceremony staged in the center of the Glienicker-Brucke Bridge between West Berlin and East Germany, Abel and Powers were exchanged.

Powers returned to the United States and was received, not as a hero, but rather as a mercenary. He was criticized by some Americans for having not committed suicide upon being captured. In 1970, Powers wrote *Operation Overflight,* his account of the incident in which he defended his behavior. He stated that the CIA had never advised suicide and criticized the agency for implying that it had.

The rest of Powers' career was spent working for Lockheed, then for a Los Angeles radio station as a traffic reporter pilot. Briefly, he left to work for an aircraft communications manufacturer, but returned to broadcasting with station KNBC in Los Angeles as a reporter using his helicopter to achieve special vantage points. On August 1, 1977, after videotaping scenes of a brush fire, Powers and his cameraman were heading back to their base when their helicopter crashed in Encino, California. The cause of the crash was believed to be a lack of fuel. Powers died in the wreckage.

On May 1, 2000, exactly 40 years after he was shot down over the Soviet Union, Francis Gary Powers was awarded the Distinguished Flying Cross. He is now buried near the graves of other Americans whose careers were flight related—military aviation pioneer Lieutenant **Thomas Selfridge** and astronauts **Virgil Grissom, Roger Chaffee, Don Eisele,** and **James Irwin.**

Mary Randolph
Author, First Burial at Arlington
(August 9, 1762–January 23, 1828)
Sec. 45, Special lot near the Custis Walk, T–36

Just below Arlington House along Custis Walk is a solitary grave surrounded by a red brick wall.

This is the final resting place of Mary Randolph; it also is the oldest grave on the Arlington estate.

Mary Randolph was a descendant of one of the oldest and most distinguished families in Virginia. A direct descendant of Pocahontas, she was a cousin to **Mary Lee Fitzhugh Custis,** the wife of the builder of Arlington House, and to Robert E. Lee. Mary Randolph also claimed among her many cousins Thomas Jefferson, whose daughter was married to Mary Randolph's brother, Thomas Mann Randolph, a former governor of Virginia. Mary Randolph is believed to be the godmother of Mary Anna Custis Lee, the wife of Robert E. Lee. She was married to David Mead Randolph.

She was considered the quintessential mistress of the plantation, publishing a book entitled *The Virginia Housewife,* a domestic

As a friend and relative of the Custis family, Mary Randolph was the first person buried at Arlington in 1828.

guide which included recipes, instruction on candle making, herbal cures, and even how to dress a turtle. The book, a bestseller in its time, is still in print today.

The beautiful stone which graces Mary Randolph's tomb was provided by her youngest son, Burwell Starke Randolph, who had been a midshipman in the United States Navy when he fell from a mast and suffered severe permanent injuries. He believed that his mother's death was hastened by her tireless caring for him and his needs. The stone reads:

Sacred to the memory of Mrs. Mary Randolph. Her intrinsic worth needs no eulogium. The deceased was born the Ninth of August 1762 at Ampthill near Richmond, Virginia and died the 23rd of January, 1828 in Washington City. A victim of maternal love and duty. As a tribute of filial gratitude this monument is dedicated to her exulted virtues by her youngest son. Requiescat in pace.

When Mary Randolph died in 1828, **Washington Custis** allowed her burial on the Arlington estate because of her special ties to his wife and daughter, and because of her affection for the estate.

Vinnie Ream (Hoxie)
Sculptor of Abraham Lincoln
(September 25, 1847–November 20, 1914)
Sec. 3, Lot 1876, Grid T–16

President Abraham Lincoln was accustomed to hearing special requests from senators and congressmen, so when Senator James Rollins of Missouri approached him in 1864 indicating that he had a request, Lincoln was not surprised. Yet Rollins' request was truly extraordinary. A member of the Senator's constituency wanted permission to have personal sittings by the president to make sketches for a statue of Lincoln... and the constituent was a 17-year-old girl. President Lincoln quickly dismissed the idea. There was a war on, and besides, "Why should anyone want a picture of a man so homely?" he asked. Rollins pressed the point. The young lady was very talented and she would be heartbroken if she lost the chance, he said. Lincoln didn't budge. Finally Rollins pointed out that the young girl came from a very poor background. The president began to stir. "She is poor, is she?" the president asked. "Well, that is nothing against her. I will sit for the model," Lincoln said with a nod. With that nod, Vinnie Ream began her sessions with Abraham Lincoln. They continued almost daily until she saw him for the last time on April 14, 1865, the day he was assassinated.

Vinnie Ream was born in Madison, Wisconsin, in 1847. Soon after her birth her family moved to Columbia, Missouri, where she met Senator Rollins. Then they moved again, this time to Washington, D.C., where her father worked as a surveyor for the Land Office while Vinnie took a job at the Post Office sorting mail to and from the front.

Vinnie's interest in sculpting began when Senator Rollins introduced her to Clark Mills, a well-known sculptor who had designed and cast the figure of Freedom which adorns the top of the United States Capitol. Impressed with her natural ability, Mills offered Vinnie free instruction. Soon she was making likenesses of many famous clients, including George Armstrong Custer, Thaddeus Stevens, and Horace Greeley.

The sittings with Lincoln took place at the White House, usually during lunch. Ream recounted later that the president brooded much during this time and talked little. When he did speak, it was about his young son, Willie, who had died at the age of 11 in February 1863. Sometimes he wept. This was the man Vinnie Ream captured in her sketches.

Following President Lincoln's death, Congress authorized a competition for a sculpture of Lincoln to be placed in the rotunda of the Capitol. In July 1866, after much ado, Vinnie Ream was awarded the commission and $10,000. She was the first woman ever awarded a government commission, but she was not without her critics. Several members of Congress even suggested that she had compromised her morals to secure the commission. About her detractors, Vinnie indignantly replied, "These people know nothing of art."

The statue was completed in 1870, and was unveiled amidst great excitement and expectation on January 7, 1871. As the drape fell from the sculpture, the crowded rotunda erupted into tumultuous applause. Vinnie Ream had captured the essence of Abraham Lincoln, the man. Today her statue stands proudly in the Capitol rotunda.

Vinnie Ream's career flourished after she

Although Vinnie Ream's grave is marked with a reproduction of her sculpture, Sappho, her best-known work of Abraham Lincoln sits in the rotunda of the United States Capitol.

finished the sculpture of Lincoln. Other works around Washington include the statue of Admiral David Farragut in Farragut Square and the Native American Sequoia, also located in the Capitol. In 1878, Vinnie married Lieutenant **Richard Hoxie,** an army engineer who often helped her with her work. Ream saw herself as a pioneer for women sculptors and encouraged them at every opportunity. When she died in 1914, as a military spouse, she was buried in Arlington National Cemetery. Her grave, which is shared with her husband, is marked by a pedestal bearing a bas-relief of herself on its side and a bronze reproduction of her work, the poet *Sappho,* on its top.

Walter Reed
Pioneer Bacteriologist
(September 13, 1851–November 22, 1902)
Sec. 3, Lot 1864, Grid TU–16/17

Walter Reed dedicated his life to the study and prevention of disease, and is credited with the discovery of a cure for yellow fever; but his own life was cut tragically short by another onetime widespread killer: appendicitis.

Like many children living in the South during the Civil War, Walter Reed was forced to delay his education until the end of the war. Ultimately, he left his home in Belroi, Virginia, entering the University of Virginia where in 1869, he earned his medical degree. After graduation, he moved to New York City and earned a second medical degree from Bellevue Hospital Medical College in 1870. For the next five years, he served as an intern at Kings County Hospital.

In 1875, Reed enlisted in the Army Medical Corps and was commissioned a first lieutenant, assistant surgeon. After serving at various posts for the next 14 years, including the Arizona Territory, he continued his studies in bacteriology and pathology in 1890 at Johns Hopkins University in Baltimore. In 1893, he was transferred to Washington, D.C., to accept the post of curator of the U.S. Army Medical Museum while also serving as professor of bacteriology and clinical microscopy at the newly organized Army Medical School. By 1895, he had been selected as chairman of the Department of Bacteriology and Pathology at Columbian (now George Washington University) Medical School.

After the war with Spain erupted in 1898, many American soldiers contracted yellow fever while serving in tropical zones. Dr. Reed was named by Surgeon General **George M. Sternberg** to chair a commission to investigate the causes and transmission of that dreaded disease. Reed advanced the theory that the fever was transmitted by the stegomyia mosquito, rather than simply by contaminated water. He established an experimental station near Havana, Cuba, and after seven months of study—which included exposing himself and others to the disease—Reed and his commission members conclusively proved his mosquito theory. Yellow fever cases were reduced from 1,400 in 1900 to only 37 in 1901, and there was not a single case in 1902.

Reed returned to resume his work at the Army Medical School in 1901. A sudden attack of appendicitis on November 22, 1902, claimed his life at the age of 51. General **Leonard Wood,** the military governor of Cuba, said of Walter Reed, "I know of no other man on this side of the world who has done so much for humanity as Dr. Reed. His discovery resulted in saving more lives than were lost in the Cuban War."

William Hubbs Rehnquist
Army Sergeant, Supreme Court Chief Justice
(October 1, 1924–September 3, 2005)
Sec. 5, Lot 7049, W-36

When William H. Rehnquist joined the Supreme Court as an associate justice in 1972, he often found himself as the lone conservative voice on the Court despite the presence of three other Republican appointees. However, by the time he died in 2005, Chief Justice Rehnquist had witnessed—and often directed—a distinctly conservative shift in the Court.

William Hubbs Rehnquist was born in Milwaukee on October 1, 1924. His father was a wholesale paper broker and his mother, who was fluent in several languages, worked as a translator. Rehnquist grew up in nearby Shorewood, attending public schools with his sister Jean. Rehnquist enrolled at Kenyon College in Gambier, Ohio, but he left school to enlist in the Army Air Corps during World War II, serving as a weather observer in North Africa. He was discharged in 1946 with the rank of sergeant.

After the war, Rehnquist attended Stanford University on the GI Bill, earning both a bachelor's and master's degrees in political science. He went on to receive a second master's degree in government from Harvard University and returned to Stanford for his law degree in 1950, where his graduated first in his class. While in law school, Rehnquist met Supreme Court Justice Robert Jackson, who eventually selected the young lawyer to be his clerk on the Court. (Also while at Stanford, Rehnquist dated his classmate, Sandra

Day, who graduated third in the class. Later, Sandra Day O'Connor served with Rehnquist on the Supreme Court.)

It was during his clerkship in Washington, D.C., that Rehnquist met **Natalie Cornell**, another Stanford graduate, who worked for the Central Intelligence Agency. They married in 1953, moved to Phoenix, and had a son and two daughters. In Phoenix, Rehnquist joined a law firm and became involved in local Republican politics where he met Richard Kleindienst, another Phoenix attorney who later worked on Richard Nixon's presidential campaign.

Kleindienst eventually became deputy attorney general under Nixon, and recommended Rehnquist for a position as deputy attorney general in the Office of Legal Counsel. It was a high-visibility position requiring Rehnquist often to testify before Congressional committees. He also worked with Kleindienst and Attorney General **John Mitchell** to vet potential Supreme Court nominees to succeed retiring Associate Justice John Harlan. Frustrated by his failure to find an appropriate candidate, Mitchell recommended Rehnquist for the Court, and President Nixon concurred.

On January 7, 1972, along with new Justice Lewis Powell, William H. Rehnquist joined the Supreme Court as its 100th justice. It did not take long for Rehnquist to establish himself as a strong conservative voice, often as a lone dissenter. He believed the only rights the Constitution protects are those the document names specifically. With that belief in mind, he joined Justice Byron White in 1973 as the only dissenters in the landmark *Roe v. Wade* case, which established that a woman's right to privacy protects her right to an abortion.

When Chief Justice **Warren Burger** announced his retirement in 1986, President Ronald Reagan nominated Rehnquist to succeed Burger. Although opposed by many liberals and subjected to five days of often-contentious Senate hearings, Rehnquist prevailed and on September 26, 1986, Rehnquist became the nation's 16th chief justice. Antonin Scalia was sworn in as Rehnquist's successor as associate justice.

During his tenure as chief justice, Rehnquist presided over a Court that heard many controversial cases, including issues of privacy, criminal rights, gay rights, and free speech. The Court also decided the 2000 presidential election by denying Democrat Al Gore a recount in a closely contested vote in Florida, handing the victory to Republican George W. Bush. The controversial 5-4 decision held that a lack of uniform standards for counting ballots from county to county meant that the recount would violate the constitutional guarantee of equal protection. Rehnquist voted with the majority.

As chief justice, William Rehnquist also presided over the five-week impeachment trial of President Bill Clinton in 1999, only the second chief justice to so preside. Clinton was acquitted. (In 1868, Salmon P. Chase presided over the impeachment trial of President Andrew Johnson.) Later when asked about his role in the trial, Rehnquist borrowed a line from a Gilbert and Sullivan operetta, "I did nothing in particular and I did it very well."

As chief justice, William Rehnquist led the closed-door conferences where the Court discussed and voted on cases. He also made assignments for writing majority opinions, managed the Court's docket, controlled open-court arguments, and supervised more than 300 Court employees. His efficient management of the Court won the respect and admiration of his colleagues regardless of their ideological persuasions.

In October 2004, Rehnquist announced that he had thyroid cancer. He received treatments for the illness and returned to the Court several months later. Although weakened by his illness, he refused to step down and refuted all rumors of his pending retirement. He died on September 3, 2005, and was succeeded by John G. Roberts as chief justice.

Following funeral services at St. Matthew's Cathedral in Washington, Chief Justice Rehnquist was buried next to his wife Natalie at Arlington National Cemetery. Natalie Rehnquist died in 1991. Three former chief justices also are buried at Arlington—**William Howard Taft, Earl Warren, and Warren Burger.**

REVOLUTIONARY WAR VETERANS

Although the American Revolution ended nearly 80 years before Arlington National Cemetery was established, 11 veterans of that war have been reinterred at Arlington. Arlington is the only national cemetery to claim veterans buried within its walls from every war in American history. Many of these men had been deceased more than a century when requests were made to allow their burial at Arlington. Nine of them are buried in Section 1 between Arlington House and the Fort Myer Gate. **Pierre Charles L'Enfant** and **Hugh Auld** are buried in Section 2. What follows is a brief remark about each of these men who fought, not to defend our nation, but to create it. The lives of two of these veterans, **Pierre Charles L'Enfant** and **James McCubbin Lingan,** are discussed in separate profiles.

Hugh Auld
(1745– December 17, 1813)
Sec. 2, Lot 4801, Grid U–31

Hugh Auld served as a lieutenant in the Talbot County Militia in 1780. He died at Deep Water Point Farm, near Clairborne, Maryland, and was buried in a family plot there. He was reinterred in Arlington on April 11, 1935. Buried next to Auld is his son and namesake who was a veteran of the War of 1812, and who died on November 2, 1820.

William Ward Burrows
(January 16, 1758–March 6, 1805)
Sec. 1, Lot 301-B, Grid NO–33/34

William Ward Burrows was born in Charleston, South Carolina in 1758 and, as a young man, served in the Revolutionary War. He was named commandant on the newly established U.S. Marine Corps in 1798 by President John Adams. Among other Corps institutions, he is credited with creating the U.S. Marine Corps Band. His contemporary, author Washington Irving, described Burrows as "a gentleman of accomplished mind and polished manner."

Burrows died in Washington, D.C., in 1805, and was buried in the Presbyterian Cemetery in Georgetown. His remains were reinterred in Arlington on May 12, 1892. The epitaph on his tombstone states:

> His death and such, Oh reader, with thy own,
>
> Has free from terrors and without a groan,
>
> His spirit to Himself, the almighty drew,
>
> Mild as a [illegible] exhales the [illegible] dew.

Joseph Carleton
(1754–1812)
Sec. 1, Lot 299, Grid MN–33/34

Joseph Carleton was born in Longmanthby, Cumberland County, England. He came to the colonies and served as a paymaster in the American Army during the Revolution. After the war, he worked as a merchant and lived in Georgetown, now a part of Washington, D.C. When he died in 1812, he was buried in the Presbyterian Cemetery in Georgetown, and was reinterred at Arlington on November 13, 1907.

John Follin
(1761–1841)
Sec. 1, Lot 295, Grid MN–33/34

John Follin, a native of Fairfax County, Virginia, joined the American Navy in 1778 at the age of 17. He was captured by the British while at sea, and held as a prisoner of war for three years, including a year on Gibraltar. He was exchanged at the close of the Revolution. His wives, **Catherine Sandford Follin** (1785–1813) and **Mary Barker Follin** (1785–1863) are buried with him.

John Green
(1730–1793)
Sec. 1, Lot 503, Grid KL–34/35

John Green's monument proudly boasts that Green was born and died at his family home, Liberty Hall, in Culpepper County, Virginia, and that he commanded one of the first companies of minutemen of that county. He rose to the rank of colonel of the Tenth Virginia Volunteers, and was a founding member of the Society of the Cincinnati. His tombstone also indicates that he was presented a sword by the Continental Congress for meritorious service. He originally was interred at Liberty Hall, and was reinterred at Arlington on April 23, 1931. John Green has been deceased longer than any other person buried at Arlington National Cemetery. His wife, **Susannah Blackwell Green**, is buried with him.

John Green is one of 11 Revolutionary War veterans buried at Arlington.

James House
(1761–1834)
Sec. 1, Lot 297-A, Grid MN–33/34

James House enlisted in the Continental Army on March 14, 1777, at the age of 15, and served as a matross (artillery gunner) in Captain Drury Ragsdale's Company of Artillery assigned to the State of Virginia. Originally buried in the Old Presbyterian Cemetery in Georgetown (now a part of Washington, D.C.), General House was reinterred at Arlington on May 12, 1892.

Thomas Meason
(1726–1813)
Sec. 1, Lot 297-B, Grid MN–33/34

General Thomas Meason was born in Uniontown, Pennsylvania, the birthplace of another great American General, **George C. Marshall.** He was a resident of Georgetown, in the District of Columbia, when he died on March 10, 1813. He was buried in the Old Presbyterian Cemetery before he was reinterred at Arlington on May 12, 1892. Thomas Meason was born before any other person buried in Arlington National Cemetery, making him the oldest person buried here.

William Russell
(1735–1793)
Sec. 1, Lot 314-A, Grid MN–34/35

Commissioned a colonel on December 19, 1776, William Russell became a brigadier general of the Thirteenth, Tenth, Fifth, and Eleventh Virginia Regiments. During the winter of 1777–78, he was stationed at Valley Forge. Following the fall of Charleston, South Carolina, he was taken prisoner and held from January 1, 1783, until May of that year. Following the Revolutionary War, he resided in Fincastle County, Virginia, and served in the Virginia State Senate. He died while visiting his son in Front Royal, Virginia, and was buried in a homemade walnut coffin on their family plot. He was reinterred at Arlington on July 7, 1943.

Caleb Swan

(Died November 29, 1809)
Sec. 1, Lot 301-C, Grid MN–33/34

Originally from Massachusetts, Caleb Swan served as an ensign in the Third and Eighth Massachusetts Regiments. He rose to the rank of paymaster general of the Army, and was given a land grant for his service. Originally buried in the Old Presbyterian Cemetery in Georgetown in the District of Columbia, Swan was reinterred at Arlington on May 12, 1892.

Frank Reynolds

Television Newscaster
(November 29, 1923–July 20, 1983)
Sec. 7A, Lot 180, Grid TU–23/24

Few of the millions of Americans who watched his national news broadcasts knew much about Frank Reynolds. Of course he was seen as a competent, compassionate journalist, but few people knew of his many awards for excellence in broadcast journalism, his devotion to his family, and his distinguished military record.

Frank Reynolds was born in East Chicago, Indiana, and attended Wabash College in downstate Crawfordsville, dropping out after his first year of studies to enlist in the United States Army during World War II. In that war, he rose to the rank of staff sergeant and was wounded, for which he was awarded a Purple Heart.

Reynolds' career in broadcast journalism began in 1947 when he joined station WJOB in Hammond, Indiana. Later, he worked for the CBS affiliate in Chicago (WBBM), and then for the ABC affiliate (WBKB, now WLS). After 14 years in Chicago, Reynolds was promoted in 1965 to the network news division of ABC, and served as that network's White House correspondent. He later coanchored the national evening news with Howard

K. Smith, but lost the anchor job when Harry Reasoner joined the ABC news team. In 1978, Reynolds returned to the anchor's desk as chief anchor on the "World News Tonight" program, and held that post until his death in 1983.

Reynolds was an innovative broadcast journalist. He anchored the forerunner to ABC's "Nightline" program, which evolved from special late night coverage of the crisis in Iran in 1979 when 53 Americans were held hostage. From 1965 until his death, he covered each of the national political conventions and each of the manned space flights for ABC television. In 1979, he was awarded the coveted George Foster Peabody Award for excellence in broadcast journalism, and in 1980, Reynolds was again honored by his peers with an Emmy award for his coverage of that year's national election.

Illness forced Reynolds from his anchor desk in April 1983. He never recovered from his illness, dying in his suburban Washington, D.C., home on July 20.

Reynolds was eulogized by his friend, President Ronald Reagan, as a "very decent man, not only in the way he lived, but in the way he did his job." A measure of the worldwide impact of Frank Reynolds' death was evident in a letter sent from the Vatican which was read at his funeral. Sentiments from that letter are immortalized on his tombstone. The inscription reads:

A man who cared

Beloved Husband and Father

Dedicated Journalist

Edmund Rice
Medal of Honor Winner, Weapons Inventor
(1842–July 20, 1906)
Sec. 3, Lot 1875, Grid T–16

Many tombstones in Arlington attempt to tell the story of the persons whose graves they mark, but no stone does it better than that marking the grave of Edmund Rice. Cited for "conspicuous bravery on the third day of the battle of Gettysburg," Rice was granted our nation's highest award, the Congressional Medal of Honor. A simple granite rock proudly displays, in beautiful detail, a bronze replica of that medal, which once graced the uniform of this Civil War hero.

Rice enlisted in the Union Army in his hometown of Cambridge, Massachusetts, during the early days of the Civil War. In July 1861, he was appointed captain of the Nineteenth Massachusetts Infantry. It was at Gettysburg in 1863 that he displayed his uncommon courage. Under attack by General George Edward Pickett's troops, Rice led his division in a countercharge against overwhelming odds. When the battle dust settled, Rice found himself severely wounded behind enemy lines, but his counterattack had been successful.

Rice mustered out of the Army as a colonel on June 30, 1865. Unhappy with civilian life, he reenlisted the following year, and remained a soldier until 1903, when he retired with the rank of brigadier general. Rice is well known for his invention of several military weapons, including the trowel bayonet, stacking swivel, and the knife-intrenching bayonet.

His simple but descriptive grave is located among several unusual tombstones in the area at the end of Miles Drive in the southwestern section of Arlington.

An unsculpted granite boulder marks the grave of Edmund Rice. A reproduction of his Medal of Honor proudly recounts his bravery at the battle of Gettysburg.

Hyman G. Rickover
Admiral, "Father of the Nuclear Navy"
(January 27, 1900–July 8, 1986)
Sec. 5, Lot 7000, Grid VW–36

Hyman Rickover's naval career spanned more than 60 years, during which time he became one of the U.S. Navy's most important scientists and administrators. Rickover's tenacious and farsighted viewpoints inspired both plebes and presidents. Yet, it was that same tenacity which resulted in his forced retirement at the age of 82.

Born to Jewish parents in the czarist Russian village of Makow, about 50 miles north of Warsaw, Hyman Rickover immigrated to the United

States when he was just 6 years old. Raised in Chicago, Rickover earned an appointment to the U.S. Naval Academy in 1918, graduating in 1922, 106th in a class of 539. His first assignment was aboard the battleship *Nevada* where he served for five years. That tour of duty was followed by postgraduate study at Annapolis and at Columbia University in New York City.

The only sea command of Rickover's long career came in 1937 when he was named captain of a minesweeper *Finch,* which was stationed in China. During World War II, Captain Rickover directed the electrical section of the Navy's Bureau of Ships. Although he spent most of the war ashore, he did manage a ship repair base on Okinawa toward the end of the war. Perhaps the most important assignment in Rickover's career came in 1946 when he was named to a special team of scientists to study the feasibility of a nuclear propulsion system for the Navy. This work resulted in the development of the world's first nuclear-powered submarine, *Nautilus,* which was launched in 1954.

The success of the *Nautilus* revolutionized the U.S. military's sea power. With a nuclear propulsion system, a vessel could travel tens of thousands of miles without the necessity of refueling. In 1957, the *Nautilus* cruised for 62,500 miles on its first load of nuclear fuel. In 1958, on a voyage from Hawaii to Great Britain, it became the first submarine to pass under the North Pole's icecap.

While Hyman Rickover was pivotal in bringing nuclear power to the Navy's submarine and surface fleet, his achievements did not result in his advancement in rank. It was not until 1958—and only after a congressional investigation—that Rickover was promoted to flag officer rank as a vice admiral. He was named a full admiral in 1973 at the age of 73. But despite his age Rickover had no intention of retiring. He was able to remain on active duty well beyond the normal retirement age, in part because of the considerable influence he wielded on Capitol Hill. However, by 1982, his influence had diminished and—now 82 years old—Rickover was forced into retirement.

Admiral Rickover considered himself a maverick and nearly everyone he worked with agreed. During one interview in 1984, Rickover recounted that he never kept a copy of the Navy regulations in his office. "One time some guy brought it in," Rickover confessed, "and I told him to get the hell out and burn it." A brilliant scientist, Rickover was unrelenting in his demands upon his subordinates. Yet, he was able to instill in those who worked with him a desire for excellence. President Jimmy Carter recalled that next to his parents Admiral Rickover had influenced his life more than anyone else.

The great esteem in which Admiral Rickover was held was evidenced during his retirement dinner in 1982 when three former presidents—Jimmy Carter, Gerald Ford, and Richard Nixon—appeared at the dinner to show their respect for the admiral. In July 1985, Hyman Rickover suffered a stroke and remained in ill health until his death on July 8, 1986, at his home in Arlington, Virginia. He was buried with simple military honors at Arlington National Cemetery. A memorial service was later held at Washington's National Cathedral.

Mary Roberts Rinehart
Mystery Writer, Playwright, War Correspondent
(August 12, 1876–September 22, 1958)
Sec. 3, Lot 4269, Grid X–17/18

Mary Roberts Rinehart had studied nursing, married a doctor, and looked forward to spending her life caring for the sick when in 1906 she wrote a few stories to earn some money. The result: she quickly became America's premier mystery writer. And when World War I broke out in Europe, she landed a position as this country's first female war correspondent.

Mary Roberts, born in Pittsburgh in 1876, was the recipient of a typical Victorian upbringing. A nursing student, she married doctor **Stanley Marshall Rinehart,** just four days after her graduation from nursing school. It seemed that she would spend her life attending her husband's patients, but in actuality, he retired from his medical practice to attend to her writing career.

A family financial squeeze in 1906 prompted Rinehart to try her hand at writing, an almost unheard of action for a woman. Fortunately, her work proved highly popular. Her first story, "The Man in Lower Ten," was serialized by The Saturday Evening Post in 1907. It was her first novel, however, that brought her national attention. "The Circular Staircase," published in 1908, was heralded as a breakthrough in crime fiction for its innovative melding of humor and horror.

It was also The Saturday Evening Post that approached Rinehart about being their correspondent to cover the war in Europe. After what Rinehart herself called "grave consultations" with her husband, she finally agreed to undertake the assignment. Undaunted at being the only woman correspondent, she fearlessly covered the action, imbuing her war stories with the same flare and excitement that had been the hallmarks of her novels.

Following the war, Mary Rinehart returned to the United States, and successfully tried her hand as a playwright. Collaborating with Avery Hopwood, she produced "The Bat," a stage hit in 1920. By 1921, the Rineharts had moved to Washington, D.C., and her husband forsook his medical career to manage his wife's thriving business affairs. Roughly ten years later, in 1932, Dr. Rinehart died, and Mary moved to New York where she continued to bask in the limelight as America's best mystery writer, still writing baffling whodunits into her 70s.

Mary Roberts Rinehart died in 1958 at the age of 82 in New York City. She is buried in Arlington with her husband, who had attained the rank of major in the United States Army.

THE RODGERS FAMILY
A Naval Dynasty
Sec. 1, Lot 130, Grid 0–32/33

S ince the United States Navy was founded in 1798, the Rodgers family has produced outstanding naval officers. The first was Commodore John Rodgers (1773–1838) who was the highest ranking naval officer during the War of 1812. Although he is not buried at Arlington, two of his grandsons and his great-grandson are buried together in Section 1 of the cemetery: **John Augustus Rodgers, Thomas Slidell Rodgers,** and **John Rodgers.**

John Augustus Rodgers
(July 26, 1848–March 2, 1933)

John Augustus Rodgers was born in Havre-de-Grace, Maryland, the brother of Rear Admiral Frederick Rodgers. He was appointed to the Naval Academy, class of 1868, and saw action during the Civil War on the ironclad *Marion* in its pursuit of the Confederate steamers *Florida* and *Tallahassee* in the summer of 1864. From 1868 until 1880, Rodgers served in the Pacific Squadron, then was stationed at the Washington Navy Yard. During the Spanish-American War, he took part in the famous battle against the Spanish Admiral Cervera at Santiago, Cuba, serving under **William T. Sampson** and **Winfield Scott Schley.** For "eminent and conspicuous conduct" in that battle, he was advanced five numbers in rank. Upon his retirement on July 26, 1910, he had attained the rank of rear admiral. John Augustus Rodgers returned to his home in Havre-de-Grace where he died on March 2, 1933, at the age of 84.

Thomas Slidell Rodgers
(August 18, 1858–February 28, 1931)

Born in Morristown, New Jersey, Thomas Slidell Rodgers graduated from Annapolis in 1878. During the Spanish-American War he served on the *Bennington* and *Monterey,* and was commissioned executive officer on board the new *Maine* from 1902 until 1905. Rodgers was named chief of Naval intelligence between 1912 and 1913, and director of the Naval War College from 1915 through 1916. On June 13, 1916, he was promoted to rear admiral, and given command of Division Seven Battleship Force, Atlantic Fleet. Thomas Slidell Rodgers retired from active duty on July 19, 1916, and died 15 years later, on February 28, 1931.

John Rodgers
(January 15, 1881–August 27, 1926)

John Rodgers, the son of **John Augustus Rodgers** and nephew of **Thomas Slidell Rodgers,** is the youngest of the Rodgers family buried at Arlington. Also counted among his ancestors is Commodore Matthew C. Perry, naval hero of the War of 1812.

John Rodgers, born in Washington, D.C., attended and graduated from the U.S. Naval Academy in 1903. As a lieutenant, he served aboard the *Nebraska* in 1908, and turned his dreams from ships to planes in 1911 when he was assigned to the flying school operated by the Wright brothers. Rodgers became only the second Naval officer in history to qualify as a pilot, and helped to organize the Naval Air Station at San Diego. During the early days of World War I, Rodgers commanded the Submarine Division One of the Atlantic Fleet, and earned a Distinguished Service Medal for dangerous minesweeping activities in the Atlantic. Later named commanding officer of the submarine base at New London, Connecticut, Rodgers was promoted to commander and placed in charge of the Naval Air Station at Pearl Harbor, Hawaii.

Perhaps Rodgers' greatest adventure came when he was chosen to command one of two experimental Navy seaplanes to fly nonstop from San Francisco to Hawaii. He took off in the PN-9 biplane from California on August 31, 1925, with a crew of four. The companion plane ditched about 300 miles after takeoff, but Rodgers was determined that his plane would continue the mission alone. Flying all night, his craft ran out of fuel just 400 miles short of Hawaii, and Rodgers was forced to ditch in the Pacific. For nine days, he and his crew drifted on the open sea, uncertain of their fate. Rodgers fashioned a makeshift sail from the canvas of the wing and was able to sail toward Hawaii. Fatigued and sunburned, he and his crew were finally picked up by a submarine just 15 miles off shore. Although he did not complete the flight, he still set the distance record for seaplane navigation.

Rodgers later served as chief of the Bureau of Aeronautics, then commanded an experimental seaplane squadron. On August 27, 1926, he was on board an inspection flight from Washington, D.C. to Philadelphia when his plane went down in the shallow waters of the Delaware River, the impact of the crash pinning Rodgers in the cockpit. He suffered severe injuries and died of his wounds.

William Starke Rosecrans
Civil War General, Congressman
(September 6, 1819–March 11, 1898)
Sec. 3, Lot 1862, Grid T–16/17

If there had not been a sinister interception of a telegram to President Lincoln from General William Starke Rosecrans, there is little doubt that Rosecrans would have been the 17th president of the United States.

During the 1864 presidential campaign, many Republicans were encouraging Rosecrans to oppose Lincoln for their party's nomination for president. With the Union far from victory over the Confederacy, members of the Republican Party felt that perhaps a new candidate was needed to head their ticket. Rosecrans chose not to oppose the president and Lincoln, seeking to gain support both within the ranks of his party and among the general public, decided to ask Rosecrans to be his running mate.

On the president's behalf, James Garfield wired the request to General Rosecrans, who was with his troops in the field, and Rosecrans responded favorably. However, control of the telegraph lines in wartime fell under the jurisdiction of the secretary of war, Edwin M. Stanton—a man considered by many to be the second most important and clearly the most ambitious person in Washington. Stanton did not want Rosecrans on the ticket, and so he did not convey the general's response to Lincoln. Failing to receive that reply, the president assumed that Rosecrans did not want the position, offering it instead to Andrew Johnson. The rest is history. When Lincoln died in April 1865, Vice President Johnson assumed the presidency. Had it not been for Edwin Stanton's interception of Rosecrans' acceptance of Lincoln's offer, Rosecrans would have become the vice president and our nation's 17th president.

William Starke Rosecrans, a native of Kingston Township, Ohio, graduated from West Point in 1841, ranked fifth in his class despite having received only sporadic education prior to his entry into the military academy. During the Civil War, he showed great promise as an officer, gaining promotion to brigadier general in May 1861.

During 1862, he served under General Ulysses S. Grant, but failed to carry out Grant's plan to trap retreating Confederate soldiers at Iuka, Mississippi. This failure resulted in a rift between Grant and Rosecrans that lasted the remainder of their lives. Grant later fired Rosecrans when he retreated at Chickamauga and suffered numerous casualties. Rosecrans resigned from the army in 1867 to serve as minister to Mexico, a position he lost when Grant became president.

Turning his attention to mining and railroad interests in California, he served in Congress from 1881 until 1885, becoming chairman of the House Committee on Military Affairs. In that position, he was one of the few people who opposed restoring Grant to the rank of general after he had suffered severe financial losses, and even after it was disclosed that Grant was dying of cancer. William Starke Rosecrans died in Los Angeles in 1898, and was buried in Section 3 of Arlington National Cemetery.

William Thomas Sampson
Naval Hero
(February 9, 1840–May 6, 1902)
Sec. 21, Lot S-9, Grid MN–20/21

William T. Sampson produced one of the greatest naval victories in American history, or did he? When American naval forces defeated the Spanish fleet under the command of Pascual Cervera y Topeta at Santiago, Cuba, during the Spanish-American War, it sounded a death knell for Spain's war effort. Sampson was commander of those forces, but during the battle, he was away from the fighting, conferring with the commander of U.S. land forces. By the time he returned to the scene, Cervera's fleet had been completely disarmed by the American naval vessels under the immediate command of **Winfield Scott Schley.** A national controversy arose as to whether Schley, who was in command during the battle, or Sampson, who had outlined the general battle plans, should be credited with the victory. That question threw the United States Navy, the American press, and the American people into an often-heated debate.

The press appeared to take the side of Schley, but the special Navy Inquiry Board headed by the revered naval hero, Admiral George Dewey, found that Sampson had acted properly and should, therefore, as commander in chief of the forces, be credited with the victory. Even Schley acknowledged that as commanding officer Sampson was entitled to the victory. That did not end the controversy, however. As a result, the Navy promoted both Sampson and Schley to the rank of rear admiral in 1899.

Sampson, a native of Palmyra, New York, entered the Naval Academy in 1857. Ranked first in his class, he graduated in 1861. During the Civil War, he served in and around the Washington, D.C. area, seeing action aboard the *Potomac* in the Gulf of Mexico. In 1862, he served as an instructor at the Naval Academy, which had been temporarily moved to Newport, Rhode Island. In 1864, he was executive officer aboard the new ironclad, *Patapsco,* as part of the South Atlantic Blockading Squadron when it was sunk by a Confederate torpedo.

Following the war, Sampson held various posts on land and at sea. He headed the Department of Physics and Chemistry at the Naval Academy, served aboard frigates, and was superintendent of the Naval Observatory in Washington, D.C. Later, while assigned to the torpedo station at Newport, Sampson urged the creation of a Naval War College, returning to the Naval Academy to serve as superintendent. He also was chief of the Bureau of

Ordnance from 1893 until 1897. In 1897, he was given command of the new battleship, *Iowa,* and was promoted to commander in chief of the North Atlantic Squadron.

When the Spanish-American War began in April 1898, Sampson moved his squadron toward a blockade of Cuba. Although **Winfield Scott Schley,** who headed the Flying Squadron at that time, technically outranked Sampson, he was placed under Sampson's command. Sampson ordered Schley into a blockade position of Santiago Harbor, hoping to keep the Spanish Admiral Cervera from entering the harbor while Sampson returned to Key West, Florida, to convoy Army troops. Schley did not move directly to the blockade position, allowing Cervera to sail his fleet into the safety of the harbor.

Sampson joined Schley on June 1, and as commander, Sampson established the blockade—which included searchlights trained on the narrow harbor entrance at night—to keep Cervera from escaping. Sampson also launched reconnaissance operations to obtain more information regarding Cervera's intentions. On July 3, Sampson was aboard the *New York* seven miles east of the harbor to meet with General William Rufus Shafter to coordinate land forces. It was at this moment that Cervera chose to attempt his escape from the harbor. He was met by the guns of the American fleet under the direct command of Schley aboard the *Brooklyn.* In less than four hours, the entire Spanish fleet was sunk or run ashore while the Americans suffered only minimal casualties. Sampson did not arrive on the scene until near the end of the battle.

Following the war, Sampson's health began to decline, though he did retain command of the North Atlantic fleet for another year. In 1899, he was named commandant of the Boston Navy Yard, but retired soon thereafter. He died in Washington, D.C. on May 6, 1902.

Winfield Scott Schley
Naval Hero
(October 9, 1839–October 2, 1909)
Sec. 2, Lot 1207, Grid TU–31/32

Winfield Scott Schley took part in some of the greatest American naval exploits of the 19th century. Yet his greatest battle took place not on the high seas, but in the arena of public opinion. That public battle resulted from the overwhelming defeat of the Spanish fleet at Santiago Harbor, Cuba, during the Spanish-American War.

Schley was commander of the Flying Squadron in 1898 when he was ordered to join the naval forces under the command of **William T. Sampson,** an officer technically ranked below Schley. Sampson, who was searching for the Spanish fleet under Admiral Pascual Cervera y Topeta, had ordered Schley to commence a blockade of Santiago Harbor while Sampson convoyed Army troops from Key West, Florida. Slow to respond, Schley's squadron allowed Cervera's forces to gain the security of the harbor before Schley established the blockade. On June 1, Sampson joined Schley on the scene and kept the Spanish vessels trapped within the harbor for over a month. Under Sampson's direction, searchlights were fixed on the narrow harbor entrance and reconnaissance operations were undertaken.

Finally, on July 3, Cervera made his move. Sampson, however, was on board the *New York* at that moment, seven miles east of the harbor entrance, meeting with General William Rufus Shafter to coordinate the land force operations. The American naval vessels were under the direct command of Schley, who greeted Cervera with a barrage of cannon fire. Within four hours, the entire Spanish fleet had been sunk or run aground. Sampson arrived on the scene just as the battle ended. News of the American victory erupted on the front pages of every newspaper in the U.S., igniting a heated debate over who deserved the credit for the spectacular American victory. Was it Schley, who was in command during the battle? Or Sampson, who had outlined the general battle plans?

The controversy grew to such a fever pitch that a special Naval Inquiry Board was impaneled with the venerable Admiral George Dewey as its chair. Although the press appeared to favor Schley, the Board ruled that Sampson was proper in his command, and, as such, should be given credit for the military operation. Even Schley himself acknowledged Sampson's right to claim the victory, but the controversy was slow to die. Finally, the Navy resolved the debate by promoting both men to the rank of rear admiral in 1899.

Long before the Spanish-American War erupted in 1898, Schley's career had been filled with adventure. A namesake of the famous Mexican War general, Winfield Scott, Schley was born in Frederick County, Maryland, and graduated from the U.S. Naval Academy with the class of 1860. He served along the Atlantic seaboard during the Civil War and was given his first command when he sailed the captured Confederate vessel, *General Parkhill,* to the Admiralty Court in Philadelphia.

Following the Civil War, he served as a professor of modern languages at the Naval Academy from 1867 through 1869. Fifteen years later, Schley gained national attention when he undertook the hazardous command of the

Thetis on a daring rescue mission to the Arctic. In 1881, Army Lieutenant **Adolphus Washington Greely** had begun an expedition to the north of Greenland with a crew of 24. By 1883, there had been no communication from them, so Schley sailed into the treacherous frozen seas of the North Atlantic. There, on June 23, 1884, at Cape Sabine in northern Greenland, Schley found Greely and six other survivors near death, rescuing them and bringing them safely back to America. Schley returned to the United States a hero, earned promotion to commander, and was named chief of Equipment and Recruiting.

In 1891, Schley was involved in another incident that became the focus of international attention. A liberty party from his ship, *Baltimore,* which was docked in Valparaiso, Chile, was attacked by a mob; two of his sailors were killed. This ignited an international incident between the United States and Chile.

Following the Spanish-American War, Schley was named commander in chief of the South Atlantic Station where he remained until reaching the mandatory retirement age of 62 on October 9, 1901. After his retirement, Schley traveled widely, enjoying fame as a popular hero. Just seven days before his 70th birthday, Schley died in 1909.

Thomas E. Selfridge
First Military Aviation Fatality
(February 8,1882–September 17, 1908)
Sec. 3, Lot 2158, Grid QR–13/14

Just five years after the Wright brothers' first successful flight at Kitty Hawk, the United States Army invited them to Fort Myer, Virginia, to demonstrate their new "flying device" for possible military applications. The U.S. Army was interested in a craft that could carry two people a distance of 125 miles at a speed of 40 miles per hour, and the Wrights were confident that their airplane could meet the specifications.

Daily test flights began on September 3, 1908, from the Fort Myer parade ground immediately adjacent to Arlington National Cemetery. The spectacle of men flying in heavier-than-air machines attracted crowds of spectators from nearby Washington, D.C., so the Army planned a special Labor Day program of aerial displays. Among those attending the program were Secretary of War **William Howard Taft** and inventor Alexander Graham Bell.

On September 17, following two weeks of successful flight demonstrations, Orville Wright suggested that an Army observer be allowed to accompany him on one of the flights. Quick to volunteer for the duty was 26-year-old Army Lieutenant Thomas Selfridge. Permission granted, Selfridge was strapped into the open seat next to Wright and they began their ascent. For three minutes, Selfridge enjoyed a flawless flight. Then suddenly, while soaring at an altitude of 110 feet, the plane began to shake violently, causing Wright to lose control of the aircraft. The crowd of 2,500 spectators watched in horror as the propeller broke from the plane. Scrambling to regain some maneuverability as they fell toward the earth, Wright turned off the engine as a last hope to glide the plane toward a controlled landing. Within a minute, however, the plane crashed out of control onto the parade ground severely injuring Wright, and requiring the immediate evacuation of Selfridge to Walter Reed Hospital. He was pronounced dead three hours later.

Thomas Selfridge—the nephew and namesake of Rear Admiral Thomas O. Selfridge—was born in San Francisco in 1882. Young Selfridge attended the United States Military Academy at West Point, graduating with the class of 1903. It was soon clear to Army officials that Selfridge displayed a great interest in flying, which prompted one Army official to call Selfridge the "most enthusiastic aeronautical expert" in the Army. Selfridge worked with several well-known aviators and inventors, including balloonist **Thomas Scott Baldwin** of Quincy, Illinois, and Alexander Graham Bell. Selfridge worked with Bell on the June Bug Project, which was the first attempt by the U.S. Army to put a man aloft by use of a kite.

Lieutenant Selfridge was buried with military honors in Section 3 of Arlington National Cemetery, just a few hundred yards from the site of the airplane crash that cost him his life, and cost the U.S. military its first aviation fatality. Since Selfridge's death, other pioneers of flight have been interred in Section 3 at Arlington. Buried near his grave are two of the three Apollo One astronauts—**Virgil Grissom** and **Roger Chaffee**—who were killed on January 27, 1967, while performing a simulated launch for their space flight. Another pilot, **Francis Gary Powers,** also is buried in Section 3. He was the American reconnaissance airman shot down over the Soviet Union in 1960, and later convicted as an American spy.

In these never-before-published photographs, Lt. Thomas E. Selfridge, top left, joins aviation pioneer Orville Wright as they prepare for take-off from the parade grounds of Ft. Myer adjacent to Arlington National Cemetery. Just minutes later, Selfridge is being carried from the wreckage of the plane, which fell out of control from a height of more than 100 feet, seriously injuring Wright and killing Selfridge.

Philip Henry Sheridan

Civil War General, General in Chief of the Army
(March 6, 1831–August 5, 1888)
Sec. 2, Lot S-1, Grid ST–33/34

A rlington National Cemetery was established in 1864 as a result of the Civil War. Many of those buried here are fallen heroes of that war, including generals from both the North and South. Prominent among these historic graves is that of Philip Henry Sheridan, generally considered to be the third most important Union general, ranking behind only Ulysses S. Grant and William Tecumseh Sherman.

The son of Irish immigrants and one of six children, Sheridan was born in Albany, New York. He attended the U.S. Military Academy, but his record there was less than sterling. Only after the original appointee failed to qualify was Sheridan accepted for admission, and then he was suspended for a year after lunging at an upperclassman with a bayoneted rifle. He finally graduated with the class of 1853, and spent his early years on the Western frontier.

When the Civil War began, Sheridan was a relatively unknown 30-year-old lieutenant of Infantry serving in Oregon. His involvement in the war as a troop commander did not commence until April 1862 when he was named quartermaster of the staff of Henry Wager Halleck, supreme commander of the Western Theatre. With Halleck, Sheridan took part in the campaign against Corinth, Mississippi, was soon promoted to colonel, and given command of a cavalry brigade that he led on a successful raid against Booneville, Mississippi. Further successes at Perryville, Kentucky, and Stone's River, Tennessee, earned him a rapid and steady rise in rank and in command. By September 1863, "Little Phil," a nickname that fit his 5' 5" frame, had attracted the attention of General **William Starke Rosecrans,** and he was promoted to brigadier general. Although suffering defeat with Rosecrans at Chickamauga, Sheridan later rallied his forces to record a major victory at Missionary Ridge. Impressed with Sheridan's performance, General Grant promoted him to commander of the Cavalry of the Army of the Potomac.

In 1864, Sheridan led a raid on Richmond, Virginia, which resulted in the death of General J.E.B. Stuart, one of the South's great cavalry leaders. Sheridan's best-known victory occurred shortly after he was given command of the Army of the Shenandoah in August 1864. It occurred at Cedar Creek, Virginia, and has been immortalized in the poem, "Sheridan's Ride," by Thomas Buchanan Read. Sheridan's army was camped at Cedar Creek, but the general was about

15 miles north in Winchester on his way back from Washington, D.C. Awakened before dawn to the sounds of distant gunfire, Sheridan rode quickly out of Winchester, and was greeted by the sight of his own army fleeing the battle site. Though a short man, Sheridan cut a very authoritarian figure when mounted on his stallion. He commanded his troops to regroup and counterattack. They obeyed his orders, eventually routing the Confederate troops from the Shenandoah Valley. For this Sheridan was promoted to major general and received the express gratitude of the U.S. Congress.

For Sheridan, the rest of the war must have seemed like a mopping up exercise. He kept constant pressure on General Robert E. Lee's forces in Virginia, and on April 1, 1865, won a key victory at Five Forks, blocking Lee's retreat to the South. On April 9, 1865, Sheridan himself was present to witness Lee's surrender at Appomattox Court House.

After the Civil War, Sheridan was given command of the Division of the Gulf, which pressured the army of Napoleon III to end its occupation of Mexico, and which hastened the fall of his puppet emperor, Maximilian, in 1867. President Andrew Johnson named Sheridan military commander of Louisiana and Texas during Reconstruction, but the president soon removed him because of Sheridan's harsh administration. He was returned to the Western frontier, promoted to lieutenant general in 1869, and given command of the Division of the Missouri.

In 1884, after the death of William Tecumseh Sherman, Sheridan was named general in chief of the Army, the highest ranking position in the American Armed Forces. Then in 1888, Sheridan was promoted to full general. He never retired from the Army, dying in 1888 while still on active duty. He finished his autobiography, the two-volume *Personal Memoirs of P.H. Sheridan,* just before he died.

Philip Henry Sheridan is buried at Arlington just south and east of Arlington House, but his tomb is not easily recognized because it is surrounded by several trees and cannot be read from the walkway above the grave. His marker bears a large bas-relief of the General. Only the word "Sheridan" is written on the stone. Sheridan's wife and several of his children are buried near him.

THE SHUTTLE *CHALLENGER* ASTRONAUTS

Across the country the scenes were reminiscent of the 1960s—schoolchildren huddled around television sets, watching a rocket carry Americans into space. But it was not the 1960s, it was the 1980s when reusable manned orbiters were launched into space and returned to earth with regularity. For most Americans, space flight had become commonplace. To the millions of schoolchildren watching this launch, however, there was nothing commonplace about it. This mission had generated a great deal of publicity, because included among its crew was America's first "ordinary citizen in space," schoolteacher Christa McAuliffe. In the months preceding the launch, Christa McAuliffe had rekindled an interest in space exploration, not only among the nation's schoolchildren, but among all its citizens. She personified the belief that Americans could accomplish anything if they just put their minds to it. So it was McAuliffe's presence among the seven crew members of the space shuttle *Challenger* that brought millions of Americans to their television screens on January 28, 1986.

At 11:38 a.m. EST, the *Challenger* lifted off from Pad 39-B of the Kennedy Space Center at Cape Canaveral, Florida. Slowly but steadily the shuttle cleared the tower, heading for its mission among the stars. Suddenly, 73 seconds and nine miles into the flight, as millions of American schoolchildren watched in horror, the orbiter exploded into a vast, billowing white cloud, pierced by red and orange flames. As thousands of pieces of debris fell into the Atlantic Ocean, two booster rockets trailed away from the explosion sight, leaving many spectators believing that the shuttle had been able to clear the explosion, and was heading for the emergency landing strip nearby. But that soon proved not to be the case. The

A memorial to the seven shuttle *Challenger* astronauts marks the common grave that contains the remains of the astronauts that were recovered but could not be identified. Dedicated March 21, 1987, the memorial is located in Section 46 next to the grave of shuttle Commander Dick Scobee. Grid O-23/24.

valiant crew of the space shuttle *Challenger* lost their lives as a result of that explosion. Along with Christa McAuliffe, the crew included shuttle commander **Francis R. (Dick) Scobee,** pilot **Michael J. Smith,** mission specialists Ellison S. Onizuka, Judith A. Resnik, and Ronald E. McNair, and payload specialist Gregory B. Jarvis.

It was several agonizing weeks after the explosion before the remains of the shuttle crew were finally located and identified. On April 29, 1986, those remains were released to the families of the astronauts for private burial services. Unfortunately, not all of the recovered remains could be positively identified. Therefore, in a private ceremony on May 20, 1986, those unidentified remains were placed in a single, common grave at Arlington, dedicated to the memory of all seven shuttle astronauts. Two crew members whose remains were identified—mission commander Dick Scobee and shuttle pilot Mike Smith—were buried at Arlington in May 1986.

Francis R. (Dick) Scobee
(May 19, 1939–January 28, 1986)
Sec. 46, Lot 1129-4, Grid O–23/24

Francis Richard Scobee was born in the little Washington town of Cle Elum (a Native American name meaning "swift water"). The son of a railroad engineer, he graduated from nearby Auburn High School in 1957. Following graduation, Scobee went to work for the giant aircraft manufacturer, Boeing, which had been the principal employer in the area since World War II. But Scobee left Boeing in October of that year, enlisting in the United States Air Force.

Stationed at Kelly Air Force Base in San Antonio, Texas, Scobee was trained as an aircraft mechanic. It was while he was in San Antonio that he met June Kent whom he married the following year; he was 20, she was 16. Dick Scobee juggled his Air Force duties to find the time to join his wife as a night student at nearby San Antonio College.

By 1963, Dick had earned two years credit toward his degree when he first learned of the Air Force's Airman's Education and Commissioning Program, aimed at making officers out of enlisted men. He was quickly accepted, and enrolled at the University of Arizona where he received a degree in aerospace engineering in 1965. In September of that year, he was commissioned a lieutenant and entered pilot training school at Moody Air Force Base in Georgia.

During the mid-1960s American military involvement in Southeast Asia escalated sharply, increasing the need for trained pilots. Scobee left for Vietnam in November 1967, assigned to the 535th Tactical Airlift Squadron. During his tour of duty in Vietnam, Scobee earned many military decorations, including the Distinguished Service Cross and the Air Medal.

In July 1971, Dick Scobee made his first contact with America's space program when he entered the Aerospace Research Pilot School at Edwards Air Force Base in California. Following 700 hours of study on the ground and 150 hours in the air, Captain Scobee was awarded his test pilot's wings in June 1972. It only seemed natural to Scobee that he would then apply for astronaut training, which he did in 1977. The following year, when NASA was selecting a new group of astronauts to fly the space shuttles, Dick Scobee was among them. After 22 years he retired as a major from the Air Force, moving his family to Houston, to concentrate on his NASA duties. While there, June Scobee received her PhD from Texas A & M University, and was named a visiting assistant professor at the University of Houston.

In April 1984, Dick Scobee made his first journey into space as second in command of one of NASA's most successful flights. As pilot of the *Challenger*, he maneuvered the spacecraft so that his fellow crew members could retrieve the broken Solar Max satellite. After it was repaired on board the shuttle, the satellite was returned to its correct orbit. Scobee and the other members of the crew later appeared at an in-flight press conference sporting T-shirts which read Ace Satellite Repair Co.

Dick Scobee was chosen to command Mission 51-L, the 25th space shuttle flight scheduled for January 20, 1986. The mission assumed celebrity status when it was announced that included among its crew would be schoolteacher Christa McAuliffe. On January 28, 1986, after five delayed launches, the rocket's main engines roared into action at 11:38 a.m. Seventy-three seconds later, nine miles above the Atlantic Ocean, the mission ended in a fiery explosion.

On May 19, 1986, Dick Scobee would have celebrated his 47th birthday. Instead, he was buried at Arlington National Cemetery

Francis "Dick" Scobee was commander of the space shuttle *Challenger.* **He was buried at Arlington on his 47th birthday anniversary.**

during a brief, solemn ceremony. His grave is marked by a regulation headstone, bearing the Air Force's astronauts' insignia. Immediately adjacent to his grave are the graves of three airmen killed in 1980 during an aborted attempt to rescue American hostages held in Iran.

Michael J. Smith

(April 30, 1945–January 28, 1986)
Sec. 7A, Lot 208-1, Grid TU–23/24

Michael J. Smith grew up on a small farm outside Beaufort, a small fishing village on the North Carolina coast. The family farm was located near the Beaufort-Morehead City airport, providing Mike with a vantage point from which to watch the planes taking off and landing. He began taking flying lessons before most people learn to drive. On April 30, 1961, he made his first solo flight; it was his 16th birthday.

Mike Smith graduated from Beaufort High School in 1963, gaining an appointment to the United States Naval Academy at Annapolis. In 1967, he graduated 108th in his academy class of 893 students. Ten days later he married Jane Jarrell, a young girl from Charlotte, North Carolina, whom he had met several years earlier. The next stop for Smith was the U.S. Naval Postgraduate School in Monterey, California. He had been one of 12 students chosen to study aeronautical engineering in a newly formed accelerated program.

Michael Smith was on his first space mission when he died aboard the space shuttle *Challenger*.

Following the completion of his graduate studies in March 1968, Smith began an extended period of flight training followed by a tour of duty aboard the *USS Kitty Hawk* during the Vietnam War. After his arrival in Vietnam in 1972, Smith flew 225 combat missions and was awarded, among other decorations, the Navy Distinguished Flying Cross, the Vietnamese Cross of Gallantry with Silver Star, and 13 Strike Flight Air Medals. In 1973, Smith returned to the United States, entering the U.S. Navy Test Pilot School at Patuxent River, Maryland. Five years later he applied for the position he had always hoped for—astronaut. But he was not accepted. Smith applied again. This time his dream was realized when he was asked to enter the astronaut class of 1980.

Mike Smith acclimated quickly to NASA and the space program. In 1985, his familiarity with the program led to his assignment to assist civilian astronaut Senator Jake Garn during Garn's preparation for a 1985 Shuttle flight. The senator affectionately referred to Smith as "my mother hen." For Mike Smith, his first mission was Flight 51-L aboard the shuttle *Challenger*. Although it had been scheduled to liftoff on January 20, 1986, it was delayed five times before given the go-ahead on January 28.

As pilot of the *Challenger*, Smith and Commander Dick Scobee were busy on the flight deck reviewing checklists and monitoring computers, readying themselves for the mission that would carry the first ordinary citizen into space, schoolteacher Christa McAuliffe. As the *Challenger* left Pad 39-B, the external fuel tank ruptured and highly flammable rocket fuel began leaking. One minute and twelve seconds into the flight that fuel ignited, causing the explosion that destroyed *Challenger* and killed its crew.

Michael J. Smith was granted a posthumous promotion to captain and was buried with full military honors at Arlington National Cemetery on May 3, 1986. The Navy astronaut insignia—depicting Navy pilot wings and a shooting star—adorns his black marble headstone.

Following the explosion of the *Challenger*, President Ronald Reagan immediately appointed a blue-ribbon commission headed by former Attorney General and Secretary of State **William P. Rogers** to investigate the shuttle explosion. On June 9, 1986, the Rogers Commission made their report public. The cause of the *Challenger* accident was determined to be the failure of O-rings on the right-hand booster rocket. A joint in that rocket had failed to contain the pressure of hot gases produced by burning rocket fuel. Flames burned through the booster rocket's wall, causing the booster rocket to tear away from the external fuel tank which ruptured, spilling highly flammable liquid hydrogen and liquid oxygen. When ignited, these liquid fuels caused the massive explosion which destroyed the *Challenger*.

A memorial to the seven shuttle *Challenger* astronauts marks the common grave that contains remains of the astronauts which were recovered but could not be identified. Dedicated March 21, 1987, the memorial is located in Section 46 next to the grave of shuttle Commander Dick Scobee. (Grid O-23/24).

THE SHUTTLE *COLUMBIA* ASTRONAUTS

During Shuttle *Columbia's* launch on January 16, 2003, a piece of foam insulation broke off the orbiter's external fuel tank and struck the leading edge of *Columbia's* left wing. Although there was some concern at NASA about possible damage to the spacecraft, they decided to continue the flight because they believed there was little that could be done at that point.

Following a successful 16-day scientific and research mission in space, the *Columbia* began its return to Earth at about 8:15 a.m. (EST) on February 1 with a scheduled landing at 9:16 a.m. at the Kennedy Space Center in Florida. The descent began 175 miles above the Indian Ocean. By 8:44, the orbiter had reentered the Earth's atmosphere, now 76 miles over the Pacific. At 8:54, as the *Columbia* crossed the coast of northern California, Mission Control received its first abnormal sensor readings, but continued normal communications with the flight crew. Within two minutes, *Columbia* had crossed California, Nevada, Utah, Arizona, and New Mexico.

At 8:58, it crossed into Texas airspace 39 miles above the Earth. At 8:59, NASA received its last verbal communication and telemetry signal. While managers at Mission Control were uncertain about what was happening aboard the *Columbia*, observers on the ground in Texas saw the orbiter disintegrating above them.

A recovery mission began immediately with NASA warning the public to stay away from any debris because of possible contamination. Eventually 42,000 pieces of debris were recovered from more than 2,000 debris fields stretching across eastern Texas, southern Arkansas, and western Louisiana.

Calling the *Columbia* crew "heroes for our time and all times," NASA administrator Sean Casey dedicated the *Columbia* Memorial on Feb. 2, 2004, one year and a day after the disaster that claimed the lives of its seven-member crew. It is near the memorial that honors the crew of the shuttle *Challenger* who died when their orbiter exploded shortly after launch on January 28, 1986. (Grid O-22/23)

The remains of the crew members were found, identified, and returned to their families. *Columbia* carried seven astronauts: Commander Rick D. Husband (U.S.A.F. colonel, also piloted the first space shuttle to dock with the International Space Station in 1999), Pilot William C. McCool (U.S.N. commander and scientist on his second shuttle mission), Payload Commander Michael P. Anderson (U.S.A.F. lieutenant colonel, on his second shuttle flight), Mission Specialist 1 David M. Brown (U.S.N. captain, pilot and doctor on his first shuttle mission), Mission Specialist 2 Kalpana Chawla (a civilian with a Ph.D. in aerospace engineering on her second space shuttle mission), Mission Specialist 4 Laurel Blair Salton Clark (U.S.N. captain and doctor on her first shuttle mission), and Payload Specialist I Ilan Ramon(an Israeli Air Force colonel, Israel's first astronaut on his first space mission). Astronauts Anderson, Brown, and Clark are buried at Arlington Cemetery.

NASA appointed a special panel to investigate the tragedy led by former NATO Supreme Allied Commander Admiral Harold W. Gehman, Jr. The *Columbia* Accident Investigation Board found that "physical and organizational causes played an equal role in the *Columbia* accident—that the NASA organizational culture had as much to do with the accident as the foam that struck the Orbiter on ascent." The Board made 29 recommendations for improving the shuttle and NASA's organizational structure.

NASA returned to space on July 26, 2005, with the launch of shuttle *Discovery.*

Michael P. Anderson
(December 25, 1959–February 1, 2003)
Sec. 46, Lot 1180-1 (Grid O-24)

For Michael Anderson, a career as an astronaut was perfect; it allowed him to pursue simultaneously his two greatest lifelong interests—science and aviation. Born in Plattsburgh, New York, but raised in Cheney, Washington, Anderson was the son of an Air Force veteran. Growing up as America was preparing to land a man on the moon, he knew at an early age that he wanted to travel in space.

Anderson earned a bachelor's degree in physics and astronomy from the University of Washington in 1981 and a master's in physics from Creighton University in 1990. After a stint as an EC 135 pilot flying the Strategic Air Command's airborne command post code-named "Looking Glass," he entered the space program in 1995. He worked in the Astronaut Office, Flight Support Branch until he was chosen as a crew member on shuttle *Endeavor* in 1998.

As a mission specialist, Anderson was on board when *Endeavor* docked with *Mir*, the Russian orbital station. During that mission the *Endeavor* crew delivered 9,000 pounds of scientific equipment, hardware, and water. In 2003, Anderson was payload specialist aboard the shuttle *Columbia,* completing approximately 80 experiments during the 16-day mission. He died when the orbiter broke apart during re-entry, but he ended his life fulfilling his greatest dreams—conducting scientific experiments while traveling in space. He was posthumously awarded the Congressional Space Medal of Honor.

David M. Brown
(April 16, 1956–February 1, 2003)
Sec. 46, Lot 1180-3 (Grid O–24)

Throughout his life, David Brown earned many titles, including gymnast, circus acrobat, doctor, scientist, and pilot, but the title he cherished most was astronaut.

Born in Arlington, Virginia, Brown earned a bachelor's of science degree in 1978 from the College of William and Mary where he was on the gymnastic squad. During college he made good use of his acrobatic talents riding a 7-foot unicycle and being a stilt walker for a local circus. In 1982, he received his medical degree from Eastern Virginia Medical School in Norfolk. He joined the navy after his medical internship and completed his flight surgeon training in 1984.

In 1988, Brown became the first flight surgeon in ten years to qualify for pilot training, graduating first in his class in 1990. After serving aboard the *USS Independence* in Japan, he was selected for astronaut training in 1996. Brown qualified as a mission specialist and was assigned to support payload development for the International Space Station. In September 2000, Brown learned that he had been chosen to fly on his first space flight—STS-107, the shuttle *Columbia's* science and research mission scheduled for launch in July 2001.

Following many delays, the mission finally took off on January 16, 2003. After 16 days and nearly 80 scientific experiments later, the *Columbia* was just 16 minutes from landing when it broke apart over eastern Texas, killing the entire crew. David Brown is buried in the nation's most important military cemetery in the town where he was born. He was posthumously awarded the Congressional Space Medal of Honor.

Laurel Blair Salton Clark

(March 10, 1961–February 1, 2003)

Sec. 46, Lot 1180-2 (Grid O-24)

Laurel Clark was a doctor who could practice medicine anywhere—literally. Nationally board certified, she also qualified as an undersea medical officer, diving medical officer, submarine medical officer, naval flight surgeon, radiation health officer, basic life support instructor, advanced cardiac life support provider, advanced trauma life support provider, and hyperbaric chamber advisor. No matter where she was, she was qualified to practice medicine, even in space.

Born in Ames, Iowa, and raised in Racine, Wisconsin, Clark received both her bachelor's degree in zoology in 1983 and her medical degree in 1987 from the University of Wisconsin-Madison. While in medical school, she trained with the Diving Medicine Department. She also did postgraduate work in pediatrics at the Bethesda Naval Hospital.

After training stints in Connecticut and Florida, Clark was assigned as the Submarine Squadron Fourteen Medical Department Head in Holy Loch, Scotland, where she dove with U.S. Navy divers and performed numerous medical evacuations from submarines. She then underwent aeromedical training in Pensacola, Florida, to become a flight surgeon, and was stationed in Arizona and the Western Pacific. By 1996, she had been selected by NASA to begin astronaut training.

Clark qualified as a mission specialist, and for three years she worked in the Astronaut Office, Payloads/Habitability Branch. In 2000, she was chosen to join the crew of the shuttle *Columbia*, which launched on January 16, 2003. Following a busy 16-day scientific mission, the *Columbia* was heading for a landing when it broke apart during re-entry, killing the seven-member crew. Her remains were recovered and she was buried with full military honors at Arlington. Along with her crewmates, she was posthumously awarded the Congressional Space Medal of Honor.

Daniel Edgar Sickles
General, Congressman, Murderer
(October 20, 1819–May 3, 1914)
Sec. 3, Lot 1906, Grid ST–16

There are few people buried at Arlington National Cemetery whose lives were as colorful and controversial as Daniel Sickles—a career politician, decorated veteran, and murderer.

A native of New York City, Sickles attended New York University, studied law, and was admitted to the bar in 1846. At the age of 28, Sickles was elected to the New York state assembly. The assembly later censured him for bringing a well-known bordello operator onto the floor of the assembly for a tour.

With his Tammany Hall connections, Sickles was named corporation counsel for the city of New York in 1853, at the age of 34. He resigned later that year when President Franklin Pierce named him secretary of the U.S. legation in London.

He returned to the United States in 1855, serving in the New York state senate from 1856 to 1857. On March 4, 1857, he took the oath of office as a Democratic member of the United States Congress. It was during his first tenure as a congressman that Daniel Sickles was tried for the murder of the son of an American hero.

Following his election to Congress, Sickles purchased a home on Lafayette Square across the street from the White House. In 1859, he found his young wife in a compromising situation with Francis Barton Key, son of Francis Scott Key, the author of "The Star-Spangled Banner." Sickles chased young Key from his house onto Lafayette Square, where, in front of dozens of witnesses, he drew a pistol, shot, and killed Barton Key.

Sickles was charged with murder. For his attorney, he hired Edwin M. Stanton (later President Lincoln's secretary of war who appropriated Arlington to be a cemetery in 1864). Stanton knew he faced an up-hill battle after his client reportedly declared, "Of course I killed him. He deserved it."

So Stanton presented a novel defense, arguing that Sickles was temporarily insane when he committed the crime, and asked the court to acquit him by reason of his insanity. The court concurred, and the United States Supreme Court later upheld the acquittal—the first time the defense ever had been used successfully. Sickles returned to Congress, and to his wife.

When the Civil War broke out in 1861, Daniel Sickles raised New York's Excelsior Brigade. He was promoted to brigadier general and given command of the brigade. Sickles led the brigade through several campaigns, culminating at Gettysburg. There, defying direct orders, he led his men on a devastating maneuver that cost him both his command and his right leg. Undaunted, Sickles retrieved his amputated leg, donating it to the Army Medical Museum, where it can be seen today at the Walter Reed Medical Center in Washington.

After the war, Daniel Sickles diverse career continued. In 1865, he undertook a special diplomatic mission to South America, returning to serve as military governor of the Carolinas during Reconstruction. He retired from the Army with the rank of major general in 1869 in order to accept President Ulysses Grant's appointment as minister to Spain, where he served from 1869 to 1873. There he distinguished himself by having a liaison with the former queen of Spain, Isabella.

He served as chair of the New York Civil Service Commission in 1888 and 1889 and as sheriff of New York City in 1890. Sickles returned to Congress in 1893, but was defeated for reelection. In 1897, he was awarded the Congressional Medal of Honor for his service in the Civil War.

After leaving Congress, Daniel Sickles chaired the New York State Monuments Commission. During this time, he used his influence to help create the National Battlefield Park at Gettysburg. However, he was removed from the monuments commission in 1912 for allegedly misusing funds.

By 1914, Daniel Sickles had alienated most of his family and friends and was considered incompetent. His colorful and controversial life ended in his home in New York City on May 3, 1914. He was 94 years old.

Walter Bedell Smith

General, Ambassador, CIA Director
(October 5, 1895–August 9, 1961)
Sec. 7, Lot 8197-A, Grid VW–24

The administrative and diplomatic abilities of Walter Bedell Smith received great recognition both during and after World War II. Despite an investigation regarding his handling of intelligence related to a possible attack on Pearl Harbor, Smith continued to serve in vital U.S. government posts, including positions as ambassador to the Soviet Union, director of the CIA, and undersecretary of state.

Walter Bedell Smith first entered military service in 1913 when he joined the National Guard in his home town of Indianapolis. He had studied at Butler University in Indianapolis, but was forced to withdraw when his father became seriously ill. During World War I, Smith was commissioned a second lieutenant in the Army Reserve. Called to action in France, Smith took part in the battle of the Marne and was later wounded during the battle of Aisne.

In 1920, Smith joined the regular Army and was assigned to the new Bureau of Military Intelligence. Throughout that decade, Smith worked for the Military Bureau of the Budget, and later commanded native troops in the Philippines, earning promotion to captain. During the 1930s, Smith acquired most of his formal military training. He completed the courses of study at the Infantry School at Fort Benning, Georgia, the Command and General Staff School at Fort Leavenworth, Kansas, and the Army War College in Washington, D.C. While at Fort Benning, Smith became acquainted with then-Colonel **George C. Marshall.** This proved to be a lifelong friendship.

When Marshall was named Army chief of staff in 1939, he brought Smith with him to Washington. Smith assumed the duties of secretary to the General Staff, and subsequently served as secretary to the Anglo-American Joint Chiefs of Staff after the United States entered World War II.

Smith's career was threatened briefly in 1941, following the Japanese attack on Pearl Harbor. On Saturday, December 6, 1941, the day before the infamous attack, Smith decided not to deliver a routine intelligence pouch to Chief of Staff General Marshall, who was spending the weekend outside of Washington. He took it upon himself to hold the material until the following Monday. Smith stated that he was led to believe the pouch contained only a partially decoded Japanese cable, and that the cable was not urgent. It was later shown to contain information about an impending attack. Smith, however, was exonerated by President Franklin Roosevelt, General Marshall, and the Congress following a thorough investigation.

Promoted to brigadier general in 1942, he was named chief of staff for General Dwight Eisenhower in North Africa. Smith negotiated the surrender of Italy in 1943, and signed the formal surrender papers on behalf of the United States. Following his success in North Africa, Smith was named chief of staff for the Supreme Headquarters of the Allied Expeditionary Forces. As Eisenhower's emissary, he participated in the Malta Conference, and was a member of the Allied group that accepted Germany's formal surrender.

After the war, President Harry Truman appointed Smith to succeed W. Averell Harriman as U.S. ambassador to the Soviet Union in the early years of the Cold War. It was during his tenure in Moscow that the Berlin Crisis occurred. As ambassador, Smith also served as an official delegate to the Paris Peace Conference in 1946, and to all the foreign ministers' conferences until 1949.

Having gained special permission from Congress to retain his military status while serving in a diplomatic post, Smith returned to the U.S. in 1949 to assume command of the First Army. That command was short-lived, however, because President Truman named Smith as the second director of the CIA, mandating him to reorganize the agency. While director, Smith was promoted to full general.

Unlike most officials of the Truman administration, Smith did not leave the government when Dwight Eisenhower assumed the presidency. Rather, he was named by President Eisenhower to be undersecretary of state, under **John Foster Dulles.** This time Smith resigned his military commission to take the diplomatic position. Then in 1954, he resigned from government service to enter the private sector.

As a civilian Smith served on the boards of directors for several major companies, including NBC, RCA, United Fruit Company, and Corning Glass Works. During his illustrious career, he not only received the Distinguished Service Medal from this country, but also was decorated by 13 other countries, including Great Britain, France, and the Soviet Union. Walter Bedell Smith died in Washington, D.C. in 1961, and is buried in Arlington near his mentor and close friend, George C. Marshall.

Robert Dean Stethem
"Young American Hero"
(November 17, 1961–June 15, 1985)
Sec. 59, Lot 430, Grid EE–25

Robert Stethem was a 23-year-old steelworker second class in the United States Navy assigned to the Navy's underwater construction team. He enjoyed his work because it gave him a chance to travel, as it did in early June 1985. Then Seaman Stethem joined an inspection and repair project on a U.S. military facility in Nea Makri, Greece. It had been a routine assignment and after completing it, Stethem boarded TWA Flight 847 in Athens to fly home to America.

Shortly after takeoff, a group of fanatic Shiite Muslims commandeered the plane, triggering a tragic drama that resulted in the brutal beating and murder of young Stethem. Soon after taking over the plane, the Arab hijackers realized that Stethem was a U.S. serviceman and made him the target of their hatred of the United States. Yet even when his very life was threatened, Stethem never denied his American military status. Courageously, Robert Stethem withstood the brutal attack the air pirates directed at him. The other passengers, after their eventual release, recounted Stethem's bravery, marveling at his ability to maintain his dignity, never forgetting that as a serviceman he represented the United States of America. Frustrated by their inability to destroy Stethem's proud spirit, the hijackers shot the young sailor at point blank range, and as the world watched in horror, threw his body from the plane onto the tarmac at Beirut Airport.

The hostage drama continued for two weeks following the killing of Robert Stethem, but finally all the other passengers and crew were freed. Robert Stethem's body was returned to the United States, and he was buried with full military honors at Arlington National Cemetery.

This young man from Waldorf, Maryland, was recalled by one neighbor as "just the kind of kid you'd like to have as your own son." Polite and athletic, Stethem had played defensive back on the varsity football team at Thomas Stone High School, where he graduated in 1980. The son of two career Navy parents, Robert enlisted in the Navy within six months of his high school graduation.

President Ronald Reagan, speaking on behalf of all Americans, called Robert Stethem "a young American hero."

Stethem's bravery and ultimate sacrifice for his country were further recognized when his parents, Richard and Patricia Stethem, accepted the Purple Heart on their son's behalf. On April 25, 1986, Robert Stethem was posthumously awarded the Bronze Star. He is buried in Section 59 of Arlington amid the graves of the 22 Marines who also were the victims of terrorism when their barracks in Beirut were bombed by Arab extremists in October 1983.

Potter Stewart
Supreme Court Justice
(January 23, 1915–December 7, 1985)
Sec. 5, Lot 40-2, Grid W–36

It was a most unusual decision for a Supreme Court justice in good health to retire at the age of 66. Appointed for life, many justices serve into their 70s and beyond. Yet Potter Stewart knew the constant demands of time and energy made by our nation's highest court, and after 23 years on the Supreme Court, he decided to more fully devote himself to his family. With that decision, he graciously ended a highly respected career.

Born in Jackson, Michigan, Stewart grew up in Cincinnati, Ohio, where he became a lifelong Reds baseball fan. Even after he moved to Washington in 1958, he continued to consider the Cincinnati Reds as "invincible." Still, even as a child, the law was his greatest love. His father James Garfield Stewart was a justice on the Ohio Supreme Court.

Following his cum laude graduation from Yale University in 1937, he studied for a year at Cambridge University in England as a Henry Fellow. Then he returned to Yale to receive his law degree in 1941. Stewart saw active sea duty with the Navy in the Atlantic, Caribbean, and Mediterranean theatres during World War II. He retired as a lieutenant in 1945.

Then Vice President George Bush and members of the Supreme Court headed by Chief Justice Warren Burger (at left) attend the graveside services for former Justice Potter Stewart in December 1985.

After the war, he practiced law in New York City, later returning to his home in Cincinnati where he served on the city council from 1950 to 1953 and as vice mayor in 1952 and 1953.

In 1954, at age 39, he was appointed by President Eisenhower to the United States Court of Appeals for the Sixth Circuit, becoming the youngest federal judge serving at that time. In 1958, he was again appointed by President Eisenhower, this time to the United States Supreme Court, replacing another Ohio native, Justice Harold H. Burton. Forty-three years old, Stewart became the fifth youngest justice to serve on our nation's highest court.

Justice Stewart rendered some of the most important decisions in the Court's history, especially those rulings related to the First Amendment, criminal law, and capital punishment in America.

He served under two chief justices, **Earl Warren** and **Warren Burger.** When he retired in 1981, he was succeeded by the first woman appointed to the Court, Sandra Day O'Connor.

Justice Stewart remained active after he left the Court. He served on many commissions, visited numerous law schools, and read law books for Recordings for the Blind. He is among 12 Supreme Court justices buried at Arlington, joining **Hugo Black, Harry Blackmun, William J. Brennan, Warren Burger, William O. Douglas, Arthur Goldberg, Oliver Wendell Holmes, Jr., Thurgood Marshall, William Rehnquist, William Howard Taft,** and **Earl Warren.**

The Sullivan Brothers

George Thomas, Gunner's Mate 2nd Class, born December 14, 1914
Francis "Frank" Henry, Coxswain, born February 18, 1916
Joseph Eugene, Seaman 2nd Class, born August 28, 1918
Madison "Matt" Abel, Seaman 2nd Class, born November 8, 1919
Albert Leo, Seaman 2nd Class, born July 8, 1922
Died Aboard the *USS Juneau*, November, 1942
Memorial Section C, Lots 30-34 (S-17)

During WWII, the five Sullivan Brothers of Waterloo, Iowa, became instant celebrities when they enlisted together in the U.S. Navy and requested they be assigned to the same ship. It had never occurred before, and the Navy discouraged the request knowing the risk. However, the brothers persisted, and on February 14, 1942, they were together when the light cruiser *USS Juneau* was commissioned into service. What started as an opportunity for five brothers to support their country—and each other—ended tragically nine months later when the *Juneau* was sunk by a Japanese submarine and all five brothers perished.

The Sullivan brothers were part of a large Irish-Catholic family from Waterloo, Iowa, that included their parents, Tom and Alleta, and two sisters, Genevieve, born in 1917, and Kathleen, who died in infancy in 1931.

The two oldest boys, George and Frank, had served four years in the Navy and were discharged in May 1941, but following the Japanese attack on Pearl Harbor, they reenlisted with their younger brothers on January 3, 1942, with the stipulation that they would serve together. Following four weeks of basic training at Great Lakes Naval Training Station in Illinois, they were assigned to the *USS Juneau*.

The *Juneau* operated in the Atlantic Ocean until it was ordered to the Pacific Theatre on August 22, 1942. On November 12, while battling a Japanese force off Guadalcanal, the *Juneau* was struck by a torpedo causing it to withdraw from the battle. The next day it was struck again causing a massive explosion and sinking within 20 seconds. The force of the explosion convinced officers on nearby ships that no one survived the attack and the intensity of the battle forced their retreat.

Sadly it is estimated that nearly 100 men survived—many injured and badly burned, including George Sullivan. Men slowly succumbed to their injuries, the heat, and shark attacks until the final 10 survivors were rescued eight days later. No Sullivans were among them.

Security prohibited the reporting of lost ships, but by January the family in Waterloo knew something was wrong. No mail had come from the boys, who wrote letters regularly. And a neighbor had gotten a letter from her son who expressed sympathy for the Sullivans. On January 11, naval officers arrived at the Sullivan home to inform the parents that their five sons were missing.

Sympathy poured in from around the world. President Franklin Roosevelt sent a personal letter of condolence to the parents, and Pope Pious XII sent a message of sympathy along with a religious medal and a rosary.

America honored the Sullivan brothers on April 4, 1943, when Mrs. Sullivan christened the destroyer, *USS The Sullivans*, at San Francisco. *The Sullivans* served throughout WWII and the Korean War, and is now moored at Buffalo, New York.

Today, the Sullivan brothers are honored by headstones in Arlington that read "In Memory of," a special phrase reserved for stones that mark the cenotaphs, or empty graves, of service personnel whose remains have not been recovered.

William Howard Taft

President, Chief Justice of the United States
(September 15, 1857–March 8, 1930)
Sec. 30, Grave S-14, Grid YZ-39/40

Williiam Howard Taft's career spanned 50 years, included a term as president of the United States and nearly a decade as chief justice of the Supreme Court, making him the only person in American history to serve in both positions.

When William Taft was born in Cincinnati in 1857, he became part of a family whose name has become synonymous with public service in Ohio. His father, Alphonso Taft, became attorney general of the United States in 1876 during the administration of Ulysses S. Grant. William distinguished himself as a student, graduating second in his undergraduate class at Yale in 1878, and first in his law school class at the University of Cincinnati in 1880.

He began his long and remarkable public service career as an assistant prosecuting attorney for Hamilton County, Ohio, in 1881. His first position on the bench was as an Ohio Superior Court judge in 1887, a post he held for three years until he was appointed solicitor general of the United States by President Benjamin Harrison. As solicitor general, his chief responsibility was to represent the United States in all cases before the Supreme Court. He resumed his judicial career as a U.S. Circuit Judge for the Sixth Circuit in 1892, simultaneously serving as dean of the Law Department of the University of Cincinnati until 1900.

On March 12, 1900, President William McKinley appointed Taft president of the Philippine Commission, charged with governing the islands acquired as a result of the recent war with Spain. Subsequently, Taft was named the first civilian governor of the Philippines, and served in that position until 1904. As governor, Taft introduced many needed reforms and programs to the islands, including modern roads, schools, sanitation systems, and land reform. It was during his term as governor that Taft made one of the most difficult decisions of his career. In 1902, President Theodore Roosevelt wanted to appoint Taft to fill a vacancy on the Supreme Court, a position Taft had coveted all his life. Yet Taft felt obligated to finish the work he had started in the Philippines, so he reluctantly declined Roosevelt's offer, certain that he would never sit on the high court. Instead, Roosevelt appointed a jurist from Massachusetts, **Oliver Wendell Holmes, Jr.,** who remained on the court for nearly 30 years. Taft completed his term as governor, then accepted an appointment to Roosevelt's Cabinet as secretary of war in 1904, a post that Taft's father had held 25 years earlier.

President Roosevelt, choosing not to seek reelection in 1908, turned to Taft as the man to succeed him in the Oval Office. Taft publicly declared that he did not want to be president, but bowed to the pressure of his wife, **Helen Herron Taft,** President Roosevelt, and other members of his family. After winning the Republican Party's nomination, he faced perennial Democratic nominee, **William Jennings Bryan,** in the general election. Taft won a sweeping victory and settled into the White House, a place he later described as "the lonesomest place in the world."

Taft's presidency was not known for innovative policies, but rather for its *laissez-faire* approach to government. Unfortunately, he also managed to incur the wrath of his predecessor and patron, Theodore Roosevelt. In fact, Roosevelt was so unhappy with Taft's performance that he ran against Taft for the Republican nomination in 1912. At the party's Chicago convention, the Republicans witnessed a real donnybrook. Going into the convention, Roosevelt had won the most votes during the primaries and separate state conventions. Taft, however, had gathered a majority of the delegates' support, and won the nomination on the first ballot. Never to be outdone, Roosevelt formed his own party, The Bull Moose Party, and challenged both Taft and the Democratic nominee Woodrow Wilson in the national election. With the Republican ranks deeply divided, Wilson won an easy victory, receiving 435 electoral votes to Roosevelt's 88 and Taft's meager eight votes.

Taft, whose six-foot, more than 300-pound frame made him the largest man to serve as this nation's president, was an avid sportsman and included golf among his favorite pastimes. His term as president may not be known for its great international or domestic policies, but several noteworthy

A large marble monument marks the grave of William Howard Taft and Helen Herron Taft in Section 30. Taft is the only person in American history to serve both as president and chief justice of the United States. Helen Herron Taft is one of two first ladies buried at Arlington.

events did occur during his tenure. He was the first president to throw out the first baseball of the season, in a game between the Philadelphia Athletics and the Washington Senators in 1910, thus starting a yearly tradition. Also during his presidency, both the North and South Poles were reached by manned expeditions for the first time, and the famous cherry trees were planted in Washington.

After Taft vacated the Oval Office, he joined the faculty of Yale Law School and served as president of the American Bar Association, but in 1921 his greatest dream came true when President Warren G. Harding appointed the former president chief justice of the United States. Taft led the Court with distinction, gaining special recognition as a skilled administrator. It was under his guidance and direction that the present Supreme Court Building was designed and constructed. So important did Taft consider his service as chief justice that he once said, "The truth is that in my life I don't ever remember that I was president."

He retired from the high court on February 3, 1930, due to ill health, and died five weeks later. He was both the first American president and first Supreme Court chief justice to be buried at Arlington. His grave is marked by a Stoney Creek Granite monument which rises fourteen-and-one-half feet. Commissioned by Taft's widow and sculpted by James Earl Frazer, it is in the Greek Stele form, surmounted by a carved ornamental device in the acroteria motif.

President Taft's wife **Helen Herron Taft** died in 1943 at the age of 82, and is buried beside her husband. It was Mrs. Taft who succeeded in bringing the cherry trees to Washington's Tidal Basin. She and **Jacqueline Kennedy Onassis** are the only former first ladies interred in Arlington National Cemetery.

Hoyt Sanford Vandenberg
Air Force Chief of Staff
(January 24, 1899–April 2, 1954)
Sec. 30, Lot 719, Grid WX–38/39

Hoyt Sanford Vandenberg was born in Milwaukee, Wisconsin, just before the turn of the 20th Century and graduated from West Point in 1923. His early career was spent becoming a crack pilot; by 1929 he had achieved command of the Sixth Pursuit Squadron at Schofield Barracks (named for Secretary of War **John Schofield**) in Hawaii. Ten years later Vandenberg completed instruction at the Army Command and General

Staff School as well as at the Army War College. Assigned to the Plans Section of the Air Corps Headquarters, he worked daily with General **Hap Arnold** to draft contingency plans in case the United States entered the war then raging in Europe. Vandenberg rose to the rank of colonel on January 27, 1942; in August of that year, he was named chief of staff of General **James Doolittle's** Twelfth Air Force in England.

Later involved in the North African campaign and the invasion of Sicily and Italy, Vandenberg received special recognition from General Dwight Eisenhower, and was promoted to brigadier general. In August 1943, he was appointed deputy chief of the Army Air Force Headquarters Staff in North Africa. Vandenberg took part in the early planning of the invasion of Europe, and following his promotion to major general in March 1944, he joined General Eisenhower's staff.

His contributions to the American war effort continued. In July 1944, Vandenberg was selected by General **George C. Marshall** to command the Ninth Air Force, which was ultimately the largest Air Force in Europe. As commander, he orchestrated the air support for General **Omar Bradley's** Twelfth Army Group in its drive across Europe. For his spectacular performance, General Eisenhower promoted him once again, this time to lieutenant general.

Following the war, President Harry Truman named Vandenberg as director of the Central Intelligence Group, the forerunner to the CIA. Then in April 1947, he left the intelligence group and returned to Air Force duty, soon taking the post of deputy commander in chief of the Air Staff. In October of that year, he was promoted to full general and became the first vice chief of staff in the newly organized United States Air Force. Six months later, upon the retirement of General Carl Spaatz, Vandenberg was elevated to chief of staff of the U.S. Air Force.

During his tenure as Air Force chief of staff, Vandenberg conducted the Berlin Airlift, and oversaw the new Air Force's first test in combat—the Korean War. Vandenberg retired a highly decorated airman in June 1953, and died of cancer the following year in Washington, D.C., at the age of 55. After his death, the sprawling Air Force base in Southern California was renamed as a lasting tribute to General Vandenberg.

His wife **Gladys Vandenberg** started the Arlington Ladies (see page 323), a group that represents the chief of staff of each branch of the U.S. Armed Forces at every funeral at Arlington. When no immediate family members can attend the burial service, family members of the deceased gain comfort knowing that someone is always present at the interment of their loved one.

Jonathan Mayhew Wainwright

General, World War II POW
(August 23, 1881–September 2, 1953)
Sec. 1, Lot 358-B, Grid L/M–35/36

When General Jonathan Mayhew Wainwright was taken prisoner by the Japanese in May 1942, he was the highest ranking POW in the Pacific Theatre. He had been forced to abandon his defense of the Bataan Peninsula in the Philippines when he ran out of food and equipment, and his position was overrun by a much larger Japanese force. For three years in POW camps in the Philippines, on Taiwan, and in Manchuria, Wainwright suffered from the belief that he had disgraced himself and his country by his surrender. He was beaten by his captors and suffered merciless humiliation in front of his fellow prisoners. However he refused to be broken, maintaining his dignity as a commander and as a man until Soviet troops liberated him in August 1945. He returned to the United States to receive not only a hero's welcome from the American public, but also the Congressional Medal of Honor from President Harry Truman.

Wainwright was the product of a family that had produced military heroes for generations. His grandfather was a Union naval officer killed in action in Galveston Harbor during the Civil War; his uncle was killed while fighting pirates off the coast of Mexico in 1870; and his father, a veteran of the American Indian frontier and Spanish-American War, died on active duty in Manila in 1902. Born in Walla Walla, Washington, Wainwright attended West Point as had his father before him. He graduated in 1906, and made his first tour of duty in the Philippines in 1908.

During World War I, Wainwright participated in the St. Mihiel and Meuse-Argonne offensives in France. He returned to the United States in 1920, spending much of the period between the world wars learning the textbook side of professional soldiering. He graduated with honors from the Command and General Staff School in 1928, and was recommended for advance command training. In 1934, he completed study at the Army War College, and by 1940 he had risen to the rank of major general on his way back to Manila, this time to assume command of the Philippine Division.

After the Japanese attack on Pearl Harbor, he became field commander of U.S. and Filipino forces under Douglas MacArthur. When MacArthur left for Australia, Wainwright was ordered to defend the Bataan Peninsula where he and his men earned the name "the battling bastards of Bataan." Against overwhelming odds, Wainwright's forces fought gallantly until they were forced to surrender to General Tomobumi Yamashita on Corregidor Island. Although he waited three years to be rescued, his liberation came in time for him to be airlifted to the deck of the *USS Missouri* in Tokyo Bay to witness the surrender of General Yamashita on September 2, 1945.

Following the war, Jonathan Mayhew Wainwright was given command of the Fourth Army at Fort Sam Houston, Texas. In 1946, he published his autobiography *General Wainwright's Story,* then retired from the Army the following year. Out of uniform, Wainwright became an insurance company executive. On September 2, 1953, exactly eight years after the surrender of Japan, he died of a massive stroke in San Antonio, Texas. In recognition of his outstanding military record, he was granted the extraordinary posthumous honor of lying in state in the vaulted chapel of the Memorial Amphitheatre at Arlington. General Wainwright is now buried in Arlington near another hero: his father, **Robert Powell Wainwright.**

Earl Warren
Governor, Vice Presidential Candidate, Chief Justice
(March 19, 1891–July 9, 1974)
Sec. 21, Lot S-32, Grid M–20/21

E arl Warren's public career spanned nearly half a century, from 1920 until 1969. During that time, he held elective offices on the local and state levels, ran for vice president, and sought his party's nomination for president. After more than 30 years in elected office, Warren undertook his most important task, Chief Justice of the United States.

Earl Warren's father was an immigrant from Norway; his mother a native of Sweden. Born in Los Angeles, Earl worked at odd jobs in order to pay his tuition at the University of California. After spending time as

a railroad call boy, a freight hustler, and a truck driver, Warren graduated from college in 1912. Two years later, he earned his law degree and entered private practice. Warren enlisted in the Army during World War I, attaining the rank of first lieutenant. He returned to his private practice, but left it in 1920 to

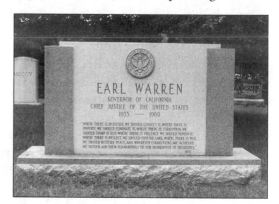

become a deputy assistant city attorney for the city of Oakland, California. He never again engaged in the private practice of law.

In 1925, Warren was appointed district attorney of Alameda County, California, and was reelected to that position in 1926, 1930, and 1934. During his tenure as district attorney, he gained a reputation as an effective crime fighter, sending a city manager and several city councilmen to jail on graft charges.

In 1938, Earl Warren undertook his first campaign for statewide office, seeking election as attorney general. Although he was a Republican, Warren took advantage of a California law allowing candidates to crossfile under several party labels. In that primary election, he also ran on the Democratic Party and Progressive Party tickets. Warren won all three primaries, and went on to win the November general election. But during his campaign, Warren suffered a devastating personal tragedy—the murder of his father.

Early on a Saturday evening, his father was sitting home alone in his chair reading the paper. It was a warm evening and apparently his father fell asleep, leaving the doors and windows open. The evidence later showed that someone had come into the house, and struck his father on the head with a short piece of pipe, crushing his skull. His father's body had been dragged into the bedroom, where the killer had left him on the bed to die. It was the next morning before the crime was discovered. No one was ever arrested for the murder. While many theories were advanced, Earl Warren subscribed to the belief that a vagrant traveling on the trains that passed near his father's house had seen his father alone, entered the house, killed him, and stole his father's wallet. The wallet was found a short distance from the house. It had been the only thing missing.

Warren served one term as California's attorney general, then set his sights on the governor's mansion. Winning the Republican primary, he was pitted against a strong Democratic incumbent. Despite being rated the underdog, Warren won the election with 57 percent of the vote. He stood for reelection in 1946, again winning easily. As governor of California, he was viewed as a political conservative because he denounced "communistic radicals" and supported the wartime internment of all persons of Japanese ancestry. However, following the war, he developed a progressive image, proposing a state program of prepaid medical insurance accompanied by liberal welfare and pension benefits.

In 1948, the Republican nominee for president, Governor Thomas Dewey of New York, chose Warren to be his running mate. Although the polls predicted an easy win for the Dewey-Warren ticket, and some newspapers printed headlines proclaiming a Dewey win, President Harry Truman won a second term, sending Warren back to the statehouse in California. That election was the only loss Earl Warren ever suffered during his 30 years in elective office.

Warren ran for a third term as governor in 1950, this time facing a formidable opponent, James Roosevelt, son of the late President Franklin Roosevelt. Nonetheless, Warren won by a two-to-one margin. Two years later, a presidential election year, Warren indicated that he was interested in the Republican Party's nomination for president.

By the time the nominating convention began, it was clear to Warren that the race was between former General Dwight Eisenhower and Ohio Senator Robert Taft. Waiting until just the right moment, Warren threw his support behind Eisenhower, a move that helped the former general win the nomination. Eisenhower was in Warren's political debt and it did not take long after his election for President Eisenhower to repay his colleague.

On September 8, 1953, U.S. Supreme Court Chief Justice Fred Vinson died in office. President Eisenhower considered a successor to Vinson, first offering the position to **John Foster Dulles,** but Dulles preferred to remain in his post as secretary of state. Eisenhower then offered the position to New York Governor Thomas Dewey, but Dewey also declined, citing his desire to retire from public life. Only then did the president offer the position to Earl Warren. Warren was sworn in as the 14th chief justice on October 5, 1953.

Earl Warren's service on the United States Supreme Court continued for nearly 16 years, during which time the Court undertook numerous landmark cases dealing with racial equality, discrimination, voting rights, housing, prisoners' rights, defendants' rights, and reapportionment. Chief Justice Warren delivered many of those decisions, often disappointing conservatives who had expected a far less progressive attitude from the chief justice. Not the least vocal among his critics was the man who appointed him, Dwight Eisenhower. Asked about his nomination of Warren after he left the White House, Eisenhower characterized it as "the biggest damn fool mistake I ever made."

It was during Warren's tenure as chief justice that President **John F. Kennedy** was assassinated in Dallas in 1963. President Lyndon Johnson, shortly after he was sworn in to succeed the slain president, appointed Earl Warren to chair a special commission to investigate the Kennedy assassination. The Warren Commission, as it came to be known, found that Lee Harvey Oswald had acted as a lone assassin when he shot President Kennedy, and that Jack Ruby had also acted alone when he killed Oswald. That commission came under strong criticism for not probing more deeply into the possibility of a conspiracy.

In June 1968, Chief Justice Warren decided to retire. However he did not immediately leave office because a Senate filibuster prevented a vote on President Johnson's nominee to succeed him, Associate Justice Abe Fortas. When that nomination was finally withdrawn, Warren agreed to stay on the bench until the end of the summer term of 1969. His successor, **Warren Burger,** was sworn in on June 23, 1969.

Earl Warren died on July 9, 1974, ending a distinguished public service career. He was buried with military honors at Arlington National Cemetery.

John Wingate Weeks
Senator, Secretary of War
(April 11, 1860–July 12, 1926)
Sec. 5, Lot 7064, Grid W–35/36

Near the tomb of **John F. Kennedy** is a large granite monument that marks the grave of one of the most influential men of the early twentieth century, John Wingate Weeks.

Born in Lancaster, New Hampshire, Weeks graduated from the United States Naval Academy in Annapolis in 1881. Following his military service, Weeks moved to Boston and joined his family's prestigious banking and brokerage firm, Hornblower and Weeks. He was elected to Congress in 1904, and remained in the House as a Massachusetts representative until 1913 when he was elected to the U.S. Senate.

Weeks sought the Republican nomination for president at the Chicago convention in 1916, but was defeated by Charles Evans Hughes who ultimately lost the general election to Woodrow Wilson. John Wingate Weeks served as secretary of war in the administrations of Warren G. Harding and Calvin Coolidge. He died at the age of 66 in Washington, D.C.

George Westinghouse
Inventor, Manufacturer
(October 6, 1846–March 12,1914)
Sec. 2, Lot 3418, Grid U–29/30

George Westinghouse was born in Central Bridge, New York, and by the time he died 67 years later he had patented hundreds of inventions, organized more than 50 companies, and was president of 30 corporations, including Westinghouse Electric.

Young George developed his great interest in machines while working in his father's shop as a boy. His insatiable curiosity and his powerful creative drive resulted in his development of a rotary engine when he was only 15 years old. At age 16, he joined thousands of other boys who enlisted in the Army at the outbreak of the Civil War to save the Union. During that war, he served in both the Army and Navy. Within a year of the war's end, Westinghouse was again busy inventing.

Many of his inventions were directed toward the burgeoning railroad industry. By 1866, he had already perfected two important machines for the railroads. The first was a device to replace derailed railroad cars. Still a relatively young industry, railroads suffered regularly from train derailments, which would block tracks for days. The second invention, known as a "railroad frog," helped modernize the rail industry. The frog allowed trains to switch from one track to another, enabling trains to pass each other.

Perhaps his most important railroad invention was his perfection of the air brake. Not only did this provide for a more efficient way to stop trains, but it improved their safety. His air brake proved so successful that he organized a company to manufacture it. Following the enactment by the U.S. Congress of the Railroad Safety Appliance Act of 1893, Westinghouse standardized the air brake, allowing equipment from different lines to work together.

Among other significant Westinghouse inventions was a system to safely pipe natural gas into homes and the gas meter that allows the utility company to record a household's natural gas consumption. Finally, among his other hundreds of inventions was his introduction of alternating current (AC) for electric power transmission. It was this interest in electricity that led him to develop one of the nation's largest corporations, Westinghouse Electric Company. He lost control of the corporation during a financial panic in 1907, and within four years, he severed all ties with the company.

George Westinghouse's health failed soon after his divestiture in Westinghouse Electric. He died in New York City on March 12, 1914, and was buried a few days later in Arlington National Cemetery.

Joseph Wheeler

Confederate General, Congressman, U.S. Army General
(September 10, 1836–January 25, 1906)
Sec. 2, Lot 1089, Grid ST–32/33

Although a well-known general in the Confederate Army, Joseph Wheeler came to symbolize the move by former Confederate soldiers to reunite the nation after the Civil War. He served eight terms in the United States Congress representing the state of Alabama, and became chairman of the powerful Ways and Means Committee.

The grandson of General William Hall of Revolutionary War fame, Joseph Wheeler was born and raised in Augusta, Georgia. He graduated from the U.S. Military Academy in 1859, then attended the Cavalry School at Carlisle Barracks, Pennsylvania. By 1860, he was promoted to lieutenant and assigned to the Regiment of Mounted Riflemen at Fort Craig in the New Mexico Territory. Immediately after Georgia voted to secede from the Union in 1861, Wheeler resigned his commission and accepted a position in the armed forces of his native state.

Only 24 years old, standing 5'5" tall, and weighing just 125 pounds, Wheeler was promoted to colonel and named commander of the Nineteenth Alabama Infantry under General Braxton Bragg. In February 1862, Wheeler's units were part of the Confederate forces concentrated near Corinth, Mississippi. He led his men into combat at Shiloh, and was widely praised for successfully covering the Confederate withdrawal. In July of the same year, the cavalry of the Army of the Mississippi was placed in Wheeler's charge. Following his successes at Perryville, he was promoted to brigadier general and named to head the cavalry in the new Army of the Tennessee. Before the war's end, Wheeler had risen to the rank of lieutenant general, had been wounded three times in battle, and had survived 16 horses which had been shot out from under him.

In May 1865—soon after Lee's surrender at Appomattox Courthouse but before all hostilities had ceased—Wheeler was captured by Union soldiers as he attempted to prevent the capture of Jefferson Davis, president of the Confederacy. For his actions, Wheeler spent two months in a federal prison before being paroled.

After the war, Wheeler worked for a time in the hardware business in New Orleans, but spent his spare time studying law, eventually being admitted to the Louisiana state bar. He moved to Alabama where he was persuaded to run for the United States House of Representatives in 1883. He won a seat in the Forty-Seventh Congress. During his eight terms in Congress, among his other legislative accomplishments, Wheeler served on the Military Affairs Committee with his former military nemesis, Union General **William Starke Rosecrans.** He came to represent many of the viewpoints of postwar Southerners: favoring a paternal attitude towards blacks but opposing civil rights, encouraging whites to forget the divisions brought about by the war, and concentrating on the industrialization of the South.

Many of the sectional wounds produced by the Civil War still existed, when war with Spain was declared on April 25, 1898. Recognizing the opportunity to again demonstrate his desire for reconciliation between North and South, Wheeler, then 61 years old, resigned his seat in Congress and volunteered for military service. Sharing his hope for unity, President William McKinley commissioned Wheeler a major general in the U.S. Army, and gave him command of volunteer forces in the invasion of Cuba. Showing daring and independence, Wheeler's forces launched a successful attack against the Spanish at Las Guasimas that cleared the way for an American advance on Santiago. Only illness kept Wheeler from taking part in the renowned march up San Juan Hill.

After the Spanish-American War, Wheeler was unable to regain his seat in Congress, but was promoted to brigadier general and assigned to the Philippines. He later was recalled to serve in the United States, retiring from the Army in September 1900. Joseph Wheeler died in New York City in 1906.

The only other Confederate general buried at Arlington is **Marcus Joseph Wright**, who is interred at the foot of the Confederate Monument in Section 16 (see page 248). Apparently determined to carry on his crusade for reconciliation between North and South even posthumously, General Wheeler chose not to be buried among the Confederate soldiers at Arlington; rather his grave is near such famous Union soldiers as **Philip Henry Sheridan, John Lincoln Clem, John McAllister Schofield,** and **George Crook.** His son, **Joseph J. Wheeler, Jr.,** a West Point graduate and U.S. Army colonel, is buried with his father. Also of note: Joseph Wheeler represents the state of Alabama in the Capitol's Statuary Hall.

Leonard Wood

Rough Rider, Colonial Governor, Presidential Candidate
(October 9, 1860–August 7, 1927)
Sec. 21, Lot S-10, Grid N–20

Planning to follow in his father's footsteps, Leonard Wood left his Winchester, New Hampshire, home to enter Harvard Medical School in 1880. Following his graduation in 1883, Wood began his private practice only to find it too mundane a lifestyle to fit his ambitions. On a whim, he accepted a commission as a medical officer in the U.S. Army in 1885, hoping to fulfill his desire for more adventure. He was not disappointed. His military career not only took him around the world, but also elevated him to the highest post in the United States Army, and fueled his run for the presidency.

Leonard Wood's first assignment was to the Arizona Territory where he served under General **George Crook,** and assisted in the capture of Apache Chief Geronimo in 1886. He was awarded the Congressional Medal of Honor for his role in that historic action, though some controversy erupted over whether he played a major enough role to warrant his award.

In 1895, Wood became White House physician to President Grover Cleveland and later held the same post under President William McKinley. It was while he was serving in Washington that Wood developed a close friendship with the young assistant secretary of the Navy, Theodore Roosevelt, a friendship that would serve Wood well when the war with Spain broke out in 1898. At that time, through Roosevelt's help, Wood was given command of the First Volunteer Cavalry, better known as the Rough Riders. Contrary to widespread popular belief, Roosevelt never commanded the

Rough Riders, although he was with them when they fought on San Juan Hill near Santiago de Cuba.

Following the armistice with Spain, Wood was named governor of Cuba, and began a career as a colonial administrator. As governor from 1899 to 1902, he prepared the island for independence, building roads and schools and assisting Dr. **Walter Reed** in stamping out yellow fever by clearing vast swamps and marshes. On May 20, 1902, Wood relinquished his authority as the military governor to the popularly elected civilian president, Tomas Estrada Palma.

By the time Wood relinquished his role as Cuban governor, he had become a brigadier general, and his friend Teddy Roosevelt was president. In 1904, Roosevelt appointed Wood governor of the Moro Province in the Philippine Islands. There Wood quelled the combative Moros, gained promotion to major general, and was named commander of the Philippine Division. In 1910, President **William Howard Taft,** who also had served as Philippine Governor in 1904, named Wood as Army chief of staff, thereby completing Wood's meteoric rise in rank. In less than a decade Wood had advanced from a captain in the Medical Staff to the highest post in the Armed Forces.

Wood resigned as chief of staff in 1914. When World War I erupted in Europe during that same year, Wood became a vocal advocate for peacetime preparedness, often differing publicly with President Woodrow Wilson over the conduct of the war. Then in 1920, Leonard Wood sought the Republican nomination for President. Facing Warren G. Harding, Wood entered the nominating convention as the leading candidate. After ten ballots, however, Harding was named the winner. Wood, offered the presidency of the University of Pennsylvania in 1921, turned it down in hopes of an appointment as secretary of war in President Harding's Cabinet. That appointment never came. Instead Wood reluctantly accepted the position as colonial governor of the Philippines.

In 1927, at the age of 66, Wood returned from Manila to New York to seek surgical treatment of a tumor which had resulted from an earlier head injury. Sadly, he died on the operating table. Leonard Wood is buried near the monument to the Rough Riders and near the gravesites of many of the soldiers with whom he fought side by side in the Spanish-American War. Also, an army base in southern Missouri bears his name in tribute to his distinguished service to our country.

Other Notable Persons Buried at Arlington

Creighton Abrams, Jr. (1914—1974) General, U.S.A.; U.S. WWII tank commander; chief of staff of I Corps, IX Corps, X Corps during Korean War; U.S. forces commander in Vietnam; Army chief of staff, Sec. 21, Lot S–33 (M/N-20)

Julius Ochs Adler (1892–1955) Major General, U.S.A.; Decorated WWI and WWII veteran; general manager of the New York Times, Sec. 2, Lot 2957 (W-32/33)

Augusta Alexander (1825–1890) Major, U.S.A.; Civil War veteran; first African-American Army surgeon, 7th U.S.C.T., Sec. 1, Lot 124 (J-34)

William R. Anderson (1921–2007) Captain, U.S.N.; protégé of Admiral **Hyman Rickover**; captain of the *USS Nautilus* when it traveled from the Pacific Ocean to the North Atlantic under the North Pole on August 3, 1958; U.S. Congressman from Tennessee; Vietnam War opponent, Sec. 66, Lot 62 (G-14/15)

William R. Arnold (1881–1965) Major General, U.S.A.; WWII chief of chaplains; first chaplain to attain rank of general; Catholic auxiliary bishop of New York City, Sec 2E, Lot 85 (X-28)

John Axton (1870–1934) Colonel, U.S.A.; YMCA general secretary, 1893–1902; first Army chief of chaplains, officiated at interment of the Unknown Soldier (WWI), Sec 2E, Lot 152 (WX-28/29)

Fay Bainter (Venable) (1893–1968) 1938 Academy Award-winning actress (as Aunt Belle in *Jezebel* with Bette Davis); appeared in many films, on Broadway, and on television; married U.S.N. Lt. Commander **Reginald Venable** on June 8, 1921, Sec. 3, Lot 2456-1 (MN-12/13)

Bernt Balchen (1899–1973) Colonel, U.S.A.F.; attempted trans-Atlantic flight with **Richard E. Byrd, Jr.,** 1927; piloted first flight for Byrd over the South Pole, 1929, Sec. 2, Lot 4969-2 (WX-32/33)

Thomas Scott Baldwin (1856–1923) Major, U.S.A. Air Service; pioneer balloonist from Quincy, Illinois, Sec. 1, Lot 1285 (LM-33)

Beatrice V. Ball (1902–1963) Commander, U.S.C.G.R., senior officer in SPARS during WWII, Sec. 8, Lot 115 (AA-9)

Alan B. Banister (1905–1963) WWII submarine commander, Sec. 34, 158 (VW-12/13)

Julian Bartley, Sr. (1944–1998) Consul general killed in Nairobi, Kenya, embassy attack, August 7, 1998; also killed was his son, **Julian Bartley, Jr.** (1977–1998), who was working as a summer intern in the embassy; they are buried together, Sec. 39, Lot 1243 (AA-44)

Charles A. Bassett II (1931–1966) Major, U.S.A.F.; Gemini 9 astronaut; died with fellow astronaut **Elliott See** when their T-38 jet crashed during landing in St. Louis, Missouri, Feb. 28, 1966, Sec. 4, Lot 195 (AA-11/12)

Mario Batista (?–1946) WWII Italian prisoner of war who died while in American custody, Sec. 15, Lot 347-4, (H-25)

Sosthenes Behn (1884–1957) Lt. Colonel, U.S.A.; WWI veteran; founder of International Telephone & Telegraph, Sec. 3, Lot 2573 (Q-15)

Hugh Reid Belknap (1860–1901) Major, U.S.A.; Illinois congressman, 1895–1899; killed in action during the Philippine Insurrection; buried with his father **William Worth Belknap,** Sec. 3, Lot 2231 (P-13)

William Worth Belknap (1829–1890) General, U.S.A.; Civil war veteran, impeached while serving as Ulysses S. Grant's secretary of war, 1876, Sec. 3, Lot 2231 (P-13)

Stephen Vincent Benet (1827–1895) General, U.S.A., Civil War veteran; grandfather of poet Stephen Vincent Benet, Sec. 1, Lot 154 (N-22/23)

Floyd Bennett (1890–1928) Warrant Officer, U.S.N.; aviator who accompanied **Richard E. Byrd, Jr.** to the North Pole on May 9, 1926, Sec. 3, Lot 1852 (S-16/17)

Ollie Josephine Prescott Baird Bennett (1874–1957) Surgeon, U.S.A. Medical Corps; first woman surgeon in WWI, Sec. 10, Lot 10938 (Z-20/21)

Joseph "Jumpin' Joe" Beyrle (1923–2004) Staff Sergeant, U.S.A., a member of the 101st Airborne Screaming Eagles, parachuted into France on "D-Night, " the night before D-Day, only person to fight for both the U.S. and Russia (after he escaped from a Nazi POW camp) in WWII, Sec. 1, Lot 73A (N-33)

Anthony Drexel Biddle (1896–1961) Brigadier General, U.S.A.; U.S. ambassador to Norway, 1935–1937, Poland, 1937–1941, seven governments in exile, 1941–1945, and Spain, 1961, Sec. 30, Lot 1172 (S-37)

Charles F. Blair, Jr. (1909–1978) Brigadier General, U.S.A.F.; first pilot to fly solo across the Arctic Ocean and the North Pole from Norway to Alaska, May 21, 1951; married to actress Maureen O'Hara from 1968 until his death, Sec. 2, Lot 4966 (V-32/33)

Jeremy Michael Boorda (1939–1996) Admiral, U.S.N.; first enlisted sailor to become Chief of Naval Operations; committed suicide following investigation into his right to wear Vietnam War medals; posthumously declared eligible to wear the decorations, Sec. 64, Lot 7101 (MM-17)

George Scratchley Brown (1918–1978) General, U.S.A.F.; first Air Force general to be chairman of the Joint Chiefs of Staff, 1973–1978, Sec. 21, Lot S-34 (N-20/21)

Ronald Brown (1941–1996) Captain, U.S.A.; U.S. commerce secretary, 1993–1996, killed when his plane crashed in Croatia, April 3, 1996, Sec. 6, Lot 8389 (VW-22/23)

Frank W. Buckles (1901–2011) Corporal, U.S.A.; last surviving veteran of World War I; lied about his age (16) to enlist in August 1917; died at the age of 110; buried near General John J. Pershing, Sec. 34, Lot 579-A (T-12/13)

William Francis Buckley (1928–1985) Lt. Colonel, U.S.A.; taken hostage while posted to the U.S. embassy in Beirut as CIA station chief in 1984; held for 15 months during which time he was tortured and died; his remains were returned to the U.S. on December 28, 1991; buried with full military honors, Sec. 59, Lot 346 (EE-26)

Omar Bundy (1861–1940) General, U.S.A.; Commander VI and VII Corps during World War I, Sec. 3, Lot 2521 (PQ-15/16)

Charles "Chic" Burlingame III (1949–2001) Captain, U.S.N.; USNA graduate; pilot of American Airlines Flight 77 that was hijacked and flown into the Pentagon on September 11, 2001, Sec. 35, Lot 4288 (O-19)

Archibald Willingham Butt (1864–1912) Major, U.S.A.; aide to Theodore Roosevelt and **William Howard Taft;** lost at sea when the *Titanic* sank, April 15, 1912, cenotaph located in Sec. 3, Lot 1734, (Q-15)

Marion E. Carl (1915–1998) Major General, U.S.M.C.; distinguished WWII Marine aviator; also served in Korea and Vietnam; murdered in his home at age 82, Sec. 4, Lot 160 (U-9)

John A. Cash, Sr. (1936–1998) Colonel, U.S.A.; Vietnam veteran who wrote about experiences of African Americans in the U.S. military, Sec. 67, Lot 3090 (EE-11)

Jacob Chestnut (1940–1998) Master Sergeant, U.S.A.; U.S. Capitol police officer killed in the line of duty on July 24, 1998, Sec. 4, Lot 2765 (U-9)

William Christman (?–1864), Private, U.S.A., first military burial at Arlington, 1864 (see page 22), Sec. 27, Lot 19 (CC-47/48)

Bennett "Champ" Clark (1890–1954) U.S. senator from Missouri, 1933–1945, Sec. 2, Lot 3435 (UV-29/30)

Clark Clifford (1906–1998) Captain, U.S.N.R.; advisor to four presidents; U.S. secretary of defense, 1969, Sec. 7A, Lot 35 (U-24)

Leslie William Coffelt (1910–1950) Private, U.S.A.; White House policeman killed protecting President Truman from an assassin at Blair House, Sec. 17, Lot 17719-59 (I-20)

William Colby (1920–1996) Major, U.S.A., CIA director, 1973–1976; drowned while canoeing near his home in Maryland, April 27, 1996, Sec. 59, Lot 655 (EEFF-23/24)

J. Lawton Collins (1896–1987) General, U.S.A.; WWII commander of VII Corps; fought at Guadalcanal and Utah Beach on D-Day; Army chief of staff, 1949–1953; U.S. ambassador to Vietnam, father of lunar astronaut Michael Collins, Sec. 30, Lot 422-LH (ZAA-38)

Lucien E. Conein (1919–1998) Lt. Colonel, U.S.A.; veteran spy; served with OSS in WWII; landed behind German lines to deliver weapons to French insurgents; participated in the 1963 assassination of South Vietnam's President Diem; former colleague of Watergate mastermind E. Howard Hunt who considered recruiting him for Watergate break-in, Sec. 66, Lot 851 (FF-18)

Charles P. "Pete" Conrad (1930–1999) Captain, U.S.N.; astronaut; copilot of Gemini 5, 1965; command pilot of Gemini 11, 1966; commanded Apollo 12 and was third person to walk on the Moon on November 19, 1969; aboard Skylab 2 mission, 1973; died in motorcycle crash near Ojai, California, July 8, 1999, Sec. 11, Lot 113-3 (N-15)

John Sherman Cooper (1901–1991) U.S. senator from Kentucky, 1946–1949, 1952–1955, 1956–1973; U.S. Ambassador to the United Nations, 1949, 1968; to India and Nepal, 1955–1956, to Germany, 1974–1976, Sec. 7A, Lot 103 (U-23/24)

Raymond J. Costanzo (1923–2002) Sergeant, U.S.A., WW II POW, superintendent of Arlington National Cemetery, 1975–1990, Sec. 7, Lot 191 (U-24)

Ernest K. Coulter (1871–1952), Lt. Colonel, U.S.A., advocate of children's rights; founder of Big Brothers of America (now Big Brothers/Big Sisters of America), Sec. 3, Lot 4480-A-1 (S-13)

Louis Cukela (1888–1956) Sergeant, U.S.M.C.; One of only five Americans to earn both Army and Navy Congressional Medals of Honor; was serving with the 5th Marine Regiment at Villers-Cotterets, France, during WWI, Sec. 1, Lot 427, (J-35)

Benjamin O. Davis, Sr. (1877–1970) Brigadier General, U.S.A., first African-American Army general; Spanish-American War veteran; professor at Tuskegee Institute, Sec. 2E, Lot 478 (W-31/32)

Cushman Kellogg Davis (1838–1900) Civil War veteran; Minnesota governor, 1874–1887; U.S. senator, 1887–1900, member of Spanish-American War peace commission, Sec. 1, Lot 362 (L/M-36)

Dwight Filley Davis (1879–1945) Lt. Colonel, U.S.A.; secretary of war, 1925–1929, governor of the Philippines, 1929–1932, founded tennis' Davis Cup, Sec. 2, Lot 4962 (WX 32/33)

Jacob Devers (1887–1979) General, U.S.A.; WWII commander of Army ground forces in Europe, Sec. 1, Lot 149-F (MN-33/34)

Edward P. Doherty (1840–1897) Captain, U.S.A., commanded patrol that captured John Wilkes Booth, Sec. 1, Lot 690 (J-33)

Samuel N. Drew (1948–1995) Director of European Affairs for the National Security Council, killed while carrying a peace proposal during Bosnian civil war, Sec. 6, Lot 8607 (V-21)

Adolph Dubs (1920–1979) Lt. Commander, U.S.N., WWII veteran; career diplomat; U.S. ambassador to Afghanistan; kidnapped by Afghan rebels and killed during exchange of gunfire between kidnappers and Afghan troops, Sec. 5, Lot 149 (VW-37)

John Porter East, PhD (1931–1986) First Lieutenant, U.S.M.C.; East Carolina State University professor, 1964–1980; U.S. senator from North Carolina, 1981–1986; committed suicide on June 21, 1986, Sec. 7A, Lot 207 (TU-23/24)

Donn Eisele (1930–1987) Colonel, U.S.A.F.; Apollo 7 astronaut; director of the Peace Corps in Thailand, died December 1, 1987, while on business in Japan, Sec. 3, Lot 2503-G-1 (Q-15)

Irene Englund (1916–2002) Women Airforce Service Pilot (WASP); one of 1,074 women who piloted military aircraft on domestic flights during WWII to free male pilots for combat duty overseas; logged more than 1,200 hours in flight of variety of aircraft during 18-month period; first WASP to earn military burial honors, Columbarium, Court 4, Sec. 0, Niche 3-4 (NN-21)

Robert Fechner (1876–1939) Private, U.S.A.; first director of Civilian Conservation Corps, 1933–1939, Sec. 22, Lot 15540 (L-22)

Walter Flowers (1933–1984) First Lieutenant, U.S.A.; Alabama congressman, Watergate Committee member, Sec. 7A, Lot 182 (TU-23)

Joseph J. Foss (1915–2003) Brigadier General, U.S.A.F.; Medal of Honor recipient; shot down 26 enemy aircraft during WWII; South Dakota governor; American Football League commissioner; NRA president; hosted ABC's "American Sportsman," Sec. 7A, Lot 162 (TU-23/24)

Robert C. Frasure (1942–1995) U.S. ambassador killed while carrying a peace proposal during Bosnian civil war, Sec. 4, Lot 3033 (YZ-11/12)

Theodore C. Freeman (1930–1964) Captain, U.S.A.F.; astronaut; died October 31, 1964, when his T-38 jet crashed during training at Ellington Air Force Base, Houston, Texas, Sec. 4, Lot 3148 (AA-11)

Kathryn George Frost (1948–2006) Major General, U.S.A., commander of Army and Air Force Exchange Service, highest ranking woman in the Army at the time of her retirement in 2005, and highest ranking Army woman buried at Arlington, Sec. 64, Lot 7077 (MMNN-17)

Ruth M. Gardiner (1914–1943) Second Lieutenant, U.S.A.; first Army nurse killed in WWII, Sec. 21, Lot 197 (M-19/20)

John Gibbon (1827–1896) Major General, U.S.A.; commanded the "Iron Brigade" during the Civil War; commanded party that found and buried General George Custer's troops at Little Big Horn, Montana, 1876, Sec. 2, Lot 986 (T-31)

Francis M. Gibson (1847–1919) Captain, U.S.A.; commanded Custer relief party but arrived too late, Sec. 1, Lot A-107 (J-32/33)

John M. Gibson (1956–1998) U.S. Capitol police officer; killed in the line of duty on July 24, 1998, Sec. 28, Lot 140 (U-41)

George Graham (1757–1830) Captain, U.S.A.; U.S. secretary of war under presidents Madison and Monroe, 1816–1817, reinterred from Congressional Cemetery, Sec. 3, Lot 1989 (RS-14/15)

S. David Griggs (1939–1989) Rear Admiral, U.S.N.; shuttle astronaut; died when the WWII vintage plane he was piloting crashed during an air show near Earle, Arkansas, on June 17, 1989, Sec. 7A, Lot 81 (TU-23)

Leslie Groves (1896–1970) Lt. General, U.S.A., directed construction of the Pentagon, military administrator of the Manhattan Project, Sec. 2, Lot 3754 (R-31)

M. Robert Guggenheim (1885–1959) Colonel, U.S.A., ambassador to Portugal, Sec. 2, Lot 4732 (V-33)

David Hackworth (1930-2005) Colonel, U.S.A., highly decorated Korean and Vietnam wars veteran—Purple Heart (8), Distinguished Service Cross (2), Silver Star (10), and Bronze Star (8), military reformist, author, journalist, and U.N. Medal of Freedom recipient, Sec. 34, Lot 417A (T-13)

Putnum Welles Hangen (1930–1970) First Lieutenant, U.S.A.; NBC reporter who was killed in Cambodia by the Khmer Rouge; his remains were recovered in 1992, Columbarium, Court 3, Sec. W, Niche 13-3 (NN-19)

Rupert Vance Hartke (1919-2003) Lieutenant, U.S.N., U.S. Senator from Indiana, 1959-1977, Medicare advocate, anti-Vietnam War presidential candidate in 1972, Sec. 5, 7043-A (W-36)

Richard Helms (1913–2002) Lt. Commander, U.S.N., interviewed Adolph Hitler as a UPI reporter in 1930's; OSS officer; joined CIA at its inception in 1947; CIA director, 1966–1973; U.S. ambassador to Iran, 1973–1976, Sec. 7, Lot 8142-1 (W-24)

Lewis B. Hershey (1893–1977) General, U.S.A., director of Selective Service System, 1936–1970, only four-star general never to serve in combat, Sec. 7, Lot 8197-D (VW-24)

Anton Hilberath (?–1946) First sergeant, German Army, WWII prisoner of war, who died while in American custody, Sec. 15, Lot 347 (H-25)

John Hinkel (1906–1986) Colonel, U.S.A., Arlington Cemetery historian and author, Sec. 7A, Lot 153 (U-24)

Juanita R. Hipps (1912–1979) Lt. Colonel, U.S.A.; WWII nurse; wrote the bestseller, *I Served on Bataan,* Sec. 21, Lot 769 (NO-20/21)

Kara Spears Hultgreen (1965–1994) Lieutenant, U.S.N.; first woman combat pilot in U.S. history who died when her F-14 fighter jet crashed during training exercises aboard *USS Abraham Lincoln* on Oct. 25, 1994, Sec. 60, Lot 7710 (GG-20)

Robert Green Ingersoll (1833–1899) Colonel, U.S.A.; nationally recognized orator; agnostic philosopher, civil rights advocate, Sec. 3, Lot 1620 (S-16/17)

James B. Irwin (1930–1991) Colonel, U.S.A.F.; Apollo 15 astronaut; eighth person to walk on the Moon, 1971; led expeditions to Mount Ararat, Turkey, in search of Noah's Ark, 1982–1983, Sec. 3, Lot 2503-G-2 (Q-15/16)

Brian J. James (1957–1992) Major, U.S.M.C.; served in Lebanon, 1984; astronaut, died when the V-22 Osprey aircraft he was piloting crashed into the Potomac River near Washington, D.C., July 20, 1992, Sec. 60, Lot 4436 (FF-21)

Bernard T. Janney (1843–1916) Captain, U.S.A., Civil War veteran, prominent educator in the District of Columbia, Janney School is named for him, Sec. 3, Lot 2127 (Q-15)

Louis Vaughn Jones (1895–1965) African-American concert violinist; Howard University professor, Sec. 43, Lot 511 (W-44)

Prabhi G. Kavaler (1952–1998) Foreign Service Officer, Dept. of State; killed in Nairobi, Kenya, embassy attack, August 7, 1998, Sec. 36, Lot 1471 (AA/BB-41)

Kenneth Keating (1900–1975) Brigadier General, U.S.A.; New York congressman, 1947–1959; U.S. senator, 1959–1965; unseated by **Robert F. Kennedy;** ambassador to India, 1969–1972; ambassador to Israel, 1973–1975, Sec. 5, Lot 141 (W-36/37)

William Pitt Kellogg (1830–1918) Colonel, U.S.A.; Nebraska chief justice, 1861; Louisiana U.S. senator, 1868–1872, 1877–1883; governor, 1883–1887; congressman, 1887–89, Sec. 3, Lot 2538 (P-16/17)

Burton Kennedy (1922–2001) Lieutenant, U.S.A.; highly decorated WWII veteran; wrote and directed westerns with John Wayne, Kirk Douglas, Henry Fonda, Glenn Ford, and Robert Mitchum; also worked on TV series, including *Combat, Simon and Simon,* and *Magnum P.I.,* Sec. 7A, Lot 15 (U-24)

Otto Kerner (1908–1976) Brigadier General, U.S.A., governor of Illinois, 1961–1968; headed Kerner civil rights commission; U.S. Court of Appeals justice, Sec. 3, Lot 2547 (P-16/17)

Harley Kilgore (1893–1956) Colonel, U.S.A.; U.S. senator from West Virginia, 1941–1956, Sec. 30, Lot 536 (Y38)

Michael Kilian (1939–2005) Corporal, U.S.A., Chicago Tribune columnist; author; co-writer of Dick Tracy comic strip, Columbarium, Court 8, Sec. G, Niche 15-3 (00-22)

Ivory Kimball (1843–1927) Private, U.S.A.; founding member of Grand Army of the Republic; judge; instrumental in securing authorization and funding for Arlington's Memorial Amphitheatre, Sec. 3, Lot 1538 (Q-15)

Iven C. Kincheloe, Jr. (1928–1958) Captain, U.S.A.F.; served in Korea, 1950–1951, won aviation's MacKay Trophy for setting a new altitude record when he flew a Bell X-2 rocket plane to 126,000 feet, Sept. 7, 1956; astronaut; died July 26, 1958, when his F-104 jet crashed in the Mojave Desert near Edwards Air Force Base, California, Sec. 2, Lot 4872-1 (V-32/33)

Jeff King (1860–1964) Sergeant, U.S.A.; cavalry scout, second oldest person buried at Arlington (See Mark Matthews below), Sec. 35, Lot 1566 (OP-20/21)

Harry Klein, Jr. (1944-2002) Major, U.S.A., Sec. 66, Lot 7164 (DD-18)

Bertram Korn (1918–1979) Rear Admiral, U.S.N.; rabbi; highest ranking Jewish chaplain in the United States Armed Forces, Sec. 2, Lot 186 (W-28/29)

Joseph J. Kruzel (1945–1995) Deputy assistant secretary of defense; killed while carrying a peace proposal during Bosnian civil war, Sec. 30, Lot 621 (WX-39)

Thomas G. Lanphier, Jr. (1915–1987) Colonel, U.S.A.F.; WWII pilot who shot down the plane carrying Admiral Isoroku Yamamoto, commander in chief of the Japanese Imperial Navy and architect of the attack on Pearl Harbor, Sec. 11, Lot 789-2 (P-14)

Emery "Swede" Larson (1899-1945) Colonel, USMC; legendary football coach at the U.S. Naval Academy, 1939–1941, "Never lost to Army," Sec. 2-E, Lot 4789 (UV-31)

Evelyn Lincoln (1909–1995) Personal secretary to President **John F. Kennedy,** wife of U.S.A. Tech Sergeant **Harold W. Lincoln,** Columbarium, Court 4, Sec. A, Niche 16-3 (NN-21)

Peter Lisagor (1915–1976) Sergeant, U.S.A.; newspaper columnist; long-time Chicago Daily News bureau chief in Washington, D.C., Sec. 2, Lot 4968-B (W-32/33)

John Davis Lodge (1903–1985) Captain, U.S.N.; lawyer; actor; WWII veteran; Connecticut congressman, 1947–1951; governor, 1951–1955; U.S. ambassador to Spain, 1955–1961; to Argentina, 1969–1974; to Switzerland, 1983–1985, president, Junior Achievement, Inc., 1963–1964, Sec. 30, Lot 8966 (AA-39)

James Longstreet, Jr. (1865–1922) Lt. Colonel, U.S.A and **Robert Lee Longstreet** (1863–1940) Major, U.S.A.; sons of Confederate General James Longstreet, Sec. 15, Lot 32 (I-24/25)

Allard Lowenstein (1929–1980) Private, U.S.A.; New York congressman, 1969–1971, U.S. ambassador to the United Nations for Special Political Affairs, assassinated in his office on March 14, 1980; at his request, he has the closest grave to JFK, Sec. 30, Lot 2005-1 (TU-35/36)

Francis Lupo (1895–1918) Private, U.S.A; first WWI MIA whose remains were identified by the Joint POW/MIA Accounting Command using DNA testing; died during the Second Battle of the Marne; remains were found by a French archeological team, Sec. 66, Lot 7489 (DD-14)

John Roy Lynch (1847–1939) Major, U.S.A.; former slave; Mississippi congressman, 1873–1877, 1882–1883; chair of Republican National convention, 1884, Sec. 4, Lot 2747 (YZ-10)

Melvin J. Maas (1898–1964) Major General, U.S.M.C.; Minnesota congressman, 1927–1933, 1935–1945; national commander of the Disabled American Veterans, Sec. 34, Lot 4-A (VW-12/13)

Peter Makohin (Prince Leon Bogun Mazappa Razumowski) (1880–1956) Second Lieutenant,U.S.M.C.; Russian prince who fled to America after an assassination attempt in 1907; took the name of the man he credited for saving his life; WWI veteran, Sec. 1, Lot 558 (J-34)

Michael J. Mansfield (1903–2001) Seaman, U.S.N., U.S.M.C., Private, U.S.A.; U.S. senator from Montana, longest-serving senate majority leader, 1961–1977, U.S. ambassador to Japan; Presidential Medal of Freedom recipient, Sec. 2, Lot 4969 FLH (WX-32/33)

Martin, William F. (1926–1966) Staff Sergeant, U.S.A.,; WWII veteran, Sec. 51, Lot 575 (DD-45)

Ilona Massey (Dawson) (1912–1974) Opera singer turned movie and TV actress. Appeared with Peter Lorre, Lon Chaney, Walter Pidgeon, George Raft, Roddy McDowall, and the Marx brothers. Hosted her own TV show in 1954. Fourth husband was Air Force Major General **Donald Dawson,** Sec. 5, Lot 7056 (V-36)

Mark Matthews (1894–2005) First Sergeant, U.S.A.; buffalo soldier; at 111 years old, oldest person buried at Arlington Cemetery; served under **John Pershing** in Mexico in 1916; in the South Pacific during WWII; honored by Secretary of State Colin Powell in 2002, Sec. 69, Lot 4215 (MM-10)

David M. May (1945–1971) Major, U.S.A.; helicopter pilot shot down in Cambodia in 1971; his remains were recovered and buried at Arlington in January 2000, Sec. 34, Lot 753 (U-12)

Geraldine Pratt May (1895–1997) Colonel, U.S.A.F.; first woman to earn the rank of colonel; first director of Women in the Air Force (WAF), 1948–1951, Columbarium, Court 4, Sec. MM, Niche 16-1 (NN-21)

William Gibbs McAdoo (1863–1941) Lieutenant, U.S.N.; developed tunnels between New York City and New Jersey; U.S. secretary of the treasury, 1913–1918; married Woodrow Wilson's daughter in White House ceremony, May 7, 1914; chair of the Federal Reserve Board, 1918; unsuccessful candidate for president in 1920 and 1924; U.S. senator from California, 1933–1939, Sec. 2, Lot 4969 (W-32/33)

John S. McCain (1884–1945) Admiral, U.S.N.; as commander of Task Force 38 during WWII, planes under his command sank 49 ships in one day; witnessed Japanese surrender on board the *USS Missouri,* September 2, 1945, Sec. 2, Lot 4356 (V-15)

John S. McCain, Jr. (1911–1981) Admiral, U.S.N.; while commander in chief of U.S. forces in the Pacific (1968–1972), his son, Navy pilot John S. McCain III, was shot down and taken prisoner of war in Vietnam where he remained for more than five years; John S. McCain III was later elected to the United States Senate from Arizona. Sec. 3, Lot 4001 (U-15)

George B. McClellan, Jr. (1865–1940) Lt. Colonel, U.S.A., son of Civil War General George McClellan (see McClellan Arch, page 252); New York congressman, 1895–1903; New York City mayor, 1903–1909; Princeton University professor, 1912–1931, Sec.2, Lot 3394 (UV-29)

Anita Newcomb McGee (1864–1940) Assistant Surgeon, U.S.A.; first woman Army surgeon, 1898; founded Army Nurse Corps, 1901; director of the Daughters of the American Revolution Hospital Corps; daughter of **Simon Newcomb** (see page 150), Sec. 1, Lot 526-B (KL-34/35)

Kathleen McGrath (1952–2002) Captain, U.S.N.; first woman to command a U.S. warship, *USS Jarrett,* in 2000; died of cancer; wanted to follow her father's Air Force career but recruiter was out to lunch, so Navy recruiter signed her with offer of overseas travel, Sec. 66, Lot 7274 (DD-17)

Richard Leroy McKinley (1933–1961) Specialist 4th Class, U.S.A.; only nuclear accident fatality in U.S. history; in Idaho, buried in a lead-lined casket at the direction of the Atomic Energy Commission, Sec. 31, Lot 472 (X-37/38)

Paul V. McNutt (1891–1955) Colonel, U.S.A.R.; governor of Indiana, U.S. high commissioner to the Philippines, 1937–1939, Sec. 2, Lot 4969-B (W-33)

John C. Metzler (1909–1990) Sergeant, U.S.A.; superintendent of Arlington National Cemetery, 1951–1972; played vital role in preparation and administration of funeral and burial for President **John Kennedy** in 1963 (see pages 111-112); his son, John J. Metzler, Jr., became superintendent of Arlington in 1991, Sec. 7A, Lot 86 (U-24)

William Miller (1914–1983) First Lieutenant, U.S.A.; New York congressman, 1951–1965; chair of the Republican National Committee, 1961; 1964 GOP vice-presidential candidate with Senator Barry Goldwater, Sec. 5, Lot 93 (W-36)

John Mitchell (1913–1988) Lieutenant Jr. Grade, U.S.N.; two-time Purple Heart recipient; commanded **John F. Kennedy's** PT boat unit; U.S. attorney general under Richard Nixon, 1969–1972; served two years in prison for conspiracy and obstruction of justice for the Watergate scandal, Sec. 7A, Lot. 121 (U-24)

Thomas H. Moorer (1912–2004) Admiral, U.S.N., chairman of the Joint Chiefs of Staff, 1970–1774, Sec. 1, Lot 171-H (N-33)

Ben Moreell (1892–1978) Admiral, U.S.N.; "Father of the Seabees," Sec. 4, Lot 2616 (T-9)

Daniel Patrick Moynihan (1927–2003) Lieutenant (JG), U.S.N.; **John Kennedy's** assistant secretary of labor; ambassador to India; U.S.

ambassador to the U.N.; U.S. senator from New York, 1977–2001, succeeded by Hillary Clinton; recipient Presidential Medal of Freedom, Sec. 36, Lot 2267 (AA-41)

Edmund Sixtus Muskie (1914–1996) Lieutenant, U.S.N.; governor of Maine, 1955– 1959; U.S. senator, 1959–80; 1968 Democratic vice-presidential candidate; secretary of state, 1980–81, Sec. 6, Lot 8724 (W-21)

Michael Musmanno (1897–1968) Rear Admiral, U.S.N.R.; judge at Nuremburg trials, Pennsylvania chief justice, Sec. 2, Lot 4735-E (UV-33/34)

Alfred Bayard Nettleton (1838–1911) Brigadier General, U.S.A.V.; assistant secretary of the treasury, 1890–1893; managing editor of the *Philadelphia Inquirer;* founder of the *Minneapolis Tribune,* Sec. 1, Lot 127 (O-32/33)

Arthur D. Nicholson, Jr. (1947–1985) Major, U.S.A.; killed while member of American Military Liaison Group in East Germany, Sec. 7A, Lot 171 (U-23/24)

William B. Nolde (1929–1973) Colonel, U.S.A.; highly decorated soldier and last official fatality of the Vietnam War, Sec. 3, Lot 1775-B

William O'Dwyer (1890–1964) Brigadier General, U.S.A; New York City mayor, 1945–50, U.S. ambassador to Mexico, 1952–1953, Sec. 2, Lot 889 (R-31/32)

Joy Bright Hancock Ofstie (1898–1986) Yeoman, U.S.N: WWI pilot; first director of Women Accepted for Volunteer Emergency Services (WAVES), 1946–1953, wrote "Lady in the Navy," three-time Navy widow, Sec. 30, Lot 2138 (TU-36)

Richard Oliver (1934–1966) Lt. Commander, U.S.N., pilot, U.S. Navy's precision flying Blue Angels; crashed during an exhibition at the annual Canadian National Exhibition air show, Sec. 3, Lot 2405-A (P-12)

Robert F. Overmyer (1936–1996) Colonel, U.S.M.C., astronaut; pilot of first fully operational shuttle, STS-5, 1982; commander of Shuttle *Columbia* Spacelab-3, 1985; headed *Challenger* recovery operations; served on *Challenger* inquiry board; died in the crash of an experimental kit airplane in Duluth, Minnesota, March 22, 1996, Sec. 23, Lot 22469 (M-22)

Joseph Medill Patterson (1879–1946) Captain, U.S.A.; publisher of the Chicago Tribune, 1914–1925, and the New York Daily News, 1925–1946, Sec. 6, Lot 5681 (V-22)

Robert Patterson (1891–1952) Major, U.S.A.; secretary of war, 1945–1947, Sec. 30, Lot 612 (X-39/40)

George Smith Patton (1923–2004) Major General, U.S.A., son and namesake of WWII armored commander, 3 tours in Vietnam, awarded Purple Heart and Distinguished Service Cross (2), Sec. 34, Lot 784 (X-13)

Lemuel Penn (1915–1964) Lt. Colonel, U.S.A.R., prominent African-American educator, assistant supt. of Washington, D.C. public schools. Murdered by members of the Ku Klux Klan while returning to D.C. from Army Reserve training at Ft. Benning, Ga. His killers were first convictions under the 1964 Civil Rights Act., Sec. 3, Lot 1377 (LM-19)

George Edward Picket, Jr. (1864–1911) Major, U.S.A.; son of Confederate General George E. Pickett; served in the Philippines; died at sea, April 11, 1911, Sec. 3, Lot 2030 (RS-14/15)

Spotswood Poles (1887–1962) Sergeant, U.S.A.; Negro League all-star outfielder called "the black Ty Cobb;" credited with a .400 lifetime batting average; earned a Purple Heart during WWI, Sec. 42, Lot 2324 (U-46)

Valentine "Val" Pringle (1937–1999) Specialist 3, U.S.A., actor, starred in British TV series, "Sapphire and Steele," and many movies, including "Ragtime"; singer; songwriter; murdered when he confronted two burglars in his South African home, Sec. 5-F, Lot 2 (V-36)

Arcangelo Prudenza (?–1946) Corporal, Italian Army, WWII prisoner of war who died while in American custody, Sec. 15, Lot 347 (H-25)

John Pruitt (1896–1918) Corporal, U.S.M.C.; one of only five Americans to earn both Army and Navy Congressional Medals of Honor while serving in the 6th Regiment Marines in Blanc-Mont, France, during WWI; died on his 22nd birthday just 28 days before the armistice was signed, Sec. 18, Lot 2453 (O-9)

Lewis B. Puller, Jr. (1945–1994) First Lieutenant, U.S.M.C.; Vietnam veteran who lost both legs and parts of both hands when he stepped on an enemy land mine in Vietnam in 1968; his autobiography,

"Fortunate Son," won a Pulitzer Prize in 1991; son of General Lewis "Chesty" Puller, Sr., the most decorated Marine in U.S. history; the younger Puller committed suicide on May 11, 1994, succumbing to depression and alcoholism, Sec. 3, Lot 2229 (P-13)

Barbara Allen Rainey (1948–1982) Lt. Commander, U.S.N.; first woman pilot in the Navy and first woman to receive prestigious Wings of Gold, 1974; resigned from the Navy in 1977; died at age 34 in a plane crash at Middleton Field near Evergreen, Alabama, Sec. 6, Lot 5813-A-7 (XY-22)

Wallace Fitz Randolph (1841–1910) Major General, U.S.A.V.; Civil War and Spanish-American War veteran; only gravesite in Arlington to be marked with a piece of artillery, Sec. 1, Lot 132 (N-33)

Arnold P. Raphel (1943–1988) Foreign Service Officer; U.S. ambassador to Pakistan; killed when his aircraft exploded while accompanying Pakistani President Mohammed Zia ul-Haq on August 17, 1988, Sec. 5, Lot 151 (W-36)

John A. Rawlins (1831–1869) Major General, U.S.A.; confidant of Ulysses S. Grant; secretary of war, 1869, Sec. 2, Lot 1007 (S-32/33)

Prince Leon Bogun Mazappa Razumowski (see Peter Makohin)

Donald T. Regan (1918–2003) Lt. Colonel, U.S.M.C, secretary of treasury and chief of staff for Ronald Reagan, author of "View from the Street," Sec. 35, Lot 4953 (ST-18)

Jon Eric Reid (1945–1971) Chief Warrant Officer, U.S.A.; helicopter pilot shot down in Cambodia in 1971; his remains were recovered and buried at Arlington in January 2000, Sec. 34, Lot 753 (U-12)

Lorimer Rich (1890–1978) Private, U.S.A.; designed Tomb of the Unknowns, Sec. 48, Lot 288 (S-23)

Matthew Ridgeway (1895–1993) General, U.S.A; led 82nd Airborne invasion of Europe in WWII; replaced Douglas MacArthur as commander of UN forces during Korean War; Supreme Commander of NATO forces in Europe, 1951–1953; Army chief of staff, 1953–1955, Sec. 7, Lot 8196-1 (VW-24)

Russell Rippetoe (1975–2003) Captain, U.S.A.; first casualty of Operation Iraqi Freedom to be buried at Arlington; victim of a suicide bomber, Sec. 60, Lot 7860 (F-21)

Henry M. Robert (1837–1923) Brigadier General, U.S.A.; wrote "Robert's Rules of Order," Sec. 3, Lot 3945 (V-16)

Kenneth L. Roberts (1885–1957) Captain, U.S.A.; WWI veteran; wrote "Northwest Passage" and other novels; awarded Pulitzer Prize. Sec. 2, Lot 3426 (TU-29/30)

Roscoe Robinson, Jr. (1928–1993) General, U.S.A.; Vietnam War veteran; first African-American Army four-star general, Sec. 7A, Lot 18 (U-24)

William P. Rogers (1913–2001) Lt. Commander, U.S.N., President Eisenhower's attorney general; helped establish Justice Department's Civil Rights Division; secretary of state under Richard Nixon, chaired panel that investigated the shuttle *Challenger* disaster, Sec. 30, Lot 817 LH (XY-40/41)

Finn Ronne (1899–1980) Captain, U.S.N.R.; made four expeditions to the Antarctic, twice with Admiral **Richard E. Byrd, Jr.;** awarded two Congressional Medals of Honor; the Ronne Ice Shelf is named for him, Sec. 2, Lot 4957 (V-32/33)

Stuart A. Roosa (1933–1994) Colonel, U.S.A.F.; Apollo 14 astronaut; piloted the *Kitty Hawk* space module around the Moon in 1971 while astronauts Alan Shepard and Edgar Mitchell landed on the lunar surface, Sec. 7A, Lot 73 (TU 23/24)

Marie T. Rossi-Clayton (1959–1991) Major, U.S.A.; first woman combat pilot to die in action, 101st Airborne Division, Operation Desert Storm, Persian Gulf War, March 1, 1991, Sec. 8, Lot 9872 (CC-10/11)

Albert Bruce Sabin (1906–1993) Lt. Colonel, U.S.A.; worked with U.S. Army Medical Corps during WWII studying viral diseases affecting troops; his oral polio vaccine, developed in 1955, has prevented an estimated 5 million cases of polio and 500,000 deaths. Sabin is buried near **Walter Reed,** Sec. 3, Lot 1885 (T-15)

Pierre Salinger (1925–2004) Lieutenant (JG), U.S.N., White House press secretary for **John F. Kennedy** and Lyndon Johnson, establishing the first live presidential news conference, 1961; U.S. senator from California, 1964; Paris bureau chief for ABC News, Columbarium, Court 6, Sec. PP, Niche 7-3 (NN00-21)

John Scali (1918–1995) Journalist; ABC television news broadcaster; unofficial U.S.-Soviet go-between during Cuban missile crisis, 1962; U.S. ambassador to the United Nations, 1973-1975, Sec. 8, Lot 10322, (CC-8)

John McAllister Schofield (1831–1906) Lt. General, U.S.A.; professor at Washington University in St. Louis, Missouri; Civil War general; Congressional Medal of Honor recipient; secretary of war, 1868–1869; general in chief of the army, 1888–1895; established precedent for civilian control of the military, Sec. 2, Lot 1108 (T-31)

Hugh Doggett Scott, Jr. (1900–1994) Captain, U.S.N.; congressman from Pennsylvania, 1941–1945, 1947–1959, U.S. senator, 1959–1977; was part of the Republican congressional delegation that met with President Richard Nixon to tell him he could not survive impeachment, Sec. 7A, Lot 139 (U-24)

Robert R. Scott (1915–1941) Machinist Mate First Class, U.S.N., Congressional Medal of Honor recipient who sacrificed his life when he continued to operate a compressor to provide air for his fellow crew members trapped below deck on the *USS California* during the Japanese attack on Pearl Harbor, December 7, 1941, Sec. 34, Lot 3939 (N-16)

Elliot M. See, Jr. (1927–1966) Commander, U.S.N.R.; astronaut; died with fellow astronaut **Charles Bassett** when their T-38 jet crashed during landing in St. Louis, Missouri, Feb. 28, 1966, Sec. 4, Lot 208 (T-9)

Philip Henry Sheridan, Jr. (1880–1918) Major, U.S.A.; son of Civil War General Philip Sheridan; aide to Theodore Roosevelt, Sec. 2, Lot 1 (ST-33/34)

Leslie Sherman (1987–2007) Daughter of military veterans Anthony and Holly Sherman; Virginia Tech student in history and international relations; victim of shooting spree that killed 32 students on April 16, 2007, Sec. 34, Lot 3366-2 (W-11)

Charles Dwight Sigsbee (1845–1923) Rear Admiral, U.S.N.; captain of the *USS Maine* when it was sunk in Havana Harbor, February 15, 1898; also captain of *USS Brooklyn* when it carried remains of John Paul Jones from France to the U.S. Naval Academy, Sec. 2, Lot 941 (RS-31/32)

Albert Merriman Smith (1913–1970) UPI White House correspondent whose reports first alerted the world to the assassination of **John F. Kennedy;** one of four reporters who saw President Kennedy after he was shot; also witnessed Lyndon Johnson's oath of office aboard Air Force One; buried next to his son, Army Captain **Albert Merriman Smith, Jr.,** whose helicopter crashed in Vietnam on February 18, 1966, Sec. 32, Lot 823 (VW–34)

Johnny Michael Spann (1969–2001) Captain, U.S.M.C.; CIA officer; first casualty of the war in Afghanistan, Sec. 34, Lot 2359 (U-13)

Ellis Spear (1834–1917) Brigadier General, U.S.A.V; colonel, Maine 20th Infantry; second in command to General Joshua Chamberlain at Little Round Top during the battle of Gettysburg, July 1863; career government official including U.S. commissioner of patents, Sec. 2, Lot 4699 (WX-32)

William H. Standley (1872–1963) Admiral, U.S.N.; chief of naval operations, 1933–1937; U.S. ambassador to the Soviet Union during WWII, 1941–1943, Sec. 2, Lot 1188-2 (T-31)

George M. Sternberg (1838–1915) Brigadier General, U.S.A.; Army surgeon general, 1890–1902, established Army Medical School, Sec. 2, Lot 994 (S-32/33)

Theodore Fulton "Ted" Stevens (1923–2010) Lieutenant, U.S.A. Air Corps; served in the 14th Air Force Transport Section with Lt. General Claire Chennault in China during WWII; U.S. Senator from Alaska, 1968–2009, Sec. 30, Lot 281-LH (Z-40/41)

Samuel S. Stratton (1916–1990) Captain, U.S.N.; WWII veteran of the Pacific theatre; interrogated Japanese Supreme Commander General Tomoyuki Yamashita; Naval Intelligence School instructor, 1951–1953; Schenectady, New York mayor, 1956–1959; U.S. congressman, 1959–1989, Sec. 7A, Lot 58 (U-24)

James A. Tanner (1844–1927) Corporal, U.S.A., lost both legs at second Battle of Bull Run; stenographer present at Lincoln's death bedside providing historic record; founding member of the Grand Army of the Republic, Sec. 2, Lot 877 (PQ-31/32)

 **Maxwell D. Taylor** (1901–1987) General, U.S.A., WWII commander 101st Airborne Division; supt. of West Point, 1945–1949; commandant in Berlin, 1949–1951, deputy Army chief of staff, 1951–1953, Eighth Army commander in Korea, 1953–1954, Army chief of staff, 1955–1959, chairman, Joint Chiefs of Staff, 1962–1964, ambassador to South Vietnam, 1964–1965, Sec. 7A, Lot 20 (U-24)

Luther Terry (1911–1985) Surgeon General, U.S.P.H.S.; issued warning that cigarette smoking is a health hazard, 1964, Sec. 3, Lot 1829 (RS-16)

Stephen D. Thorne (1953–1986) Lt. Commander, U.S.N.; astronaut; died when the stunt plane in which he was a passenger, being piloted by NASA flight control engineer James Simons, crashed near Santa Fe, New Mexico, on May 24, 1986, Sec. 7A, Lot 135 (U-24)

Carl P. Thorpe (1927–1986) Lt. Colonel, U.S.A.; son of football legend and Olympic gold medalist Jim Thorpe; career Army officer, Sec. 8, Lot 9790-5 (VV-8/9)

Eli Karin Turner (1838–2000) Wife of former admiral and CIA director Stansfield Turner, Sec. 7A, Lot 130-C (U-24)

Ernest Karl Turner (1914–1950) Sergeant, U.S.A; first soldier killed during the Korean War, July 28, 1950, Sec. 12, Lot 6829 (Y-26/27)

John Tyler, Jr. (1819–1896) Captain, U.S.A., colonel, C.S.A.; one of 15 children of President John Tyler; served as his personal secretary while president; originally placed in private vault at Congressional Cemetery, interred at Arlington five months later, Sec. 1, Lot 779 (I-34)

Matt Urban (1919–1995) Lt. Colonel, U.S.A.; awarded Congressional Medal of Honor from Jimmy Carter 35 years after heroic conduct in WWII, lost paperwork cited as reason for the delay; also received seven Purple Hearts, Sec 7A, Lot 40 (U-23)

Jack Valenti (1921–2007) First Lieutenant, U.S.A.; WWII Army Air Corps bomber pilot with 51 missions over Europe; special assistant to Lyndon Johnson; aboard Air Force One when LBJ took the oath of office; president of the Motion Picture Association of America, 1966–2004; helped implement voluntary movie rating system, 1968, Sec. 32, Lot 516 (W-34)

Cyrus Vance (1917–2002) Lieutenant, U.S.N., secretary of the army under **John Kennedy** and Lyndon Johnson; Jimmy Carter's secretary of state, Sec. 64, Lot 6551 (NN-16)

James Van Fleet (1892–1992) General, U.S.A.; led ground troops on D-Day at Utah Beach and Battle of the Bulge; commander, 8th Army during the Korean War, 1951–1953, Sec. 7, Lot 8195-A (VW-24)

James Van Fleet, Jr. (1925–1952) Captain, U.S.A.F., son of General James Van Fleet; shot down and presumed dead during the Korean War, memorialized on his parents' headstone, Sec. 7, Lot 8195-A (VW-24)

Leigh Wade (1897–1991) Major General, U.S.A.F.; pilot of the *Boston,* first aircraft to make a round-the-world flight, 1924, Sec. 11, Lot 147-C (MN-16/17)

David M. Walker (1944–2001) Captain, U.S.N., astronaut; pilot of shuttle Discovery, 1984; commander of shuttle missions in 1989, 1992, and 1994, including 1989 Atlantis voyage that launched first spacecraft from a shuttle–the Magellan probe that mapped the surface of Venus; died of cancer, Sec. 66, Lot 5191 (EE-16)

Vernon A. Walters (1917–2002) Lt. General, U.S.A.; with President Truman when he fired Douglas MacArthur; spoke seven languages, served as translator for President Eisenhower, deputy director of the CIA, 1972–1976; U.S. ambassador to the United Nations, 1985–1988; ambassador to West Germany, 1988–1991, Sec. 1, Lot 73-D (N-33)

Keith Ware (1915–1968) Major General, U.S.A; WWII Congressional Medal of Honor recipient; killed in combat in Vietnam, Sec. 30, Lot 258-3 (YZ-40)

Herbert N. Wassom (1938–1988) Brigadier General, U.S.A.; killed when his aircraft exploded while accompanying Pakistani President Mohammed Zia ul-Haq and U.S. Ambassador Arnold Raphel on August 17, 1988, Sec. 5, Lot 151 (W-36)

Charles J. Watters (1927–1967) Major, U.S.A.; chaplain killed while rendering aid to his fallen comrades in Vietnam; Medal of Honor recipient, Sec. 2E, Lot 186 (VW-29/30)

Caspar Weinberger (1917–2006) Captain, U.S.A.; WWII intelligence officer for General Douglas MacArthur; Richard Nixon's chair of Federal Trade Commission, director of management and budget and secretary of health, education and welfare; Ronald Reagan's secretary of defense, Sec. 30, Lot 835-1 (Y-46)

Earle Gilmore Wheeler (1908–1975) General, U.S.A.; chairman of the Joint Chiefs of Staff during the Vietnam War, 1964–1970, Sec. 30, Lot 434-1 (AA-39)

Nancy Dickerson Whitehead (1927–1997) First woman television news correspondent, CBS, 1960; Peabody Award-winning producer, married to veteran Naval Reserve officer **John C. Whitehead**, Sec. 3, Lot 1316-A-LH (LM-18/19)

Harvey Washington Wiley (1844–1930) Corporal, U.S.A.; pioneer of pure food and drug laws; "Father of the Pure Food and Drug Act;" first director of the FDA; established the Good Housekeeping Seal of Approval, Sec. 13, Lot 5959 (K-31/32)

Charles Wilkes (1798–1877) Rear Admiral, U.S.N; led 1840 expedition that confirmed Antartica is a continent, Sec. 2, Lot 1164 (TU-32)

Clifton C. Williams, Jr. (1932–1967) Major, U.S.M.C.; astronaut; died when his T-38 jet crashed on Oct. 5, 1967, Sec. 3, Lot 2503 (Q-15)

Robert R. Williams (1911–1993) Captain, U.S.N., commanded the WWII submarine *Finback* that rescued Navy pilot, later President George H. W. Bush on September 2, 1944, Columbarium, Court 3, Niche FF-6-4 (NN-20)

Ernest "Boojum" Wilson (1894–1963) Corporal, U.S.A.; inducted to the Baseball Hall of Fame, 2006, with 17 other Negro League players and Chicago Cubs pitcher Bruce Sutter; played with Homestead Grays and other teams, 1922–1945; .351 career batting average, Sec. 43, Lot 114 (U-43/44)

Orde Wingate (1903–1944) Major General, British Army; WWII commander, Zionist commando, Sec. 12, Lot 288 (XY-24/25)

Earnest Wrentmore (1904–1983) Colonel, U.S.A.F.; youngest soldier to serve with American Expeditionary Forces in WWI at the age of 12; also served in WWII and Korea, Sec. 65, Lot 4102 (GG-17)

Horatio Gouveneur Wright (1820–1899) General, U.S.A.; directed completion of the Washington Monument, 1884, then the tallest structure in the world, Sec. 45, Lot S-4 (ST-34/35)

Jerauld Wright (1898–1995) Admiral, U.S.N.; youngest graduate of the U.S. Naval Academy at age 20; WWI veteran; aide to presidents Coolidge and Hoover; veteran of WWII's European and Pacific theatres; U.S. Atlantic Fleet commander and NATO Atlantic supreme commander, 1954–1960; U.S. ambassador to Taiwan, 1963–1965, Sec. 2, Lot 4955 (V-32/33)

Horatio Wright's
headstone

Samuel B. M. Young (1840–1924) Lt. General, U.S.A.; Civil War private who became the first U.S. Army chief of staff, 1903–1904, Sec. 3, Lot 1852 (Q-14)

Luther W. Youngdahl (1896–1978) Second Lieutenant, U.S.A.; WWI veteran; Minnesota Supreme Court justice; governor, 1947–1951; U.S. District Court judge for the District of Columbia, 1951–1978, Sec. 30, Lot 402 (Z-40)

Edward F. Younger (?–1942) Sergeant, U.S.A.; WWI veteran who selected one of four caskets of unknown soldiers to be buried in the Tomb of the Unknowns (see page 277), Sec 18, Lot 1918 (LM-12/13)

Arlington's Major Monuments and Memorials

S ince its founding in 1864, Arlington National Cemetery has evolved from a paupers' cemetery–hastily established to satisfy the overwhelming demand for burial space during the Civil War–into our country's most important national shrine. The placement at Arlington of many of America's most cherished memorials has contributed to the cemetery's honored status. Described below are the major monuments that can be seen in Arlington. Each has been dedicated to the memory of a particular cause or event in American history or to a special group of individuals.

America the Beautiful Memorial Grove (Persian Gulf War Memorial)
Sec. 5, 30, 31, Grid (WX-37)

O n August 2, 1990, Iraqi forces invaded its neighbor, Kuwait, and Iraqi President Saddam Hussein soon declared Kuwait the 19th providence of Iraq. When Iraq failed to meet the February 22, 1991, deadline set by the United Nations to withdraw unconditionally, President George H.W. Bush ordered offensive action. In a lightning-fast campaign, U.S.-led coalition forces defeated Hussein's forces in only four days. "Operation Desert Storm" included 532,000 American forces; 293 lost their lives.

On May 7, 1996, former President Bush dedicated a living memorial at Arlington to the men and women who served in "Operation Desert Storm." Mounted on a pink granite stone, the plaque reads:

AMERICA THE BEAUTIFUL

MEMORIAL GROVE

THIS GROVE IS A LIVING TRIBUTE TO ALL

WHO SERVED IN THE PERSIAN GULF WAR

AND AN ENDURING SYMBOL

OF PEACE AND STRENGTH FOR ALL

Dedicated by George Bush, May 7, 1996
President of the United States of America, 1989–1993

Argonne Cross
Sec. 18, Grid K–12/13

The Argonne Forest region in northeast France near the Belgian border was the scene of some of the fiercest fighting during the last days of World War I. The American Expeditionary Force lost thousands of men and women in the Argonne region. The bodies of many of the American casualties were not returned home but instead were buried in France. Following the war, the remains of many of those Americans were disinterred and reburied, either in military cemeteries in Europe or returned to the United States. More than 2,000 of the men and women who gave their lives in France for the defense of freedom are now buried in Arlington National Cemetery, primarily in Section 18. In a corner of that large section with its many rows of simple white headstones rises the simple white rood known as the Argonne Cross.

A grove of 19 pine trees forms an emerald grotto that surrounds the 13-foot marble cross. These trees represent the trees of the Argonne Forest where so many lost their lives.

On November 17, 1921, Secretary of War **John Wingate Weeks** approved the idea of a memorial to those who died in France, regardless of where they are presently buried. Through the efforts of the Argonne Unit American Women's Legion, that stately cross now stands with an eagle and wreath engraved on its face.

Planted nearby is a memorial tree dedicated on April 28, 1985, by the Prelacy of the Armenian Apostolic Church on behalf of Armenian survivors of World War I.

Buffalo Soldiers Memorial
Section 22, Grid KL–21

O n June 28, 1866, the United States Congress authorized the creation of six regiments of African-American soldiers, then known as the United States Colored Troops. They eventually became the 9th and 10th Calvary and the 24th and 25th Infantry regiments. The 9th Calvary Regiment was activated in Greenville, Louisiana, under the command of Colonel Edward Hatch on September 21, 1866. The same day, Colonel Benjamin Grierson took command of the 10th Calvary Regiment at Fort Leavenworth, Kansas.

The first tours of duty of the USCT were on the Western frontier, building forts and roads, stringing telegraph lines, escorting stages and trains, and protecting settlers and cowboys.

The name "buffalo soldiers" is believed to have originated with the Native Americans in the region. As the legend goes, the Native Americans respected the soldiers' discipline and courage, which they equated to the strengths of the buffalo.

At a time when nearly a third of all Army enlistees deserted, these soldiers had the U.S. Army's lowest desertion and court-martial rates. From 1870 to 1890, 14 Buffalo Soldiers were awarded Congressional Medals of Honor.

When war with Spain was declared in 1898, the Buffalo Soldiers were sent to Cuba. There again, they distinguished themselves as they fought along side the legendary Rough Riders.

In 1998, a monument was dedicated at Arlington marking the centenary of the Buffalo Soldiers' participation in the Spanish-American War. It reads:

BUFFALO SOLDIERS
CENTENNIAL CEREMONY
JULY 1, 1898–JULY 1, 1998

DEDICATED TO THE BUFFALO SOLDIERS, 9th AND 10th
CALVARY, AND THE 24th AND 25th INFANTRY REGIMENTS
(COLORED TROOPS) FOR VALIANT SERVICE IN THE
SPANISH-AMERICAN WAR. THEY CHARGED UP SAN JUAN
HEIGHTS AND EL CANEY, CUBA WITH TEDDY ROOSEVELT
AND THE ROUGH RIDERS.

As in war, the monuments to the Buffalo Soldiers and the Rough Riders are side by side.

The Buffalo Soldiers also served under **John J. Pershing** in the 1916 Mexican campaign to capture Pancho Villa. It was Pershing's advocacy of these soldiers that earned him the nickname "Black Jack." The regiments remained a part of the U.S. Army until President Harry S Truman ordered the desegregation of the United States military in 1948.

Canadian Cross (Cross of Sacrifice)
Sec. 46, Grid 0–24/25

Few countries enjoy the bonds of goodwill and friendship that the United States and Canada share. Our common border remains the longest unguarded frontier on earth, and our nations have shared triumphs and tragedies throughout history. It was in this spirit of friendship that in 1925 Canadian Prime Minister MacKenzie King first proposed a memorial to the large number of United States citizens who enlisted in the Canadian Armed Forces, and lost their lives during World War I. Because the Canadians entered the war long before the United States, many Americans enlisted in Canada to join the fighting in Europe.

On June 12, 1925, President Calvin Coolidge approved the request, and on Armistice Day 1927 the monument near the Memorial Amphitheatre was dedicated. Designed by Canadian architect Sir Reginald Bloomfield, the monument consists of a bronze sword adorning a 24-foot gray granite cross.

The inscription on the cross reaffirms the sentiment expressed by Prime Minister King regarding Americans who served in the Canadian Armed Forces. Following World War II and the Korean War, similar inscriptions on other faces of the monument were dedicated to the Americans who served in those conflicts.

Chaplains' Hill
Sec. 2, Grid X–28

Tall oak trees rise majestically above the area of Arlington known as Chaplains' Hill, so named because chaplains who have served in war rest here. These chaplains, representing many different faiths, brought spiritual–and often physical–aid and comfort to American servicemen stationed throughout the world.

Chaplains' Monument

The keystone to this special area of Arlington is the Chaplains' Monument, dedicated to the 23 chaplains who lost their lives in World War I. Although it stands only five-and-a-half feet tall, its purpose is immeasurable for it recognizes the invaluable services rendered by men of faith in all wars. Erected by chaplains who served in the Great War, it was dedicated on May 5, 1926.

Among the men who went into battle unarmed, and who are now buried on this grassy hill, are Colonel **John T. Axton,** the Army's first chief of chaplains; and World War II's Chief of Chaplains **William R. Arnold,** the first chaplain to attain general's rank. He later served as a Catholic auxiliary bishop of New York City.

Representative of the chaplains who served during the Vietnam War is Major **Charles Joseph**

Watters (Sec. 2E, Lot 186-A, Grid VW–29/30) who was posthumously awarded the Congressional Medal of Honor for his actions on November 19, 1967. With complete disregard for his own safety during an assault on Hill 875 near Dak To, Chaplain Watters, unarmed, was rendering aid to his fallen comrades when he was killed by a nearby bomb explosion.

Inscribed on the face of the Chaplains' Monument is the quote from the Bible (John 15:13): "Greater love hath no man than this, that a man lay down his life for his friends."

Catholic Chaplains' Memorial

Eighty-three Catholic chaplains lost their lives during World War II, the Korean War, and in Vietnam. On May 21, 1989, a memorial was dedicated in their honor. The nearly seven-foot monument is made of unpolished granite. On its face is a bronze plaque that lists the names of the 70 priests who gave their lives during World War II, six who died during the Korean War, and the seven who died in Vietnam.

Confederate Monument
Sec. 16, Grid I–23

T he history of Arlington National Cemetery is steeped in the Civil War, for it was this great national struggle that necessitated the establishment of this cemetery to bury its many dead. For many years following the war, the bitter feelings between North and South remained, and although hundreds of Confederate soldiers were buried at Arlington, it was considered a Union cemetery. Family members of Confederate soldiers were denied permission to decorate their loved ones' graves and in extreme cases were denied entrance to the cemetery.

These ill feelings were slow to die, but over time they finally began to fade. Many historians believe it was the national call to arms during the Spanish-American War that brought Northerners and Southerners together at last. In that war, numerous Confederate veterans volunteered their services and joined their Northern brothers on the battlefield in the common defense of our nation. In June 1900, in this spirit of national reconciliation, the United States Congress authorized that a section of Arlington National Cemetery be set aside for the burial of Confederate dead. By the end of 1901, all the Confederate soldiers buried in the national cemeteries at Alexandria, Virginia, and at the Soldiers' Home in Washington had been brought

The solemn figure of a woman representing the South extends a laurel wreath toward her fallen sons. Peaked headstones that mark the graves of Confederate soldiers surround the Confederate Monument in Jackson Circle.

together with the soldiers buried at Arlington and reinterred in the Confederate section. Among the 482 persons buried, there are 46 officers, 351 enlisted men, 58 wives, 15 Southern civilians, and 12 unknowns. They are buried in concentric circles around the Confederate Monument, and their graves are marked with headstones that are distinct for their pointed tops. Legend attributes these pointed-top tombstones to a Confederate belief that the points would "keep Yankees from sitting on them."

To further honor these citizens of the South, the United Daughters of the Confederacy petitioned to erect a major monument to the Confederate dead. On March 4, 1906, Secretary of War **William Howard Taft** granted their request. The cornerstone was laid on November 12, 1912, at a ceremony featuring speakers **William Jennings Bryan** and **James A. Tanner,** a former Union corporal who lost both legs at the second Battle of Bull Run. Tanner was commander in chief of the Union veterans group, The Grand Army of the Republic. That same evening, now-President William Howard Taft addressed the United Daughters of the Confederacy at a reception held in the Daughters of the American Revolution's Centennial Hall.

Chosen to design the memorial was the world-renowned sculptor, **Moses Ezekiel.** Ezekiel brought more than just his artistic talents to this project for he also was a Confederate veteran who knew firsthand the horrors of the Civil War. He is now buried at the base of the famous monument he created.

The Confederate Monument was unveiled before a large crowd of Northerners and Southerners on June 4, 1914, the 106th anniversary of the birthday of President of the Confederacy Jefferson Davis. President Woodrow Wilson delivered an address and veterans of both the Union and Confederacy placed wreaths on the graves of their former foes, symbolizing the reconciliation between the North and the South that is this memorial's central theme.

Ezekiel created a monument rich in symbols. Standing atop the 32-foot monument is a larger-than-life figure of a woman representing the South. Her head is crowned with olive leaves; her left hand extends a laurel

Former Confederate and Union officers join President Woodrow Wilson (left) at the dedication ceremonies for the Confederate monument in 1914. With its dedication, Arlington became a truly national cemetery.

wreath toward the South, acknowledging the sacrifice of her fallen sons. Her right hand holds a pruning hook resting on a plow stock. These symbols bring to life the biblical passage inscribed at her feet: "And they shall beat their swords into plow shares and their spears into pruning hooks." The plinth on which she stands is embossed with four cinerary urns symbolizing the four years of the Civil War.

Supporting the plinth is a frieze of 14 inclined shields, each shield depicts the coat of arms of one of the 13 Confederate states and Maryland, which did not join the Confederacy, but supported the South in the war.

Below the plinth is another frieze of life-sized figures depicting mythical gods and Southern soldiers. At the front of the monument, the panoplied figure of Minerva, goddess of war and wisdom, attempts to hold up the figure of a fallen woman (The South) who is resting upon her shield, The Constitution. Behind The South, the Spirits of War are trumpeting in every direction calling the sons and daughters of the South to aid their falling mother. On either side of the fallen woman are figures depicting those sons and daughters who came to her aid, and who represent each branch of the Confederate service: Soldier, Sailor, Sapper, and Miner.

Completing the frieze are six vignettes illustrating the effect of the war on Southerners of all races. The vignettes include a faithful black slave following his young master; an officer kissing his infant child in the arms of her mammy; a blacksmith leaving his bellows and workshop as his sorrowful wife looks on; a robed clergyman bidding farewell to his wife and young son; a young lady binding the sword and sash on her beau; and a young officer standing alone.

The base of the memorial features several inscriptions. On its front face are the seal of the Confederacy and a tribute by the United Daughters of the Confederacy, followed by the Latin phrase: *Victrix Causa Diis Placuit Sed Victa Caton.* Translated this phrase means: "The Victorious Cause was Pleasing to the Gods, But the Lost Cause to Cato." On the rear of the monument is an inscription attributed to the Reverend Randolph Harrison McKim, who was a Confederate chaplain, and who served as pastor of the Epiphany Church in Washington for 32 years. It reads:

> Not for fame or reward
> Not for place or for rank
> Not lured by ambition
> Or goaded by necessity
> But in simple
> Obedience to duty
> As they understood it
> These men suffered all
> Sacrificed all
> Dared all–and died

In addition to Moses Ezekiel, three other Confederate soldiers are buried at the base of the monument. They are Lt. **Harry C. Marmaduke** who served in the Confederate Navy, Captain **John M. Hickey** of the Second Missouri Infantry, and Brigadier General **Marcus J. Wright** who commanded brigades at Shiloh and Chickamauga.

The Hiker
United Spanish War Veterans Memorial
Memorial Drive, Grid LL–40

Approaching Arlington National Cemetery along Memorial Drive, the first monument on the left is the United Spanish War Veterans Memorial, known as the Hiker. The solitary figure is an American veteran dressed in the uniform worn by the Army during the Spanish-American War. Displayed on its front face are the dates of that conflict, 1898-1902. Mounted on the base of the memorial is a bronze cross bearing the names of the four theatres of service for the war: Cuba, Puerto Rico, the United States, and the Philippine Islands. This memorial was erected by the United Spanish War Veterans, and was dedicated at a special ceremony on July 24, 1965.

Korean War Veterans Memorial
Section 48, Grid QR–26

On June 25, 1950, North Korean troops streamed across the border into South Korea. Just three days later they captured its capital, Seoul. By September 1950, U.S.-led United Nations forces had counterattacked, retaking Seoul. Within a month, U.N. forces had captured the North Korean capital of Pyongyang. But almost immediately Communist Chinese forces entered the war, forcing a U.N. retreat. Although cease-fire negotiations began in July, 1951, the war dragged on until an armistice was signed on July 27, 1953. By the time the war had ended, 5.7 million Americans had served in Korea.

On July 27, 1987—the 34th anniversary of the signing of the Korean War armistice—No Greater Love and the Korean War Veterans Association dedicated a gray marble bench as the first international memorial to those Americans who died fighting that war.

On the back of the bench, these words are inscribed:

"The Beginning of the End of War Lies in Remembrance"
– Herman Wouk

IN SACRED MEMORY OF THOSE AMERICANS WHO GAVE
THEIR LIVES DURING THE KOREAN WAR, 1950–1953

54,246 DIED   8,177 MISSING IN ACTION
389 UNACCOUNTED FOR POWS

FIRST INTERNATIONAL TRIBUTE, JULY 27, 1987
GIVEN BY NO GREATER LOVE AND THE KOREAN WAR
VETERANS ASSOCIATION

Beside a shady walkway near the Memorial Amphitheatre, this inviting respite offers weary visitors a peaceful place to rest and reflect–a noble offering in stark contrast to the struggle that cost so many Americans their lives a half a century ago.

The Lockerbie Memorial Cairn
(Pan Am Flight 103 Memorial)
Section 1, Grid NO–33/34

O n December 21, 1988, Pan American Airways Flight 103 was enroute from Frankfurt, Germany, via London to New York. It left London's Heathrow Airport at 6:25 p.m., local time. At 7:02 p.m., Flight 103 was ripped apart by a violent explosion. Blazing fragments of the plane rained down on the city of Lockerbie, Scotland. A wing section complete with engines landed on a residential section of Lockerbie, creating a crater 155 feet by 196 feet. In total, 259 passengers from 22 countries and 11 people on  the ground were killed. After a painstaking reconstruction of the aircraft and a lengthy international investigation, the cause of the explosion was determined to be a bomb planted in the cargo hold of the plane.

On November 3, 1995, President Bill Clinton unveiled the Lockerbie Memorial Cairn at Arlington National Cemetery. Among those present at the ceremony were victims' family members, residents of Lockerbie, American and British law enforcement officers, and many people who simply wanted to honor those who were killed.

The monument is a 12-foot conical tower representing a traditional Scottish cairn or memorial. It is made of 270 blocks of red Scottish sandstone. Each stone represents one life lost when Flight 103 crashed. The names of the victims are engraved on the marble collar at the base of the tower. The following words also are engraved on the base:

On 21 December 1988, a terrorist bomb destroyed
Pan American Airlines Flight 103 over Lockerbie, Scotland,
killing all on board and 11 on the ground.
The 270 Scottish stones which compose this memorial cairn
commemorate those who lost their lives in
this attack against America.

A bronze plaque on the side of the cairn states:

IN REMEMBRANCE OF
THE TWO HUNDRED SEVENTY
PEOPLE KILLED IN THE
TERRORIST BOMBING OF
PAN AMERICAN AIRWAYS
FLIGHT 103 OVER LOCKERBIE,
SCOTLAND
21 DECEMBER 1988
PRESENTED BY
THE LOCKERBIE AIR DISASTER TRUST
TO THE UNITED STATES OF AMERICA

McClellan Arch
Grid CC–27/28

Following the establishment of Arlington National Cemetery in 1864, the grounds were enclosed. Several gates provided pedestrian and vehicular access. The main entrance to the cemetery was located where the McClellan Arch currently towers 30 feet above the roadway.

The arch was constructed during the 1870s as a tribute to Civil War General George B. McClellan whose wartime headquarters were located at

Arlington house. It was a tribute to General McClellan, not a memorial. McClellan did not die until October 29, 1885. Although McClellan is not buried at Arlington, his son, **George B. McClellan, Jr.,** is buried in Section 2. (See page 231.)

Atop the arch facing east, the word "McClellan" is inscribed in gold. Below that is the phrase:

> "On fame's eternal camping ground
>
> their silent tents are spread,
>
> And glory guards with solemn round,
>
> the bivouac of the dead."

The west face of the arch is inscribed with the words:

> "Rest on embalmed and sainted dead,
>
> dear as the blood ye gave,
>
> no impious footsteps here shall tread
>
> on the herbage of your grave."

Memorial Amphitheatre
Grid Q–23

By the turn of the twentieth century, Arlington National Cemetery had won its place in the hearts of Americans as a special site for honoring the valiant men and women who have served our country. It no longer was considered just a pauper's cemetery, a graveyard for people who had nowhere else to go. By 1900, many of the great soldiers of the Civil War–generals and privates alike–chose Arlington as their final resting place. Veterans of the Spanish-American War, including 229 crewmen from the *USS Maine,* had been buried here. Since 1868, it had become a gathering place each Memorial Day for solemn ceremonies honoring the nation's dead. And in 1914, with the dedication of the Confederate Monument, Arlington had truly become a national cemetery.

The Old Amphitheatre near Arlington House had provided a rostrum for speakers for 40 years, but it could no longer accommodate the size of the crowds that were coming to attend the larger memorial ceremonies at Arlington. Therefore in 1908, a movement was launched by the Civil War

A rare aerial view of the Memorial Amphitheatre during its final stages of construction in 1919. Also shown in the *USS Maine* Memorial (above and to the right of the Amphitheatre) and the Confederate Monument in Jackson Circle (upper right). The Spanish-American War Memorial is shown upper left.

veterans group, Grand Army of the Republic, to construct a larger permanent facility. With a membership in excess of 300,000, the GAR approached Congress and expressed their sentiment that Arlington National Cemetery had become a national shrine for all time. Representing the GAR, Judge **Ivory G. Kimball** (Sec. 3, Lot 1538) stated in a hearing before Congress, "Arlington is not for today; it is not for the Grand Army of the Republic alone; it is not for the Spanish War veterans alone, but during all time as long as this nation lasts Arlington will be unique and will be the burial place for our soldiers."

On May 30,1908, a commission was authorized by an act of Congress to oversee the planning and construction of the Arlington Memorial Amphitheatre. The necessary appropriations were not made, however, until five years later on March 4, 1913, and bids were finally let on February 11, 1915. Such great importance was attributed to this structure that President Woodrow Wilson laid the cornerstone on October 13, 1915, in the presence of thousands of spectators, including veterans from the Civil War and the Spanish-American War.

Even before its completion, the Amphitheatre became a place of assembly. Memorial Day services were held in the unfinished amphitheatre in 1919 almost a year before it was dedicated on May 15, 1920. A memorable day of festivities accompanied that dedication. Grand Marshall for the event was the 80-year-old former general in chief of the Army, **Nelson Appleton Miles.** President Woodrow Wilson, unable to attend the dedication because of his ill health, was represented by Secretary of War Newton D. Baker.

The Memorial Amphitheatre remains today much as it was on the day it was dedicated in 1920. Frederick D. Owens, of the New York architectural firm of Carrere and Hastings and chief architect of the structure, endeavored to "obtain a classic and serious character in order to express the dignity of the [amphitheatre's] purpose." Such classic structures as the Theatre of Dionysus at Athens and the Roman Theatre at Orange were studied with the desire to meld classic design with the colonial character of the other buildings in Washington, such as the White House and the U. S. Capitol.

Made of white marble from Danby, Vermont, the central feature of the structure is the large amphitheatre formed by a 152-by-200-foot ellipse which seats approximately 5,000 people. Forty-two special seating boxes are provided around the inside Doric marble colonnade that encircles the Amphitheatre. There are entrances at the four principal axes, with the main entrance from the east leading onto a stage large enough to accommodate between 250 and 300 people.

Inscriptions of quotations from presidents Washington and Lincoln, as well as the names of prominent military figures and battle sites, adorn both the interior and exterior walls of the Amphitheatre. On the apse is carved the quote from George Washington's statement to the Provincial Congress in New York on June 26, 1775: "When We Assumed The Soldier We Did Not Lay Aside The Citizen."

The arch above the stage bears the inscription from Abraham Lincoln's Gettysburg Address: "We Here Highly Resolve That These Dead Shall Not Have Died In Vain." On the two piers supporting the arch above the stage are inscribed the names of 14 Army commanders and 14 Navy commanders, all from the period prior to World War I when the Amphitheatre was built. The names of all the men are listed chronologically from the War of

Independence through the Spanish-American War. Each of the piers is filled to capacity precluding the addition of more recent names. The names of these 28 military leaders, of whom three are buried at Arlington, were approved by the Arlington Memorial Commission. Around the exterior wall above the colonnade are inscribed the names of 44 major battles from the War of Independence, the War of 1812, the Mexican War, the Civil War, and the Spanish-American War.

The Memorial Amphitheatre now serves a variety of important functions. Many memorial services are held here annually, particularly on Memorial Day and Veterans' Day. The Amphitheatre has been used for funeral services on special occasions. Three of those occasions were to bury the Unknowns who now rest on the East plaza of the Amphitheatre. The other six services held in the Amphitheatre were for Sculptor **Moses Ezekiel,** who created the Confederate Monument, March 30, 1921; Colonel **Charles Young** (Sec. 3, Lot 1730, Grid RS- 16/17), June 1, 1923, the first black graduate of the U.S. Military Academy; Ignace Jan Paderewski, July 5, 1941, the Polish statesman; General of the Armies **John J. Pershing,** July 19, 1948; Secretary of Defense **James V. Forrestal,** May 25, 1949; and General **Henry "Hap" Arnold,** first Air Force chief of staff, January 18, 1950.

In the lower level of the Amphitheatre is a vaulted chapel which is used for various religious functions. Among the services held here was the funeral for five U. S. airmen shot down over Yugoslavia in September 1946, and a service for General **Jonathan Mayhew Wainwright.**

Forming part of the east entrance to the Amphitheatre is a large hall, presently used as a Memorial Display Room. On the first floor of this area are the decorations, commendations, plaques, and other memorabilia associated with the Unknowns who have been buried on the plaza directly east of the Memorial Amphitheatre. Included are the flags which have draped the caskets of each of those servicemen, the Medal of Honor that each has been awarded, and the numerous American and foreign awards presented on their behalf. Together with these many awards is a pictorial history of the Unknowns' interment ceremonies.

On the second floor of the pavilion is the Medal of Honor Room, designed and used solely to display and honor the names of all service personnel who have been awarded the Medal of Honor, the highest of military decorations. Also located in the Amphitheatre is a carillon presented on October 25, 1949, by AMVETS to the People of the United States in memory of those who died during World War II. The carillon was rededicated during a ceremony on April 2, 1978.

On March 15, 1969, in honor of the fiftieth anniversary of the American Legion, President Richard Nixon dedicated the lighting system for the Tomb of the Unknowns, which was provided by the American Legion and the American Legion Auxiliary. A plaque honoring the occasion is located in the Amphitheatre.

Memorial Entrance to Arlington National Cemetery

The entrance to Arlington National Cemetery extends across the Potomac River to near the Lincoln Memorial at the eastern edge of the Memorial Bridge. The Memorial Bridge, Memorial Drive (the parkway which leads into Arlington Cemetery), and the magnificent entrance to the cemetery were designed as a single project and were dedicated together on January 16, 1932 by President Herbert Hoover.

The Memorial Bridge was intended as a symbolic link, binding the North and the South together into one great Union. The theme of national unity continued as Architects McKim, Meade & White designed the bridge to extend along an axis joining two great symbols of our nation: the Lincoln Memorial and the Robert E. Lee Memorial at Arlington House.

Connecting the bridge to the cemetery gates is a parkway known as Memorial Drive. Along this parkway is the rotary intersection with the George Washington Memorial Parkway, which leads to the first president's home at Mt. Vernon. At night, as visitors approach Arlington along Memorial Drive, the eternal flame, which marks President **John Kennedy's** grave, is visible on the hillside. Also located along Memorial Drive are several memorials and monuments not formally part of Arlington Cemetery. These

.abees Memorial, the Mechanized Armor Memorial, the United : Veterans Memorial (the Hiker), the monument to Admiral **rd**, and the 101st Airborne Division Memorial. Near the Seabees Memori.. .s the Arlington Cemetery Metro subway stop. Memorial Drive ends in a sculpted court that has been partially excavated from the steep hillside below Arlington House.

At the western end of the court is the Hemicycle, a semicircular retaining wall which rises 30 feet and is 226 feet in diameter. In the center of this wall is a large semicircular niche that measures 20 feet across and 30 feet high. In the center of the niche is a bas-relief of the Great Seal of the United States. On either side of the Great Seal are seals of the Department of the Army and the Department of the Navy, with the Army on the south side and the Navy on the north.

The Hemicycle now forms the exterior wall of the Women in Military Service for America Memorial. The memorial was dedicated in 1997 to honor nearly two million women who have served in the United States Armed Forces. (See page 295.)

From the court, roads lead both north and south through a pair of large ornate wrought iron gates in each direction. The set of gates on the north is called Schley Gate after Admiral **Winfield Scott Schley.** The set on the south side is called Roosevelt Gate in honor of President Theodore Roosevelt. In the center of each gate is mounted a gold wreath, 30 inches in diameter. Set within each wreath is a shield with the seal of one of the military services. On the Roosevelt Gate are the seals for the U.S. Marine Corps and the U.S. Army. Mounted on the Schley Gate are the U.S. Navy and U.S. Coast Guard seals. When the gates were installed, the United States Air Force was still a branch of the Army and so its own seal does not appear.

The Memorial Bridge, Memorial Drive, the memorials, and monuments which line that drive, the Memorial Entrance, and the Robert E. Lee Memorial (Arlington House) all fall within the jurisdiction of the National Park Service, U.S. Department of the Interior.

Memorial Sections
Sections 2, 3, and 13

In Arlington Cemetery there are 11 Memorial Sections where the tombstones bear the special phrase, "In the Memory of...," This phrase is not found on the standard regulation headstone. These stones mark the cenotaphs, or empty graves, of those service personnel whose bodies could not

be recovered, but whose deaths have been certified by the United States Department of Defense. These cenotaphs memorialize more than 1,200 dead from World War II, Korea, and Vietnam in Arlington. These are not graves of unknowns, but rather of persons whose identities are established, but whose remains cannot be located. In the Memorial Sections, the headstones are placed more closely together and are usually located on steeper terrain that would prohibit the burying of caskets. The cenotaph of popular orchestra leader **Glenn Miller** is located in Section 13 (Lot 464-A). (See page 144.) Miller's plane disappeared on a flight from London to Paris in 1944. The plane was never found. And the five **Sullivan Brothers**, who died together when their ship was destroyed during WWII, are buried in Section 3 (Lots 30-34). (See page 205.)

Memorial to the Servicemen Killed in Beirut, 1983
Sec. 59, Grid EE–26

In the summer of 1983, the United States agreed to take part in an effort to restore peace to Lebanon, a country shaken by civil war. Together with French and Italian troops, American forces were deployed near the International Airport in Beirut. Both Marines and Sailors were stationed in a temporary military compound.

Early on the morning of October 23, 1983, in a suicidal assault, a terrorist crashed a munitions- laden truck through the security gate of the compound and into the barracks where hundreds of American servicemen lay sleeping. The resulting explosion

"LET PEACE TAKE ROOT"

THIS CEDAR OF LEBANON TREE GROWS IN LIVING MEMORY OF THE AMERICANS KILLED IN THE BEIRUT TERRORIST ATTACK AND ALL VICTIMS OF TERRORISM THROUGHOUT THE WORLD.
DEDICATED DURING THE FIRST MEMORIAL CEREMONY FOR THESE VICTIMS.

GIVEN BY NO GREATER LOVE
OCTOBER 23, 1984
A TIME OF REMEMBRANC

hurled debris hundreds of yards in every direction. When at last the rubble could be cleared and an accounting made of missing Americans, 161 U.S. servicemen lay dead. These men, dedicated to keeping the peace, had no chance to defend themselves. The bodies of the servicemen were returned to the United States, accompanied by military honor guards.

Twenty-two of these men are now buried at Arlington National Cemetery in Section 59.

On October 23, 1984, a ceremony was held to honor those 161 servicemen by the organization called No Greater Love. In memory of these men, a cedar of Lebanon tree was planted and a monument dedicated. Entitled "Let Peace Take Root," the monument proclaims that this cedar tree was placed as a living memory of those men who died in Beirut.

The monument also is dedicated to all victims of terrorism throughout the world. One such victim was Seaman **Robert Stethem,** who was serving in the United States Navy at the time this tree was planted. On June 15, 1985, Stethem was murdered by extremists when they discovered he was an American military serviceman traveling on the civilian airline flight they had hijacked. He is buried nearby. (See page 200.)

Memorial to the Servicemen Who Died During the Attempt to Rescue American Hostages Held in Iran, 1980
Sec. 46, Grid OP–23/24

The fall of 1979 was a turbulent period in Iran. The Shah had been deposed by Islamic fundamentalists under the Ayatollah Khomeini, and although diplomatic relations still existed between the United States and Iran, these relations were strained. On November 4, 1979, hundreds of Iranians seized the U.S. embassy and took 66 Americans hostage. For days nothing was known of the hostages' condition until their captors finally released all female and black hostages. Later, one other man was released for medical reasons, leaving 53 Americans captives of the Iranian Islamic fundamentalists.

By spring of 1980, the situation had reached a virtual standstill, with all diplomatic channels apparently exhausted. In the absence of diplomatic options, President Jimmy Carter authorized a secret military operation on April 25, 1980, designed to rescue those remaining American hostages. The plan called for a rendezvous of helicopters and cargo planes at a remote desert site in Iran before attempting the actual rescue of the hostages. However, the mission was

aborted when a freak accident caused two of the aircraft to collide. The ensuing explosion and fire claimed the lives of eight American service personnel. Their bodies could not be recovered before the surviving aircraft had to abandon the desert staging area. Shortly thereafter the eight bodies were returned to the United States, but the remaining 53 hostages were not freed until January 20, 1981, 444 days after they had been captured.

A monument dedicated to the memory of those gallant servicemen, who died in the valiant effort to rescue the American hostages, has been erected near the Memorial Amphitheatre at Arlington National Cemetery. The white stone marker bears a bronze plaque listing the names and ranks of the three Marines and the five airmen. Three of those men—Major **Richard Bakke**, Major **Harold Lewis, Jr.**, and Sergeant **Joel Mayo**—are now buried at Arlington in a grave marked by a common headstone located about 25 feet from to the group memorial.

Military Order of the Purple Heart Memorial
Amphitheatre, Sec. 35, Grid PQ-22

The Purple Heart was the first military decoration established by General George Washington during the Revolutionary War. Revived by President Herbert Hoover in 1932, its award was made retroactive to service during World War I. On May 30, 1984, the Military Order of the Purple Heart, a congressionally chartered organization, planted a tree and placed a plaque on the south side of the Memorial Amphitheatre, declaring the area a Historic Site of the Order.

Mothers' Tree
Amphitheatre, Sec. 48 (P-24/25)

The American Legion Auxiliary planted a tree on a site north of the Memorial Amphitheatre on May 8, 1932, to pay tribute to all mothers who had suffered the loss of a child during active military service.

Netherlands Carillon
Located just north of the Ord-Weitzel Gate of Arlington

Following World War II, the people of the Netherlands wished to show their deep appreciation for the assistance provided by the United States, both during and after the war. It was decided that a carillon, made in the Netherlands, would be presented to the people of the United States. A drive was undertaken to raise the funds. Contributions were received from Netherlanders young and old and from every walk of life. After years of planning, on May 5, 1960, dedication ceremonies were held, and on behalf of her people, the Netherlands' beloved Queen Juliana presented the bell tower to the people of the United States. There were 49 bells with the smallest weighing 42 pounds and the largest weighing more than six tons. The unique bells were cast in three different Netherlands foundries.

In 1995, to celebrate the 50th anniversary of the liberation of the Netherlands from the Nazis, a group of Dutch citizens raised the necessary funds to refurbish the aging carillon and to add a 50th bell to celebrate 50 years of freedom enjoyed by the Dutch people. It was dedicated on May 5, 1995.

The Netherlands Carillon is approximately 127 feet high, 25 feet deep and 36 feet wide, standing on a quartzite plaza 93 feet square and surrounded by thousands of tulips. It is located on a beautifully landscaped site directly north of the Ord-Weitzel Gate of Arlington Cemetery, near the Iwo Jima monument. The music of these famous bells can be heard throughout the cemetery during concerts performed at the Carillon on Saturdays and national holidays from May through September. Visitors are welcome to climb the tower to watch the carillonneur perform and view the city of Washington and other surrounding features. For more information about the concerts, visit the National Park Service Web site at http://www.nps.gov/archive/gwmp/carillon.htm.

Nurses Memorial
Sec 21, Grid M–19/20

On the gentle sloping hillsides in Section 21 hundreds of nurses are buried. They served American troops from the time of the Spanish-American War until today. On a nearby knoll, rising above the simple headstones of these women, the figure of a nurse stands like a guardian angel keeping watch over her fellow medics. Frances Rich's sculpture captures the compassion, the gentleness, and the strength, which are exemplified by the nurses of the United States Armed Forces.

In 1937, Army and Navy nurses began a drive to raise funds for a monument at Arlington National Cemetery dedicated to all nurses who had served in the United States Armed Forces. On May 4, 1937, permission was granted by Secretary of War Harry H. Wooding, to plan and erect the monument. On the afternoon of November 8, 1938, during a moving dedication ceremony, the eight-and-one-half-foot marble statue was unveiled to the reverent applause of the scores of nurses assembled. Its simple inscription: Army and Navy Nurses.

On November 20, 1970, a rededication ceremony was held to extend its commemoration to include all nurses who had served since 1938, as well as to include all Air Force nurses.

Old Amphitheatre and Rostrum
Section 26, Grid P–32

Near Arlington House, in a section of what was once the garden of Mary and Robert E. Lee, is the old Amphitheatre and Rostrum. Completed in 1868 in compliance with the order of General John A. Logan, it was dedicated as part of the first observance of Decoration Day (now Memorial Day) on May 30 of that year. The featured speaker on that occasion was General James A. Garfield, later president of the United States.

The Amphitheatre is encircled by a colonnade which supports a latticed roof, once covered with thick vines. In the center of the Amphitheatre is a dais known as "the Rostrum," made of white marble in a classic design and inscribed with the phrase, *E pluribus unum* (Out of many, one). The Old Amphitheatre held 1,500 seats and served as the principal area of assembly before the current Memorial Amphitheatre was completed in 1921. Among the great speakers who graced its podium was **William Jennings Bryan.**

This 1868 photograph (left) shows the Old Amphitheatre and Rostrum where hundreds of people would gather for large memorial services before the new Amphitheatre was opened in 1921. The Old Amphitheatre is located near Arlington House. Right, the Old Amphitheatre as it looks today.

Pearl Harbor Survivors' Memorial
Amphitheatre, Sec. 48, Grid R-24

On December 7, 1984, the 43rd anniversary of the Japanese attack on Pearl Harbor, the Pearl Harbor Survivors Association planted a tree on the north side of the Memorial Amphitheatre in memory of all persons who survived that attack, but who have since died.

POW/MIA Memorial
Amphitheatre, Sec. 48, Grid Q-24

On October 9, 1983, No Greater Love planted a tree on the north side of the Memorial Amphitheatre in honor of persons who have fought in any war and who are listed as "Missing In Action" or as a "Prisoner of War."

Pyramid of Remembrance Living Memorial

A simple red granite block under a magnolia tree is dedicated to the memory of service personnel who have died in missions other than declared wars. Dedicated on May 11, 2004, the memorial was conceived by students at Riverside High School in Painesville, Ohio, after they saw news reports of the body of a soldier being dragged through the streets of Mogadishu, Somalia, in 1993. U.S. troops had been sent to Mogadishu to help quell violence in the Somali capital. A Black Hawk helicopter was downed during the operation and one or more of the bodies of U.S. casualties were dragged through the streets by civilians.

The high school students decided to spearhead a drive to construct a 40-foot memorial pyramid on the National Mall in Washington dedicated to U.S. service personnel who have died in operations other than declared wars. It was finally decided to place a living memorial at Arlington National Cemetery.

The memorial reads:

FAITH * HONOR * VIRTUE
THIS LIVING MEMORIAL IS DEDICATED TO THE

BRAVE MEN AND WOMEN OF THE UNITED STATES

ARMED FORCES WHO HAVE PERISHED DURING

TRAINING ACCIDENTS, PEACEKEEPING MISSIONS,

HUMANITARIAN EFFORTS, COVERT OPERATIONS

AND TERRORIST ATTACKS.

DEDICATED IN 2004

BY

AMERICA'S YOUTH

WE WILL ALWAYS REMEMBER YOUR SACRIFICE

The Roads and Walkways of Arlington National Cemetery

Within the confines of Arlington National Cemetery, there are 45 roads and walkways stretching more than 15 miles. These arteries are named in honor of well-known American military figures, each of whom is noted below. Although not all of these famous Americans are buried at Arlington, the names of those whose graves are here appear in bold.

Arnold Drive
World War II General of the Air Force **Henry "Hap" Arnold**
Capron Drive
Named in honor of several family members
Clayton Drive
Civil War Brigadier General **Powell Clayton**
Crook Walk
Civil War Major General **George Crook**
Custis Walk
Arlington estate founder **George Washington Parke Custis**
Dewey Drive
Spanish-American War Admiral George Dewey
Doubleday Walk
Civil War Major General **Abner Doubleday**
Eisenhower Drive
General of the Army and President Dwight David Eisenhower
Farragut Drive
Civil War Admiral David Glasgow Farragut
Garfield Drive
Civil War Brigadier General and President James Abram Garfield
Grant Drive
Civil War General and President Ulysses S. Grant

Halsey Drive
World War II Fleet Admiral **William "Bull" Halsey**
Hobson Drive
Spanish-American War Rear Admiral Richmond P. Hobson
Humphreys Drive
Civil War General Andres A. Humphreys
Jackson Circle
Confederate Civil War General Thomas "Stonewall" Jackson
Jesup Drive
Major General Thomas S. Jesup, War of 1812
King Drive
World War II Fleet Admiral Ernest J. King
Lawton Drive
Civil War Major General Henry W. Lawton
Leahy Drive
World War II Fleet Admiral **William D. Leahy**
Lee Drive
Confederate Civil War General Robert E. Lee
L'Enfant Drive
Revolutionary War Captain **Pierre Charles L'Enfant**
Lincoln Drive
President Abraham Lincoln
MacArthur Circle
Lieutenant General **Arthur MacArthur**
MacArthur Drive
World War II General of the Army Douglas MacArthur
Marshall Drive
World War II General of the Army **George C. Marshall**
McClellan Drive
Civil War Major General George B. McClellan.
McKinley Drive
Civil War Major and President William McKinley
McPherson Drive
Civil War Major General James McPherson
Meigs Drive
Quartermaster Major General **Montgomery Meigs**
Memorial Drive
For all Americans who have served in the Armed Forces of the United States

Miles Drive
    Civil War Lieutenant General **Nelson A. Miles**
Mitchell Drive
    Army Air Corps Major General William Mitchell
Nimitz Drive
    World War II Fleet Admiral Chester Nimitz
Ord-Weitzel Drive
    Civil War Major Generals **Edward O. C. Ord** and Godfrey Weitzel
Patton Drive
    World War II General George S. Patton, Jr.
Pershing Drive
    General of the Armies **John J. Pershing**
Porter Drive
    Civil War Admiral **David Dixon Porter**
Roosevelt Drive
    Rough Rider Colonel and President Theodore Roosevelt
Schley Drive
    Spanish-American War Rear Admiral **Winfield Scott Schley**
Sheridan Drive
    Civil War General **Philip Henry Sheridan**
Sherman Drive
    Civil War General William Tecumseh Sherman
Sigsbee Drive
    Spanish-American War Rear Admiral **Charles Dwight Sigsbee**
Weeks Drive
    U.S. Secretary of War **John Wingate Weeks**
Wilson Drive
    President Thomas Woodrow Wilson
York Drive
    Sergeant Alvin C. York, World War I hero

Rough Riders Memorial
Sec. 22, Grid KL–21

T hey became one of the best-known cavalry units in American history, though few people remember their official title, the First U.S. Volunteer Cavalry. But mention the name "Rough Riders," and visions come to mind of the charge up San Juan Hill, led by **Leonard Wood** and Teddy Roosevelt. The Rough Riders served with distinction during the Spanish-American War. This monument was erected to their memory by the members and friends of the regiment in 1906.

It is a large, dark-gray granite stone that displays the insignia of the First U.S. Volunteer Cavalry on its west face. It also lists the battles in which the Rough Riders took part–Las Guasimas, San Juan, and Santiago. The names of all the officers and enlisted men of the First Cavalry who lost their lives during the Spanish-American War are engraved on the imposing granite stone.

Seabees Memorial
Memorial Drive, Grid KK–40/41

W hen the United States was suddenly and dramatically pulled into World War II following the Japanese attack on Pearl Harbor in December 1941, there was an acute shortage of military bases to support American combat forces deployed in Europe and the Pacific. To alleviate the shortage, the United States Navy established an engineering and construction force known as the U.S. Naval Construction Battalion, or C.B.

Soon its members were universally known by the nickname derived from those initials, the Seabees.

Along Memorial Drive near the Arlington Cemetery Metro stop is a monument dedicated to the men who have served as Seabees. A larger-than-life figure dominates the monument depicting the momentous contributions made by the Construction Battalion. The image is that of a Seabee, who in

the midst of a construction project, stops to make friends with a young child. Below the figures are the words, "With Compassion for Others We Build–We Fight for Peace With Freedom."

On a semicircular bronze bas-relief, sculptor Felix de Weldon (who also sculpted the Iwo Jima monument) depicted scenes of Seabees at work in various construction trades. Prominently displayed is the Seabee slogan "Can Do." This graphic memorial was dedicated on May 27, 1974.

Second Schweinfurt Memorial
Amphitheatre, Sec. 35, Grid Q-22

A maple tree and a plaque have been placed on the south side of the Memorial Amphitheatre by the Second Schweinfurt Memorial Association, and have been dedicated to the memory of the airmen of the U.S. Army Eighth Air Force who attacked and destroyed a ball bearing factory in Schweinfurt, Germany, on October 14, 1943.

September 11th Memorial
Sec. 64, Grid NN-15

Tuesday, September 11, 2001, was a sunny, warm day. By 9:00 a.m., more than 24,000 people were at work inside the Pentagon, the U.S. military headquarters in Arlington, Virginia. Suddenly at 9:37 a.m. a Boeing 757 aircraft traveling at 345 miles per hour and carrying 10,000 gallons of fuel exploded into the west side of the building.

It was American Airlines Flight 77, which had departed Dulles International Airport at 8:20 a.m. with 58 passengers and six crew members on board. Just 30 minutes into the flight, five passengers hijacked the plane over the Ohio-West Virginia border and turned the aircraft back toward Washington. It was one of four planes hijacked that day in a coordinated terrorist attack. Two planes struck the World Trade

Center towers in New York City and a third plane crashed in Pennsylvania. In addition to the 64 people on board Flight 77, 125 military and civilian employees inside the Pentagon lost their lives.

On September 12, 2002, Secretary of Defense Donald Rumsfeld dedicated a memorial to the 184 victims of the Pentagon tragedy. It is located in Section 64 within sight of the Pentagon. The names of the victims are inscribed on the five-sided, 4-foot-5-inch marker. The monument also marks the grave which holds the remains of victims that could not be identified. For five victims, this is their only memorial. None of their remains were identified, including a 3-year-old passenger aboard Flight 77. Sixty-four victims of the tragedy are buried at Arlington; 50 of them are nearby with others buried throughout the cemetery or inurned at the Columbarium.

Spanish-American War Memorial
Sec. 22, Grid N–21

When the United States declared war on Spain in 1898, it was the first major conflict fought by our country since the Civil War. Many Civil War veterans, both Union and Confederate, volunteered to fight. President William McKinley realized that many of the enduring wounds between the North and the South could be healed by uniting the country behind a common enemy, so he offered commissions to former Confederate officers in the United States Armed Forces. Many of these veterans accepted as the country joined forces against the Spanish.

Following the war, the National Society of the Colonial Dames of America petitioned the quartermaster general of the Army to erect a monument within Arlington National Cemetery. It was to be the first memorial to all American veterans who fought side by side in combat since the Civil War. The petition gained quick approval, and on May 21, 1902, the Spanish-American War's most famous veteran–President Theodore Roosevelt–dedicated the monument.

The monument is a Corinthian column of Barre granite standing nearly 50 feet tall. Atop the column is a sphere of Quincy granite on which a bronze eagle is mounted. On the tablet attached to the rear base of the memorial is an inscription honoring the soldiers and sailors of the United States who gave their lives for their country in the war with Spain.

In 1964, the Colonial Dames desired to honor those Americans who lost their lives in the wars fought since the Spanish-American War. Accordingly, a rededication of the monument was held and a second bronze tablet was unveiled. Its special inscription reads:

TO THE GLORY OF GOD AND

IN GRATEFUL REMEMBRANCE

OF THE MEN AND WOMEN OF

THE ARMED FORCES WHO IN

THIS CENTURY GAVE THEIR

LIVES FOR OUR COUNTRY

THAT FREEDOM MIGHT LIVE

THIS TABLET IS DEDICATED BY THE

NATIONAL SOCIETY OF THE

COLONIAL DAMES

OF AMERICA

OCTOBER 11, 1964

Behind the memorial are four guns mounted on concrete stands. The two inner guns were captured from the Spanish forces during that war; they are flanked by two American naval guns.

Spanish-American War Nurses Memorial
Sec. 21, Grid L–20

T he Spanish-American War was the first war involving the United States in which nurses were organized and assigned as a special, quasi-military unit. During that war, many nurses lost their lives. Many of those who served are now buried in Section 21 of Arlington National Cemetery.

The Society of Spanish American War Nurses has erected a memorial to those brave nurses who died during that war. The Maltese cross, which serves as the insignia of the Society, rests atop a large granite megalith dedicated to the memory of their "brave comrades."

Tomb of the Unknowns
World War I   World War II
Korean War   Vietnam War
Grid ST–22/23

W ithin the walls of Arlington National Cemetery can be found tombs of unknown servicemen from every war in American history, except the American Revolution. The official Tomb of the Unknown of the Revolutionary War is located in the burial grounds of the Presbyterian Meeting House in Alexandria, Virginia. The Tomb of the Unknown Civil War Dead (see page 283) is in Section 26, and the Tomb of the Unknown Dead of the War of 1812 (see page 284) is in Section 1.

Following are the stories of the tombs of the four unknowns located on the East Plaza of the Memorial Amphitheatre at Tomb of the Unknowns.

World War I

On November 11, 1918, an armistice was declared, ending World War I. It was to be the war to end all wars. So pandemic were its effects that only when the fighting had finally stopped could Americans pause to remember the thousands of men and women who had given their lives in that global struggle. Throughout the country, local memorial services were held to

The Tomb of the Unknowns on the East Plaza of the Memorial Amphitheatre as seen from Roosevelt Drive.

commemorate those who had died and to honor those who had returned. Yet there were hundreds of Americans who did not return because their remains could not be identified despite employing every known means to determine their identities. The bodies of more than 1,600 Americans were interred in France where they lost their lives. They are buried in four American cemeteries created for them.

Still reeling from the effects of the greatest war the world had ever known, many Americans felt that something special needed to be done to remember—not the war, but what the war had cost our nation. Finally, in response to public sentiment, Congress followed the example of our allies and approved a resolution providing for the burial of an unidentified American soldier at Arlington National Cemetery. On March 4, 1921, the last day of his presidency, Woodrow Wilson signed the bill and an elaborate procedure began for choosing that honored unknown soldier.

The Unknown was to be symbolic of all persons who had given their lives during that war. Every American could pay homage to this fallen soldier, believing him to be the son, husband, brother, or friend who did not come home. To achieve this general feeling, it was imperative that there be no means to discover the soldier's actual identity. Even revelation of the name of the cemetery from which he was chosen for reinterment might compromise the secrecy surrounding the unknown soldier's selection. So one candidate-unknown was chosen from each of the four American cemeteries in France. On October 22, 1921, each of the four bodies were exhumed and transported under honor guard to the city hall at Chalons-sur-Marne, France, for final random selection. During that night the honor guard shifted the positions of the four identical caskets so that no one–not even the graves registration detail–could differentiate among them. As a last guarantor of secrecy, all burial records of these four servicemen were destroyed. On October 24, Army Sergeant **Edward F. Younger** of Chicago, who had been wounded in combat and highly decorated for valor, was given the honor of selecting the Unknown Soldier of World War I by placing a spray of white roses on one of the caskets. That spray of white roses accompanied the Unknown to Arlington and these flowers are buried with him. Sergeant Younger also is buried at Arlington National Cemetery (Sec. 18, Lot 1918-B, Grid LM–12/13).

The three remaining unknown soldiers were reinterred in the Meuse-Argonne Cemetery in France while the chosen Unknown began his journey home, symbolic of those who could not make that journey. The Unknown was placed in a special, American-made casket which bears the inscription, "An unknown soldier who gave his life in the Great War." The cortege containing the Unknown Soldier and his honor guard traveled from Chalons through Paris on its way to Le Havre. There the Unknown was placed on the *Olympia*, which had been Admiral Dewey's flagship during the Spanish-American War.

On its way to Washington, the *Olympia* received full salutes and honors from every vessel it encountered on the high seas. Finally, on November 9, 1921, it docked at Washington, D.C. where the Unknown was greeted by his former commander, General of the Armies **John J. Pershing.** Pershing led the procession to the United States Capitol, where the Unknown was to lie in state until Armistice Day, November 11. Nearly 100,000 mourners paid their respects on November 10, the single intervening day; many more were turned away when the guards were ordered to close the doors at midnight.

The next day, November 11, 1921, President Warren G. Harding led the nation in solemn services held at Arlington in the new Memorial Amphitheatre. Following his remarks, the president placed the Congressional Medal of Honor and the Distinguished Service Cross on the casket. Also present were representatives of America's allies in World War I to pay tribute and to award the Unknown their highest honors–the Victoria Cross of the British Empire, the Croix de Guerre of France, the Order of Leopold of Belgium, the Gold Medal of Bravery of Italy, as well as the highest honors of Romania, Poland, Cuba, and Czechoslovakia.

All of these military decorations are now housed at Arlington in the Trophy Room adjacent to the Tomb of the Unknowns. Following these presentations, the remains were carried to the gravesite on the terrace just east

During a spectacular ceremony in the new Memorial Amphitheatre in 1921, President Warren G. Harding awards the Congressional Medal of Honor to the Unknown Soldier of World War I prior to his interment on the East Plaza.

of the Amphitheatre. At the bottom of that grave was placed a two-inch layer of soil from the battlefields of France.

Just before the remains were buried forever, a final honor was bestowed upon the fallen soldier by Native Americans. The 74-year-old chief of the Crow Nation, Plenty Coups, stepped forward. In his native tongue, he offered a stirring prayer for all fallen soldiers, "I hope that the Great Spirit will grant that these noble warriors have not given up their lives in vain and that there will be peace to all men hereafter." With that, he placed upon the grave his coup stick and ancient headdress which had been with his tribe for generations. This was the highest tribute of his proud people. The headdress and coup stick from the Crow Nation are also kept in the Trophy Room at Arlington.

Although America's first Unknown Soldier was laid to rest in November 1921, it was not until 1926 that Congress authorized the completion of the monument. What resulted from that enactment was the magnificent sarcophagus placed in 1931, that has been viewed by millions of visitors for decades. Although simple in its design, the sarcophagus' dimensions are impressive. The large white marble monument, which weighs 50 tons, was quarried in Colorado and rough-hewn in Vermont. It is relieved at the corners by neo-classic pilasters, or columns, set onto the surface. Sculpted into the east side facing Washington, D.C. are three figures which represent Peace, Victory, and Valor. On the west face are inscribed the immortal words:

HERE RESTS IN

HONORED GLORY

AN AMERICAN

SOLDIER

KNOWN BUT TO GOD

Immediately after the interment of the World War I Unknown, Americans offered homage to the hero buried at Arlington, unparalleled in our nation's history. In addition to the thousands of visitors who poured into the cemetery, flowers, Christmas cards, birthday cards, and letters arrived all addressed to the Unknown. Tragically, among the letters were inquiries from mothers and wives wondering if the Unknown was in fact their son or husband. Despite the extraordinary precautions taken against discovery of the Unknown's identity, and the widespread publicity about those precautions, still the letters of inquiry came. Proffering clues of a birthmark or a gold tooth, they hoped against hope that this soldier was their lost loved one. It is the belief that this soldier might be any American unknown that adds a special dimension to this symbolic memorial. This honored-yet-anonymous hero represents all the unknowns who died in brave service to our country during World War I.

World War II, The Korean War

The Great War, in which the Unknown had given his life, did not end all wars. On September 1, 1939, Germany invaded Poland and a second worldwide conflagration began. Virtually no corner of the world was unscarred. When World War II ended in 1945, formal plans were made to inter at Arlington an unknown from that war; the ceremony was to take place on Memorial Day, 1951. Unfortunately, before the date of that official ceremony arrived, America became embroiled in hostilities again, this time in Korea. So the plans to inter a World War II Unknown at Arlington were postponed.

On August 3, 1956, President Dwight D. Eisenhower signed legislation to select and pay tribute to the Unknowns of both World War II and the Korean War. Again following the same procedures used after World War I, great precautions were taken to ensure the complete anonymity of these two unknowns.

The World War II candidate-unknowns were exhumed from cemeteries in Europe, Africa, Hawaii, and the Philippines. In two separate ceremonies in France and Hawaii, a candidate-unknown for the European Theatre and for the Pacific Theatre were chosen. The Korean Unknown was chosen from four sets of unidentified remains of those who fought in Korea and who were buried in the National Cemetery of the Pacific in Hawaii. Army Master Sergeant Ned Lyle was granted the privilege of selecting the Unknown.

The three unknowns were brought together aboard the *Canberra*, off the Virginia Capes. There, Hospitalman First Class William R. Carette, then the Navy's only active-duty enlisted Medal of Honor recipient, selected the Unknown of World War II. The candidate not chosen was given a full honors burial at sea, while the Unknowns from World War II and Korea sailed on to Washington, D.C., docking on May 27, 1958.

The next morning the two caskets were removed to the Rotunda of the United States Capitol, where they lay in state for 48 hours while thousands of Americans filed past paying their final respects. On Memorial Day, the Unknowns were taken from the Capitol to Arlington, just as the first Unknown had been taken 37 years earlier. The ceremonies at Arlington were solemn and brief. President Eisenhower spoke only 26 words. "On behalf of a grateful people, I now present Medals of Honor to these two unknowns who gave their lives for the United States of America." As in 1921, representatives of governments from around the world presented their highest honors to America's fallen heroes. These military decorations also can be viewed in the Trophy Room. The Unknowns were then laid to rest on the terrace next to the Unknown of World War I.

The Vietnam Era

As a tribute to the members of the United States Armed Forces who served in Southeast Asia during the 1960s and 1970s, Secretary of Defense **Caspar Weinberger** announced on April 13, 1984, that an Unknown from the Vietnam Era would be interred at Arlington National Cemetery on Memorial Day 1984.

The selection process took place at the National Cemetery in Hawaii on May 17, 1984. The Unknown arrived in Washington on May 25 and was taken to the United States Capitol where he lay in state. Again, thousands of Americans filed past the casket to pay their respects. During funeral and interment services at Arlington, President Ronald Reagan awarded the Congressional Medal of Honor to the Unknown on behalf of the American people.

On May 14, 1998, the unknown American of the Vietnam Era was exhumed from the Tomb for possible identification. Using the most sophisticated science available, the unknown was identified as First Lieutenant Michael J. Blassie, U.S. Air Force. In accordance with the wishes of his family, he was reinterred in Jefferson Barracks National Cemetery near St. Louis, Missouri.

The crypt at the Tomb of the Unknowns is empty, a marble tablet marking the crypt states:

HONORING AND KEEPING FAITH WITH

AMERICA'S MISSING SERVICEMEN, 1958–1975.

A member of the U.S. Army Third Infantry, known as the Old Guard, provides a continuous honor guard for the Tombs of the Unknown. Engraved on the Tomb of the World War I Unknown are the words: HERE RESTS IN HONORED GLORY AN AMERICAN SOLDIER KNOWN BUT TO GOD.

The Tomb Guard

Although the Tomb of the Unknowns is guarded at present by members of the crack Third Infantry, this was not always the case. The first guard established for the Tomb was a civilian watchman in November 1925. In 1926, a military guard was posted for the first time, but only during daylight hours when the cemetery gates were open to the public. In 1937, a 24-hour military guard was established. Finally in 1948, the guardianship of the Tomb was assumed by the Third United States Infantry, known as the Old Guard.

The Changing of the Guard

This simple but impressive ceremony takes place every half-hour from April 1 through September 30, and every hour on the hour from October 1 through March 31 during daylight hours. At night, the guard changes every hour throughout all seasons of the year.

At his or her post, the sentinel crosses the walkway in exactly 21 steps; turns to face the Tomb for 21 seconds; turns again, pausing an additional 21 seconds, then retraces the steps taken. The number "21" is symbolic of the highest salute afforded dignitaries in military and state ceremonies. The guard will speak or change his or her pattern only under exceptional circumstances, including the issuance of a warning to anyone who attempts to enter the restricted area around the Tomb.

The Old Guard, the U.S. Army's official ceremonial unit, is the oldest active infantry unit of the Army. Often referred to as the President's Own, the Old Guard is the Army honor guard and escort for the president. Its soldiers participate in more than 3,500 ceremonies annually at the White House, Pentagon, and numerous other national memorials. Headquartered in the adjacent Fort Myer Army installation, they also perform military funeral rites in Arlington and participate in state funerals. In 1996, the first woman qualified to join the elite Old Guard following a 1994 directive from Secretary of Defense William Cohen to allow women to apply.

President Bill Clinton honors the American Unknowns by laying a wreath during Veteran's Day services at the Tomb of the Unknowns.

Wreath-Laying Ceremonies

Throughout the year, more than 2,000 wreath-laying ceremonies take place at the Tomb of the Unknowns. As a gesture of respect to the United States, and in honor of our gallant dead, groups from every quarter of our country and every walk of life come to Arlington to participate in this time-honored tradition. Since 1921, every American president has made the pilgrimage to the Tomb at least once, and countless foreign dignitaries representing every nation on earth have placed wreaths here.

Tomb of the Unknown Civil War Dead
Sec. 26, Grid QR–32/33

Near Arlington House, in what was once part of its famous rose garden, stands a monument dedicated to the unknown soldiers who died in the Civil War. The monument, dedicated in September 1866, stands atop a masonry vault containing the remains of 2,111 soldiers gathered from the fields of Bull Run and the route to the Rappahannock. The remains were found

In 1866, a monument (above) was erected in the former rose garden of Arlington House honoring more than 2,000 unknown dead of the Civil War. The original stone was replaced with the current monument (below).

scattered across the battlefields or in trenches and brought here. This monument was the first memorial at Arlington to be dedicated to soldiers who had died in battle, and who later could not be identified. Because in some instances only a few bones or a skull were recovered, it is assumed that the vault contains the remains of Confederate soldiers as well as Union troops.

Quartermaster General **Montgomery Meigs** ordered that these bodies be gathered and buried on this particular site, knowing that the presence of graves here would prevent the Lee family from inhabiting their house again.

Tomb of the Unknown Dead of the War of 1812
Sec. 1, Lot 299, Grid N–33/34

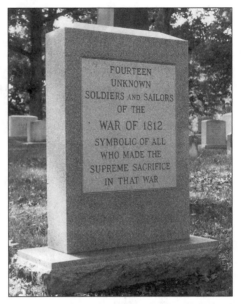

On this site rest 14 soldiers from the War of 1812, identities unknown. Although they are now buried in this mass grave, they were not originally buried on this site. Their remains were discovered in 1905 during excavation work near the old Washington Barracks (now the Washington Navy Yard). The reinterment to this site took place that same year.

On April 8, 1976, the National Society of the United States Daughters of the War of 1812 dedicated the large granite monument that now marks the tomb. The memorial displays the relevant dates of the War of 1812, and declares that these unknown soldiers are "Symbolic of All Who Made the Supreme Sacrifice in That War."

United States Air Force Memorial
South of Arlington Cemetery

The United States Air Force Memorial dramatically captures the image of the contrails of the Air Force Thunderbirds' "bomb burst" maneuver–three stainless steel spires arcing against the wild blue yonder. While the maneuver usually includes four aircraft, this striking memorial overlooking Arlington Cemetery appropriately depicts the missing-man formation traditionally reserved for funeral fly-overs.

In 1992, the Air Force Memorial Foundation was established to create a memorial honoring those who have served in the United States Air Force and its predecessors, from the Aeronautical

Photo courtesy of Department of the Air Force

Division of the U.S. Signal Corps in 1907 to today's U.S. Air Force, which was established by the National Security Act of 1947. Throughout its history, more than 54,000 Air Force personnel have died in combat.

The memorial was dedicated on October 14, 2006, before a crowd of more than 30,000 people. According to the architect, James Ingo Freed, the three spires—the tallest of which is 270 feet—represent the three core values of the Air Force: integrity first, service before self, and excellence in all that is done.

Embedded in granite beneath the three central spires is the Air Force "star," which has long been emblazoned on Air Force aircraft and serves as the rank insignia of every enlisted member of the Air Force, according to the Air Force Memorial Foundation. Other key elements of the memorial include a "Runway to Glory" at the site entrance, a bronze Honor Guard statue developed by the renowned sculptor Zenos Frudakis, two granite inscription walls located at either end of the central lawn, and a Glass Contemplation Wall that honors fallen airmen.

United States Coast Guard Memorial
Sec. 4, Grid XY–9/10

Two tragic episodes in United States Coast Guard history prompted the construction of this memorial, which sits atop a hill near the southern edge of the cemetery. On September 21, 1918, the cutter *Seneca* was lost while attempting to salvage the British steamer, Wellington, which had been torpedoed in the Bay of Biscay. All officers and crew of the *Seneca* were lost.

Just five days later, on September 26, 1918, the cutter *Tampa* was sunk by an enemy submarine in the Bristol Channel, and all on board that ship were lost as well. The names of these vessels and their crewmen, as well as of all Coast Guard personnel who lost their lives during the Great War, are inscribed on the sides of the monument. The United States Coast Guard Memorial at Arlington was dedicated on May 23, 1928.

The Coast Guard was formed as the successor to the Revenue Cutter Service and the Life Saving Service on June 28, 1915. By law, both the *Tampa* and the *Seneca* were ordered to operate as part of the Navy when the United States entered World War I on April 6, 1918.

In the monument's rock foundation and pyramid design, architect George Howe and sculptor Gaston Lachaise have captured the spirit of the Coast Guard's legendary steadfastness. A bronze sea gull poised with its wings uplifted alights below the Coast Guard motto *Semper Paratus* (Always Prepared). This bird further symbolizes the tireless vigil that the United States Coast Guard maintains over our nation's maritime territory.

United States Marine Corps Memorial
Iwo Jima Monument
Located just north of the Ord-Weitzel Gate of Arlington

The United States Marine Corps Memorial was established to honor the thousands of Marines who have given their lives in the defense of this great nation, and in the pursuit of liberty around the world. Although the memorial depicts just one of the hundreds of battles in which Marines have taken part, it vividly illustrates the courage, determination, and skill with which the Marines have performed their duties for more than two centuries, since the Marine Corps' founding on November 10, 1775.

Chosen to represent the contribution of all Marines is the famous scene of the flag-raising on Mount Suribachi during the Battle of Iwo Jima in World War II. This scene was first immortalized by a chance photograph taken by Associated Press photographer Joe Rosenthal on February 23, 1945, as the Marines planted the U.S. colors during the raging battle for control of the strategically situated island of Iwo Jima.

Although Iwo Jima was a small island (less than five miles long and two miles wide), it held military importance because of its two Japanese-built airfields. Just 660 miles from the mainland of Japan, it served as a base for Japanese fighters to attack American bombers on sorties to the major military-industrial centers of Japan. If wrested from enemy control, those airfields would prove invaluable as a staging area for the American aerial campaign. For these reasons, the decision was made that the Fourth and Fifth Marine Divisions would undertake an assault of the island.

Prior to the Marines' landing, Navy and Army Air Force planes subjected the island to "the longest and most intensive" bombing in the Pacific theatre during World War II. The island had been fortified by 642 blockhouses, pillboxes, and other gun positions, and it was the intent of this massive, 74-day bombing campaign to weaken the firm Japanese defense of the island. Unfortunately, bad weather nullified some of the effect of the bombing raids.

On February 19, 1945, American Marines scrambled from their carriers and waded through an ankle-deep sea of volcanic ash to establish a beachhead. After gaining a hold on the beaches, it was their goal to take Mount Suribachi, the 550-foot volcanic peak on the southern tip of the island. Although the beachhead was established against only minor resistance, the Japanese emerged from underground shelters to unleash extensive firepower once the initial barrage was over.

The most famous photograph of WWII (above) earned photographer Joe Rosenthal a Pulitzer Prize. The flag-raising on Iwo Jima Island on February 23, 1945, inspired the construction of the U.S. Marine Corps Memorial (below) located just north of Arlington National Cemetery.

It was the Twenty-eighth Marines of the Fifth Marine Division who were ordered to take the hill, which they had managed to isolate from the rest of the island by the end of the first day of fighting. For four days the battle raged, until finally on February 23, a 40-man American combat patrol reached the rim of the crater, secured a small U.S. flag (45 by 28 inches) to a length of iron pipe left behind by the Japanese, and proudly raised the Stars and Stripes. The sight of the U.S. colors flying atop the summit inspired the thousands of Americans still below.

But this was not the historic flag-raising that Rosenthal captured on film. Once the original flag was raised on that summit, a larger flag (96 by 56 inches) was taken from one of the landing craft. Photographer Rosenthal immediately realized the purpose of this second flag and closely pursued its bearer. Sergeant **Michael Strank,** Corporal Harlan Block, Private Franklin Sousley, and Private **Ira Hayes** carried the colors up the hill. As they reached the summit, commanding officer Lieutenant Harold G. Schrier ordered that the second flag be raised and the first flag be lowered. Sergeant Strank found a second length of pipe and fastened the larger flag to it. Seeing that the four men were having trouble raising the flag on the rugged terrain, two men standing nearby—Pharmacist's Mate Second Class John H. Bradley and Private **Rene A. Gagnon**—came to their aid. As the six men struggled to raise the colors, Rosenthal snapped the picture, which has been called the single most famous photograph ever taken, and for which he was awarded the coveted Pulitzer Prize.

Although the flag-raising inspired the forces trying to take the tiny island, it could not minimize the heavy casualties suffered by the Americans. Before the battle ended on March 25, more than a month after the capture of Mount Suribachi, 17,372 Marines had been wounded and 5,931 Marines had lost their lives in an effort to take an area only one-eighth the size of Washington, D.C.

Nevertheless, the photo sent American morale soaring. When President Franklin Roosevelt saw the photograph, he ordered that the identities of the six men be determined and that they be recalled to the United States. He realized that both the photograph and the men had become a boon to national morale. The scene became the subject of a poster during the Seventh War Bond Loan drive, and a three-cent commemorative postage stamp was issued. The six men in the photo became instant celebrities. It was not long, however, before the world was to learn that only three of those brave men survived the battle for Iwo Jima. Sergeant Michael Strank, Corporal Harlan H. Block, and Private Franklin R. Sousley were among the nearly 6,000 men killed in later phases of the fighting for control of the island.

These six men, hailing from very diverse backgrounds, shared one brief, immortalized moment in their lives. Three of them (Rene Gagnon, Ira Hayes, and Michael Strank) are now buried in Arlington National Cemetery. Their lives are outlined in the profile section of this book. The remaining Marines are introduced below:

Harlan Henry Block was born in Yorktown, Texas, on November 6, 1924. He had graduated from Weslaco High School in 1943, and was drafted on February 18, 1943. He qualified as a parachutist on May 22, and was promoted to first class the same day. After taking part in the Bougainville campaign, his unit disbanded and Block joined the 28th Marines on March 1, 1944.

Promoted to corporal on October 27, 1944, Block landed on Iwo Jima on February 19, 1945. He was killed on the island on March 1 while attacking Nishi Ridge. Originally buried on Iwo Jima, his body was returned for private burial at Weslaco, Texas.

John Henry Bradley was the last surviving member of the six men who planted the flag on Iwo Jima. Born in Antigo, Wisconsin, on July 10, 1923, he graduated from Appleton (Wisconsin) High School in 1941. He enlisted in the Navy on January 13, 1943, and following boot camp, was assigned to the Hospital Corps School. Promoted to pharmacist's mate second class, Bradley attended Field Medical School and was assigned to the 28th Marines on April 15, 1944. He was with the 28th when they landed on Iwo Jima, for his first and only military campaign. Bradley was wounded on March 12, 1945, on Iwo Jima, and was medically discharged from the Marine Corps on November 13, 1945. He died on January 11, 1994, in Antigo, where he is buried.

Franklin Runyon Sousley was a native of Flemingsburg, Kentucky, where he was born on September 19, 1925. Following his graduation from high school, he moved to Dayton, Ohio, where he entered the Marine Corps Reserve through the Selective Service System on January 5, 1944. After boot camp in San Diego, he was assigned to the Twenty-eighth Marines of the Fifth Marine Division as an automatic rifleman and was promoted to first class on November 22, 1944. He landed on Iwo Jima on February 19, 1945, and was killed one month later on March 21 during fighting around Kitano Point. Private Sousley was initially buried on Iwo Jima, but was reinterred at Elizaville, Kentucky.

Joe Rosenthal's photo generated widespread encouragement for the American war effort in 1945. Yet its most lasting inspiration was the creation of the Marine Corps Memorial which now stands near Arlington National Cemetery. Shortly after the news photo was released, sculptor Felix de Weldon, then on duty with the Navy, constructed a scale model, followed by a life-size model of the historic scene on Iwo Jima. These models were used for the bond drive poster and the postage stamp. Moved by these reproductions of the Iwo Jima flag-raising, friends of the Marine Corps proposed a monument to the memory of all Marines, a monument which would include the stirring scene in heroic proportions.

Sculptor de Weldon, who later designed and created the Seabees Memorial and the Memorial to Admiral **Richard Byrd** (both located on Memorial Drive near the main entrance to Arlington), began his formidable task in 1945. Recognizing that a work of this magnitude would require the detailing of every aspect of the figures from facial expressions to clothing and equipment, one of his first projects was to elicit the help of the three survivors, all of whom agreed to assist him. Using these three live models, together with all available pictures and physical data of the other three Marines, de Weldon cast their faces first in clay and later in plaster. A steel frame resembling the bone structure of a human body was assembled to support the huge figures under construction. Initially the figures were molded nude so that muscular strain would be evident after clothing was added. When the statue was finished in plaster, it was carefully disassembled and taken in 108 pieces to the Bedi-Rassy Art Foundry in Brooklyn, New York. There, for three years, the artisans cast the pieces in bronze.

In 1954, the finished bronze sections were trucked to and reassembled on a seven-and-one-half-acre tract just north of Arlington National Cemetery. The 100-ton monument, which is the largest cast bronze figure in the world, was dedicated by President Dwight D. Eisenhower on November 10, 1954, to coincide with the 179th anniversary of the founding of the Marine Corps. The total cost of the monument was $850,000, underwritten privately by U.S. Marines, former Marines, Marine Corps Reservists, friends of the Marine Corps, and U.S. Navy personnel.

Starting at the bottom of the flagpole and working upward, the six men depicted are: Corp. Harlan H. Block, PFC Rene Gagnon (whose downturned head is near Block's left elbow on the opposite side of the pole), PM2/C John H. Bradley (facing forward behind Block), SGT Michael Strank (leaning over Gagnon's back), PFC Franklin Sousley (immediately behind Bradley), and PFC Ira Hayes (the rear figure whose outstretched hands are not quite touching the flagpole).

The figures of the six men stand 32 feet high; the flagpole they are planting is 60 feet long. The rocky base on which they stand rises approximately six feet above a ten foot base, making the entire structure nearly 78 feet tall. To further illustrate the immensity of the monument, the M-1 rifle carried by Ira Hayes is sixteen feet in length, and the carbines are 12 feet long. The canteen, if filled, would hold 32 quarts of water. The interior of the statue is reinforced by extruded bronze supports, which required that the statue be bolted and welded from the inside. The workmen entered the statue through a "trap door" in a cartridge belt which is now welded shut. The concrete base is covered with blocks of polished Swedish black granite with the names and dates of every major Marine Corps engagement burnished into it. Also inscribed is the tribute by Fleet Admiral Chester W. Nimitz regarding the Marines on Iwo Jima, "Uncommon Valor Was a Common Virtue."

By a proclamation signed by President **John F. Kennedy** on June 12, 1961, the United States flag now flies 24 hours a day on the lighted monument. In the summer months the Marine Corps Drum and Bugle Corps and Marine troops conduct ceremonies on the adjacent parade grounds.

The monument and the parade grounds are part of the National Capital Parks, which are administered by the National Park Service, U.S. Department of the Interior.

USS *Maine* Memorial
Sec. 24, Grid MN–23/24

In the latter half of the 1890s, the United States resisted pressures to intercede on behalf of Cuba in its struggle for independence from Spain, but by 1898 the situation had grown dangerously unstable. In an effort to counter that growing instability, the U.S. Navy ordered the *USS Maine* to Havana Harbor, believing that the presence of an American battleship would promote peace, but, if necessary, could be used in the evacuation of American citizens. On January 25, 1898, the battleship under the command of Captain **Charles Dwight Sigsbee** sailed into Havana Harbor.

At that time, the *Maine* carried a crew of 355 men, including 26 officers, 290 sailors, and 39 Marines. All was quiet for the crew during the first three weeks, but that changed on the evening of February 15 when, without warning, a violent explosion ripped through the *Maine.* Officers and crew scrambled to evacuate the ship. Captain Sigsbee abandoned the vessel only after all surviving crew members were safely aboard rescue boats. He was taken aboard the pleasure ship, *City of Washington,* where he reported the night's events by message to the secretary of the navy:

> *Maine* blown up in Havana Harbor at nine-forty tonight and destroyed. Many wounded and doubtless more killed or drowned. Wounded and others on board Spanish Man-of-War and Ward Line Steamer. Send Light House Tender from Key West for crew and a few pieces of equipment above water. No one has clothing other than that upon him. Public opinion should be suspended until further notice.

The mast of the *USS Maine* is all that can be seen above the water in Havana Harbor (above) following the explosion that sank the battleship in 1898. By an Act of Congress, the mast was removed from the sunken battleship and placed in Arlington National Cemetery in 1912 (right).

Finally, it was determined that two officers and 251 enlisted men were killed in the initial explosion. Seven more later died from their wounds. Of the 260 men who died, 66 were aboard the *Maine* buried beneath the sea. The remaining 194 servicemen were buried in Colon Cemetery in Havana.

The sinking of the *Maine,* coupled with other international events, brought the U.S. to the brink of war with Spain. The American press seized upon the incident, coining the popular slogan, "Remember the *Maine,* to hell with Spain!" Political pressure was exerted on Congress to recover the bodies of the American servicemen, and on March 30, 1898, Congress approved provisions for the disinterment of the victims, and for their transfer to Arlington National Cemetery. On April 24, 1898 Spain declared war on the United States, and on the following day the United States issued its declaration against Spain. Although the war with Spain lasted less than four months, it was not until December 28, 1899, that members of the *Maine's* crew were disinterred and returned to the United States. President William McKinley and Admiral George Dewey presided over the burial of those men in Section 24 at Arlington.

For more than 12 years after its sinking, the mast of the once-mighty battleship was all that could be seen rising above the water of Havana Harbor. The 66 bodies of the *Maine's* crew who had gone down with the ship in 1898 were still on board. Finally, on May 9, 1910, Congress authorized the raising of the *Maine* from the bottom of the harbor and "for the proper interment of the bodies therein in Arlington National Cemetery." In addition, Congress authorized the secretary of war to remove the *Maine's* mast and place it upon a proper foundation as a memorial in Arlington near the bodies of the crew members interred there.

It took nearly two years to raise the battleship. In March 1912, the 66 bodies were recovered and returned to the United States. Only one of those bodies could be identified and that sailor was returned to his home state for burial. On March 23, 1912, President **William Howard Taft** presided over the services as the 65 men were interred next to their comrades in Section 24. They had been disinterred earlier from Colon Cemetery in Havana. This brought the total number of victims of the *Maine* explosion buried at Arlington to 229, of which 62 are known and 167 are unidentified.

After 14 years on the bottom of Havana Harbor, all that was left of the *Maine* was a twisted, rusted shell. That shell was towed out to sea, and on March 16, 1912, the *Maine* was scuttled with full honors in water 600 fathoms deep. A Navy court of inquiry was impaneled to investigate the sinking of the *Maine,* chaired by **William T. Sampson.** The court's report that the explosion was caused by a submarine mine did not dispel widespread public doubt.

On the 17th anniversary of the sinking of the *Maine,* February 15, 1915, the *USS Maine* Memorial was dedicated at Arlington just south of the area where its 229 crewmen are buried. The base of the monument represents a battleship turret, and through its center rises the original mast of the *Maine,* now towering above the cemetery. Around the sides of the turret are inscribed the names of all those who lost their lives in the disaster. On the north side, a doorway leads into the turret and one half of the ship's bell is welded on its inner door. The inside of the turret is a burial vault which is 30 feet in diameter.

During World War II, the burial vault inside the *Maine* Memorial was used to temporarily inter the remains of leaders of countries who were allies of the United States, and who had died here while their native lands were occupied. In 1944, the president of the Philippines, Manuel Quezon y Molina, was interred in this vault when he died here in exile during the Japanese occupation of his country. Following the war, his body was returned to the Philippines for burial.

In 1941, Ignace Paderewski, the exiled president of Poland, died in New York City. President Franklin Roosevelt allowed his remains to be temporarily interred here "until Poland is free." The body of Ignace Paderewski remained within the memorial until 1992 (see page 151).

Near the *Maine* Memorial is a large anchor and two cannons. While the anchor is not the anchor from the *Maine,* it is similar and was brought especially to Arlington from the Boston Navy Yard. The cannons are captured Spanish guns.

USS Serpens Memorial
Sec 34, Grid XY–17

During the night of January 29, 1945, an explosion rocked the United States Coast Guard Ammunition Ship, *USS Serpens,* as it sat off the coast of Laguna Beach, Guadalcanal in the Solomon Islands. The devastation was so great, the destruction so immediate that nothing could be done to save the lives of the 250 American servicemen on board. Among those killed were 199 U.S. Coast Guardsmen, 50 Army servicemen, and one U.S. Public Health Service official.

Four and one-half years later, on June 15, 1949, an elaborate reinterment service was held to give these valiant men their final resting place in Arlington National Cemetery. The extraordinary nature of the catastrophe that claimed their lives made identification of the individuals aboard the *Serpens* impossible. Therefore, their remains were placed in 52 caskets and buried in 28 gravesites. Two other gravesites in the middle of the group were set aside for the monument on which all of their names are inscribed.

An octagon-shaped monument bearing the name and rank of each serviceman killed aboard the *USS Serpens* marks their collective grave near the intersection of Jesup and Grant Drives.

War Correspondents Memorial
Grid OP–23/24

On October 7, 1986, a tree was planted in memory of those "journalists who died while covering wars and conflicts for the American people." At the base of that tree stands a marble monument in the form of an open book whose pages proclaim, "One who finds a truth lights a torch."

This memorial, which honors those who went into combat armed only with pens and notebooks, was erected by The National Press Club, the Overseas Press Club, Society of Professional Journalists, Sigma Delta Xi, and No Greater Love.

Women in Military Service for America Memorial
Memorial Drive, Grid AA-37

One chilly April morning in 1775, a group of ramshackle militiamen gathered in the public square in Lexington, Massachusetts, ready to stand their ground as a squadron of British troops advanced. Against all odds they were prepared to defend their liberty. As the British neared, a shot rang out and a short battle ensued. That shot–"heard 'round the world"–ignited an armed defense of our liberty that has never ceased. As the smoke cleared, those early pioneers of freedom had been joined by their wives, mothers, and sisters in their struggle for independence. Though women could not enlist officially in the United States Armed Forces until 1901, their unsung gallantry in defense of freedom began that morning on Lexington Green.

Since the Revolutionary War, nearly two million women have served in the United States Armed Forces—each and every one of them a volunteer. For more than two centuries there was no national recognition of the service of women in the military—no memorial to honor those women who died in service, who were prisoners of war, who were honored for bravery, or who simply served their country with pride and devotion. Now at last, there is–the Women In Military Service For America Memorial.

On November 6, 1986, President Ronald Reagan signed legislation authorizing a women's memorial in or near Washington, D.C. The law also mandated the memorial be privately funded. So a nonprofit foundation was established to manage the project, and Brigadier General Wilma L. Vaught, U.S.A.F. (Retired), was chosen to head the Women In Military Service For America Foundation.

Photo by Warren Miller

The foundation envisioned a memorial that would be more than just stones and mortar. To adequately recognize the contribution of women to America's military, it must be

The Women in Military Service for America Memorial was dedicated in 1997. Vice President Al Gore presided at dedication ceremonies that drew more than 30,000 people.

a living, working tribute that would be not only a stirring memorial, but also a museum, education center, registry, and meeting place.

With this ambitious objective in mind, the foundation searched for a site worthy of such an important memorial. But the choice was obvious–Arlington National Cemetery. Here on the hallowed grounds of our nation's most revered historic site, the foundation chose 4.2 acres that included the historic Hemicycle at the Memorial Entrance to Arlington. This 226-foot semicircular retaining wall provides the facade for the 35,000-square-foot memorial. It stands at the eastern terminus of Memorial Drive, the symbolic axis that joins the Lincoln Memorial with the Robert E. Lee Memorial at Arlington House. First designed in 1927 by the architectural firm of McKim, Meade, and White, the Hemicycle rises 30 feet above a stone plaza. It was dedicated by President Herbert Hoover on January 16, 1932. (See page 259.)

Once the location was determined, the foundation turned its attention to choosing the most appropriate design from more than 130 plans submitted. In 1989, after months of consideration and meticulous review, the design of Marion Gail Weiss and Michael Manfredi, a husband-and-wife architectural team from New York, was chosen. Their design promised to transform the aging Hemicycle into a majestic memorial.

With the site determined and the design chosen, the foundation faced the daunting task of raising $21.5 million to build the memorial. The enabling legislation required the memorial to be privately funded, but because the 65-year-old Hemicycle was quickly deteriorating, Congress authorized $9.5 million to restore the aging structure. Nonetheless, construction could not begin until the additional $12 million was raised. For more than six years, the foundation solicited funds from every corner of the country. Finally, on

June 22, 1995, President Bill Clinton broke ground for the historic memorial with 6,000 cheering guests looking on.

Construction began immediately. Dozens of masons, carpenters, glaziers, and electricians went to work on the two-and-one-half-year, $21.5-million construction project, all under the supervision of two women—General Wilma Vaught and Margaret Van Voast, the Smith College graduate and on-site construction manager.

On October 19, 1997, 30,000 people gathered as Vice President Al Gore led the dedication ceremony that included Secretary of Defense William Cohen, Supreme Court Justice Sandra Day O'Connor, and Joint Chiefs of Staff Chairman Hugh Shelton. But it also included some of those veterans for whom this memorial was established–military women, including 101-year-old Frieda Mae Hardin, a WWI Navy yeoman. Speaking for many of her sister veterans, former Yeoman Hardin shouted with her heart, if not her aged voice, "I have observed many wonderful things, but none as important or as meaningful as the progress of women taking their rightful place in society."

Today, among the sites that visitors can enjoy are:

The Hemicycle and Great Niche. The 226-foot semicircular retaining wall forms the 30-foot high front facade of the memorial. In its center is the Great Niche which measures 20 feet across. The niche contains accent panels and coffers of red Texas granite. In the top center of the niche is a bas-relief of the Great Seal of the United States. To the right of the Great Seal is the seal of the Department of the Navy, and to its left is the seal of the Department of War. Originally dedicated in 1932, the Hemicycle was never completed as designed.

The facade of the Women in Military Service for America Memorial is formed from the Hemicycle, the 226-foot semicircular retaining wall originally built in 1932.

The Court of Valor, Fountain, and Reflecting Pool. The stone-paved plaza created within the Hemicycle is the Court of Valor. The court's centerpiece is a fountain in the Great Niche which empties into an 80-foot reflecting pool. The fountain contains more than 200 jets of water whose sound "represents the individual voices of women blending in a collective harmony of purpose." The water flows into the reflecting pool, "creating a unified, reflective voice in spirit."

The Upper Terrace. Four stairways lead from the Court of Valor to the Upper Terrace. The stairway entries were cut into the original Hemicycle retaining wall. They symbolize the breaking of barriers by women in the military. The Upper Terrace is lined with angled glass tablets on which are etched quotations by and about women in the military. The terrace also offers visitors spectacular views of **John Kennedy's** gravesite, Arlington House, and the national monuments across the Potomac River.

The Hall of Honor. This room honors servicewomen who were killed in action, died in the line of duty, were prisoners of war, or recipients of our nation's highest awards for service or bravery. The Daughters of the American Revolution and the United Daughters of the Confederacy donated the flags in the Hall of Honor, including the United States flag and flags from the 50 states, the District of Columbia, and U.S. territories.

Exhibit Gallery. Along the arc formed by the inside wall of the memorial are exhibits of texts, images, and memorabilia illustrating the history of women in the military from the Revolutionary War until the present. Many of these artifacts have been donated by servicewomen and their families. If visitors walk through the gallery at just the right time, they can read the quotations etched in the glass tablets on the Upper Terrace as the sun projects their shadows onto the gallery walls.

Also, visitors will notice a line of polished black granite on the floor of the gallery. This line lies on the axis between the Lincoln Memorial and the Robert E. Lee Memorial at Arlington House, symbolically uniting North and South.

Theater. A 196-seat theater offers films depicting stories of women in the military. The theater, along with the memorial's conference room, helps fulfill the memorial's role as a conference and meeting center.

The Registry. The computer registry is the memorial's most unique, and perhaps most important feature. It provides an ongoing, ever-growing tribute to women in military service. By continuously gathering data from women who have served, the memorial is building the most comprehensive history of women in the military, one story at a time. The memorial also is collecting servicewomen's photographs, military histories, diaries, newspaper clips, and other anecdotal information. But it's not easy work.

Because privacy laws and regulations prohibit the United States Armed Forces from disclosing personnel information, all the data must be collected individually.

Nearly two million women have served in the military, but fewer than one quarter of them have been registered in the memorial's database. Any servicewoman, her family members, or friends can register. Information can be submitted in one of several ways:

1. In person. Simply stop by the information desk in the Registration Room at the memorial.
2. By mail. Request a registration form, complete it, and return it to The Women's Memorial, Dept. 560, Washington, D.C. 20042-0560
3. By telephone. Call 1-800-222-2294, request a registration form, complete it, and return it to The Women's Memorial, Dept. 560, Washington, D.C. 20042-0560
4. Online. Visit their Web site at http://www.womensmemorial.org.

The Registry is a valuable resource for visitors, family members, students, researchers, genealogists, and historians. It offers visitors a singular opportunity to locate former colleagues, learn about servicewomen, and study our nation's history through the lives of the women who so generously served our country.

Gift Shop. Just inside the main entrance to the memorial, the gift shop offers visitors a wide variety of gifts, the largest collection of women's service memorabilia, and books about women in the military.

Visit the Women's Memorial Web site at: http://www.womensmemorial.org.

The Women In Military Service for America Memorial is administered by The Women In Military Service for America Foundation. The grounds of the memorial, Memorial Bridge, Memorial Drive, the memorials and monuments that line that drive, the Memorial Entrance, and the Robert E. Lee Memorial (Arlington House) all fall within the jurisdiction of the National Park Service, U.S. Department of the Interior.

Woodhull Flagpole
Sec. 35, Grid PQ-21

The Woodhull flagpole rises 90 feet above the south lawn of the Memorial Amphitheatre and is one of only two flagpoles located in Arlington National Cemetery. The other stands in front of Arlington House. Erected in 1924, the Woodhull flagpole is dedicated to the memory of Commander Maxwell Woodhull, who served in the United States Navy from 1813 to 1863.

The flags on the Woodhull flagpole and the Arlington House flagpole fly at half-staff, commencing one-half hour before the first burial service of the day. They remain at half-staff until one-half hour after the last service.

World War I Memorial
Section 34, Grid TU-12

Near the grave of General of the Armies **John J. Pershing** is a stone tablet honoring the men and women who gave their lives during World War I. The charcoal gray stone bears an engraving of the combat helmet worn by American doughboys during the Great War.

Provided by No Greater Love and the Veterans of World War I of the USA, the memorial states simply:

YOU ARE REMEMBERED

116,516 BRAVE AMERICANS

WHO DIED IN WORLD WAR ONE

"Their devotion, their valor and their

sacrifice will live forever

in the hearts of their grateful countrymen."

– General of the Armies John J. Pershing

The monument was dedicated on November 11, 1989, the seventy-first anniversary of the signing of the armistice that ended the war.

101st Army Airborne Division Memorial
Memorial Drive, Grid CC–38

This memorial commemorates the men of the 101st Airborne Division, popularly known as the "Screaming Eagles." A large bronze eagle with its wings uplifted proudly symbolizes the 101st which valiantly served this nation during World War II, the Vietnam War, and which continues to serve today. The campaigns in which the 101st participated in during World War II and Vietnam are listed on its gray granite base, which is emblazoned on all sides with the division's insignia.

Also inscribed on the base is the often-quoted phrase of Major General William C. Lee, who predicted on August 19, 1942, that the 101st "has no history but has a rendezvous with destiny."

Behind the statue, architect Harold J. Schaller and sculptor Bernhard Zukerman placed a low semicircular wall of granite on which the various areas of action of the Division are noted.

This monument was the scene of memorial services for the 101st following the death of the 248 members of the Screaming Eagles who were killed when their transport plane crashed in Gander, Newfoundland in December 1985.

3rd Infantry Division Memorial
Section 46, Grid OP-23/24

The Third Division was established on November 21, 1917, as the United States continued to build its troop strength during World War I. By April 1918, all units of the division were in France where they distinguished themselves in defense of the Marne River near Chateau-Thierry in July 1918. Their strong defense earned them the moniker, "Rock of the Marne," a motto they carry proudly today.

During World War II, the 3rd Division became the 3rd Infantry Division where they fought heroically in North Africa, Italy, France, and Austria. WWII's most decorated soldier, **Audie Murphy,** was a member of the 3rd Infantry Division, and is buried nearby. (See page 147.)

The 3rd also fought bravely during the Korean War where they helped recapture and hold the capital city of Seoul, earning the new nickname, "Rock of Seoul." After the war, the 3rd returned to Ft. Benning, Georgia, where they are stationed today. They have also served in the Persian Gulf and Iraqi wars.

On September 29, 1988, President George H.W. Bush approved the construction of the 3rd Infantry Division Monument at Arlington. The tall obelisk was dedicated on August 15, 1990, "In memory of our war dead." A plaque on the monument tells the proud history of the division during WWI, WWII, and Korea:

	Campaigns	*Killed*	*Wounded*	*Missing*
WW–I (1917–1918)	6	3,401	12,764	691
WW–II (1941–1945)	10	5,558	18,766	554
KOREA (1950–1953)	8	2,160	7,939	292

4th Infantry Division Memorial
Memorial Drive, Grid FF-39/40

Approaching Arlington National Cemetery along Memorial Drive, visitors can see the 4th Infantry Division Memorial on the left. Also known as the Ivy Division, this stately monument proudly displays the division's insignia four ivy leaves extending from a center circle alluding to the division's numerical designation. "Ivy" was chosen as the division's nickname because, as pronounced, it also refers to the Roman numeral IV, or 4.

The monument also displays the division's motto, "Steadfast and Loyal." The 4th Infantry Division was formed at Camp Greene, North Carolina, on December 10, 1917, just prior to the United States' entry into World War I. The 4th Infantry Division also served with distinction in World War II, Vietnam, and Iraq. The monument was dedicated in 2000.

Arlington's Living Memorials: Tree Dedications

For many years trees have been planted on the grounds of Arlington National Cemetery as living memorials to a special group of people or an event. They include:

Air Force Arlington Ladies Memorial
Sec. 30 (WX-38)

Airborne Memorial (50th Anniversary Foundation)
Sec. 2 (T-29)

America the Beautiful Memorial Grove
Secs. 31, 30, 5 (see page 243)

American Defenders of Bataan & Corregidor Memorial
Sec. 48 (ST-24)

American Ex-Prisoners of War Memorial
Sec. 33 (X-30/31)

American War Mothers Memorial
Sec. 35 (T-17-18)

American-Armenian Volunteers at Argonne Memorial
Sec. 18 (K-13)

American-Soviet Link-Up at the Elbe River Memorial
Sec. 7A (T-23/24)

Amphibious Scouts and Raiders of WWII Memorial
Sec. 31 (Y-33/34)

Army Air Force Orchestra/Glenn Miller Memorial
Sec. 13 (O-29/30)

Army Arlington Ladies Memorial
Sec. 13 (MN-25)

Bataan & Corregidor Memorial, American Defenders of
Sec. 48 (ST-24)

Battle of the Bulge Veterans Memorial
Sec. 46 (0-23)

Battlefield Commissions, National Order of
Sec. 37 (QR-29)

Beirut, Memorial to the Servicemen Killed in 1983
Sec. 59 (EE-26) (see page 261)

Berlin Airlift Veterans Memorial
Sec. 12 (T-19)*

Buffalo Soldiers Memorial
Sec. 22 (KL-21) (see page 245)

Chaplains' Memorial
Sec. 2E (X-28) (see page 247)

China-Burma-India Veterans Memorial
Sec. 2E (X-28)

Civil Air Patrol Memorial
Sec. 33 (Y-33)

Counterparts Memorial
Sec. 2E (W-30)

Danish Flight for Freedom Grove
Sec. 24 (MN-24/25)

Daughters of American Colonists
Memorial
Sec. 1 (M-35)

Daughters of Founders and
Patriots of America Memorial
Amphitheatre (P-21/22)

Daughters of the American
Revolution Memorial
(Arlington chapter)
Sec. 30 (Z-39)

Daughters of the American
Revolution Memorial
(National)
Sec. 31 (YZ-33/34)

El Salvador Memorial
Sec. 12 (DD-26/27)

Elbe River, American-Soviet
Link-Up
Sec. 7A (T-23/24)

Ex-POWs of the Korean War
Memorial
Sec. 2 (RS-29)

Frogmen (Underwater Demolition
Team) Memorial
Sec. 31 (AABB-34/35)

Gilbert Azaleas Memorial
Amphitheatre (ST-22/23)

Glider Pilots, WWII Memorial
Sec. 33 (Y-33)

Gold Star Mothers Memorial
Sec. 2 (VW-33)

Indigenous People of America/
Vietnam Era Veterans/Indian
Warriors Memorial
Section 8 (BBCC-8/9)

Jumping Mustangs, 1st Battalion,
8th Calvary Memorial
Sec. 48 (TU-25)

Khe Sanh Veterans Memorial
Sec. 2 (W-32)

Korean Mountain Ash
Amphitheatre (Q-24/25)

Korean Pine
Amphitheatre (Q-24/25)

Korean War Ex-POWs Memorial
Sec. 2 (RS-29)

Landing Craft Support Ships
Memorial
Sec. 46 (OP-25)

Lexington Minutemen Memorial
Sec. 1 (O-34)

Marshall Plan Memorial
Sec. 7 (UV-23)

Medal of Honor Grove
Sec. 2 (O-31/32)

Memorial to the Servicemen
Killed in Beirut, 1983
Sec. 59 (EE-26) (see page 261)

Merill's Marauders (5307th
Composite) Memorial
Sec. 13 (OP-74)

Military Order of the Purple
Heart Memorial
Amphitheatre, Sec. 35 (PQ-22)
(see page 263)

Military Order of the World Wars
Memorial
Sec. 12 (Z-28)

Glenn Miller/Army Air Force
Orchestra Memorial
Sec. 13 (O-29/30)

Montford Point Marines Memorial
Sec. 23 (KL-24/25)

Mothers' Tree
Amphitheatre Sec. 48 (P-24/25)
(see page 263)

Nagata Japanese Cherry Trees
Sec. 54 (HH-32)

National Arborist Association
Memorial
Sec. 54 (DDEE-30/31)

National Order of Battlefield
Commissions Memorial
Sec. 37 (QR-29)

Naval Order of the United States
(Seafarers) Memorial
Amphitheatre Sec. 48 (RS-
24/25)

Navy Arlington Ladies Memorial
Sec. 34 (XY-17/18)

Navy Bombing Squadron 104
Sec. 12 (Y-28)

Operation Restore Hope Memorial
(Somalian Campaign)
Sec. 60 (II-18/19)

Operation Tiger Memorial
Sec. 13 (M-25)

Pearl Harbor Survivors' Memorial
Amphitheatre Sec. 48 (R-24)
(see page 266)

Persian Gulf War Memorial
Sec. 60 (GG-20/21) (see page
243)

Polish Legion of American
Veterans and Auxiliary
Sec. 24 (N-23/24) (see Ignace
Jan Paderewski, page 151)

Postal Unit Memorial (144th
Army Postal Unit)
Sec. 32 (XY-33)

POW/MIA Memorial
Amphitheatre, Sec. 48 (Q-24)
(see page 267)

Prelacy of the Armenian Apostolic
Church Memorial
Sec. 18 (K-12/13) (see Argonne
Cross, page 243)

Purple Heart Memorial
Amphitheatre, Sec. 35 (PQ-22)
(see page 263)

Pyramid of Remembrance
(see page 267)

Rakkasans 187th Airborne
Memorial
Sec. 7A (U-23)

Rangers Advisors Memorial
Sec. 13 (OP-25)

The Retired Officers Association
(TROA) Memorial
Sec. 48 (T-26)

Reuben H. Tucker Chapter, 82nd
Airborne Memorial
Sec. 31 (Z-34)

Russian Orthodox Church
Memorial
Sec. 13 (N-25)*

Seafarers Memorial (Naval Order
of the United States)
Sec. 48 (RS-24/25)

Second Schweinfurt Memorial
Amphitheatre Sec. 35 (Q-22)
(see page 272)

Somalian Campaign, Operation
Restore Hope Memorial
Sec. 60 (II-18/19)

Special Operations Memorial
Sec. 46 (OP-24)

Swiss Internees Memorial
Sec. 12 (XY-25/26)

Take Pride in America Memorial
Grove
Administration Bldg. (GG-34)

Triple Nickels (555th Parachute
Infantry Division) Memorial
Sec. 23 (LM-24/25)

TROA (The Retired Officers
Association) Memorial
Sec. 48 (T-26)

Tuskegee Airmen Memorial
Sec. 46 (NO-24/25)

Underwater Demolition Team
Memorial
Sec. 31 (AABB-34/35)

Unit K-West and B-East Memorial
Sec. 2E (X-31)

U.S. Colored Troops and Freed
Slaves Memorial
Sec. 27 (AA-48/49)

USS Houston and HMAS *Perth*
Memorial
Sec. 12 (BB-27/28)

USS Iowa Victims Memorial
Sec. 60 (FF-19)

USS Underhill Memorial
Sec. 33 (X-31)

Vietnam War Memorial (No
Greater Love)
Sec. 28 (U-43)

Vietnam Era Veterans/Indian
Warriors Memorial/Indigenous
People of America
Section 8 (BBCC-8/9)

Vietnam Veterans Memorial
(Veterans of Foreign Wars
Auxiliary)
Amphitheatre Sec 48 (PQ-
25/26)

War Correspondents Memorial
Sec. 46 (OP-23/24) (see page
295)

World War I Memorial
Sec. 34 (TU-12) (see page 300)

World War II Memorial
Sec. 30 (AA-39)

World War II Glider Pilots
Memorial
Sec. 33 (Y-33)

1st Armored "Old Ironsides"
Division Memorial
Sec. 46 (O-25)

1st Calvary Division Memorial
Sec. 33 (X-30)

4th Infantry (Ivy) Division
Memorial
Sec. 21 (N-21)

13th Airborne Division Memorial
Sec. 33 (Z-28)

17th Airborne Division Memorial
Sec. 33 (AA-28)

23rd Infantry Regiment Memorial
(Korea)
Sec. 31 (BB-35/36)

56th Field Artillery Battalion, 8th
Infantry Division Memorial
Sec. 33 (X-32/33)

82nd Airborne Division Golden
Brigade Memorial
Sec. 7 (VW-27/28)

82nd Airborne Division Memorial
Sec. 48 (TU-24/25)

82nd Airborne Memorial, Reuben
H. Tucker Chapter Memorial
Sec. 31 (Z-34)

93rd Bombardment Group
Memorial
Sec. 2E (W-31/32)

94th Infantry Division Memorial
Sec. 46 (OP-25)

104th Timberwolf Division,
WWII Memorial
Sec. 32 (X-33)

144th Army Postal Unit Memorial
Sec. 32 (XY-33)

199th Light Infantry Brigade
Memorial
Sec. 31 (AA-34/35)

325th Glider Regiment Memorial
Sec. 7 (WX-27/28)

385th Bomb Group, 8th Air Force,
WWII Memorial
Sec. 46 (OP-23)

416th Bombardment Group (L)
Memorial
Sec. 48 (T-24/25)

454th Bombardment Group
  Memorial
  Sec. 2E (VW-31)

455th Bombardment Group
  Memorial
  Sec. 2E (W-32)

484th Bombardment Group
  Memorial
  Sec. 33 (Y-30)

487th Bombardment Group
  Memorial
  Sec. 9 (U-28)

508th Parachute Infantry
  Regiment Memorial
  Amphitheatre, Sec. 35 (R-22)

511th Parachute Infantry
  Regiment Memorial
  Sec. 48 (TU-24/25)

551st Parachute Infantry Battalion
  Memorial
  Sec. 33 (BB-34)

555th Parachute Infantry Division
  (Triple Nickels) Memorial
  Sec. 23 (LM-24/25)

Arlington:
A Visitor's Guide

Arlington National Cemetery performs two diverse, yet vital functions. It is not just a revered national shrine, but also an active modern cemetery where thousands of burials are conducted annually, while accommodating millions of visitors.

A Large Active Cemetery

The United States maintains 153 national cemeteries, of which only Arlington and the cemetery at the Soldiers Home in Washington, D.C. are under the jurisdiction of the United States Army. The remaining cemeteries are administered by the Veterans Administration (137) and the National Park Service (14). Arlington is not the largest cemetery. It ranks second behind Long Island National Cemetery in New York in the number of graves located within its walls. Arlington National Cemetery occupies an area of 657 acres, which is approximately one-half of the original Arlington estate owned by

The view from Bryan Circle of that section of Arlington Cemetery that was formerly the South Post of Fort Myer. The Washington Monument can be seen across the Potomac River.

George Washington Parke Custis. The remainder of the estate is now Fort Myer, a U.S. Army installation adjacent to Arlington and closely connected to the cemetery's operations. Originally Arlington House was included in the 200-acre tract designated as a cemetery by Secretary of War Edwin M. Stanton in 1864. Today, however, Arlington House and its immediate environs are no longer part of Arlington Cemetery. Instead, they are administered as the Robert E. Lee Memorial by the National Park Service. Between 1864 and 1999, numerous parcels of land were annexed to the original Arlington Cemetery 200-acre tract until it had grown to 657 acres.

In 1999, President Bill Clinton signed legislation transferring the neighboring 37-acre Navy Annex property and another eight acres from Fort Myer to the cemetery. These additional 45 acres could yield as many as 30,000 new gravesites. At the time, Arlington had fewer than 60,000 sites available.

Arlington National Cemetery has evolved over a period of nearly 150 years from a simple potter's field to a major national shrine. With the addition of numerous tracts of land, the result has been a network of diverse gravesite arrangements and a confusing mixture of numerical gravesite designations, which have become a modern superintendent's conundrum. For this reason, the sectional outline of the cemetery does not, at times, appear to progress in any logical order. However, to help minimize confusion when looking for a particular gravesite, cemetery officials provide the section and lot number of any gravesite, and supply visitors with a coordinated map to pinpoint the specific location. A map using the same coordinates as the map made available at the cemetery appears on the inside back cover of this book.

Soldiers from Every War

Interred within Arlington's walls are veterans from every American war, a fact that makes Arlington unique among national cemeteries. Although Arlington was not established until 1864, veterans from the American Revolution, the War of 1812, and the Mexican War have been reinterred here. Among these honored dead are 4,725 unknown persons, most of whom died during the Civil War. In addition, there are more than 45 foreign nationals interred within Arlington's walls, including British Field Marshall Sir **John Dill** and World War II German POW **Anton Hilberath** (Sec. 15C, Lot 347, Grid H–25). Also at Arlington are gravesites dedicated to the memories of those service personnel whose deaths were officially verified but whose remains were never recovered. (See Memorial Sections, page 260)

Cemetery Flagpoles

There are two official flagpoles located within Arlington. One stands majestically on the hill in front of Arlington House, while the other, the Woodhull Memorial Flagpole, is located on the south lawn of the Memorial Amphitheatre. On days when a burial service is taking place within the cemetery, both flags are lowered to half-staff one-half hour before the beginning of the first service, and in tribute to the persons being buried, they remain at half-staff until one-half hour after the final service.

Visiting Dignitaries

Among the nearly four million visitors who make the pilgrimage to Arlington each year are people from every corner of the globe. Thousands of international travelers join Americans as they pay their respects at the Tomb of the Unknowns and to view the graves of many of our national heroes. These visitors include kings and queens, presidents and prime ministers, military chiefs and diplomats who lay a wreath in honor of all who have served this nation at the Tomb of the Unknowns.

On Veteran's Day 1985, Prince Charles and the late Princess Diana of Great Britain laid a wreath at the Tomb of the Unknowns.

The Amphitheatres

Many organizations utilize both the Old Amphitheatre and the larger Memorial Amphitheatre (see descriptions under Monuments and Memorials) for various patriotic and religious functions throughout the year. Ceremonies on Veteran's Day and Memorial Day traditionally draw thousands of visitors who come to hear addresses by the president or other high-ranking government officials.

Section 60

Following the first fatalities of the Iraq War in 2003, Arlington designated Section 60 as the final resting place for most of these American heroes. Located in the southeastern portion of the cemetery, Section 60 was away from the

usual routes taken by visitors. But by 2008, more than 450 casualties of the wars in Iraq and Afghanistan had been buried here, and Section 60 has become a destination site for thousands of family members, friends, colleagues, and grateful citizens who come to honor these fallen heroes.

Burial Regulations

By 2008, 300,000 people had been interred or inurned in Arlington National Cemetery. With an average of more than 27 burials per weekday, current estimates predict that the cemetery will be filled to capacity by the year 2060. Nevertheless, burial at Arlington is no longer an option available to all current or former military personnel. Certain restrictions have been imposed and a special procedure must be followed to gain admission. To request an interment or inurnment at Arlington, the person making funeral arrangements should contact the Office of the Superintendent as soon as possible. Cemetery personnel will verify eligibility and notify the person making the request. Military honors and the selection and engraving of headstones also will be arranged at the time of the request for interment. Information regarding specific burial regulations and how to request an interment or inurnment can be found in Appendix III on page 333.

Ground Burials

Following the death of President **John F. Kennedy,** requests for interments at Arlington rose dramatically. Cemetery officials were forced to make the difficult decision to limit eligibility for burial at Arlington. While the range of persons eligible is still quite broad, interested parties are well-advised to consult the cemetery's formal regulations. An official copy of the eligibility requirements issued by Arlington Cemetery can be found in Appendix III on page 333, or visit the cemetery's Web site at http://www.arlingtoncemetery.org.

Family Gravesites

Normally only one gravesite will be issued to a family requiring the interment of family members at different levels in a single grave. Exceptions, however, are made in cases where one site cannot accommodate a large family.

Reserving Gravesites

Prior to 1962, eligible parties could reserve burial sites at Arlington; such "reservations" remain valid today. However, allocation of a gravesite is now made only when the need arises. If the spouse or eligible child of a primary eligible party dies first, space is assigned for the spouse or child, provided the primary party agrees in writing to be buried in the same site. The cemetery cannot usually allow the family to choose a particular burial site. With nearly 24 burials per weekday, logistics require that spaces be allocated to accommodate concurrent burial services. However, the cemetery does try to accommodate family members who wish to be buried near relatives, if a space is available next to or near that relative.

Cremations and the Columbarium

In addition to ground burials, Arlington National Cemetery provides for the inurnment of cremated remains within a Columbarium and the cemetery's boundary wall. The Columbarium, located in Section 63 in the southeastern corner of the cemetery, was dedicated on April 26, 1980. When completed, the Columbarium will offer 67,000 niches. In 2008, construction began on a new boundary wall along the east and south edges of the cemetery. Niches for cremated remains are being embedded within sections of the wall, which will eventually surround portions of the cemetery, adding as many as 25,000 niches.

Photo courtesy of Department of the Army

The gravesites in the eastern part of Section 54 (at the top of the photo) are 5' x 5' to accommodate inurnments. Section 54's western section, shown at the bottom of the photo, contains the standard 5' x 10' gravesites.

Currently more than 60 percent of the remains received at Arlington are cremated although more than half of these still receive ground burials. To accommodate these inurnments, and to conserve space, the cemetery designated that gravesites in Section 54 be 5' x 5' rather than the standard 5' x 10' sites found throughout the cemetery.

Burial by Military Rank or Race

When Arlington was first established in 1864, burial was by race and rank, reflecting the structure of the military at that time. Burial sections were divided between officers and enlisted men, and between white and African-American servicemen. African-American soldiers, primarily members of the United States Colored Troops, were buried in Sections 23 and 27. Many of the tombstones in these sections bear the "U.S.C.T." designation. African-American civilians were buried in Section 27. Following the United States Armed Forces' elimination of

A grave in Section 13 shows the United States Colored Troops (U.S.C.T.) designation.

segregated units in 1948, burials by race also were eliminated at Arlington.

Although Arlington began as a cemetery for unknowns and for soldiers from modest backgrounds, soon after the Civil War more and more officers began requesting burials at Arlington, increasing the prestige of the cemetery. As the honor of an Arlington burial increased, competition developed for securing the most prominent sites within the cemetery. This led to a *de facto* separation of officers from enlisted men. Concurrent with the change in regulations regarding headstones in 1947, all differentiation between separation of officers and enlisted men was eliminated.

Expenses

Certain services related to burial at Arlington are provided without expense to the party. There is no cost for the site itself and the cemetery personnel prepare the grave and place the regulation headstone. The cemetery also provides normal maintenance for the grave as part of its overall maintenance program. Additionally, in those cases where private funeral services have taken place outside Arlington and the body has been transported to the cemetery at private expense, burial arrangements are also provided at no cost. Other services and expenses may also be provided for persons who die while on active duty in the Armed Forces. Such benefits should be determined by the family at the time of death.

Gravesite Decorations

In an attempt to maintain the dignity of Arlington National Cemetery, and to provide for the uniform regulation of gravesite decorations, the following guidelines have been adopted:

Floral Tributes

Fresh cut flowers may be placed on graves at any time, but artificial flowers may only be placed on graves between October 10 and April 15.

Planting of any flowers, shrubs, or trees is prohibited.

Potted plants are permitted during the period that begins 10 days before and ends 10 days after Easter.

Christmas wreaths are permitted during the Christmas season.

Floral items will be removed from the graves as soon as they become faded or unsightly.

Floral tributes may not be secured to the headstone or marker.

There will be a general cleanup of all floral items on graves 10 days after each holiday—Easter, Memorial Day, and Veterans Day.

Permanent Flower Containers

Permanent flower containers, which are placed below ground level and have telescoping flower vases, are permitted. However, the container must be placed in the ground by the cemetery staff. The government assumes no responsibility for damaged or missing flower containers.

Other Decorations

Statues, vigil lights, flags, or any type of commemorative items are not permitted on graves except for flags placed on the graves by the government.

Flags

All graves are decorated with small flags during the 24-hour period preceding Memorial Day. No other flags are permitted on the graves at any time.

Headstone Regulations

History

The establishment of a cemetery at Arlington in 1864 was necessitated by the tragic and wholesale loss of life in the Washington vicinity during the Civil War. Dozens of burials took place every day. As row after row of fallen soldiers were interred, only simple whitewashed wooden headboards marked their graves. Within a few short years, time and nature had taken their toll on those boards, causing their decay. Quartermaster General **Montgomery Meigs,** realizing that continuous replacement at a cost of $1.23 per headboard was impractical, ordered the study of an alternative marker. He proposed markers made of cast iron and coated with zinc to prevent rusting and placed several such markers in the cemetery. However, these iron markers were rejected by

other government officials in favor of more traditional stone markers. Finally in 1873, the U.S. Congress voted to utilize the marble headstones which are still in use today. Only one of the original cast iron markers still exists. It marks the grave of Captain **Daniel Keys** (Sec. 13, Lot 13615, Grid G-29/30).

Seemingly endless rows of wooden headboards dot the landscape in section 13 of Arlington National Cemetery in this vintage 19th century photograph.

Private Headstones

It has always been the policy of the United States government to provide a headstone for any person interred in a national cemetery. However, unlimited use of private monuments also was allowed, provided they were erected and maintained at private expense. That policy regarding use of private headstones was altered in 1947 when the government's Fine Arts Commission adopted regulations regarding the size, placement, and maintenance of headstones to maintain and ensure the dignified character of Arlington National Cemetery. All sections of the cemetery that have been opened since that time display only the simple, white regulation headstone. Should a party desire a private monument, that decision must be made at the time of interment because such monuments can only be placed in one of the sections where they already exist.

Likewise, the size and shape of the monument also must meet certain guidelines. An official copy of these guidelines can be obtained from the cemetery.

Government-Issue Headstones

The United States government will supply a headstone for each gravesite at Arlington. The regulation stone is made of white marble, and measures 13 inches wide, four inches thick, and 42 inches tall. Twenty-four inches of the white marble headstone remain above ground.

The government will engrave certain

A Civil War-era soldier adorns the only remaining cast iron marker in Arlington Cemetery, located in Section 13, Grid G-29/30.

information on the stone at no cost. If the person being buried is a military person, his or her name, dates of birth and death, rank, branch of service, and any war service will be included on the stone. If desired, one of 37 religious symbols will be inscribed near the top of the stone.

Prior to 1980, the home state of the deceased military person, as well as major military decorations, were also engraved on the stone at no expense. Now, however, a request must be made to permit the inclusion of a military decoration on the stone, and once verified and with space permitting, it can be added at private expense.

For the spouse or eligible dependent of the military person, the back of the headstone will include his or her name, dates of birth and death, and relationship to the primary party. These general rules are modified under certain circumstances, such as when there are more than two family members in a single gravesite.

Due to the high regard given to recipients of the Congressional Medal of Honor, the graves of these men and women are marked with headstones engraved in gold.

A glossary of all terms and abbreviations, including those used to describe military rank, military decorations, and religious symbols, can be found in Appendix I and II of this book.

The remains of shuttle *Challenger* Captain Michael J. Smith are borne on a horse-drawn caisson, one of the military honors granted some veterans buried at Arlington National Cemetery.

Military Honors and Burial Services

A ny former or current member of the United States Armed Forces is entitled to certain honors at the time of burial, if desired. Such honors, however, are never required and are often omitted. The honors bestowed during a military burial are steeped in tradition and reflect the deep respect accorded a person who has served our nation.

History

Anyone who has ever witnessed a military funeral is struck by the precision and grandeur that even the simplest of these services evokes. The use of a caisson to transport the casket, the riderless horse, and the rifle salute are honors that find their origins in military history. The caisson is an ammunition wagon which has evolved from the 16th century when it was used to remove bodies from the battlefields. A riderless horse, with boots reversed in the stirrups and carrying a blackhandled sword in a silver scabbard, signifies a fallen soldier who will never ride again. A three-shot volley fired over the grave is another ancient tradition used originally to signal opposing forces that the truce called to allow the recovery of fallen soldiers was ended, and that the armies were prepared once again to do battle. Another custom is the playing of "Taps" by a lone bugler. While final musical tributes are ancient in their origins, the use of "Taps" began only during the Civil War, first as a "lights out" signal at the end of the day and then as a "good sleep" salute to fallen comrades.

Available Honors

At Arlington, four types of burial services are available, each involving military honors provided by the branch of the military in which the deceased served.

1. **Full Honors.** Every member of the Armed Forces with a rank equivalent to warrant officer or above is entitled to the following honors:
   - a color guard
   - an escort platoon (which varies in size commensurate to rank)
   - a military band
   - a casket team
   - a firing party
   - a bugler
   - a flag over the casket

In addition, a flag officer (general or admiral) is also entitled to a caparisoned or riderless horse and a cannon salute. Each branch of the service may also designate its own variations on these honors.

At any military service, a military chaplain will conduct the service if requested by the family.

2. **Standard Honors.** Any current or former member of the Armed Forces of any rank is entitled to the following honors:
   - a casket team
   - a firing party
   - a bugler
   - a flag over the casket.

In addition, if the military personnel had been mounted during service, a caparisoned horse can also be provided. As always, each branch of the military service may provide special variations on these honors and a military chaplain will conduct the services, if requested.

3. **Body Bearers.** When the spouse or other dependent of a current or former member of the Armed Forces is buried at Arlington, the military branch in which the primary party served will provide a casket team for the services and, if desired, a military chaplain. In such a case, no other military honor would be provided because the deceased was never a member of the U.S. Armed Forces.

4. **Combined Armed Forces Honors.** These honors are provided on rare occasions when the deceased exercised command authority over more than one branch of the service. These combined honors are usually reserved for current or former presidents of the United States (as commander in chief), secretaries of defense, chairmen of the Joint Chiefs of Staff, or an unusual officer granted multiple command, usually in a combat situation.

These honors include escort platoons from each branch of the service over which the officer exercised command. President John F. Kennedy was awarded such honors in 1963, as was General Omar Bradley at his funeral in 1981.

Arlington: A Visitor's Guide

A visit to Arlington National Cemetery is an important part of any visit to Washington, D.C., and every American is encouraged to view its many landmarks and monuments. But it is important to remember that while Arlington is a national public shrine, it is also a hallowed burial ground. Visitors are reminded to afford the cemetery the dignity and respect it deserves and to refrain from littering or disfiguring the grounds. Food and beverages are not permitted within the cemetery.

Visitors Center

Located just inside the main gate to Arlington is the Visitors Center. Here, visitors can obtain brochures and maps of the cemetery, as well as specific information about the location of particular gravesites.

Hours

Arlington National Cemetery is open every day of the year. The hours vary between winter and summer:

April 1 through September 30, 8:00 a.m. to 7:00 p.m.
October 1 through March 31, 8:00 a.m to 5:00 p.m.

Vehicles

Visitors are not allowed to drive into the cemetery, and so must park their vehicles in one of the lots provided. If, however, persons wish to visit the grave of a relative or friend, a temporary pass allowing them to drive to a gravesite may be obtained at the Visitors Center. Permanent passes are also available for the next of kin of persons interred at Arlington. These may be obtained by writing to the Office of the Superintendent, Arlington National Cemetery, Arlington, Virginia 22211.

Metro Subway

Because of the large amount of vehicular traffic around Washington and at Arlington, visitors are encouraged to utilize the capital area's Metro subway system. The Metro stop for Arlington Cemetery is located approximately 200 yards from the main entrance to the cemetery.

Tours

Normally, visiting the cemetery must be done on foot. However, a commercial tour bus operates within Arlington Cemetery, and for a fee, transports visitors among any of four stops: the Visitors Center, the grave of President **John F. Kennedy,** the Tomb of the Unknowns, and Arlington House (the Robert E. Lee Memorial).

Web Site

A great deal of interesting and practical information about Arlington National Cemetery, including burial regulations, eligibility requirements, and much of the information contained in this chapter, can be found on the cemetery's official Web site at http://www.arlingtoncemetery.org.

The Arlington Ladies

A member of the Arlington Ladies personally represents the chief of staff of each branch of the United States Armed Forces at every funeral conducted at Arlington. Begun as a service for Air Force families in 1948 by **Gladys Vandenburg**–wife of Chief of Staff **Hoyt Vandenburg**–the Arlington Ladies now include the United States Army, Navy, and Air Force. At graveside services, the representative of the Arlington Ladies presents the next of kin with a personal note of sympathy on behalf of the chief of staff and the branch of service.

But it is on those occasions when no family member is able to attend the ceremonies that the Arlington Ladies provide their most important service. When family members live hundreds, perhaps thousands of miles from Arlington, and are unable to attend the burial ceremonies, they take great comfort in knowing that an Arlington Lady is always present at the interment of their loved one.

Appendix I
Glossary of Terms, Abbreviations, and Symbols Found on Headstones
(Excluding abbreviations for military rank.)

General Terms and Abbreviations

A.F.C.   Air Force Cross

A.M.   Air Medal

A.N.C.   Army Nurse Corps

ARCOM.   Army Commendation Medal

B.S.M.   Bronze Star Medal

C.I.B.   Combat Infantry Badge

CITIZEN   This term appears primarily on tombstones for persons buried during the Civil War in Section 27. The person buried here was a free person, regardless of race.

CIVILIAN   Any person buried with this designation was nonmilitary, regardless of whether the person was a free person or considered a slave.

C.S.A.   Confederate States of America indicates a Confederate soldier.

D.F.C.   Distinguished Flying Cross

D.S.C.   Distinguished Service Cross awarded to Army personnel.

D.S.M.   Distinguished Service Medal

G.S.   Gold Star (Navy, Marines, and Coast Guard)

IN MEMORY OF...	Designates a cenotaph or empty grave. There are no remains buried here. The marker was placed as a memorial. (See Memorial Sections.)
L.M.	Legion of Merit
Mex. Bor.	Mexican Border Campaign
M.O.H.	Congressional Medal of Honor
M.S.M.	Meritorious Service Medal
N.C.	Navy Cross–awarded to Navy or Marine personnel
O.L.C.	Oak Leaf Cluster (Army and Air Force)
P.H.	Purple Heart
S.A.W.	Spanish-American War veteran
S.S.	Silver Star
UNKNOWN	The remains of the person buried here could not be positively identified.
U.S.A.A.C.	United States Army Air Corps
U.S.C.T.	United States Colored Troops. An African-American soldier who served in the United States military during that period prior to 1948 when the U.S. Armed Forces were segregated.
USS MAINE	The person buried here was a member of the crew of the *USS Maine* at the time it was destroyed in 1898. (See *USS Maine* Memorial.)
W.A.A.C.	Women's Army Auxiliary Corps
W.A.C.	Women's Army Corps

Nonreligious Symbols

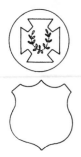

The Confederate States of America Symbol. It denotes that the person buried here was a member of the Confederate Army.

An engraved shield which covers the front face of a tombstone indicates that the person buried here was a member of the United States Armed Forces prior to and including the Spanish-American War.

Religious Symbols

Any persons buried at Arlington National cemetery whose grave is marked with a regulation tombstone is entitled to have a religious affiliation symbol engraved on the top front face of his or her tombstone. Twenty-six such symbols are available:

Aeronic Order	Atheist	Bahai	Christian (Latin Cross)
Christian Church	Christian Reformed Church	Eckankar	Episcopal
Greek	Hindu	Konko-Kyo Faith	Lutheran

Mormon-L.D.S.

Muslim

Native American
of North America

Presbyterian

Community
of Christ

Russian
Orthodox

Seicho-No-Ie

Serbian
Orthodox

Star of David
(Jewish)

Sufism
Reoriented

Tenrikyo

Unitarian

United Church
Religious Science

United
Methodist

United Moravian
Church

Wheel of
Righteousness
(Buddhist)

World Messianity
(Izunome)

Christian &
Missionary
Alliance

United Church
of Christ

Humanist
Emblem of
Spirit

Presbyterian
Church
(USA)

Izumo
Taishakyo
Mission of
Hawaii

Soka Gakkai
International-
USA

Sikh
(Khanda)

Wiccca
(Pentacle)

Not shown because of copyrights:
Christian Scientist (Cross & Crown)
Muslim (Islamic 5 Pointed Star)

Appendix II
Guide to American Military Rank

On April 19, 1775, the first shots for American independence were fired at Lexington, Massachusetts. Since that time American military rank has continued to change and evolve. As visitors view the ranks listed on headstones at Arlington, it is important to consider the era in which a person served in order to fully appreciate that person's military rank. For example, a person with the rank of Lieutenant General in 1985 would not have attained as high a position as a Lieutenant General in 1885 when it was the highest rank in the U.S. Army. Also, during the nineteenth century there was a system of promotions known as "breveting." A soldier would be temporarily advanced in rank because of special circumstances, such as when a commanding officer might be disabled in combat, allowing a subordinate to be brevetted to a higher rank to assume command. Since the promotion was only temporary, the soldier would revert to his original rank once the special situation ended. Many of the tombstones of persons who served during the nineteenth century depict brevet rank. In numerous instances persons who were brevetted to a higher rank during the Civil War, for example, reverted to their lower rank once the war ended. It would then take as long as 30 years to again achieve the high rank they enjoyed during the war. This led to great confusion and ultimately to the elimination of brevet ranks.

What follows is a general chart of American military rank for officers as it has evolved throughout our nation's history. It is important to remember that each branch of the United States Armed Forces has its own designation of rank and that the Air Force was part of the Army until 1947.

1776–1800

Army	**Navy**	**Marines**
Ensign	Midshipman	
Lieutenant	Sailing Master	Lieutenant
Captain	Lieutenant	Captain
Major	Lieut. Commanding	Major
Lieutenant Colonel	Master Commandant	
Colonel	Captain	
Brigadier General	Commodore	
Major General	Rear Admiral	
Lieutenant General	Vice Admiral	

1800–1850

Army	**Navy**	**Marines**
Coronet	Midshipman	
Second Lieutenant		Second Lieutenant
First Lieutenant	Master	First Lieutenant
Captain	Lieutenant	Captain
Major	Lieut. Commanding	Major
Lieutenant Colonel	Master Commandant	Lieutenant Colonel
Colonel	Captain	Colonel
Brigadier General	Commodore	
Major General	Rear Admiral	
Lieutenant General	Vice Admiral	

1850–1900

Army	**Navy**	**Marines**
Second Lieutenant	Ensign	Second Lieutenant
First Lieutenant	Lieut., Jr. Grade	First Lieutenant
Captain	Lieutenant	Captain
Major	Lieutenant Commander	Major
Lieutenant Colonel	Commander	Lieutenant Colonel
Colonel	Captain	Colonel
Brigadier General	Rear Admiral, lower	Brigadier General
Major General	Rear Admiral, upper	Major General
Lieutenant General	Vice Admiral	
General	Admiral	

1900–Present

Army	Navy	Air Force	Marines
Second Lieut.	Ensign	Second Lieut.	Second Lieut.
First Lieut.	Lieut., Jr. Gd	First Lieut.	First Lieut.
Captain	Lieutenant	Captain	Captain
Major	Lt. Commander	Major	Major
Lt. Colonel	Commander	Lt. Colonel	Lt. Colonel
Colonel	Captain	Colonel	Colonel
Brig. General	Commodore	Brig. General	Brig. General
Major General	Rear Admiral	Major General	Major General
Lt. General	Vice Admiral	Lt. General	Lt. General
General	Admiral	General	General
Gen. of the Army	Fleet Admiral	Gen. of the Air Force	

Appendix III
Arlington Burial and
Tombstone Regulations*

Eligibility for Interment (Ground Burial)

The persons specified below are eligible for ground burial in Arlington National Cemetery. The last period of active duty of former members of the Armed Forces must have ended honorably. Interment may be casketed or cremated remains.

a. Any active duty member of the Armed Forces (except those members serving on active duty for training only).

b. Any veteran who is retired from active military service with the Armed Forces.

c. Any veteran who is retired from the Reserves is eligible upon reaching age 60 and drawing retired pay; and who served a period of active duty (other than for training).

d. Any former member of the Armed Forces separated honorably prior to October 1, 1949, for medical reasons and who was rated at 30% or greater disabled effective on the day of discharge.

e. Any former member of the Armed Forces who has been awarded one of the following decorations:

   1. Medal of Honor
   2. Distinguished Service Cross (Air Force Cross or Navy Cross)
   3. Distinguished Service Medal
   4. Silver Star
   5. Purple Heart

f. The President of the United States or any former President of the United States.

* *To insure current regulations, visit www.arlingtoncemetery.org.*

g. Any former member of the Armed Forces who served on active duty (other than for training) and who held any of the following positions:

  1. An elective office of the U.S. Government
  2. Office of the Chief Justice of the United States or of an Associate Justice of the Supreme Court of the United States.
  3. An office listed, at the time the person held the position, in 5 USC 5312 or 5313 (Levels I and II of the Executive Schedule).
  4. The chief of a mission who was at any time during his/her tenure classified in Class I under the provisions of Section 411, Act of 13 August 1946, 60 Stat. 1002, as amended (22 USC 866) or as listed in State Department memorandum dated March 21, 1988.

h. Any former prisoner of war who, while a prisoner of war, served honorably in the active military, naval, or air service, whose last period of military, naval or air service terminated honorably and who died on or after November 30, 1993.

i. The spouse, widow or widower, minor child, or permanently dependent child, and certain unmarried adult children of any of the above eligible veterans.

j. The widow or widower of:

  1. a member of the Armed Forces who was lost or buried at sea or, officially determined to be missing in action.
  2. a member of the Armed Forces who is interred in a US military cemetery overseas that is maintained by the American Battle Monuments Commission.
  3. a member of the Armed Forces who is interred in Arlington National Cemetery as part of a group burial.

k. The surviving spouse, minor child, or permanently dependent child of any person already buried in Arlington National Cemetery.

l. The parents of a minor child, or permanently dependent child whose remains, based on the eligibility of a parent, are already buried in ANC. A spouse divorced from the primary eligible, or widowed and remarried, is not eligible for interment.

m. Provided certain conditions are met, a former member of the Armed Forces may be buried in the same grave with a close relative who is already buried and is the primary eligible.

Eligibility for Interment of Cremated Remains in Unmarked Area

Any veteran who is eligible for interment (ground burial) and their dependent(s) may have their cremated remains placed in a designated unmarked area of the cemetery. Family members must be placed in this area once one member has had their remains placed here. The ashes must be in a biodegradable container or placed without container directly into the ground.

Application for an Exception to the Interment/Inurnment Policy

A letter requesting an exception to policy should be submitted to the Superintendent, Arlington National Cemetery, Arlington, VA 22211. A request for an exception to policy will not be considered until the death of the individual. Letters may be faxed to the Superintendent on telephone number (703) 697-4967. The letter should contain the following information:

a. Name of the deceased.

b. Reason(s) why the deceased should be favorably considered for an exception to policy. All relevant information regarding military service or service to the nation should be included. All documentation of service should be included (i.e., DD Form 214, award certificates, orders, etc.)

c. If interment is to be in the same grave as someone already interred, provide the full name of the previously interred person and the section/grave number where interred, if known. Include the relationship of the deceased to the previously interred person.

d. Include a point of contact and both a daytime and evening telephone numbers for questions concerning additional information and notification purposes.

e. Family member or personal representative will read and sign the public disclosure form and forward it with the exception request. Copies of the public disclosure form are available at the Administration Building or you may telephone for a copy of the form on telephone numbers (703) 695-3175 or 695-3191.

Decisions generally provided within 24 to 48 hours after receipt of the request.

Burden of Proof in Establishing Eligibility

The estate of the deceased (or next-of-kin/personal representative) is responsible for providing the appropriate documentation to verify the veteran's eligibility for interment or for inurnment. The cemetery staff may offer assistance in verifying the veteran's eligibility. However, the veteran or their spouse must be deceased prior to the cemetery staff assisting with the verification. Verification by the cemetery staff may take up to three workdays.

Veterans who desire copies of their military records should write to National Personnel Records Center, Attention: Military Personnel Records, 1 Reserve Way, St Louis, Missouri 63132. Please allow six to eight months for a response from the National Personnel Records Center (NPRC).

Some example documents for establishing eligibility are: DD Form 214 (all branches starting in the 1950's); WD AGO Form 53, 53-55, or 53-98 for Army; NAVPERS Form 553 for Navy; and NAVMC Form 553 for the Marines during the 1940's. (Both front and back of the forms are needed.) A Record of Service provided by the NPRC is also acceptable. The preceding represents a partial listing of forms used during the 1940's. Some of the preceding documents do not describe the character of service. A copy of the discharge certificate which describes the character of service as "honorable" or "under honorable conditions" will meet this requirement.

Active Duty Deaths

Any member of the Uniformed Services who dies while on active duty (other than for training) will generally have their affairs processed by a casualty assistance officer from their respective branch of service. An active duty statement from the commanding officer will be required for verification of eligibility.

Contacting the Department of Veterans Affairs (VA)

For burial eligibility or information, you may contact your local VA Office, the nearest VA National Cemetery, or you may write to the VA at the US Department of Veterans Affairs, National Cemetery System (402B), 810 Vermont Avenue, N.W., Washington, DC 20420. http://www.va.gov

Eligibility for Inurnment in the Columbarium

The following persons are eligible for inurnment in the Columbarium. The last period of active duty (other than for training) of former members of the Armed Forces must have ended honorably.

a. Any member of the Armed Forces who dies on active duty.

b. Any former member of the Armed Forces who is retired from active duty.

c. Any former member of the Armed Forces who served on active duty (other than for training).

d. Any member of a Reserve Component of the Armed Forces who dies while he/she is:

1. On active duty for training or performing full-time service under Title 32, United States Code.
2. Performing authorized travel to or from that duty or service.
3. On authorized inactive duty training including training performed as a member of the Army National Guard or the Air National Guard (23 USC 502).
4. Hospitalized or being treated at the expense of the United States for injury or disease incurred or contracted while he/she is on that duty or service, performing that travel or inactive duty training, or undergoing that hospitalization or treatment at the expense of the United States.

e. Any member of the Reserve Officers' Training Corps of the Army, Navy, or Air Force whose death occurs while he/she is:

1. Attending an authorized training camp.
2. On an authorized practice cruise.
3. Performing authorized travel to or from that camp or cruise.
4. Hospitalized or receiving treatment at the expense of the United States for injury or disease incurred while attending camp or cruise, performing that travel, or receiving that hospitalization or treatment at the expense of the United States.

f. Any citizen of the United States who, during any war in which the United States has been engaged, served in the Armed Forces of any government allied with the United States during that war; whose last service ended honorably by death or otherwise; and who was a citizen of the United States at the time of entry into that service and at the time of death.

g. Certain commissioned officers of the National Oceanic and Atmospheric Administration (formerly United States Coast and Geodetic Survey).

h. Certain commissioned officers of the US Public Health Service.
i. Spouses and minor and certain adult children of those eligible above.
j. Any person eligible for ground burial.
k. A former member of a group that has been certified as active military service for the purpose of receiving VA benefits under the provisions of Section 401, Public Law 95-202.

Appendix IV
United States Military
Decorations and Medals

Listed below–in order of importance–are the major military awards granted to American service personnel, and which are listed on many headstones at Arlington National Cemetery. Those recipients of an award or decoration which appears in **bold** print are eligible for burial at Arlington National Cemetery.

Congressional Medal of Honor	Gallantry in action
Distinguished Service Cross	Exceptional heroism in combat
Navy Cross	Exceptional heroism in combat
Air Force Cross	Exceptional heroism in combat
Distinguished Service Medal	Exceptional meritorious service in a duty of great responsibility
Silver Star	Gallantry in action
Legion of Merit	Exceptionally meritorious service in peace or war
Distinguished Flying Cross	Heroism or extraordinary achievement in flight
Soldier's Medal	Heroism not involving conflict with the enemy
Navy and Marine Corps Medal	Heroism not involving conflict with the enemy
Airman's Medal	Heroism not involving conflict with the enemy
Coast Guard Medal	Heroism not involving conflict with the enemy
Bronze Star	Heroic or meritorious achievement during military operations
Air Medal	Meritorious achievement in flight
Meritorious Service Medal	Meritorious service in war or peace
Purple Heart	Wounds or death in combat

If a person earned a decoration for the second time, a Gold Star (for the Navy, Marines, and Coast Guard) or an Oak Leaf Cluster (for the Army and Air Force) would be awarded to the recipient instead of an additional decoration.

Index

A **bold**-printed entry indicates that the person named is buried in Arlington National Cemetery. The name of a memorial or monument that is printed in **bold** means that it, too, is located in the cemetery.

An entry that is printed in ALL CAPITAL LETTERS means that the person or monument is profiled in this book.

101st ARMY AIRBORNE DIVISION MEMORIAL ("Screaming Eagles"), 301
3RD INFANTRY DIVISION MEMORIAL, 301
4TH INFANTRY MEMORIAL, 303
Abbott Hospital, 25
Abel, Rudolf, 162
Abrams, Creighton Williams, Jr., 221
Academie Royale de Peinture et de Sculpture, 120
Academy Awards: Marvin, Lee, 137; Bainter (Venable), Fay, 221
Acheson, Dean, 73
Adams, John, 170
Adler, Julian Ochs, 221
Aeronautical Division, Signal Corps, 284
AFL-CIO, 79
Alabama: Birmingham, 44; Evergreen, 235; Harlan, 44; Lexington, 129; Mobile, 91
Alabama, University of, 44, 74
Alaska: Adak Island, 84; Fairbanks, 41; Nome, 67
Alcorn A&M College, 74
Alexander, Augusta, 221
Alexander, John, 3
Alma College, 117
AMERICA THE BEAUTIFUL MEMORIAL GROVE, 243
American Astronomical Society, 151
American Bar Association, 209
American Football League, 226
American Geographical Society, 155
American Legion, i, 65, 152, 259
American Legion Auxiliary: Memorial Amphitheatre, 259; Mothers' Tree, 263
American Nurses Association, 62

American Red Cross, 62, 135
AMVETS, 258
ANDERSON, MICHAEL P., 196
Anderson, William, R., 221
Annapolis *See* United States Naval Academy
APOLLO ONE ASTRONAUTS, 37; Chaffee, Roger, 37; Grissom, Virgil, 37; White, Edward H., 37
ARGONNE CROSS, 244
Argonne Unit American Women's Legion, 245
Arizona: Gila River Indian Reservation, 94; Phoenix, 168
Arizona, University of, 191
Arkansas, Earle, 227
Arlington House (The Robert E. Lee Memorial): George Washington Parke Custis begins construction, 5; Lafayette visits, 6; Robert E. Lee becomes administrator of estate, 10; Lees leave Arlington, 14, 17; occupied by Union troops, 17; national cemetery established, 20; Custis Lee sues to recover title, 31; title transferred to U.S. Government, 32; Robert E. Lee Memorial established, 34; Women in Military Service to America, 298
Arlington Ladies, 210, 323
Army Medical School, 238
Arnold, David Lee, 42

ARNOLD, HENRY "HAP," 40 ; Bradley, Omar, 49; Hayes, Ira, 95; Marshall, George C., 134; Memorial Amphitheatre, 258; Miller, Glenn, 145; Vandenberg, Hoyt, 210
Arnold, William A., 221, 247

Arnold, William Bruce, 42
Arteaga, Melchor, 43
Arthur, Chester Alan, 125
Associated Press, 87, 93, 286
Atomic Energy Commission, 232
Auchincloss, Hugh, 103
Auchincloss, Janet, 103
AULD, HUGH, 170
Axton, John T., 221 , 247
Ayers, Romeyn E., 91

Baesell, Norman, 145
Bainter (Venable), Fay, 221
Baker, Newton D., 256
Bakke, Richard, 263
Balchen, Bernt, 221
Baldwin, Thomas Scott, 186, 221
Ball, Beatrice, 221
Banister, Alan B., 222
Barnett, George, 123
BARROW, JOE LOUIS, 128
Barrow, Lily, 129
Bartlett, Charles, 103
Bartley, Julian, Jr., 222
Bartley, Julian, Sr., 222
Baseball Hall of Fame, 69, 241
Bassett, Charles II, 222, 237
Bastista, Mario, 222
Bayh, Birch, 101
Bayh, Marvella, 101
de la Beckwith, Byron, 75
Behn, Sosthenes, 222
Belknap, Hugh Reid, 222
Belknap, William Worth, 222
Bell, Alexander Graham, 185
Bellevue Hospital Medical College, 62, 166
Benet, Stephen Vincent, 222
BENNETT, CONSTANCE (COULTER), 42
Bennett, Floyd, 55, 222
Bennett, Joan, 42
Bennett, Ollie Josephine Prescott Baird, 222
Bennett, Richard, 42
Bessette (Kennedy), Carolyn, 105, 110
Beyrle, Joseph, 222
Biddle, Anthony Drexel, 222
BINGHAM, HIRAM, 43
Bingham, Alfreda Mitchell, 43
Big Brothers, Big Sisters, 225
Big Foot, Chief, 143
Birney, David, 99
BLACK, HUGO L., 44
Black, Josephine Foster, 44
Black Sheep Squadron, 47

BLACKMUN, HARRY A., 46, Marshall, Thurgood, 137
Blackmun, Dorothy Clark, 46
Blair, Charles F., Jr., 223
Blair, Francis P., 14
Blassie, Michael J., 33, 281
Block, Harlan, 93, 288
Bloomfield, Reginald, 247
Blue Angels, 233
Bogart, Humphrey, 83
Bolivar, Simon, 43
Boorda, Jeremy Michael, 223
Booth, Edwin, 125
Booth, John Wilkes, 225
Bouvier, Janet Lee, 103
Bouvier, John Vernou, 103
Bowdoin College, 153
BOYINGTON, GREGORY "PAPPY," 47
Braddock, James J., 129
Bradley, John H., 93
Bradley, Esther "Kitty," 49
Bradley, Mary Quayle, 49
BRADLEY, OMAR NELSON, 48, Arnold, Hap, 41; Marshall, George C., 133; Vandenberg, Hoyt, 210
Bragg, Braxton, 217
Brandeis, Louis D., 70
Breckinridge, John C., 76
Brennan, Marjorie Leonard, 50
BRENNAN, WILLIAM J., 50; Douglas, William O., 72; Marshall, Thurgood, 137; Breyer, Stephen, 46
Brown v. Board of Education, 137
BROWN, DAVID M., 197
Brown, George Scratchley, 223
Brown, John, 12
Brown, Ronald, 223
Bryan, Mary Baird, 53

BRYAN, WILLIAM JENNINGS, 51, Taft, William Howard, 208; Confederate Memorial, 249; Old Amphitheatre, 266
Buchanan, James, 13
Buckles, Frank W., 223
Buckley, William Francis, 223
Buffalo Soldiers: Matthews Mark, 231; Pershing, John J. 157
BUFFALO SOLDIERS MEMORIAL, 245
Bundy, Omar, 123, 221
Bureau of Refugees, Freedman, and Abandoned Lands, 25

BURGER, WARREN, 53; Blackmun, Harry, 45; Douglas, William O., 72; Marshall, Thurgood, 137; Rehnquist, William, 168; Stewart, Potter, 204; Warren, Earl, 215
Burger, Elvera Stromberg, 53
Burial Regulations, 314, 323
Burlingame, Charles, III, 223
Burns, James, 135
BURROWS, WILLIAM WARD, 170
Burton, Harold H., 205
Bush, George H. W.: 3rd Infantry Division Memorial, 302; Doolittle, James, 68; Hopper, Grace, 93; Marshall, Thurgood, 137; Stewart, Potter, 213; Williams, Robert, 241; Persian Gulf War Memorial, 243
Bush, George W., 169
Butler, Benjamin, 24
Butler University, 200
Butt, Archibald Willingham, 223
BYRD, RICHARD EVELYN, JR., 54; Balchen, Bernt, 241; Ronne, Finn, 236; Memorial Entrance, 260; USMC Memorial, 289
Byrd, Robert, 101

Cagney, James, 149
California: Alameda County, 67, 213; Encino, 163; Fresno, 48; Hollywood, 138; Los Angeles, 116, 163, 181, 212; Monterey, 193; Oakland, 213; Pebble Beach, 68; Rockwell, 41; San Diego, 67, 94, 180; San Francisco, 41, 69, 81, 157, 186; Sonoma, 41
California, University of: Bingham, Hiram, 43; Doolittle, James, 67; Warren, Earl, 212
Cambridge University, 204
CANADIAN CROSS (CROSS OF SACRIFICE), 246
Cape Canaveral, Florida, 190
Cape Kennedy, Florida, 37
Cardozo, Benjamin, 90
Carrere and Hastings, 255
Carette, William, 280
Carl, Marion, 223
CARLETON, JOSEPH, 171
Carnegie Institute, 151
Carpenter, Scott, 40
Carswell, G. Harold, 46
Carter, Jimmy: Goldberg, Arthur, 79; Kennedy, Edward, 102; Memorial to Servicemen Killed in Iran, 262; Rickover, Hyman, 176; Urban, Matt, 239; Vance, Cyrus, 239
Casey, Sean, 195
Cash, John A., Sr., 224
Castro, Fidel, 108

CATHOLIC CHAPLAINS' MEMORIAL, 248
Central Intelligence Agency (CIA): Buckley, William, 223; Chennault, Claire, 58; Colby, William, 224; Donovan, William, 66; Helms, Richard, 227; Kennedy, John F., 108; Powers, Francis Gary, 162; Rehnquist, William, 168; Smith, Walter Bedell, 200; Spahn, Johnny, 238; Turner, Eli, 239; Vandenberg, Hoyt, 210; Walters, Vernon, 240
Cervera y Topeta, Pascual, 179, 182, 184
CHAFFEE, ROGER BRUCE, 37, Powers, Gary, 163; Selfridge, Thomas, 186
Chaing Kai-Shek, Madame, 57
Challenger, Shuttle, 190, 233, 236
Chamberlain, Joshua, 238
Chaney, Lon, 231
CHAPLAINS' HILL, 247
CHAPLAINS' MONUMENT, 247
Charles, Ezzard, 130
Charles, Prince of Wales, 313
Chase, Salmon P., 24, 169
Chawla, Kalpana, 196
Cheltenham College, England, 63
CHENNAULT, CLAIRE LEE, 56; Boyington, Gregory, 47
Chennault, John S., 57
Chesapeake & Ohio Canal, 72
Chestnut, Jacob, 224
Chicago Daily News, 230
Chicago Tribune, 229
Chimborazo Hospital, 91
Christman, William, 224, 21
Churchill, Sir Winston: Dill, John, 63; Donovan, William, 65; Marshall, George C., 134
Cincinnati, University of, 207
Civil Conservation Corps, 94, 96, 226
Clark, Bennett Champ, 224
CLARK, LAUREL BLAIR SALTON, 198
Clark, Tom C., 137
CLEM, JOHN LINCOLN, 58; Wheeler, Joseph, 218
Cleveland, Grover, 219
Clifford, Clark, 224
Clinton, Bill: Brennan, William J., 50; Lockerbie Memorial Cairn, 253; Rehnquist, William, 169; Tombs of the Unknowns, 282; Women in Service for America Memorial, 297, 312
Clinton, Hillary, 233
COBOL, 92
Cochise, Chief, 60
Coffelt, Leslie W., 224
Cohen, William, 292, 297
Colby, William, 224

Coles, Elizabeth Pennington, 136
College of William and Mary, 197
Collins, J. Lawton, 224
Collins, Michael, 224
Colorado, Colorado Springs, 97
Colorado, University of, 144
Columbarium, 315
Columbia, Shuttle, 195
Columbia University: Donovan, William, 64;
   Douglas, William, 70; Hall, Marguerite Higgins,
   87; Rickover, Hyman, 176
Columbian University (now George Washington
   University): Reed, Walter, 167
Conein, Lucien E., 224
CONFEDERATE MONUMENT, 248, 33;
   Ezekiel, Moses, 218; 249; 258
Congressional Medal of Honor: Boyington,
   Gregory, 48; Byrd, Richard E., 55; Cukela,
   Louis, 225; Donovan, William J., 64; Doolittle,
   James, 67; Foss, Joseph, 224; Greely, Adolphus
   W., 80; Henson, Matthew, 86; Kearny's Cross,
   99; MacArthur, Arthur, 130; Miles, Nelson, 142;
   Murphy, Audie, 148; Pruitt, John, 234; Rice,
   Edmund, 174; Ronne, Finn, 236; Schofield, John
   McAllister, 237; Scott, Robert R., 237; Sickles,
   Daniel, 200; Tomb of the Unknowns, 277;
   Urban, Matt, 239; Wainwright, Jonathan, 211;
   Ware, Keith, 240; Watters, Charles, 240, 248;
   Wood, Leonard, 219
Connecticut: 44; New Haven, 70; New London, 180
Conrad, Charles, P. "Pete," 224
Cook, Frederick, 155
Coolidge, Calvin: Byrd, Richard, 55; Canadian
   Cross, 246; Lejeune, John, 123; Wright, Jerauld,
   241; Weeks, John, 215
Cooper, Gordon, 40
Cooper, John Sherman, 225
Costanzo, Raymond, ii, 225
Counter, S. Allen, 86
COULTER, CONSTANCE BENNETT, 42
Coulter, Ernest, 225
Coulter, John, 42
Crazy Horse, Chief, 60
Creighton University, 196
Cremation regulations, 315, 337
CROOK, GEORGE, 60, Miles, Nelson, 142;
   Wheeler, Joseph, 218; Wood, Leonard, 219
Cukela, Louis, 225
Cushing, Richard Cardinal, 110
Custer, George Armstrong: Gibbon, John, 226;
   Gibson, Francis, M., 226; Miles, Nelson, 142;
   Ream, Vinnie, 165
Custis, Daniel Parke, 3

Custis, Eleanor Parke, 3
Custis, George Washington Parke, 3-12;
   adopted by George Washington, 3; begins
   Arlington House, 5; marries Mary Lee Fitzhugh,
   6; farmer, artist, playwright, 6-8; eulogizes
   James Lingan, 128; dies, 10; Parks, James, 151;
   Randolph, Mary, 163, 312
Custis, John Parke, 3-4
Custis, Martha Parke, 3
Custis, Mary Anna Randolph, 5
Custis, Mary Lee Fitzhugh, 5, 153, 163

Darrow, Clarence, 53
Dartmouth College, 77
Daughters of the American Revolution, 249
Daughters of the American Revolution Hospital
   Corps, 231
Daughters of the Confederacy, 249
Daughters of the War of 1812, 284
Davis, Benjamin, Sr., 225
Davis, Bette, 221
Davis, Cushman Kellogg, 225
Davis, Dwight Filley, 225
Davis, Jefferson: 20, 30; Confederate Monument,
   249; Meigs, Montgomery, 141; Miles, Nelson,
   141; Wheeler, Joseph, 217
Dawson, Ilona Massey, 231
DELANO, JANE, 62
DePaul University, 79
Devers, Jacob, 225
Dewey, George: Leahy, William D., 119; Sampson,
   William, 182; Schley, Winfield Scott, 184; Tomb
   of the Unknowns, 277; *USS Maine* Memorial,
   292; 268
Dewey, Thomas: Dulles, John Foster, 93; Warren,
   Earl, 213
Diana, Princess of Wales, 313
Dick Tracy, 83, 229
Dickerson (Whitehead), Nancy, 240
Diem, Ngo Dinh, 224
Digges, William Dudley, 121
DILL, SIR JOHN, 63, 99, 312
Disabled American Veterans, 230
Doherty, Edward P., 225
Donovan, William James, 66
**DONOVAN, WILLIAM JOSEPH "WILD
   BILL,"** 64
DOOLITTLE, JAMES, 67; Halsey, William, Jr.,
   82; Mitscher, Marc, 146; Vandenberg, Hoyt, 210
Dorsey Brothers, 144
DOUBLEDAY, ABNER, 68
Douglas, Cathleen Heffernan, 71
DOUGLAS, WILLIAM O., 70; Brennan,

William J., 50; Marshall, Thurgood, 137
Drew, Samuel N., 225
Dubs, Adolph, 225
DULLES, JOHN FOSTER, 72, Smith, Walter
  Bedell, 202; Warren, Earl, 214
Dumbarton Oaks Conference, 73

Early, Jubal, 88
East Carolina State University, 225
East, John Porter, 225
Eastern Virginia Medical School, 197
Eisele, Donn, 226, 163
Eisenhower, Dwight: Arnold, Henry, 41;
  Blackmun, Harry, 46; Bradley, Omar, 49;
  Brennan, William, 50; Burger, Warren, 53;
  Donovan, William, 66; Dulles, John Foster, 72;
  Kennedy, John F., 107; Marshall, George C.,
  134; Miller, Glenn, 145; Powers, Francis Gary,
  161; Smith, Walter Bedell, 201; Stewart, Potter,
  205; Tomb of the Unknowns, 280; United States
  Marine Corps Memorial, 290; Vandenberg,
  Hoyt, 210; Walters, Vernon, 240; Warren, Earl,
  214; 268
Emerson, Ralph Waldo, 88
Emmy Awards: Onassis, Jacqueline Kennedy, 104;
  Reynolds, Frank, 174
Englund, Irene, 226
Equestrian statues: Dill, John, 64; Kearny, Philip, 98
EVERS, MEDGAR WILEY, 73
Evers-Williams, Myrlie, 75
Exeter Academy, 125
EZEKIEL, SIR MOSES, 75; Confederate
  Monument, 249; Memorial Amphitheatre, 258

de la Falaise, Marquis Henri, 42
Farragut, David Glasgow: Porter, David Dixon,
  159; Ream, Vinnie, 166
Fechner, Robert, 226
Federal Bureau of Investigation (FBI), 84
Federal Reserve Board, 231
Fendall, Philip R., 19
Fitzgerald, John F. "Honey Fitz," 106, 114
Fitzhugh, Anna Maria, 17
Five-Star Admirals: Dewey, George; **Halsey,
  William F.** 83; King, Ernest J.; **Leahy, William,**
  119; Nimitz, Chester
Five-Star Generals: **Arnold, Henry,** 40; **Bradley,
  Omar,** 48; Eisenhower, Dwight; MacArthur,
  Douglas; **Marshall, George C.,** 133
Flagpoles at Arlington, 313
Florida: Cape Canaveral, 190; Dade City, 138;
  Jacksonville, 62, 67; Key West, 183, 184;
  Pensacola, 47, 96, 198

Flowers, Walter, 226
"Flying Tigers" (23rd Fighter Squadron):
  Boyington, Gregory, 47; Chennault, Claire, 57
Follin, Catherine Sandford, 171
Follin, Mary Barker, 171
FOLLIN, JOHN, 171
Fonda, Henry, 229
Ford, Gerald: Douglas, William, 71; Rickover,
  Hyman, 177
Ford, Glenn, 226
Foreign nationals buried at Arlington, 312
FORRESTAL, JAMES V., 77; Knox, William,
  118; Memorial Amphitheatre, 258
Forsythe, John, 42
Fortas, Abe: Blackmun, Harry, 46; Warren, Earl, 215
Foss, Joseph J., 226
Foster, John Watson, 72
Frasure, Robert C., 226
Frazer, James Earl, 209
Freed, James Ingo, 285
Freedman's Village, 24-26
Freeman, Theodore C., 226
Frost, Kathryn George, 226
Frudakis, Zenos, 285

Gable, Clark, 42
GAGNON, RENE, 93, 288
Gardiner, Ruth M., 226
Garfield, James: Lincoln, Robert Todd, 125;
  Rosecrans, William, 181; Old Amphitheatre, 266
Garn, Jake, 194
Gehman, Harold W., 196
George III, King of England, 126
George V, King of England, 81
George VI, King of England, 64
George Foster Peabody Award: Reynolds, Frank,
  174; Dickerson (Whitehead), Nancy, 240
George Washington University: Dulles, John
  Foster, 72; Onassis, Jacqueline Kennedy, 103;
  Reed, Walter, 167
Georgia: Augusta, 137, 217
Geronimo, Chief: Crook, George, 61; MacArthur,
  Arthur, 131; Miles, Nelson, 142; Wood,
  Leonard, 219
Gibbon, John, 226
Gibson, Francis, 226
Gibson, John, 226
Glenn, John, 40
Glienicker-Brucke Bridge, Berlin, 162
GOLDBERG, ARTHUR, 79
Goldberg, Dorothy Kurgans, 79
Goldwater, Barry, 232
Goldwyn, Samuel, 42

Good Housekeeping Seal of Approval, 240
Gordon, A.G., 91
Gore, Al, 168, 296
Graham, George, 227
Grand Army of the Republic (GAR), 32, 229, 238, 249, 256
Grand Canyon, 160
Grant, Cary, 42
Grant, Ulysses S.: Lee's surrender, 26; meets with Lee after the war, 29; Belknap, William, 222; Clem, John, 59; Lincoln, Robert Todd, 124; Miles, Nelson, 143; Rawlins, John, 235; Rosecrans, William, 181; Sheridan, Philip, 188; Sickles, Daniel, 200; Taft, William Howard, 207
Gravesite decorations, 317
Gray, Horace, 89
Gray, Jerry, 145
Gray, Selina, 29
Greeley, Horace, 165
GREELY, ADOLPHUS WASHINGTON, 80: Schley, Winfield Scott, 185
GREEN, JOHN, 171
Green, Susannah Blackwell, 171
Grierson, Benjamin, 245
Griggs, S. David, 227
GRISSOM, VIRGIL I. "Gus," 37; Powers, Gary Francis, 163; Selfridge, Thomas, 186
Groves, Leslie, 227
Guggenheim, M. Robert, 227

Hackworth, David, 227
Hadfield, George, 5
HALL, MARGUERITE HIGGINS, 87
Hall, William (Air Force Lt. General), 87
Hall, William (Revolutionary War general), 217
Halleck, Henry Wager, 188
HALSEY, WILLIAM FREDERICK "Bull.," 82; Doolittle, James, 67; Leahy, William D., 119
Halsey, William Frederick, Sr., 83, 119
Hamlin, Hannibal, 24
HAMMITT, SAMUEL DASHIELL, 83
Hangen, Putnam Welles, 227
Hanson, Alexander Contee, 127
Hardin, Frieda Mae, 295
Harding, Warren: Ezekiel, Moses, 76; Lejeune, John, 123; Peary, Robert, 155; Taft, William Howard, 209; Tomb of the Unknowns, 277; Weeks, John, 215; Wood, Leonard, 220
Harlan, John, 168
Harriman, W. Averell, 201
Harrison, Benjamin: Dulles, John Foster, 72; Taft, William Howard, 207

Hartke, Rupert Vance, 227
Harvard University: Bingham, Hiram, 43; Blackmun, Harry, 45; Brennan, William, J., 50; Henson, Matthew, 86; Holmes, Oliver Wendell, Jr., 88; Hopper, Grace, 92; Kennedy, Edward, 100; Kennedy, John F., 106; Kennedy, Robert F., 114; Lincoln, Robert Todd, 124; Marshall, George C., 135; Newcomb, Simon, 150; Rehnquist, William, 168; Wood, Leonard, 219
Hatch, Edward, 245
Hawaii, Honolulu, 43; Pearl Harbor, 106
Hawthorne, Nathaniel, 88
Hayden Planetarium, 154
HAYES, IRA, 94, 288
Haynes, Don, 145
Haynesworth, Clement, 46
Headstone regulations, 318
Hearst, William Randolph, 117
Heffernan (Douglas), Cathleen, 71
Hellman, Lillian, 84
Helms, Richard, 227
Henson, Anaukaq, 86
HENSON, MATTHEW, 85; Peary, Robert, 153
Henson, Lucy Ross, 86
Hershey, Lewis B., 227
Hickey, John M., 251
HIGGINS, MARGUERITE, (*See* Hall, Marguerite Higgins)
THE HIKER (The United Spanish War Veterans Memorial), 251
Hilberath, Anton, 227, 312
Hinkel, John, 227
Hitler, Adolph, 84, 151
Hipps, Juanita R., 227
Hoffa, Jimmy, 114
Holmes, Fanny Dixwell, 90
HOLMES, OLIVER WENDELL, JR., 88; Douglas, William, 71; Marshall, Thurgood, 137; Taft, William Howard, 207
Holmes, Oliver Wendell, Sr., 99
Hood, Sir Samuel, 126
Hoover, Herbert: Donovan, William, 65; Memorial Entrance, 259; Purple Heart Memorial, 263; Women in Military Service for America, 296; Wright, Jerauld, 241
Hopkins, Arthur F., 91
HOPKINS, JULIET OPIE, 90
HOPPER, GRACE MURRAY, 92
Hopper, Vincent, 92
Hopwood, Avery, 178
HOUSE, JAMES, 171
Houston, University of, 192

Howard University, 86, 136, 226
Howe, George, 286
Hoxie, Richard, 166
Hughes, Charles Evans, 215
Hultgreen Kara Spears, 228
Humphrey, Hubert: Blackmun, Harry, 46;
    Kennedy, John F., 108
Hunt, E. Howard, 224
Husband, Rick, 196
Hussein, Saddam, 243

Idaho: Coeur d'Alene, 47
Illinois: Bloomington, 160; Chicago, 61, 79, 116,
    124, 143, 144, 176, 208, 215, 277; Jacksonville,
    51; Marion County, 51; Nashville, 45; Quincy, i,
    221; Springfield, 124
Illinois College, 51
Illinois Wesleyan University, 160
"In the Memory of...," Memorial Sections, 260
Indiana: Crawfordsville, 173; East Chicago, 173;
    Hammond, 173; Indianapolis, 200; Mitchell, 38
Ingersoll, Robert Green, 228
Irving, Washington, 170
Irwin, James B., 163, 228
Isabelle, Queen, 200
Iowa: Ames, 198; Clarinda, 144; Hampton, 118;
    Waterloo, 206
IWO JIMA MARINES, 93; Gagnon, Rene, 93;
    Hayes, Ira, 94; Strank, Michael, 95
IWO JIMA MEMORIAL; See United States
    Marine Corps Memorial

Jackson, Andrew, 6
Jackson, Charles, 88
Jackson, Robert H., 168
James, Brian, 228
JAMES, DANIEL "CHAPPIE," JR., 96
Janney, Bernard T., 228
Jarvis, Gregory, 191
Jefferson Barracks National Cemetery, 33, 281
Jefferson, Thomas, 163
Johns Hopkins University: Newcomb, Simon, 151;
    Reed, Walter, 166
Johnson, Andrew: orders return of Lee's personal
    property, 28; Rehnquist, William, 169;
    Rosecrans, William, 181; Sheridan, Philip, 189

Johnson, Lyndon: Apollo One Astronauts, 39;
    Goldberg, Arthur, 79; Kennedy, John F., 106;
    Kennedy, Robert F., 115; Marshall, Thurgood,
    137; Salinger, Pierre, 234; Smith, Merriman,
    235; Valenti, Jack, 237; Vance, Cyrus, 237;

Warren, Earl, 214
Jones, John Paul, 235
Jones, Louis Vaughn, 228
Juliana, Queen of the Netherlands, 262
Junior Achievement, 228

Kansas: Abilene, 134; Leavenworth, 133, 243
Kavaler, Prabhi, 228
KEARNY, PHILIP, 201
Kearny's Cross, 99
Keating, Kenneth, 115, 228
Kefauver, Estes, 107
Kellogg, William Pitt, 228
Kennedy, Burton, 228
Kennedy, Caroline, 103
Kennedy, Carolyn Bessette, 105, 110
Kennedy, Edward M.: 100; Kennedy, John F.,
    111; Kennedy, Robert F., 116
Kennedy, Ethel, 116
Kennedy, Joan, 101
Kennedy Shriver, Eunice, 116
KENNEDY, JACQUELINE BOUVIER, See
    Onassis, Jacqueline Kennedy
KENNEDY, JOHN FITZGERALD, 106, i,
    iii, Evers, Medgar, 73; Goldberg, Arthur, 79;
    Kennedy, Edward, 100; Kennedy, Robert F., 114;
    Marshall, Thurgood, 137; Memorial Entrance,
    257; Onassis, Jacqueline Kennedy, 103; Powers,
    Gary Francis, 162; Salinger, Pierre, 236; United
    States Marine Corps Memorial, 291, 314; Vance,
    Cyrus, 239; Warren Earl, 214; Weeks, John, 215
Kennedy, John F., Jr., 105, 110
Kennedy, Joseph P., Jr., 100, 106, 116
Kennedy, Joseph P., Sr., 106, 114
Kennedy, Patrick Bouvier, 105, 109
KENNEDY, ROBERT FRANCIS, 114, Kennedy,
    John F., 107
Kennedy, Rose, 100, 106, 110, 114
Kennedy, Victoria Reggie, 102, 116
Kentucky: Elizaville, 287; Jenkins, 161;
    Flemingsburg, 287; Perryville, 131
Kenyon College, 167
Kerner, Otto, 229

Key, Francis Scott, 199
Key, Francis Barton, 199
Keys, Daniel, 318
Khmer Rouge, 227
Khomeini, Ayatollah Rubollah, 262
Khrushchev, Nikita, 161
Kilgore, Harley, 229
Kilian, Michael, 229

Kilmer, Joyce, 65
Kimball, Ivory G., 229, 254
Kincheloe, Iven C., Jr., 229
King, Ernest, 119
King, Jeff, 229
King, MacKenzie, 246
Kirksville Normal School (now Truman State
   University), 156
Kleindienst, Richard, 168
Klem, John, *See* John Clem
Knox, Henry, 120
KNOX, WILLIAM FRANKLIN, 117; Forrestal,
   James V., 77
Kopechne, Mary Jo, 102
Korean War Veterans Association, 250
KOREAN WAR VETERANS MEMORIAL, 252
Korn, Bertram, 229
Kruzel, Joseph J., 229
Ku Klux Klan, 44, 234

Lachaise, Gaston, 286
de Lafayette, Marquis: Pershing, John J., 158; visits
   Arlington House, 6
Lanphier, Thomas G., Jr., 229
Landon, Alf, 117
Lansing, Robert, 72
Larson, Emery "Swede," 229
LEAHY, WILLIAM D., 118
Lechter, John, 16
Lee, George Washington Custis: 12; inherits
   Arlington House, 30; sues for title to Arlington
   House, 30
Lee, Henry "Light Horse Harry": father of Robert
   E. Lee, 8; Lingan, James, 127
Lee, Mary Anna Custis: 5; marries Robert E. Lee,
   8; leaves Arlington at outbreak of Civil War, 17;
   seeks to protect property, 17; seeks to recover
   personal property after war, 28; makes one last
   visit to Arlington, 29; dies, 29

Lee, Robert E.: 6; marries Mary Anna Custis,
   8; appointed supt. of West Point, 10; named
   administrator of Arlington estate, 10; resigns
   Army commission, 15; leaves Arlington for
   last time, 16; named president of Washington
   College, 27; dies in 1870, 29; Chennault, Claire,
   58; Hopkins, Juliet, 91; Kearney, Philip, 99;
   Lincoln, Robert Todd, 124; Lingan, James 128;
   Meigs, Montgomery, 140; Old Amphitheatre,
   266; Parks, James, 153; Randolph, Mary, 163;
   Sheridan, Philip, 163; Wheeler, Joseph, 217
Lee, William C., 301
Lehman, Herbert, 65

L'ENFANT, PIERRE CHARLES, 120;
   Revolutionary War Veterans, 170
LEJEUNE, JOHN ARCHER, 122
Leschetizsky, Theodor, 152
"Let Peace Take Root," Memorial to Servicemen
   Killed in Beirut, 261
Letcher, John, 16
Lewis, Harold, Jr., 263
Libby Prison, 60
Lincoln, Abraham: authorizes Robert E. Lee's
   promotion, 13; calls for volunteers after Fort
   Sumter is fired upon, 14; Clem John, 58;
   Freedman's Village, 24; Gettysburg Address, v,
   255; Holmes, Oliver Wendell, Jr., 88; Lincoln,
   Robert Todd, 124; Memorial Amphitheatre, 257;
   orders more cemeteries for Washington area, 20;
   Ream, Vinnie, 164; Rosecrans, William, 180;
   Sickles, Daniel, 199; Tanner, James, 236
Lincoln, Abraham II, 126
Lincoln, Evelyn, 230
Lincoln, Harold, 230
Lincoln, Mary Harlan, 125
Lincoln, Mary Todd, 123
Lincoln Memorial: Memorial Entrance, 259;
   Lincoln, Robert Todd, 126; Women in Military
   Service for America, 298
LINCOLN, ROBERT TODD, 123, 31
Lincoln, Willie, 165
Lincoln University, 136
LINGAN, JAMES McCUBBIN, 126;
   Revolutionary War Veterans, 170
Lisagor, Peter, 230
LIVING MEMORIALS, 305
Liszt, Franz, 76

LOCKERBIE MEMORIAL CAIRN, 253
Lodge, Henry Cabot, 109
Lodge, John Davis, 230
Logan, John A., 28; Old Amphitheatre, 266;
   Proclaims first Decoration (Memorial) Day, 32
Long Island National Cemetery, 311
Longfellow, Henry Wadsworth, 88
Longstreet, James, Jr., 230
Longstreet, Robert Lee, 230
Lorre, Peter, 231
LOUIS (BARROW), JOE, 128
Louisiana: Greenville, 243; New Orleans, 58, 123,
   217; Pointe Coupee, 122
Louisiana State Normal College (Northwestern
   State University), 56
Louisiana State University, 122
Lowenstein, Allard, 230
Lupo, Francis, 230

Lusitania, USS, 52
Lyle, Ned, 280
Lynch, John Roy, 230

Maas, Melvin J., 230
MacARTHUR, ARTHUR, 130
MacArthur, Douglas: Arnold, Henry, 41; Bradley,
  Omar, 49; Hall, Marguerite Higgins, 87; Halsey,
  William, Jr., 82; MacArthur, Arthur, 131;
  Marshall, George C., 134; Mitscher, Marc, 147;
  Ridgeway, Matthew, 235; Wainwright, Jonathan,
  211; Walters, Vernon, 240; Weinberger, Caspar,
  240
Machu Picchu, 43
MacMillan, D.B., 55
MacKay Trophy, 41, 229
Madison, James, 227
Makohin, Peter, 230
Maine, USS: 33
Maine: Haven, 161; South Portland, 153
Manfredi, Michael, 296
Manhattan Project, 227
Mansfield, Michael J., 230
Martin, William F., 230
March, Frederick, 42
Marciano, Rocky, 130
Marmaduke, Harry C., 251
Marshall, Cecelia Suyat, 136
Marshall, Elizabeth Carter Coles, 136

MARSHALL, GEORGE C., 133; Arnold, Henry,
  41; Bradley, Omar, 49; Dill, John, 64; Pershing,
  John, 158; Meason, Thomas, 172; Smith, Walter,
  201; Vandenberg, Hoyt, 210
Marshall, Herbert, 42
Marshall, John, 133
Marshall, Katherine Tupper Brown, 136
Marshall, Norma, 136
MARSHALL, THURGOOD, 136
Marshall, Vivian Burey, 136
Marshall, William, 136
Maryland: Annapolis *(See* United States Naval
  Academy); Baltimore, 94, 123, 127, 136, 151,
  166; Bethesda, 137; Charles County, 85;
  Clairborne, 170; College Park, 41; Frederick
  County, 184; Green Hills, 121; Havre-de-
  Grace, 179; Patuxant River, 193; Prince Georges
  County, 121; St. Mary's County, 83; Waldorf,
  203
Marx brothers, 231
Massachusetts: Boston, 56, 88, 106, 117;
  Brookline, 106; Cambridge, 150, 174;
  Chappaquidick, 101; Lexington, 293; Martha's

Vineyard, 101, 105, 110; Newburyport, 81;
  Springfield, 101, 131; Westminster, 139
Massachusetts Institute of Technology, 67
Massey (Dawson), Ilona, 231
Matthews, Mark, 231
Maxmillian, Emperor, 189
May, David M., 231
May, Geraldine Pratt, 231
May, James, 28
Mayo, Joel, 263
McAdoo, William Gibbs, 231
McAuliffe, Christa: the Shuttle *Challenger*
  Astronauts, 190
McAULIFFE, ANTHONY, 139
McCain, John S., 231
McCain, John S., Jr., 231
McCain, John S., III, 231
McCarthy, Joseph, 114
McCLELLAN ARCH, 254
McClellan, George B., 231, 254
McClellan, George B., Jr., 231, 255
McCool, William C., 196
McCrea, Joel, 32
McDowall, Roddy, 231
McDowell, Irvin, 17
McGee, Anita Newcomb, 231
McGrath, Kathleen, 232
McKim, Rev. Randolph Harrison, 251
McKim, Meade & White, 259, 296
McKinley, Richard Leroy, 232
McKinley, William: Bryan, William Jennings,51 ;
  Lincoln, Robert Todd, 125; MacArthur, Arthur,
  132; Miles, Nelson, 143; Spanish-American War
  Memorial, 273;
  Taft, William Howard, 207; *USS Maine*
  Memorial, 292; Wheeler, Joseph, 218; Wood,
  Leonard, 219
McNair, Ronald E., 191
McNutt, Paul V., 232
MEASON, THOMAS, 172
MECHANIZED ARMOR MEMORIAL, 260
Medal of Honor, *See* Congressional Medal of
  Honor
Medical College of Virginia, 76
Meigs, John Rodgers, 23, 141
Meigs, Josiah, 142
MEIGS, MONTGOMERY, 140; Davis, Jefferson,
  141; granted jurisdiction over Arlington House,
  20; headstone regulations, 318; Tomb of the
  Unknown Civil War Dead, 283
Melville, Herman, 88
MEMORIAL AMTHITHEATRE, 255; Ezekiel,
  Moses, 76; Kimball, Ivory, 227; Korean War

Veterans Memorial, 253; Miles, Nelson, 144; Murphy, Audie, 149; Old Amphitheatre, 266; Pershing, John, 158; Purple Heart Memorial, 263; Tomb of the Unknowns, 275; Wainwright, Jonathan, 212; 313

Memorial Bridge, 260, 300

Memorial Day, 33, 280, 313

MEMORIAL ENTRANCE TO ARLINGTON NATIONAL CEMETERY, 259

MEMORIAL SECTIONS, 260

MEMORIAL TO THE SERVICEMEN KILLED IN BEIRUT, 261 ; Stethem, Robert, 202

MEMORIAL TO THE SERVICEMEN KILLED IN IRAN, 1980, 262

Meredith, Burgess, 42

Metro subway stop, 260, 271, 323

Metzler, John C., ii, 232

Metzler, John J., Jr., ii, 232

MIA/POW MEMORIAL, 267

Michigan: Alma, 117; Detroit, 129; Grand Rapids, 39; Jackson, 204

MILES, NELSON APPLETON, 142; Crook, George, 61; Memorial Amphitheatre, 257

Military honors for burial, 320

MILITARY ORDER OF THE PURPLE HEART (Purple Heart Memorial), 263

MILLER, ALTON GLENN, 144, 261

Miller, William, 232

Mills, Clark, 165

Mills, Mike, 75

Milton Academy, 100

Minnesota: Duluth, 231; Maine, 70; St. Paul, 45, 53

Minnesota, University, 53

Minton, Sherman, 50

Miss Porter's School, 103

Mississippi: Corinth, 188, 217; Decatur, 74; Iuka, 181; Jackson, 74; Lorman, 74; Newton County, 74, Vicksburg, 159

Missouri: Clark, 48; Columbia, 165; Laclede, 156; Moberly, 49; St. Louis, 9, 140, 222, 237, 281

Mitchell, Edgar, 236

Mitchell, John, 232; Rehnquist, William, 168

Mitchum, Robert, 228

MITSCHER, MARC ANDREW, 146; Halsey, William, 82

Monroe, James, 227

Montalban, Ricardo, 42

Montana, Little Big Horn, 226

Moorer, Thomas H., 232

Moreell, Ben, 232

Morgan College, 86

Morgan, John, 145

MOTHERS' TREE, 263

Mount Suribachi, 93, 287

Moynihan, Daniel Patrick, 232

MURPHY, AUDIE, 147

Muskie, Edmund Sixtus, 233

Musmanno, Michael, 233

Mussolini, Benito, 84

Napoleon III, 99, 189

National Academy of Sciences: Meigs, Montgomery, 141; Newcomb, Simon, 151

National Aeronautic and Space Administration (NASA): Apollo One Astronauts, 38; Powers, Gary Francis, 161; Shuttle *Challenger* Astronauts, 192; Shuttle *Columbia* Astronauts, 195

National Association for the Advancement of Colored People (NAACP): Evers, Medgar, 74; Marshall, Thurgood, 136

National Building Museum, 141

National Cathedral, 177

National Geographic Society: Bingham, Hiram, 43; Byrd, Richard E., 56; Greely, Adolphus W., 81; Peary, Robert, 155; Powell, John Wesley, 161

National Park Service, 260, 264, 291, 300, 311

National Press Club, 145, 295

National Security Council, 225

National Shrine of the Immaculate Conception, 97

National Society of the Colonial Dames of America, 273

National Society of the United Daughters of the War of 1812, 284

NATO, 100

Nebraska: Lincoln, 52; Omaha, 51

Nebraska, University of, 156

NETHERLANDS CARILLON, 264

Nettleton, Alfred Bayard, 233

Nevada: Lake Mead, 161; Las Vegas, 130

New Brunswick, Salisbury, 150; New Hampshire: Lancaster, 215; Manchester, 93, 126; Winchester, 219

New Jersey: Burlington, 124; Mendham, 69; Morristown, 176; Newark, 50

New Mexico, Santa Fe, 239

New York: Albany, 185; Ballston Spa, 68; Beacon, 77; Brooklyn, 290; Buffalo, 64; Central Bridge, 216; Cooperstown, 68; Katonah, 84; Montour Falls, 62; Mount Morris, 157; New York City, 42, 70, 86, 92, 105, 120, 138, 144, 148, 152, 154, 166, 176, 178, 199, 205, 216, 218, 221, 231, 233, 247, 273; Palmyra, 182; Plattsburgh, 196; Poughkeepsie, 103; Schenectady, 238; Southhampton, 103, Watertown, 72;

Woodstock, 138
New York Times, 45, 221
New York University, 199
NEWCOMB, SIMON, 150, 231
Newfoundland, Gander, 301
Niagara College, 64
Nichols, Red, 144
Nicholson, Arthur D., Jr., 233
Nimitz, Chester, 119, 291

Nixon, Richard: Black, Hugo, 45; Blackmun,
  Harry, 45; Burger, Warren, 53; Douglas,
  William, 71; Dulles, John Foster, 73; Kennedy,
  John F., 108; Memorial Amphitheatre, 259;
  Onassis, Jacqueline Kennedy, 104; Rehnquist,
  William, 168; Rickover, Hyman, 177; Rogers,
  William, 236; Scott, Hugh, 237; Weinberger,
  Caspar, 240
No Greater Love, Korean War Veterans Memorial,
  252; Memorial to the Servicemen Killed in
  Beirut, 262; POW/MIA Memorial, 267; War
  Correspondents Memorial, 295; World War I
  Memorial, 298; 232
Nobel Peace Laureate: Marshall, George C., 135
Noble, Ray, 143
Nolde, William B., 233
North American Air Defense Command
  (NORAD), 97
North Atlantic Treaty Organization (NATO), 135
North Carolina: Beaufort, 193; Charlotte, 193;
  Kitty Hawk, 185
Northwestern University, 79
Nova Scotia, Wallace, 150
Nuremburg Trials, 66, 87, 233
NURSES MEMORIAL, 265

Obama, Barack, 102
Oberlin College, 154
O'Connor, Sandra Day, 168, 205, 297
O'Dwyer, William, 233
O'Hara (Blair), Maureen, 223
Office of Strategic Services (OSS), 66
Ofstie, Joy Bright Hancock, 233
Ohio: Cincinnati, 43, 76, 204, 207; Dayton,
  60, 289; Gambier, 167; Hamilton County,
  207; Kingston Township, 181; Newark, 58;
  Painesville, 267
Oklahoma, Oklahoma City, 146
OLD AMPHITHEATRE AND ROSTRUM,
  266, 255, 313
Old Guard, 34, 282
Oliver, Richard, 233
Onassis, Aristotle, 105, 110

ONASSIS, JACQUELINE KENNEDY, 103;
  Kennedy, John F., 107; Taft, William Howard, 209
Onizuka, Ellison S., 191
Oregon: Portland, 71
Organization of American States (OAS), 135
Osborn, Chase, 117
Oswald, Lee Harvey, 214
Overmyer, Robert F., 233
Overseas Press Club, 295
Owens, Frederick, D., 257

PADEREWSKI, IGNACE JAN, 151, 258, 294
Palma, Tomas Estrada, 220
PAN AM FLIGHT MEMORIAL, 253
PARKS, JAMES, 152
Patterson, Joseph Medill, 234
Patterson, Robert, 234
Patton, George C.: Bradley, Omar, 49; McAuliffe,
  Anthony, 139
Patton, George Smith, 234
Peace Corps, 226
PEARL HARBOR SURVIVORS MEMORIAL,
  266
Peary, Josephine Diebitsch, 156
PEARY, ROBERT EDWIN, 153; Henson,
  Matthew, 85
Penn, Lemuel, 234
Pennsylvania: Chester, 159; Chester County, 136;
  Conemaugh, 95; Doylestown, 152; Gettysburg,
  v, 69, 174, 257; Gladwyne, 40; Philadelphia,
  76, 186; Pittsburgh, 177; Uniontown, 133, 172;
  Valley Forge, 172
Pennsylvania, University of: Brennan, William J.,
  50; Meigs, Montgomery, 140; Wood, Leonard,
  220
"Pentagon Papers," 45
Perry, Matthew C., 179
Pershing, Helen Warren, 156
PERSHING, JOHN J., 156; Arnold, Henry,
  41; Buffalo Soldiers Memorial, 246; Donovan,
  William, 64; Hayes, Ira, 95; Marshall, George
  C., 133; Matthews, Mark, 231; Memorial
  Amphitheatre, 258; Tomb of the Unknowns,
  277; World War I Memorial, 300
Pershing, John Warren, III, 159
Pershing, Richard W., 159
Persian Gulf War Memorial, 243
Petain, Marshall, 119
Phi Beta Kappa, 154
Pickett, George Edward, 175, 234
Pickett, George Edward, Jr., 234
Pidgeon, Walter, 231
Pierce, Franklin, 140, 199

Pious XII, Pope, 206
Pikeville College, 161
Plant, Philip, 42
Plenty Coups, Chief, 278
Pocahontas: Custis, George Washington Parke, 7; Randolph, Mary, 163
Poles, Spotswood, 234
Polish Legion of American Veterans and Auxiliary, 152
Pollack, Ben, 144
PORTER, DAVID DIXON, 159
Potter, E.C., 98
Powell, Colin, 231
Powell, Emma Dean, 161
POWELL, JOHN WESLEY, 160
Powell, Lewis, Jr., 45, 160
POWERS, FRANCIS GARY, 160, 83
POW/MIA MEMORIAL, 267
PRELACY OF THE ARMENIAN APOSTOLIC CHURCH MEMORIAL, 245
Presidential Medal of Freedom: Brennan, William J., 50; Burger, Warren, 54; Dulles, John Foster, 71; Mansfield, Michael, 230; Moynihan, Daniel, 232
Princeton University: Bingham, Hiram, 44; Dulles, John Foster, 72; Forrestal, James V., 77; McClellan, George B., Jr., 231
Pringle, Valentine, 234
Prudenza, Arcangelo, 234
Pruitt, John, 234
Pulitzer Prize Laureates: Hall, Marguerite Higgins, 87; Kennedy, John F. 107; Pershing, John J., 158; Puller, Lewis B., 235; Roberts, Kenneth, 236
Puller, Lewis B. "Chesty," 235
Puller, Lewis B., Jr., 234
Purdue University: Chaffee, Roger, 38; Grissom, Virgil, 39
PYRAMID OF REMEMBRANCE, 266

Quezon, Manual, 293

Radical Republicans, 28, 30
Raft, George, 231
Rainey, Barbara Allen, 235
Ramon, Ilan, 196
Randolph, Burwell Starke, 164
Randolph, David Mead, 163
RANDOLPH, MARY, 163
Randolph, Thomas Mann, 164
Randolph, Wallace Fitz, 235
Raphel, Arnold P., 235
Rawlins, John A., 235
Razumowski, Prince Leon, 235

Read, Thomas Buchanan, 158
Reagan, Ronald: Burger, Warren, 54; Henson, Matthew, 86; Hopper, Grace, 93; Louis, Joe, 130; Regan, Donald, 235; Rehnquist, William, 168; Reynolds, Frank, 174; Shuttle *Challenger* Astronauts, 194; Stethem, Robert, 203; Tomb of the Unknowns, 281; Weinberger, Caspar, 240; Women in Military Service for America, 295
REAM, VINNIE (HOXIE), 143, 164
Reasoner, Harry, 174
REED, WALTER, 166, Wood, Leonard, 220, Sabin, Albert, 236
Regan, Donald T., 235
Rehnquist, Jean, 167
Rehnquist, Natalie Cornell, 168
REHNQUIST, WILLIAM HUBBS: 167, Burger, Warren, 54; Marshall, Thurgood, 137
Reid, John Eric, 235
Resnik, Judith A., 191
REVOLUTIONARY WAR VETERANS, 168
REYNOLDS, FRANK, 173
Rhode Island: Newport, 100, 182
RICE, EDMUND, 174, 143
Rich, Lorimer, 235, 263
RICKOVER, HYMAN, 175, 221
Ridgeway, Matthew, 235
RINEHART, MARY ROBERTS, 177
Rinehart, Stanley Marshall, 17
Rippetoe, Russell, 235
ROADS AND WALKWAYS OF ARLINGTON NATIONAL CEMETERY, 268
Robert, Henry M., 236
Robert E. Lee Memorial *See* Arlington House
Roberts, Kenneth L., 236
Roberts, John G., 169
Robinson, Jackie, 129
Robinson, Roscoe, Jr., 236
Rockefeller, Nelson, 79
RODGERS FAMILY, 179
Rodgers, Frederick, 17
RODGERS, JOHN, 176
RODGERS, JOHN AUGUSTUS, 179
RODGERS, THOMAS SLIDELL, 179
Rogers, William P., 236, 194
Roland, Gilbert, 42
Rollins, James, 164
Ronne, Finn, 236
Roosa, Stuart A., 236
Roosevelt, Franklin: Black, Hugo, 44; Boyington, Gregory, 48; Butt, Archibald, 223; Dill, John, 63; Donovan, William J., 64; Douglas, William, 70; Forrestal, James, 77; Holmes, Oliver Wendell, Jr., 88; Knox, William, 118; Leahy,

William, 118; Louis, Joe, 128; Marshall, George C., 134; Paderewski, Ignace, 151; Smith, Walter Bedell, 201; Sullivan Brothers, 206; United States Marine Corps Memorial, 288; *USS Maine* Memorial, 293; Warren, Earl, 214

Roosevelt, James, 214

Roosevelt, Theodore: Bryan, William Jennings, 52; Buffalo Soldiers Memorial, 244; Butt, Archibald, 223; Halsey, William, Jr., 82; Holmes, Oliver Wendell, Jr., 89; Knox, William, 117; MacArthur, Arthur, 132; Memorial Entrance, 260; Sheridan, Philip, Jr., 237; Miles, Nelson, 144; Rough Riders Memorial, 271; Spanish-American War Memorial, 274; Taft, William Howard, 207; *USS Maine* Memorial, 77; Wood, Leonard, 219

ROSECRANS, WILLIAM STARKE, 93; Crook, George, 60; Sheridan, Philip, 188; Wheeler, Joseph, 216

Rosenthal, Joe: Iwo Jima Marines, 93; United States Marine Corps Memorial, 286

Rossi-Clayton, Marie T., 236

ROUGH RIDERS MEMORIAL, 271, 246

Ruby, Jack, 214

Rumsfeld, Donald, 273

RUSSELL, WILLIAM, 172

Sabin, Albert Bruce, 236

Salinger, Pierre, 236, 182

SAMPSON, WILLIAM T., 182; Leahy, William, 118; Rodgers, John, 179; Schley, Winfield Scott, 184; *USS Maine* Memorial, 293

San Antonio College, 191

Scali, John, 236

Schaller, Harold, 301

Schirra, Walter, 40

SCHLEY, WINFIELD SCOTT, 184; Greely, Adolphus, 81; Leahy, William, 118; Memorial Entrance, 260; Rodgers, John, 179; Sampson, William T., 182

Schmeling, Max, 129

Schofield, John MacAllister: 237; Miles, Nelson, 143; Vandenberg, Hoyt, 209; Wheeler, Joseph, 218

Schrier, Harold, G., 288

SCOBEE, FRANCIS (DICK), 191; Apollo One Astronauts, 191; Selfridge, Thomas, 186

Scobee, June Kent, 191

Scopes, John, 52

Scotland, Holy Loch, 198

Scott, Hugh, Jr., 237

Scott, Robert R., 237

Scott, Winfield: meets with Robert E. Lee before

Civil War, 13; serves with Robert E. Lee; Schley, Winfield Scott, 184

SEABEES MEMORIAL, 271, 56, 260, 289

SECOND SCHWEINFURT MEMORIAL, 272

Section 54, 315

Section 60, 314

Securities and Exchange Commission, 70

See, Elliott M., Jr., 237

Selective Service System, 227

SELFRIDGE, THOMAS E., 185; Apollo One Astronauts 40; Powers, Francis Gary, 163

Selfridge, Thomas, 186

SEPTEMBER 11TH MEMORIAL, 272, 35

Sequoia, Chief, 166

Seward, William H., 24

Shafter, William Rufus: Sampson, William T., 183; Schley, Winfield, 184

Shelton, Hugh, 297

Shepherd, Alan, 40, 236

SHERIDAN, PHILIP HENRY, 188; Crook, George, 60; Miles, Nelson, 143; Wheeler, Joseph, 218

Sheridan, Philip Henry, Jr., 237

Sherman, Leslie, 237

Sherman, William Tecumsah: Miles, Nelson, 143; Sheridan, Philip, 188

Shriver, Eunice Kennedy, 116

Shriver, Sargent, 116

SHUTTLE *CHALLENGER* ASTRONAUTS; Scobee, Francis (Dick), 192; Smith, Michael, 194

SHUTTLE *COLUMBIA* ASTRONAUTS, 195; Anderson, Michael P., 196; Brown, David M., 197; Clark, Laurel Blair Salton, 198

SICKLES, DANIEL, 189

Sigma Delta Xi, 293

Sigsbee, Charles Dwight, 237, 291

Simons, James, 239

Sirhan, Sirhan, 116

Sitting Bull, Chief, 143

Slayton, Donald, 40

Smith, Albert Merriman, 237

Smith, Albert Merriman, Jr., 237

Smith, Benjamin, 101

Smith, Francis L., 26

Smith, Howard K., 174

Smith, Jane Jarrell, 193

SMITH, MICHAEL, J., 193, 191, 321

SMITH, WALTER BEDELL, 200; Marshall, George C., 133

Smith College, 297

Smithsonian Institution: 29, Meigs, Montgomery, 141; Powell, John Wesley, 161

Society of Professional Journalists, 295
Society of the Cincinnati: Green, John, 171;
    L'Enfant, Pierre Charles, 120; Lingan, James, 127
Society of the Spanish-American War Nurses, 275
Soldiers Home (Washington, D.C.), Confederate
    Monument, 248
Sons of the Covenant, 76
Sorbonne, 103
Sousley, Franklin R., 93, 288
Souter, David, 50
South Carolina: Charleston Harbor, 14, 170, 172;
    Parris Island, 93
South Dakota, Black Hills, 60
South Dakota State University, 49
Southeast Asia Treaty Organization (SEATO), 73
Spaatz, Carl, 210
SPANISH-AMERICAN WAR MEMORIAL, 273
SPANISH-AMERICAN WAR NURSES
    MEMORIAL, 275
Spann, Johnny Michael, 238
Spalding, Albert G., 69
Spear, Ellis, 238
Springarn Medal: Evers, Medgar, 75; Marshall,
    Thurgood, 137
St. Paul College of Law, 53
Standley, William H., 238
Stanford University, 168

Stanton, Edwin M.: approves use of part of
    Arlington estate as cemetery, 20; Parks, James,
    153; Rosecrans, William Starke, 181; Sickles,
    Daniel, 199
Stephenson, Sir William, 65
Sternberg, George M., 238, 167
Stethem, Patricia, 203
Stethem, Richard, 203
STETHEM, ROBERT DEAN, 202; Memorial to
    Servicemen Killed in Beirut, 262
Stevens, John Paul, 71
Stevens, Theodore "Ted," 238
Stevens, Thaddeus, 165
Stevenson, Adlai: Kennedy, John F., 107; Goldberg,
    Arthur, 79
Stewart, James Garfield, 204
Stewart, Jimmy, 145
STEWART, POTTER, 204; Marshall, Thurgood,
    137
Story, Joseph, 46
STRANK, MICHAEL, 93, 95, 288
Stratton, Samuel S., 238
Stuart, J.E.B.: meets Robert E. Lee at Arlington
    House, 12; Sheridan, Philip, 188

SULLIVAN BROTHERS, George, Francis,
    Joseph, Madison, and Albert, 205, 261
Sullivan, Alleta, 206
Sullivan, Tom, 206
Sullivan, Thomas Crook, 144
Supreme Court Justices: Black, Hugo, 44;
    Blackmun, Harry, 45; Brennan, William J.,
    50; Burger, Warren, 53; Douglas, William, 70;
    Goldberg, Arthur, 79; Holmes, Oliver Wendell,
    Jr., 88; Marshall, Thurgood, 136; Rehnquist,
    William, 167; Stewart, Potter, 204; Taft, William
    Howard, 207; Warren, Earl, 212
Sutter, Bruce, 241
SWAN, CALEB, 173
Swanson, Gloria, 42

Taft, Alphonso, 207
Taft, Helen Herron, 208
Taft, Robert, 214

TAFT, WILLIAM HOWARD, 207; Bryan,
    William J., 52; Butt, Archibald, 223;
    Confederate Memorial, 249; Ezekiel, Moses,
    76; Greely, Adolphus, 81; Henson, Matthew,
    86; Holmes, Oliver Wendell, 89; L'Enfant,
    Pierre, 121; MacArthur, Arthur, 132; Peary,
    Robert, 155; Rehnquist, William, 169; Selfridge,
    Thomas, 185; *USS Maine* Memorial, 293; Wood,
    Leonard, 220
Tanner, James A., 238, 249
Taylor, Maxwell, 238, 139
Taylor, Zachary, 68
Temple of Fame, 23
Tennessee: Dayton, 52; Shiloh, 58
Terry, Luther, 238
Texas: Commerce, 56; Dallas, 105, 106, 115; El
    Paso, 157; Galveston Harbor, 211; Houston, 192,
    226; Hunt County, 147; San Antonio, 39, 59,
    191, 212; Weslaco, 289; Yorktown, 288
Texas A. & M. University, 192
Third United States Infantry (Old Guard), 34, 282
Thomas, Clarence, 1347
Thorne, Stephen D., 239
Thorpe, Carl P., 239
Thorpe, Jim, 239
Titanic, USS, 224
Tomb Guard, 281
TOMB OF THE UNKNOWN CIVIL WAR
    DEAD, 283, 23
TOMB OF THE UNKNOWN DEAD OF THE
    WAR OF 1812, 284
Tomb of the Unknown Soldier of the
    Revolutionary War, 275

TOMB OF THE UNKNOWNS, 275, 33; Axton, John, 221; changing of the guard, 281; Memorial Amphitheatre, 275; Rich, Lorimer, 235; Third Infantry (Old Guard), 281; visiting dignitaries, 313; Younger, Edward, 241

Tracy, Dick, 227, 83

Tracy, Spencer, 67

TREE MEMORIALS, 305

Triola, Michelle, 138

Truman, Harry: Arnold, Henry, 41; Bingham, Hiram, 44; Boyington, Gregory, 48; Buffalo Soldiers Memorial, 246; Coffelt, Leslie, 224; Dulles, John Foster, 73; Forrestal, James V., 78; Halsey, William, 83; Leahy, William, 119; Marshall, George, 133; Miller, Glenn, 145; Pershing, John J., 158; Smith, Walter Bedell, 201; Vandenberg, Hoyt, 210; Wainwright, Jonathan, 211; Walters, Vernon, 240; Warren, Earl, 214

Truman State University, 156

Turner, Eli Karin, 239

Turner, Ernest Karl, 239

Turner, Lana, 42

Turner, Stansfield, 239

Tuskegee Institute, 96, 225

Tyler, John, Jr., 239

Union College of Chicago, 51

United Daughters of the Confederacy: Confederate Memorial, 249; Ezekiel, Moses, 76; Women in Military Service for America, 298

United Nations, 73, 79

UNITED SPANISH WAR VETERANS MEMORIAL (THE HIKER), 251, 260

UNITED STATES AIR FORCE MEMORIAL, 284

United States Army Corps of Engineers, 9

UNITED STATES COAST GUARD MEMORIAL, 285

United States Colored Troops (U.S.C.T.), 245, 316

United States Geological Survey, 161

UNITED STATES MARINE CORPS MEMORIAL (IWO JIMA MONUMENT), 286, 56, 95

United States Military Academy at West Point: Arnold, Henry, 40; Bradley, Omar, 49; Crook, George, 60; Doubleday, Abner, 68; Lee, George Washington Custis, 30; Lee, Robert E. Lee, 8, as supt., 10; Macarthur, Arthur, 130; McAuliffe, Anthony, 139; Meigs, Montgomery, 140; Pershing, John J., 156; Rosecrans, William, 181; Selfridge, Thomas, 186; Sheridan, Philip, 188; Vandenberg, Hoyt, 211; Wainwright, Jonathan, 208; Wheeler, Joseph, 217; White, Edward, 39; Young, Charles, 258

United States Naval Academy at Annapolis: Byrd, Richard E., 54; Halsey, William, Jr., 82; Larson, Emery, 229; Leahy, William, 118; Lejeune, John, 122; Mitscher, Marc, 146; Porter, David, 160; Rickover, Hyman, 176; Rodgers, John, 179; Rodgers, John Augustus, 179; Rodgers, Thomas Slidell, 179; Sampson, William T., 182; Schley, Winfield, 184; Sigsbee, Charles, 237; Smith, Michael J., 193; Weeks, John, 215; Wright, Jernauld, 241

United States Naval Construction Battalion, *See* Seabees Memorial

United States Supreme Court: disbands the Freedman's Village, 26; orders Arlington House returned to Custis Lee, 31

UNIVAC, 92

Unknowns: American Revolution, 275; Civil War, 283; Korean War, 279; Vietnam Era, 280; War of 1812, 284; World War , 275; World War II, 279, 258

USS MAINE MEMORIAL, 291; Paderewski, Ignace, 151

USS SERPENS MEMORIAL, 294

USS Juneau, 205

USS The Sullivans, 206

USS Titanic, 223

Urban, Matt, 239

Valenti, Jack, 239

Vance, Cyrus, 239

Van Devanter, Willis, 44

Van Fleet, James, 239; Bradley, Omar, 49

Van Fleet, James, Jr., 239

Vandenberg, Gladys, 210, 323

VANDENBERG, HOYT SANFORD, 209, 323

Van Voast, Margaret, 297

Vassar College, 92, 103

Vaught, Wilma, 296

Venable, Fay Bainter, 221

Venable, Reginald, 221

Vermont, Danby, 257

Veterans Administration, 311

Veterans of World War I, 300

Victor Emmanuel, King of Italy, 76

Vilcabamba, 43

Villa, Poncho, 157, 246

Vinson, Fred, 214

Virginia: Alexandria, 8, 20, 275; Alexandria County, 31; Appomattox Courthouse, 26, 124, 189, 217; Arlington, 177, 197; Belroi, 166; Chantilly, 99; Culpepper County, 171; Fairfax County, 17, 171; Fincastle County, 172; Front Royal, 172; Harper's Ferry, 12; Jefferson County,

91; Langley Field, 57; Leesburg, 88; Lexington, 27, 29, 135; Liberty Hall, 173; Mount Vernon, 3, 4, 259; New Market, 76; Norfolk, 134, 147; Quantico, 123; Richmond, 76, 91, 164, 188; Roanoke, 149; Winchester, 54, 189
Virginia Military Institute: Ezekiel, Moses, 76; Lee, George Washington Custis, 30; Lejeune, John, 123; Marshall, George C., 133
Virginia, University of: Bennett, Constance, 42; Byrd, Richard E., 54; Kennedy, Edward, 101; Kennedy, Robert F., 114; Reed, Walter, 166
Virginia Polytechnic Institute (Virginia Tech), 237
Visitors Center, 322
Von Rundstedt, Gerd, 139

Wabash College, 173
Wade, Leigh, 239
Wagner, Robert F., 73
WAINWRIGHT, JONATHAN MAYHEW, 211; Memorial Amphitheatre, 258
Wainwright, Robert Powell, 212
Walker, David M., 240
Wallace, George, 74
Walters, Charles, 240
Walters, Vernon A., 240
WAR CORRESPONDENTS MEMORIAL, 295
Ware, Keith, 240
WARREN, EARL, 212; Burger, Warren, 53; Stewart, Potter, 205
Warren, Francis, 156
Washington and Lee University, 29
Washington, Bushrod, 4
Washington: Cheney, 196; Cle Elum, 191; Walla Walla, 70; Yakima, 70
Washington College, 27
Washington, George: Arlington House as a memorial to, 1; marriage to Martha Dandridge Custis, 3; Kennedy, Edward, 100; L'Enfant, Pierre Charles, 120; Lingan, James, 127; Memorial Amphitheatre, 257; Pershing, John J., 156; Purple Heart Memorial, 263; raising George Washington Parke Custis, 4
Washington, Martha Dandridge Custis, 3-4
Washington Monument: Wright, Horatio, 241
Washington Times-Herald, 103
Washington University, 237
Washington, University of, 47, 196
Wasson, Herbert N., 240
Watters, Charles, 240, 247
Wayne, John, 228
WEEKS, JOHN WINGATE, 215; Argonne Cross, 244

Weinberger, Caspar, 240, 280
Weiss, Marion Gail, 296
de Weldon, Felix: Byrd, Richard E., 56; Seabees Memorial, 272; United States Marine Corps Memorial, 289
Welles, Gideon, 24
West Point *See* United States Military Academy
West Virginia University, 139
WESTINGHOUSE, GEORGE, 216
Wheaton College, 160
Wheeler, Earle Gilmore, 240
WHEELER, JOSEPH, 217; Crook, George, 60
Wheeler, Joseph, Jr. 219
White, Byron, 168
Whitehead, John C., 240
Whitehead, Nancy Dickerson, 240
Whitman College, 70
Wiley, Harvey Washington, 240
Wilkes, Charles, 240
William Mitchell College of Law, 53
Williams, Clifton C. Jr., 241
Williams, Robert R., 241
Wilson, Woodrow: Bryan, William Jennings, 52; Clem, John, 59; Confederate Monument, 249; Dulles, John Foster, 72; Lejeune, John, 123; Memorial Amphitheatre, 257; Paderewski, Ignace, 152; Pershing, John J., 157; Taft, William Howard, 208; Tomb of the Unknowns, 276; Weeks, John, 215; Wood, Leonard, 220; 231
Wilson, Ernest "Boojum," 241
Wingate, Orde, 241
Wisconsin: Antigo, 289; Appleton, 289; Ashland, 185; Hillsboro, 146; Madison, 165: Milwaukee, 131, 167, 209; Racine, 198; Sherwood, 167
Wisconsin-Madison, University of, 198
Women Accepted for Volunteer Emergency Services (WAVES), 233
Women Airforce Service Pilot (WASP), 226
Women in the Air Force (WAF), 231
WOMEN IN MILITARY SERVICE FOR AMERICA MEMORIAL, 295
Wood, John, i
WOOD, LEONARD, 219, Reed, Walter, 167; Rough Riders Memorial, 272
Woodhull, Maxwell, 200
WOODHULL FLAGPOLE, 300, 313
Wooding, Harry H., 265
Woodland Cemetery, i
WORLD WAR I MEMORIAL, 300
Wouk, Herman, 252
Wrentmore, Earnest, 241

Wright brothers: Arnold, Henry, 40; Rodgers,
  John, 180; Selfridge, Thomas, 185
Wright, Horatio Gouveneur, 241, 89
Wright, Jerauld, 241
Wright, Marcus, J., 218, 251

Yale University: Bingham, Hiram, 43; Douglas,
  William, 70; Hopper, Grace, 92; Stewart,
  Potter, 204; Taft, William Howard, 209
Yamamoto, Isoroku, 229
Yamashita, General Tomobumi, 212
Yamashita, General Tomoyuki, 238
YMCA, 221
Young, Charles, 258
Young, Roland, 42
Young, Samuel B. M., 241
Youngdahl, Luther W., 241
Younger, Edward F., 241, 277

Zia ul-Haq, Mohammad, 235, 240
Zukerman, Bernhard, 301

GUIDE TO MAP

Many of America's heroes are buried at Arlington. In order to see as many of their graves as possible, the map at right has been divided into 12 shaded areas, which have been designated "A" through "L." Most of the persons, monuments, and memorials mentioned in this book are located within one of the shaded areas–although not all of them are. Please check individual listings within the book for exact grid locations. These shaded areas are meant to alert visitors of their close proximity to well-known graves.

A Henry "Hap" Arnold
Ira Hayes
George Smith Patton
John Pershing
WWI Memorial

B Apollo One Astronauts
Constance Bennett
Anthony McAuliffe
Nelson Miles
Francis Gary Powers
Vinnie Ream
Walter Reed
Edmund Rice
William Rosecrans
Thomas Selfridge
Daniel Sickles

C Creighton Abrams
Jane Delano
John Foster Dulles
Arthur Goldberg
William Sampson
Earl Warren
Leonard Wood
Buffalo Soldiers Memorial
Nurses Memorial
Rough Riders Memorial
Spanish-American War
    Memorial
Spanish-American War
    Nurses Memorial

D Audie Murphy
Ignace Paderewski
Francis "Dick" Scobee
Canadian Cross
Memorial Amphitheatre
Memorial to Servicemen
    Killed in Iran
Shuttle *Challenger* Memorial
Shuttle *Columbia* Memorial
Tomb of the Unknowns
USS Maine Memorial
War Correspondents
    Memorial
Woodhull Flagpole

E Gregory "Pappy" Boyington

Clark Clifford
James Doolittle
John East
Joe Louis
Lee Marvin
John C. Metzler
John Mitchell
Arthur Nicholson
Frank Reynolds
Matthew Ridgeway
Roscoe Robinson, Jr.
Michael Smith
Maxwell Taylor

F Ronald Brown
Richard Helms
Lewis Hershey
George C. Marshall
Edmund Muskie
Walter Bedell Smith

G William Belknap
Hiram Bingham
Jacob Devers
Abner Doubleday
Adolphus Greely
Juliet Hopkins
James Lingan
Montgomery Meigs
Simon Newcomb
John Wesley Powell
Revolutionary War Veterans
Rodgers Family
Thomas Sulllivan
Jonathon Wainright
War of 1812 Unknown Dead

H Claire Chennault
John Clem
George Crook
William Halsey
Philip Kearny
William Leahy
Pierre L'Enfant
Arthur MacArthur
David Dixon Porter
Mary Randolph
William Schley
Philip Sheridan

Old Amphitheatre
Civil War Unknown Dead
    Memorial

I Harry Blackmun
William J. Brennan
Warren Burger
Oliver Wendell Holmes
Kenneth Keating
Jacqueline Kennedy
John Kennedy
Robert Kennedy
Thurgood Marshall
Ilona Massey (Dawson)
William Rehnquist
Hyman Rickover
Potter Stewart
John Weeks

J Bernt Balchen
Richard Byrd
John Dill
William Donovan
Marguerite Higgins
Daniel "Chappie" James
William Knox
Peter Lisagor
Marc Mitscher

K Hugo Black
Omar Bradley
J. Lawton Collins
Medger Evers
James Forrestal
Joseph Kruzel
Robert Todd Lincoln
Daniel Moynihan
William Rogers
William Howard Taft
Hoyt Vandenberg
Caspar Weinberger
Earle Wheeler

L William Colby
William F. Buckley
Grace Hopper
Robert Stethem
Memorial to the Servicemen
    Killed in Beirut